THE LOCUSTS

The Portuguese-Speaking World

ITS HISTORY, POLITICS AND CULTURE

The Series Editors
António Costa Pinto (University of Lisbon)
Onésimo T. Almeida (Brown University)
Miguel Bandeira Jerónimo (University of Coimbra)

This series will publish high-quality scholarly books on the entire spectrum of the Portuguese-speaking world, with particular emphasis on the modern history, culture, and politics of Portugal, Brazil, and Africa. The series, which will be open to a variety of approaches, will offer fresh insights into a wide range of topics covering diverse historical and geographical contexts. Particular preferences will be given to books that reflect interdisciplinarity and innovative methodologies. The editors encourage the submission of proposals for single author as well as collective volumes.

PUBLISHED

The Lusophone World: The Evolution of Portuguese National Narratives
Sarah Ashby

The Politics of Representation: Elections and Parliamentarism in Portugal and Spain, 1875–1926
Edited by Pedro Tavares de Almeida & Javier Moreno Luzón

Inequality in the Portuguese-Speaking World: Global and Historical Perspectives
Edited by Francisco Bethencourt

Marcello Caetano: A Biography (1906–1980)
Francisco Carlos Palomanes Martinho

From Lisbon to the World: Fernando Pessoa's Enduring Literary Presence
George Monteiro

The First Portuguese Republic: Between Liberalism and Democracy (1910–1926)
Miriam Pereira

The Locusts: British Critics of Portugal before the First World War
Gary Thorn

FORTHCOMING

Politics and Religion in the Portuguese Colonial Empire in Africa (1890–1930)
Hugo Gonçalves Dores

The Military and Political in Authoritarian Brazil: The Aliança Renovadora Nacional (ARENA), 1965–1979
Lucia Grinberg

The Eruption of Insular Identities: A Comparative Study of Azorean and Cape Verdean Prose
Brianna Medeiros

Dictatorship and the Electoral Vote: Francoism and the Portuguese New State Regime in Comparative Perspective, 1945–1975
Carlos Domper Lasús

Literary Censorship in Francisco Franco's Spain and Getulio Vargas' Brazil, 1936–1945: Burning Books, Awarding Writers
Gabriela de Lima Grecco

On Guard Against the Red Menace: Anti-Communism in Brazil, 1917–1964
Rodrigo Patto Sá Motta

The Portuguese at War: From the Nineteenth Century to the Present Day
Nuno Severiano Teixeira

This book is dedicated to my history teachers
Cliff Wilson Alan Smith, and Royden Harrison

THE LOCUSTS
British Critics of Portugal before the First World War

GARY THORN

ACADEMIC
PRESS
Brighton • Chicago • Toronto

Copyright © Gary Thorn, 2019.

The right of Gary Thorn to be identified as Author of this work has been asserted in accordance with the Copyright, Designs and Patents Act 1988.

2 4 6 8 10 9 7 5 3 1

First published 2019 in Great Britain by
SUSSEX ACADEMIC PRESS
PO Box 139
Eastbourne BN24 9BP

Distributed in North America by
SUSSEX ACADEMIC PRESS
Independent Publishers Group
814 N. Franklin Street
Chicago, IL 60610

All rights reserved. Except for the quotation of short passages for the purposes of criticism and review, no part of this publication may be reproduced, stored in a retrieval system, or transmitted, in any form or by any means, electronic, mechanical, photocopying, recording or otherwise, without the prior permission of the publisher.

British Library Cataloguing in Publication Data
A CIP catalogue record for this book is available from the British Library.

Library of Congress Cataloging-in-Publication Data
Names: Thorn, Gary, author.
Title: The locusts : British critics of Portugal before the First World War / Gary Thorn.
Description: Brighton ; Chicago : Sussex Academic Press, 2019. | Series: The Portuguese-speaking world : its history, politics and culture | Includes bibliographical references and index.
Identifiers: LCCN 2019000243 | ISBN 9781845199616 (hbk : alk. paper)
Subjects: LCSH: Portugal—Foreign public opinion, British. | Portugal — Foreign relations—Great Britain—History—20th century. | Great Britain—Foreign relations—Portugal—History—20th century. | Portugal—History—1910–1974.
Classification: LCC DP557.P47 T47 2019 | DDC 327.469041/0904—dc23
LC record available at https://lccn.loc.gov/2019000243

Typeset and designed by Sussex Academic Press, Brighton & Eastbourne.

Contents

Series Editors' Preface   viii
Author's Acknowledgements   x
The Illustrations   xii

Introduction   1

1. 'Descending like Locusts': Britain and the First Portuguese Republic   7
2. Reporting the Revolution   27
3. Changing Places: King Manuel into Exile   50
4. The Catholic   63
5. The Disgruntled Royalist   87
6. The Lusophile   109
7. The Secretary   141
8. The Duchess   165
9. Captives, Campaigners and Citizens   186
10. The Portuguese Pimpernel   210
11. The Missionary   231

Conclusion   257

Notes   259
Bibliography   298
Index   314

Series Editor's Preface

"Portugal has been in the limelight. A swarm of writers have descended like locusts on (...) this unfortunate country." This was how Aubrey Fitz Gerald Bell, a dedicated interpreter of the Iberian Peninsula (responsible for the translation of J. P. de Oliveira Martins' *A History of Iberian Civilization* and several of Eça de Queiroz's works into English) and an active lusophile, described the significant number of British critics of Portugal in the "Preface" of his *Portugal of the Portuguese* (New York, Charles Scribner's Sons, 1916). Herein lies the critical inspiration to Gary Thorn's *The Locusts: British Critics of Portugal before the First World War*.

Not that Bell, like his friend Edgar Prestage – a fierce conservative, monarchist and anti-republican – worried about the multiplication and dissemination of voices systematically questioning the motivations of the republican political movement and the consequences of its dynamics in Portugal. Bell was imprisoned for several days in October 1913 accused of collaborating with the monarchist reaction, and certainly had much to resent. His proximity to the British Protest Committee, led by E. M. Tenison and the Duchess of Bedford, two women fostering the cause of the rights of monarchist prisoners in Portugal, is just one sign of commitment to a particular ideology.

Gary Thorn's work offers a rich and judicious account of a group of "locusts" that engaged critically with the convoluted political developments in Portugal before the beginning of the First World War. While freeing political prisoners was the British Protest Committee's main aim, anti- slavery agitation provided a vital contextual pressure. Indeed, the participation of Portugal in modalities of "modern slavery", amply exposed by the likes of Henry Nevinson and John Harris, was one of the important motivations for such recurrent criticism. (Harris is the object of an excellent chapter entitled "The Missionary" where common distrust of the Portuguese overcame substantive differences of character and approach by others involved in the campaign to free political prisoners.) This volume adds significantly to the historiography of the Portuguese Republic, namely to the appreciation of the multifaceted, consequential entanglements between the Portuguese and the British, which cannot be reduced to what surfaces from the mere opening of boxes in the respective diplomatic archives. Thorn's assessment of Bell and others – including less-known figures such as the Catholic journalist Francis McCullagh, a devoted critic of the supposed moral and social degeneration of the country brought about by the redefinition of church–state relations, or the above-mentioned E. M. Tenison – offers a captivating contribution to the understanding of the varied ways in which pressure was, at the time, exerted over domestic and foreign policy, shaping Anglo-Portuguese mutual perceptions and relations along the way. 'The Locusts' may well have been more important as bearers of neo-colonial ideology than as liberators of political prisoners. Analysis of how the 1910 Republican revolution was depicted by some mainline British newspapers is, in this respect, not only elucidating but of prime historical importance.

António Costa Pinto (University of Lisbon)
Onésimo T. Almeida (Brown University)
Miguel Bandeira Jerónimo (University of Coimbra)

Author's Acknowledgements

Historians usually incur their greatest debts to libraries and librarians. Mine are owed to those at the old British Newspaper Library at Colindale, and the British Library of Political and Economic Science, where I first came across an old pamphlet about Portuguese political prisoners. I was convinced that it must be about the Dictatorship but this source was from 1913. I knew then much less about the First Republic, indeed there is still little to be read about it in English. Yet, as I delved deeper it was clear that the issue had disturbed some very serious and influential people, although I had never heard of E. M. Tenison at that stage. My next ports of call had to be the published histories of the First Republic. Douglas Wheeler had a couple of references to the campaign in Britain that were helpful, but he directed me to John Vincent-Smith's work also from the 1970s. Vincent-Smith made me aware of other sources not only on the political prisoners' issue. I realized that there was such a broad range of opposition to the Portuguese Republic before the First World War that it might qualify as a campaign, not just to release political prisoners, but to reform and perhaps even overthrow it.

Later, I had an enormous piece of good fortune, the sort it is fair to say historians dream of. The Oxford DNB entry by Robert Innes-Smith for E. M. Tenison, mentions an unpublished autobiography. It is listed as being deposited in the University of Kent's Templeman Library. It transpired that Innes-Smith himself had deposited all Tenison's remaining papers there sometime in the late 1990s. My hunch was that an amateur historian like Tenison would have carefully preserved her papers. But I also knew from Innes-Smith that a fire had destroyed her home in 1954. What had survived and in what condition, if I could ever get access to it, heaven alone knew. My greatest research debt of all is to Sue Crabtree, emeritus Special Collections Librarian at the University of Kent, for taking me down to a basement of the Templeman Library on a cold January day to stand amazed at the complete wall of shelving that comprised the Tenison Papers. Within them was a perfectly preserved, typed manuscript describing the good lady's time as BPC secretary, as well as much personal correspondence. Without Sue's sensibly flexible professionalism I would not have been able to use the Tenison Papers. I hope she found that retirement idyll in her native Lincolnshire, from where she can rest assured that she shared in the making of this small piece of history.

My former students and a few colleagues at Birkbeck supported my occasional open seminars on Portuguese history, particularly Pamela Moir. Early drafts of Chapters 2, 6 and 8 were all piloted there. In The Open University, Bernard Waites urged me never to finish 'The Locusts' without Chapter 11. He was quite right and I hope he now reads it. Aggelic Christopoulou and Steve Poore have always taken an interest in the book, and I thank them for their encouragement across time and distance. Lucía Cooper taught me Portuguese many years ago, and invited me to many events at King's College, London. Jason Lindsay of Hedingham Castle provided useful information about E. M. Tenison's time living in Hedingham Hall. The editors of the series in which this book appears have offered valuable support; likewise, Anthony Grahame, Editorial Director at Sussex Academic. Beth Dufour worked tirelessly to obtain the necessary image permissions.

This book is dedicated to my history teachers, in case I do not manage to complete another. Cliff Wilson first taught me that history could be stranger than fiction at Old Palace Primary School in Bow, East London. At the Coopers' Company's School, Alan Smith warned me that embarking on historical research invited a lifetime of addiction. He never spoke a truer word. In the Centre for the Study of Social History at the University Warwick, Royden Harrison taught me that being a good historian involved collaboration and comradeship as well as research and writing skills. All of them taught me more than history: persistence, durability, fortitude, optimism and above all, I hope, wisdom. They are a constant reminder that history is a humanity.

The Illustrations

The author and publisher gratefully acknowledge the following for permission to reproduce copyright material. Every attempt has been made to identify the copyright owners for these works and to obtain permission to publish them. The publishers apologize for any errors or omissions in the list below and would be grateful to be notified of any corrections that should be incorporated in the next edition or reprint of this book.

FRONT COVER
Celebrating Portuguese Independence.
Postcard celebrating the Revolution of 5 October, 1910. Pictured are leading members of the Republican Cabinet, including Teófilo Braga (President), José Relvas (Minister of Finance), and Afonso Costa (Minister of Justice). The deposed King Manuel is pictured at the base being blasted out of office along with his military and religious allies.

Postcard, 1910. Copyright © Mary Evans / Grenville Collins Postcard Collection. Reproduced with permission.

Front cover insets: Philip Gibbs, Francis McCullagh, Vicente de Bragança-Cunha, E. M. Tenison.

Sir Philip Gibbs
Bain News Service. Digital file from original negative,
http://hdl.loc.gov/loc.pnp/ggbain.32082
Library of Congress, Prints & Photographs Division, ggbain 32082.

Francis McCullagh, the Catholic journalist
The *Review of Reviews for Australasia*, February, 1912, p. 563. Courtesy of University of Toronto Libraries, image from
https://archive.org/details/reviewofreviews021912steauoft

Vicente de Bragança-Cunha, the disgruntled Royalist
Tom Titt, *The New Age*, 11 April 1912, p.572. Image courtesy of Modern Journals Project, Brown University Library.

http://modjourn.org/render.php?id=1165310116406250&view=mjp_object
Rightsholder not confirmed at time of going to press.

Miss E. M. Tenison, Secretary of the BPC
Eva Mabel Tenison, on coming out, probably c. 1900–1.
Unknown photographer.
The Lady, 20 July 2010, p. 19.
Rightsholder not confirmed at time of going to press.

BACK COVER
E. M. Tenison (1880–1961). Grave, Castle Hedingham cemetery, Essex. Author's photograph.

INTERNAL ILLUSTRATIONS (after page 112)

Francis McCullagh, the Catholic journalist.

Vicente de Bragança Cunha, the disgruntled Royalist.

Colégio de Campolide – Lisboa, Portugal, where Father Torrend was a professor
Edição Rocha Lisboa – BP colorizado n°534. Postacard, 1910.
https://www.postais-antigos.com/lisboa11-colegio-de-campolide-lisboa.html
Reproduced with permission from Hugo de Oliveira.

Sir Philip Armand Hamilton Gibbs by Walter Stoneman
Sir Philip reported on Portuguese prisons in the *Daily Chronicle*.
Whole-plate glass negative, 1920. Given by Walter Stoneman, 1951.
Copyright © National Portrait Gallery, London. Reproduced with permission.

Gaby Deslys (Marie-Elise Gabrielle Caire), King Manuel's companion in 1910
Foulsham & Banfield, published by Rotary Photographic Co. Ltd, bromide postcard print, 1900s.
Bequeathed by Patrick O'Connor, 2010. © National Portrait Gallery, London. Reproduced with permission.

Ramalho Ortigão, (1836–1915), critical Republican who pleaded with his compatriots 'not to be martyrs'
https://en.wikipedia.org/wiki/Ramalho_Ortig%C3%A3o

Photographer unknown. Rightsholder not confirmed at time of going to press.

Philip Morrell with his wife and their daughter 1911
Lady Ottoline Morrell, with Philip Edward Morrell and their daughter, Julian Vinogradoff (née Morrell) by Cavendish Morton, platinum print, circa 1911.

Philip Morrell chaired the second public meeting at the Westminster Palace Hotel on 6 February, 1914.

Given by the photographer's son, Cavendish Morton, 1991. Copyright © National Portrait Gallery, London. Reproduced with permission.

Vicente de Bragança-Cunha
Tom Titt, *The New Age*, 11 April, 1912, p. 572. Image courtesy of Modern Journals Project, Brown University Library.
http://modjourn.org/render.php?id=1165310116406250&view=mjp_object
Rightsholder not confirmed at time of going to press.

Musette Majendie (1903–1981), E. M. Tenison's close friend, in her district scout commissioner's uniform.
Reproduced courtesy of J. Lindsay, Hedingham Castle.
Drslip, Hinckford History Project Wiki http://hinckford-history.wikia.com/wiki/File:10440861_10203840450910160_8697461859079749020_n.jpg

Miss E. M. Tenison, Secretary of the BPC

Adeline, Duchess of Bedford, vice-chair of the British Campaign, and prison reformer.
Adeline Duchess of Bedford by Bullingham & Co. Copyright © Historic Images / Alamy Stock Photo.
Reproduced with permission.

"Fearless but Intemperate": Rev. Campbell, minister of the City of Temple, speaker at the first public meeting on 22 April 1913, as caricatured by 'Spy' in *Vanity Fair*
Leslie Ward (1851–1922), "Men of the Day" Number 940. *Vanity Fair*, 24 November 1904,
Reproduced with permission from Storey's Ltd.

Alice Seeley Harris, missionary, photographer and campaigner with large group of Congolese children, early 1900s.
The Harris Lantern Slide Show. Copyright © Anti-Slavery International/ Autograph ABP.
http://www.liverpoolmuseums.org.uk/ism/exhibitions/brutal-exposure/alice-seeley-harris.aspx [accessed 30 June 2016].
Reproduced with permission from Anti-Slavery International.

The 'black hole of Elvas', visited by Philip Gibbs in December, 1913.
1 View from inside a cell at Forte da Graça.
2 View of courtyard at Forte da Graça.
Author's photographs.

FIGURE (page 145)
Tenison's Network. From the Campaign's base in Britain the BPC's Secretary developed a complex pattern of political relationships that connected with sympathizers in Austria and Portugal.

Act, Sire, that none of high admired degrees,
Of French, Italian, English, German land,
Can venture to assert the Portuguese
Are more to be commanded than command.
                    Luís Camões, *The Lusiads* (1572)

And then the locusts came. It had not happened for many a long year. The elders said locusts came once in a generation, reappeared every year for seven years and then disappeared for another lifetime.
                    Chinua Achebe, *Things Fall Apart* (1958)

Introduction

The British intellectual and journalist Aubrey Bell wrote in 1915:

> Since the murder of King Carlos and of the Crown Prince Luis Felipe on the 1st of February 1908, Portugal has been in the limelight. A swarm of writers have descended like locusts on the land, and the printing presses of Europe have groaned beneath the mass of matter concerning this unfortunate country.[1]

This book is an attempt to view the early years of the First Portuguese Republic from a British perspective. It uses the specific case of a small group of critics in the years before the First World War to connect to a constellation of general attitudes about Portugal and the Portuguese. These critics were either British, or working within a British context. Vicente Bragança-Cunha, a Portuguese Goan, lived and worked in Britain. Francis McCullagh was Irish. In other ways, they were a mixed bunch. Whilst they had shared views about the First Republic, they also had many differences. The issue on which all agreed – that forms the heart of this study – is that political prisoners should not be kept by a state allied to Britain and should be freed. This issue brought an otherwise disparate group together around a single organisation with a sole, declared purpose. After an existence of only about a couple of years it claimed almost total success. It may, therefore, be one of the shortest-lived pressure groups in twentieth-century Britain. Its origins, however, reach back into a long history of British neo-colonialism in Portugal and its empire.

There is scarcely an historiography of British attitudes towards the Portuguese, before the Dictatorship. Some attention has been given to Anglo-British diplomacy, but next to none to those who worked outside of official circles. It is a long time since Rose Macaulay wrote her episodic and generalised account of travellers to Portugal through the ages.[2] Some of 'The Locusts' went to Portugal, but more agitated from home. Distance has its disadvantages, of course, but so too does proximity. This book seeks to identify the historical sources of British negativity towards Portugal's First Republic.

The historiography of the First Republic in English is slight. Strangely, that is almost as true of Edwardian Britain. In the optimistic aftermath of the 1974 Revolution, Wheeler[3] attempted to correct the excessively critical approach of Bragança-Cunha.[4] More recently Schwartzman[5] has used the Republic as a laboratory for testing world systems theory. Her approach takes us closer to understanding the regime's constraints at an international level, but marginalizes individual agency within the metropole, itself. While Portugal's was the 'colonialism of the semi-colonised', in Cabral's depiction of the macro-global context,[6] at the micro-level, politicians like Afonso Costa and soldiers like Paiva Couceiro exercised crucial personal agency in shaping the 'internal war' of the 'Old Republic' to 1914. Edwardian foreign and imperial policy was also a contested enterprise. Liberalism governed between 1906 and 1914, but was divided, and without much power from 1910. Liberal Imperialism inhabited the state to the disappointment of its critics, who would have had a different kind of empire. While from within the Liberal tent Radical critics tried to move Liberal Imperialism to the left; outside it, Labour did little more than salivate over Liberal private grief. Amongst Liberals, the Republic generated more criticism than the Monarchy had. But Portugal's empire rolled on unchanged, little reformed, and much censured. Even the most sympathetic criticism from Britain carried a semi-colonialist tone. Condescension flowed readily from an established discourse of subalterneity. Portugal was 'othered' politically, analogous to her geographical marginalisation on the edge of Europe.

The book is constructed around a handful of leading campaigners because the sources lent themselves to such an approach. It is not an argument for individual agency as the dominant cause of historical change. Rather, these intersecting narratives are used as interpretational vantage points upon revisited events. As the writing progressed, it became clear that, if it was to live at all this history had to live through its characters, because they *were* extraordinary people. Bell, McCullagh, Gibbs, Bragança-Cunha were all journalists, but also 'men of letters' and powerful minds. Tenison and the Duchess of Bedford were not journalists, but historian and social reformer respectively. Each was a woman of aristocratic pedigree combined with intellectual distinction. As women, in an age of greater gender discrimination than our own, they led the Campaign through organisational ability. The British Protest Committee was a single-issue campaign on the political prisoners' question, at least in its official declarations. There were many important opponents of the First Republic who were not active members of it. Here, we confront a difficulty. The BPC had no membership list. So, who was a 'campaigner'? I have assigned membership through activism around common attitudes. This includes Braganca- Cunha and John Harris, marginal activists at best, but key access points, in contrasting ways, to the wider imperial context of the Portuguese state. Most of these people knew each other, often well. A number passed through Yokes Court, 51 Berkeley Square, or both. One or two had been incubated as 'Locusts' in the periphery; in Goa or São Tomé, for example.

What emerges is, perhaps, the shape of a 'campaign' in only the loosest sense. The political prisoners' issue galvanized a few well-connected and influential members of the 'chattering classes' to become political activists, against the grain in the case of some. In opting for activism, they were required to come to terms with the functioning of an increasingly influential press. But press power, itself, only emerged out of an evolving culture of citizenship, enabling effective public action. Here lay a contradiction of uneven development. An initiative over a specific libertarian objective (freeing political prisoners) ignited within a British imperialist culture casting condescension upon peripheral Portugal. A handful of people, who might otherwise be written off as obscure or marginal to pre-war British political society, become emblematic of the cultural biases of the imperial state. But they also shed light on some contested aspects of developing democracies: the constitutional role of monarchy, the role of religion, the rule of law, as well as the imperial conscience – the responsibilities of metropoles towards subalterns. At the same time, they expose the more regressive, institutional conservatism that defended such states as they negotiated the fraught path towards the First World War. Exposing such tensions reminds us of the limitations of linear views of modern history. The road to 1914 was a crooked line.

To have any effect on state power, the individual agency of 'The Locusts' had to swarm and collectivize into an organized campaign. At every necessary point, the Foreign Office pulled up the drawbridge of diplomacy in front of it. Some quite influential citizens were in revolt over foreign policy towards Portugal. One or two (like Tenison), were novices at the art of public protest; but others (like Harris) were long-standing subversives who knew all the tricks. Here, a British history of emerging citizenship opens out towards a comparative history from below. This campaign of British citizens was paralleled by equally modern developments in Portuguese society. In both countries, public action grew stronger on the advanced diet of citizenship. Each society wrestled with the question of what the middle classes would do about empire. A vanguard had begun to inform debate through travel. Britons increasingly went to metropolitan Portugal, but also to its empire. Sometimes this led to extraordinary encounters. Philip Gibbs met political prisoners in Lisbon in late 1913, but what he found in the 'black hole of Elvas' astounded even the stoic readers of the *Daily Chronicle*. John Harris was so appalled by what he found in São Tomé in 1912 that he called it out as 'Portuguese Slavery.' These 'Locusts' touched the lives of their readers because of the 'new journalism'. By the early twentieth century, the power of the printed word in mass circulation could challenge the state's truths. It revealed injustice and oppression across Portuguese historical sites. State and empire were reinterpreted within the public discourse as an imagined community resembling a diaspora of tyranny.

The first three chapters attempt to create the broader context of Portuguese history that incubated 'The Locusts' in Britain. Chapter 1 begins by explaining the Anglo-Portuguese historical culture from which they emerged. It then broadens out to consider how historians have written about Anglo-Portuguese relations in the century or so since 1914. It continues by focussing inwards upon the short-term causes of the Revolution of 1910. It ends by considering whether that event represents a maturation of late nineteenth-century civil society. Chapter 2 examines how selected examples of the mainstream British press reported the 1910 Revolution. It compares these sources to argue that the public was presented with a contested narrative occasioned by ideology and space. Chapter 3 examines the persistence of the Anglo-Portuguese link through one specific example: King Manuel's exile to Britain at the end of 1910. The circumstances of his departure are clarified from the conflicting accounts. Less disputed is the welcoming network that received him in Britain, and his comfortable adaptation to his new circumstances. Where else would an exiled Portuguese king end up but Twickenham?

From Chapter 4, the book focuses in on the individual contributions of the disparate group of activists I have called 'The Locusts.' The fourth chapter looks at the particularly religious motivations of the Catholic journalist Francis McCullagh, an incipient *enragé* against the Republic from 1910. He represents that group who saw the anti-clericalism of the Republican regime as indicative of Portugal's social degeneration. For them, the Revolution was a conspiracy of racially inferior, evil atheists, intent on vanquishing God and King from the state. Bragança-Cunha, the subject of Chapter 5, shared the Irishman McCullagh's Catholicism, but was a unique 'Locust' in other respects. As a Portuguese Goan, he was a different type of peripheral critic: an *émigré* in London. Yet, the sources he has left sound a deafening, silence on a personal colonial narrative he seems at pains to conceal. His backstory has been pieced together from other sources. From early 1911, he polemicized against the Republic with an angry Royalism that served to camouflage his colonial identity. An ideological soulmate of the exiled King, there seems to have been no contact between them across the capital. Like Tenison, he was also an historian of monarchy.

Aubrey Bell, the subject of Chapter 6, is pivotal. His doubts about the First Republic, expressed in a wide range of sources, exhibit a deep empathy. His personal experience, as Lisbon correspondent of the *Morning Post* from 1911, gave him a unique insight into Portuguese politics. He was much more than a journalist. A Lusophile intellectual of the first rank, Bell, was also an exile – a self-consigned one – reporting from the periphery. His writing was a bridgehead to the fulcra in the metropole: E. M. Tenison and the Duchess of Bedford. In Chapter 7 we see Tenison move from lady of leisure-cum-dilettante historian, to secretary of a political campaign in a matter of months. She was joined shortly by the Duchess of Bedford, a social reformer of national esteem, infused with an equal sense of the injustice being inflicted on Portuguese Monarchists. Like the Harrises, later, their personal narratives are entwined. Even before the Duchess got on board, Tenison had helped form the British Protest Committee (BPC) which burst into print with its captives' narratives – a subject of Chapter 9. That marked the Campaign's initial step towards maturity as a civic movement: a recognition of the power of propaganda. The amplification of print into the civic arena was realized through the public meetings of 1913–14, an expression of civic consciousness paralleled in Portugal. The BPC begins to ape the great reforming movements of the Edwardian age, notably the Anti-Slavery Society. In the absence of its own regular journal (like the *Anti-Slavery Reporter*), the BPC deploys conduits like *The Daily Chronicle*, and in Chapter 10, Philip Gibbs is recruited to reveal the full horror of Portuguese political prisons, first visited by the Duchess in the spring of 1913.

Long before then, John Harris had followed Henry Nevinson and others in attacking Portuguese integrity over 'slavery'. The penultimate chapter on Harris demonstrates the unavoidability of a centrifugal approach for understanding the broad context of the political prisoners' campaign. A methodology that links shifting historical sites necessarily takes us from South London to West Africa and back to Whitehall. Africa is always the elephant in the room of the earlier chapters. Tenison would have had it remain so. But, 'Locusts' swarmed beyond London and Lisbon, swooping also on the cocoa plantations of São Tomé and Princípe to follow the train of forced labour back to Angola. Harris is marginal to the BPC, itself, but central to the arguments of the book. He conveyed the evils of slavery from West Africa to the reading rooms and public halls of the metropole. Mab Tenison made good use of him, despite her reservations. With others, they ratcheted-up a discourse of despair about Portugal, designed to bring the regime to its senses. 'The Locusts' fought hard, and with some success, to lay waste to the 'nightmare Republic'. But, long before summer 1914, that was not a battle that the British government sought. In the circumstances of 1913–14, the imperatives of pre-war diplomacy decreed that the Foreign Office was not about to terminate the Alliance, let alone indulge in nation building. In Whitehall, 'The Locusts' found an adversary equal to any they faced in Lisbon.

CHAPTER

1

'Descending like locusts': Britain and the First Portuguese Republic

1 Neglectful condescension

Just seven years before Aubrey Bell compared critics of Portugal to a swarm of locusts, the distinguished French intellectual Jean Finot[1] wrote, in the wake of the assassination of 1908:

> No country, perhaps, has attracted less attention of late years than Portugal... I have looked in vain in recent works on the psychology of nations for any penetrating account of Portugal. There is none. Economic studies of Portugal, published in other lands, are fundamentally wrong. When they are eulogistic, they care only to preach up her credit. When they are hostile they do not scruple to cheapen even her inexhaustible resources.[2]

Finot's regret, that Portugal was a victim of both neglect and misrepresentation, is instructive. Bell's suspension of that neglect did nothing to remedy the misrepresentation. Neglect persisted into the present century. Three distinguished Portuguese historians recently observed, 'the whole of the First Republic, remains insufficiently studied overshadowed as it is in terms of both popular and academic interest by the New State.'[3]

In Britain, neglect has resulted in a relative silence that has tended to write Portugal out of history. It has suffered from, in a much borrowed phrase of E. P. Thompson's, 'the enormous condescension of posterity'.[4] When it has been attended to, Portuguese history has been subjected to a narrative of exceptionalism. A dominant discourse into the twentieth century saw Portugal's unique empire of miscegenation declining into peripheral instability and revolution.

Attributing exceptionalism to a failure to modernize is a limited perspective. Twentieth-century capitalist development proved an uneven process. The losers resided not only in Portugal, but across Southern Europe: in Italy, Greece and Spain, not to mention the East. To be acknowledged within the Western canon, Portuguese history has needed to produce exceptional moments; crises lending themselves to a 'dramatization of identity'.[5] Such exceptions occurred in 1974 (when it had a second revolution), during the Second World War (when it was of strategic importance), and perhaps during the First World War (when it was an ally for two years). The inception of the First Republic was such a pivotal moment. Yet, its reception in Britain has received little attention from historians.[6] This is surprising given that the fate of Portugal's empire raised important questions within Anglo-German relations, and therefore about the causes of the First World War. Should Germany be appeased with Portugal's African colonies? Worse for the Republic, would the Iberian peninsula not be more stable if Spain governed it all?[7] Between 1910 and 1914, Portugal mattered.

A narrow focus on diplomatic history is insufficient to explain the campaign in Britain against the Republic. Early critics had tried to turn public opinion against the forced labour system in the African colonies, frequently condemned as 'slavery'. But the Republic caused criticism to shift to Portugal, itself. In the two years before the outbreak of War, the issue of political prisoners came to dwarf even that of anti-clericalism in British politics. Republican Portugal was portrayed as a failed democracy; a virtual police state in which the rule of law was collapsing. The right of such a state to allied status was challenged. Some who preferred German Monarchism to Portuguese Republicanism would have gifted its colonies to Berlin, or even perhaps Madrid.

It has been proposed that most of this agitation was mere monarchist propaganda.[8] But, there existed a greater diversity of criticism. In the daily and periodical press, and on public platforms, men and women of conservative, Catholic, and monarchist views stood alongside those of liberal, secular and even republican persuasions. Some wanted the complete overthrow of the Republic and the restoration of Church and Monarchy; others, its reform into an improved, secular, liberal democracy. Notably absent were socialists; uncertain about a radical regime with only fragile links to the labour movement. Ramsay MacDonald dipped his toe into turbulent Portuguese waters once,[9] but withdrew after a barrage from the flamboyant *émigré* Vicente de Bragança-Cunha.[10] The British Protest Campaign's insistence that freeing political prisoners was their only concern was distrusted by Portuguese Republicans who suspected it was a dagger into the

Republic itself. Even so, the Republic's dependence on British goodwill to survive forced it to address criticism from any source.[11]

2 Incubating 'Locusts': The historical context of the First Republic

A recent summary of the historiography of the First Republic concluded:

> one can distinguish three main interpretations. For some historians, the First Republic was a progressive and increasingly democratic regime. For others, it was essentially a prolongation of the liberal and elitist regimes of the nineteenth century. A third group, finally, chooses to highlight the regime's revolutionary, Jacobin, and dictatorial nature.[12]

Into the third category fit not only historians, but many of the 'The Locusts', themselves. From the other two we can detect a narrative that traces the origins of modern Portuguese Republicanism back to the constitutional monarchy of 1820, whose liberalism survived the civil wars. A structural continuity has been established between it and early twentieth-century Republicanism, particularly through the PRP's replication of monarchical control over the electoral system.[13] The liberal monarchy handed on a modernising state, but it was one badly managed. Underlying this was a comparatively under-developed, dependent economy. Amongst small-scale industry, one-sixth of firms were foreign-owned in 1900; half of these by the British. The 'political enslavement to England' that Oliveira Marques noted,[14] was underpinned by economics.

Only Lisbon contained a middle class capable of a political challenge to the monarchical elites. The lower middle class, in particular, provided the backbone of independent Republicanism. They were moderate liberals, not Jacobins, and had recovered from late nineteenth-century depression less impoverished than many across Europe. Aspirational and free trading, they had not yet been overrun by large retail expansion. Small businesses increased, 1900–10, fostering a secure embrace of progressive politics that contrasted with the Right-turn elsewhere in Europe. In Portugal, middle-class reformers targeted little more than the corrupt excesses of the state.[15]

Through the late nineteenth century, lack of economic and demographic growth put the brake upon modernisation. Lisbon grew after 1860, but hardly anywhere else did. Under-employed Portuguese emigrated, increasingly from the 1880s, while their remittances helped to close the trade gap a little. Modernisation occurred mainly in the social and political spheres. The Laws of Separation of 1911 had been anticipated since 1834 when the religious orders were closed. At the dawn of the Republic, national illiteracy rates of around 70 percent provided the political oxygen for Republican propaganda. But, aspiring to primary education of the standard of French *lyceés* when 17.5 percent of all parishes had no school in 1911 sounded like telling starving Portuguese children to eat cake. Radical Republicans saw in this ossification, not modernisation. They blamed the monarchical regime for running politics like a pyramid scheme:

> the government appointed the civil governor of the districts, who would choose the administrator of the county, who would in turn appoint the parish alderman, who would choose the head of police. Not only did this system facilitate reciprocal complicities, it was at the service of the elites in Lisbon, nourishing the various "parties". From this resulted an entangled web of big shots, *"caciques"* and electioneers, who coerced and manipulated the will of the electorate.[16]

Portugal's emergence as a wider but rotational two-party, democracy dated from 1878.[17] But from 1911 Republicanism developed a contradictory relationship with the suffrage, itself. Having extended it in 1911, it then restricted it again in 1913. The exclusionary tool was the literacy clause that privileged better-educated urban areas, where Republican voting was strong, at a time of Monarchist insurrection. Women and members of the armed forces were also kept unenfranchized. The effect was 'a gradual democratic delegitimization' with elections continuing to be 'mere confirmation rituals', much as they had been under the Monarchy, but against the grain for Western Europe.[18]

The intellectual wing of Republicanism, from the late 1860s, was the 'Generation of 1870'. Angry young men like Teófilo Braga, Antero de Quental, Eça de Queirós, and Oliveira Martins hotly debated the 'Coimbra Question', in practice many reformist questions. Francophile, Positivist, and secular, they have been seen as the *avant-garde* of modernity,[19] influencing growing Republicanism beyond their numbers.[20] Post-1870 changes in Republican France provided a template for renewal in decadent Portugal, where inertia was blamed on the weak Monarchy in thrall to the Church.

Portugal's Francophile culture looked all the way back to the Revolution. It took on various Portuguese mutations. Republicanism was deeply marked, but the French connection spread across the 'chattering classes', and even into the royal family.[21] In literature, it is to be found in the critically measured appreciation of Paris that flowed from the pen of Eça de Queirós.[22] Eça' s day job was as a diplomat, and he served his time in Newcastle and Bristol as well as his beloved Paris. This bred witticisms about Portugal's greatest novelist never being in Portugal, which just invited his contempt: Lisbon was 'a city translated from the French into slang.'[23] Comtean Positivism ran through Portuguese bourgeois culture, exemplified by Quental's lecture on political modernisation of 27 May 1871.[24] He identified three causes of Portugal's historic decline. Morally, he pointed to the damaging effects of a conservative Catholicism. Portuguese Positivists followed Comte's teachings that true knowledge could only be obtained through science, not religion. Teófilo Braga, rather than Quental, compared Republicanism as a morally superior value-system to a hypocritical Church.[25] Freemasonry and anti-clericalism completed the challenge to Church authority. Politically, Quental argued progress towards citizenship had been damaged by the Monarchy's centralism, suppressing local autonomy. The historian, Alexandre Herculano, conferred on Quental an imaginary past that idealized local municipalism. It was a medieval construct in which local *conselhos* struggled like small republics against an oligarchic state. Republicanism inherited the municipalist mantle but became so metropolitanized that it struggled to see beyond Lisbon. Economically, Quental blamed a complacent and bloated landowning class for swallowing any gains from empire. It held back the pre-requisite for modernisation: a dynamic middle class. Quental's panacea for modernisation was, thus, to embrace science, federalise government, and promote industrialisation.

Quental and the 'Generation of 1870' were the offspring of an obsession with national regeneration. Only a nation that had fallen so far could be so fixated upon rising. To this end, Sebastianism's mythology was reconstructed to meet the needs of a Republicanism destined to replace Monarchy.[26] Catroga detects a similar tractability in national regeneration, an imaginary that penetrated all social classes, and one steeped in fear of racial decay. National redemption was reflected in interpretations of natural phenomena, and even the naming of children. The 'Generation of 1870' generated an optimism that Portuguese society could ascend from its historically low point. But Positivism became obsessed with explaining the nadir through social biologism. Portugal was imagined as a diseased, decadent society. Scientism offered treatment, although complete cure depended on returning to the perfect medication of the Enlightenment. For a deeply psychotic Portugal, this would not be easy. As a generation of medics subscribed to social biologism, the 'Generation of 1870' became honoured as doctors of society.

The 1891 crisis added to the psychosis a perception that the Empire and the *patria* were equally doomed. Pessimism took hold as neurotic Portuguese interpreted the earthquake of 1909 and the appearance of Haley's Comet in 1910 apocalyptically. One Setubal priest blamed Republicans preaching revolution for inviting God's punishment. Seven years before the Fatima apparitions of 1917, a twelve-year-old girl in Póvoa claimed the Virgin had told her that Haley's Comet would bring the end of the world. Others believed this had already been predicted by the regicide of 1908. When Armageddon failed to arrive, more couples turned optimistically towards secularism and civil marriage. Religious naming of children declined, encouraged by Republicans, although one civil governor in Braga drew the line at registering a little 'Victor Hugo Rousseau'. This revolutionary nomenclature was emblematic of a demographic for a new *patria*.[27]

The lack of national self-confidence and the drive for national regeneration had roots in the frequent British interventions in Portuguese affairs. The expulsion of the Monarchy to Brazil in 1807[28] was effectively to facilitate a military occupation to confront Napoleon. British troops were still in Portugal in the 1820s. Palmerston supported the liberal constitutionalism of Maria (Pedro's daughter) against the absolutist Miguelists through the civil wars of the 1830s. Still, the Quadruple Alliance of Britain, France, Spain and Portugal in 1834 'was essentially a device for the settlement of the affairs of the Peninsula according to British prescriptions.'[29] After a popular revolt, 1846–47, against Maria II's repressive policies temporarily overthrew her, Palmerston intervened again. The Chartist, George Julian Harney, was so appalled he stood against Palmerston in Tiverton in 1847. But as Palmerston told Queen Victoria, Maria 'should remember that England was the final arbiter in Portugal.'[30] He reiterated this in 1857 by using the Quadruple Alliance to send British troops to crush the Chartist rebellion in Porto. Palmerston managed to have it both ways. The rule of the Queen's dictator, Saldanha, was preserved but under a restored constitution and an amnesty for all rebels. Later, the BPC constructed a legitimating narrative for a Portuguese political amnesty from this Palmerstonian precedent.

The British also intervened over the slave trade. After Britain abolished it in 1807, it determined to enforce this comparative disadvantage on its competitors. An official Portuguese declaration of illegality in 1836 was *'para inglês ver.'*[31] Palmerston was not fooled, threatened Portugal with war, but failed to pass a Slave Trade (Portugal) Bill in 1839.[32] Portuguese prevarication continued until a final act in the Portuguese parliament on 25 February 1869. Still evasion continued, until the abolition of slavery in Brazil in the 1880s finally killed the trade completely.[33] Former slaves were redesignated *serviçais*, owing some forced labour by the new code of native labour, 1875. Forced labour became the norm, but was 'virtual slavery' as the editor of *The Spectator* called it.[34] The argument was really about the autonomy of empire, which Republicans shared in believing was vital to national regeneration. Defence of empire was a signifier of patriotism; questioning it implied national decadence and raised the 'regime question.'[35] The 1890 Ultimatum delivered the Monarchy into Republican hands through the Monarchy's association with national humiliation. A failed Republican rising took place in Porto in 1891. Britain's 'boundless expansion'[36] across central Africa epitomized by Rhodes' Cape to Cairo plans, intersected the vision of Portugal's 'rose-coloured map' (*mapa rosa*) of 1886 to link Angola with Mozambique. The British spread a narrative of incompetence, exacerbated by Rhodes' racist dismissal of too much land already being given away to 'a half caste Portugee.'[37] Portugal was forced to withdraw from southern central Africa. The loss impacted deeply on its national identity as a relatively minor diplomatic defeat was transformed into a disaster. Portugal succumbed to a negative self-image, an 'imagined community' that reflected a subaltern acceptance of a destiny imposed from without.[38]

In the cartoons of Raphael Bordallo Pinheiro Portuguese popular culture made light of national humiliation. Bordallo's character *Zé Povinho* satirized Portugal's two-faced diplomacy.[39] It has been argued that the Portuguese bourgeoisie's support for colonialism should be read as resistance against foreign domination.[40] But, in Bordallo's case, he abhorred Portuguese prostrations even more than British bullying. His depiction of a comic bourgeoisie of semi-colonized mimics, imitating the behaviour of the dominant colonial power throbs with social criticism.[41] Britain is caricatured as a gluttonous John Bull intent on eating Portuguese colonies. *Zé Povinho* represents the moral conscience of the Portuguese people, indignant at the complicity of their own politicians in British avarice. At Bordallo's Berlin Conference of 1885, Portuguese diplomats are trading away their country's interests in return for champagne. Despite his satire, Bordallo's bourgeois Republicanism continued to defend the colonial empire as part of the national patrimony. But it was his genius to expose hypocrisy by having *Zé Povinho* ask the national question in comic irony: 'who are your worst enemies – foreign predators, or your own rulers?' There was no hiding place from this wry debate for a Monarchy accused of turning the Portuguese into the Africans of Europe. Systemic Monarchist connivance with the British attested to a semi-colonized Portugal disempowered within the world system. Resistance was a fabrication for consumption by the domestic audience.

An agreement of 1898 mortgaged the Portuguese colonies against loan repayments to Britain and Germany. Still the Portuguese allowed passage of British arms through Mozambique during the Boer War. *Rapprochement* led to frequent royal visits. Edward VII went in 1903; Carlos came in 1904. Manuel went in 1909; and again in 1910, for Edward's funeral. By then, the two Treaties of Windsor (1899 and 1904) had reaffirmed the Old Alliance, and Portugal supported Britain against Germany over Morocco. But the British interpretation of *rapprochement* was flexible enough to incorporate negotiations with the Germans over the future of the Portuguese colonies, between 1911 and 1914. Secret diplomacy complicated this triangular relationship. The German strategy of betting that the Portuguese would be weakened by indebtedness backfired, and as Lichnowsky, German Ambassador in London observed, Germany, who had once aspired to inherit Portugal's colonies, could now only hope to be its medical adviser.[42] It was even suggested that the Germans wanted to keep the Republicans in power, at a time of Royalist incursions, because Republicans offered a better chance of colonial concessions.[43] In the end, the Portuguese obtained some French assistance in European capital markets.

The British evaluated the Alliance against the precariousness of Anglo-German relations. Portuguese suspicions pressured Britain into making the 1898 agreement with Germany public. The Portuguese wanted publication of its agreement of 1899 with the British, to reassure its own public that it was safeguarding the colonies. Furthermore, bartering the Portuguese colonies had raised Belgian concerns for the Congo, and French hackles in respect of the Entente. In the end, there was no Anglo-German agreement on the Portuguese colonies because negotiations foundered on German refusal to publish any agreement. The negotiations are an example *par excellence* of secret diplomacy's role in causing the First World War. Germany's emergence as a great power had not offered Portugal the alternative alliance that many Anglo-sceptics had hoped for. Germany had merely become another predator. After a period of improved relations, the early years of the Republic (1910–14) saw historic fears of Spanish incursion revive. This put an end to the flirtation with Iberianism in Republican ranks, in favour of a new realism that sought to consolidate the Old Alliance for want of a better alternative.[44]

The Old Alliance has been subject to frequent historiographical revision. In Britain, it drew upon a rich fiction preserved by collective memory, repetitively recycled to the neglect of the evidence. Charles Boxer's history master hit the nail on the head when he joked that Portugal was both our oldest ally and our worst. And, Boxer was surely right to suggest that the jest works just as well in reverse.[45] Victor Kiernan cut through the cant, too, when he observed: 'The notion of six centuries of unbroken friendship between two sea-faring nations of Europe's western fringes has a romantic savour, and would be charming if true.'[46] He dates the beginning of a modern neo-colonial relationship from the English guarantee of Portuguese independence after the Reconquest (1640), cemented by Charles II's marriage to Catherine of Bragança (1662). The Methuen Treaty (1703) secured domination of Portuguese markets for British textiles. The Napoleonic Wars saw the Portuguese compelled to exchange French rule for British. Spain was inclined to sell union as Portugal's best hope of avoiding becoming the new Canada, whilst the British feared an Iberian Union would become Francophile. To guard against renewed French, or Spanish, designs upon Portugal, the British continued to underwrite a subaltern Portuguese empire. Decadent Portuguese colonialism was kept on life support by British colonialism as a kind of hedge bet.

When Kiernan warned against falling foul of romanticism he may have had in mind Edgar Prestage's celebration of one race complementing the other's qualities, a conceptualisation most historians now find redundant. As one has said, the earlier romantics were too seduced by the durability of the Alliance.[47] However, even Prestage, acknowledged the discontinuities, such as the boarding of Portuguese slave ships through the later nineteenth century. But there is no hint of neo-colonialism in the Prestage of 1934.[48] This contrasts with Charles Boxer's realism that suggests the Alliance paved the way to the 1910 Revolution because the 1890 Ultimatum strengthened Republicanism.[49] Boxer certainly acknowledged mutual benefits, but stressed that most went to the stronger partner. His conclusion, that the Alliance remained in tact because of reciprocity, does not fundamentally differ from Prestage's, however. Neither adopted the centrifugal approach of situating Anglo-Portuguese relations within a world imperial system. Boxer looked no further than the Alliance for half the explanation of the Portuguese Empire's longevity. The other half was 'its singular record of repressive and obscurantist rule.'[50]

Since the 1970s, historians have tended to move away from Alliance theory towards assessing Anglo-Portuguese as one spoke of a wheel of imperial relations. After Wallerstein, Schwartzman (writing only months before the transition from communism to democracy in Eastern Europe) explained the Republic's collapse through Portugal's semi-peripheral status within the world system, and the compounding effects of a 'disarticulated economy.'[51] The attempt to use Portuguese history as a case study in comparative under-development fits into a school of American social science scholarship comparing Iberian with Latin American societies.[52] As a 'grand theory', it can struggle for empirical evidence at the domestic level and is inclined to marginalize both national autonomy and individual agency.[53]

The early years of the 'Old Republic' (1910–14) focused inwards, asserting a new primacy of politics over 'economic disarticulation.' The new *Cortes* was younger, more metropolitan, educated, and middle class. But continuities persisted. Most members were still the placemen of local bosses. Only in the more independent urban areas, like Lisbon and Porto, did middle-class Republicanism significantly dislodge the remnants of the old regime. Continuities with the Monarchy have led historians to question whether democracy really was the Republican project from 1910. Perhaps, regime change was little more than a shift in elite circulation? Perhaps, there was no 'long road to democracy,'[54] just a narrowing of representation through disenfranchisement and anti-clericalism. The First Republic becomes a paradoxical regime; a 'peculiar combination of limited radicalism and political exclusivism.'[55] This view engages with an older revisionism about the middle class not steering a special path towards democracy in early twentieth-century Europe.[56] It did not play a consistently progressive role everywhere. In Portugal, although membership of the political class changed, ownership of capital did not.

In 1910 Portugal was still a highly rural economy. Landed capital ranged from the *latifundists* of the South to subsistence farmers in the North. Finance capital dominated small-scale industry. Republicanism attacked institutions like the Church, without any programme of economic redistribution, so inviting labour revolt. The heartland of rural conservatism lay in the North. God fearing and Church loving, it was sceptical of Republicanism's metropolitan agenda. In 1900, 60 percent of the population worked in small-scale agriculture, where rates of illiteracy ran far above the national average of 79 percent.[57] It was here that Couceiro's risings to restore the Monarchy won support. This was the Portugal of the *longue durée*; these people who were not counted, and did not count. The new Republic produced no early programme of land reform (as the Spanish Republic did in 1931).[58] Peasants wanted something to redress the 115 percent rise in taxes on farmers' incomes over the three decades before 1908.[59] Instead, their churches were disrespected, their votes taken away.

Early twentieth-century Portugal has been described as a religious land with an unpopular church.[60] As the Catholic politician P. Zacarias de Oliveira said, 'We are Catholics because our forefathers were. And we don't want to know about any other reasons for being so.'[61] Faith was a traditional inheritance of the *longue durée*, distinct from organized religion. The Fátima apparitions of 1917 provoked an expression of popular faith the Church initially regarded as a challenge to its authority. It then co-opted and institutionalized them.[62] After a long nineteenth-century of punishment for supporting absolutism through the civil wars, the Church had re-institutionalized itself by around 1900, though it continued to denounce the twin evils of Positivism and Freemasonry. Republicanism dismissed it as a remnant of archaic superstition. A Catholic revival involving renewed Jesuit education, charity and a new Catholic press set up an antithetical relationship with Republicanism. Catholicism became more politicized, supporting both social justice and the dictatorship of João Franco. By then, the religious question had become inseparable from the regime question, all contested in a vitriolic public language.[63] Although Church schools had made little impact on literacy rates, closing them down was an act of Republican ideological purity. Lucia Santos, thirteen on 13 June 1920, claimed that the Virgin Mary told her during the second apparition that to fulfil Jesus' plans for her, she needed to learn how to read. In that year 97 percent of the females in the parish of Fátima were still illiterate, and 87 percent of the males were.[64]

The survival of the First Portuguese Republic would depend, therefore, upon how well it managed the internal dynamics of state and society. World systems theory is not designed to address such specifics,[65] but does direct us towards the global vulnerabilities of the semi-peripheral state. As it was being developed in North American universities, Amílcar Cabral was leading the resistance to Portuguese colonialism in Guinea-Bissau. He was producing some remarkably similar ideas about imperialism. Cabral was a trained agronomist, but armed struggle in Guinea-Bissau focused him upon the history of Portuguese colonialism in Africa. His experience as a revolutionary nationalist meant he 'conceived of theory as a description of reality rather than merely as a speculative exercise.'[66] He drew an analogy between the 'semi-autonomous state' in Africa in the 1960s and 1970s and Portugal's historical relationship with fully autonomous, imperialist states like Britain.[67] Cabral dated Portugal's semi-autonomous status from the Methuen Treaty. It turned eighteenth-century Portugal into 'a semi-colony of England . . . England had every interest in using the Portuguese colonies, not only to exploit their economic resources, but also to occupy them as support bases on route to the Orient, and thus to maintain absolute domination in the Indian Ocean.'[68] Portugal was reduced to a clientalist role within world imperialism. By the early twentieth century half of Angola and Mozambique's exports went to only three countries: Britain, France and Germany. The 1885 Berlin Conference had been decisive in dividing up world markets. Portugal's role was as facilitator accepting the crumbs from the table. Unable to match the developmental role taken by the bigger imperialist powers, Portugal transferred its own metropolitan backwardness onto the colonies.[69]

Cabral theorized his ideas on the nature of Portuguese imperialism very concisely at a conference in Helsinki on 20 October 1971. Originally published in a French journal, it has been neglected as a source. He argued that, since the Methuen Treaty (1703) Portugal had historically been 'not an imperialist country but a country chained to imperialism.' Its economic infra-structure had always been too undeveloped to support full imperialism. Even by the twentieth century its economy was largely foreign owned, so that it became, 'a half colony.' It could only act as an intermediary, or policeman, between the exploited peoples and the ultimate colonialists. But the modern functions of 'half colony' were only derived later, at Berlin in 1885. 'England' became the ultimate guarantor of its empire, which meant vigorous exploitation of Portugal's colonies 'as if they were her own.' 'England' was part of a 'nucleus' (or core) of fully developed capitalist states that 'On their periphery . . . created countries dominated by imperialism.' The peripheral states (like Portugal) could only reproduce a 'half', or 'a partial colonialism.' Because Portuguese colonialism was also archaic – 'the most backward of all colonialisms' – it could only survive in the modern colonialist era by acting in a subordinate capacity.[70]

Cabral's thought anticipated postcolonial studies.[71] He depicted Portugal as being in a subaltern relationship with Britain due to the disparities in imperial power and historical dependency. Britain practised what he called 'real imperialism', to which Portugal's was subordinate. Unlike the social subaltern, the state Portugal retained the autonomy to source and write its own history, but only as a 'half-colony.' Of course, it had no control over how this was interpreted in the neo-colonial partner state. Subaltern studies attends to discrepancies in power reflected by dominant and subordinate narratives, and this study is concerned with a contest of narratives between actors in the two states. There could be no single Portuguese or British narrative, but there was a dominant Republican one in Portugal, and a dominant neo-colonialist one in Britain. In crucial ways, the British narrative was more powerful than the Portuguese. Portugal was rendered subaltern in the sense that neo-colonialism shaped a dominant narrative about it within the core, international arena. Britain dominated not only through the direct economic power that Cabral observed, but also in controlling the terms of the public-international discourse. In the 'private domain' Britain was cognisant of the economic and diplomatic advantages of the Old Alliance; but in the 'public' it was presented as one of mutual interest: a false equality. Portugal possessed its own dominant (Republican) narrative, but its influence was limited to the domestic domain by the power imbalance within the Alliance. Subaltern status compelled it to avoid conflict, even to the point of accommodating the dominant narrative.

Republicanism was loathe to do this, but caution was necessary because of the semi-periphery's dependency that circumscribed Portuguese discourse. But, particularly beyond the official level, both narratives were also in a dialogue, influencing and changing each other. 'Semi-colonialism' flowed both ways as constructions of difference were moderated and mediated. One change was that the Republic proved more critical of Britain than the Monarchy, Afonso Costa being the main offender. His reputation as a trouble maker dated from 1909 when he opposed compensating the Madeira sugar manufacturer Harry Hinton after a change in taxation law. The Republican opposition used the case to lambaste the Monarchist government's subservience to British interests.[72] Such evidence adds to the pattern of Anglo-Portuguese relations being in constant renegotiation. However, the short-term focus of this study is on a period of just half a decade. If anything the BPC's construction of difference in respect of the First Republic became more extreme between 1910 and 1914, to achieve its singular goal of releasing political prisoners.

Critics have argued that theories like Cabral's run the risk of presenting Portuguese colonialism as a mere conduit for the foreign policy of the great powers. Foreign capital was a necessary evil, but did not prevent imperial policy from retaining a good deal of autonomy. Sceptics remind us that the empire was projected as the expression of the nation, itself. The persistence of practices such as forced labour need not be read as exampling a dependent backwardness. The dominant empires retained similar systems, themselves, making the difference only one of degree.[73] This is an important revision and a reminder that Portuguese historians work within their own cultural context. As the later chapter on the missionary, John Harris, concedes, the autonomy that Portugal exercised over forced labour in the Empire does not fit easily with a semi-peripheral or subaltern status. At the same time, to 1914, it was Portugal's very semi-autonomy that caused it to exploit a nationalist imaginary at home, and a deceptive diplomacy abroad.

3 The origins of the 1910 Revolution

For that astute observer Jean Finot, Carlos I was the architect of his own downfall. Mentally exhausted by party politics, in 1906, he appointed João Franco as dictator. Even Queen Amélie expressed doubts about his abuse of this power. 'Franco is in the right, but he has no tact,'[74] she complained. Carlos defended his offence to constitutionalism through an arrogant sense of mission:

> Our country ... suffers and has suffered from administrative corruption . . . when some years hence some people see what I have accomplished they will excuse my brutalities and violations of the "Constitution."[75]

But his violations engineered the dismissal of far more governments than King Luis before him. His over-active constitutionalism caused conflict and instability.[76]

Carlos had a taste for sailing and pretty women, some said of orgiastic proportions. He exhausted the Civil List on his excesses, so he practised creative accountancy by selling the royal yacht to the state at an inflated price, then loaning it back. His reputation as an accomplished marine biologist did not save him from the wrath of the Republican press.[77] On 28 January 1908 a Republican plot[78] was foiled and a host of its leaders, that read like a roll-call of the Revolution to come, jailed by Franco. They ranged from Afonso Costa, the most dangerous man in Portugal, according to Dom Manuel, to the weightlifter and fencer, João Pinto dos Santos.[79] Ramalho Ortigão, still free, pleaded with his fellow jailed Republicans:

> not to be martyrs, not to offer themselves as victims ready to shed their precious blood for the great cause – not to cherish the old idea of expiring on the barricade biting the heroic cartridge to the strains of the 'Marseillaise' amid the shouts of Liberty and Equality etc.[80]

Franco had struck at the head of the dragon, but its tail proved the real danger. Alfredo Luís da Costa was just twenty-four in 1908. He was a migrant from the village of Castro Verde, in the Baixo Alentejo region, south east of Lisbon. Rescued from illiteracy by a benevolent uncle, he took to clerking, then political journalism in the Azores. Returning to Lisbon from running a bookshop in Estremoz, he joined a well-known freemasons' lodge and returned to journalism. Manuel do Reis da Silva Buiça was older at thirty-one, the illegitimate son of a parish priest from Vinhais, near Bragança, in the north-eastern region of Trás-os-Montes. More fortunate than the offspring of Father Amaro,[81] he moved from Cavalry Sergeant to secondary school teacher. By 1908, he was a committed anarchist and member of the *Carbonário*. Buiça made a will on 28 January in case his two young children became orphans, but both he and Costa avoided arrest.[82]

On 1 February, both assassins enjoyed their last meal in the Café Gelo, a Republican haunt in the Praça do Rossio. a stone's throw from the Terreiro do Paco do Praça, where the King kept them waiting because the royal train was delayed by an hour. It terminated on the south bank of the Tagus, from where the royal family took the steamer across the river, then into an open top carriage to cross the square. Before they could reach the other side, Buiça and Costa shot the King and the Crown Prince dead. They probably intended to murder the entire royal family.[83] Instead, they were apprehended, then subjected to what seems to have been a judicial murder by the police. Afterwards, Monarchists were disgusted at the veneration of Buiça and Costa in Republican circles, where legend built them into the martyrs Ortigão had warned against. Yet, 200,000 people turned out for their funeral.[84] Republicans raised funds for Buiça's children, and they continued to live with their maternal grandmother in a fourth floor attic in Mouraria, one of Lisbon's worst slums. Although the regicide was unique in Portuguese history, it had not come completely out of the blue. Plots had been springing up since the Monarchy's national humiliation by the 1890 Ultimatum.[85] Carlos was rumoured to be going the way of the Serb King, Alexander I, assassinated in 1903. And for the portentous, a novel predicting something like this would happen had sold six thousand copies in the month before the assassination.[86]

The assassination, itself, was greeted with the silence of the grave. Jean Finot was an observer in the French Legation in Lisbon when he heard. He found the population of the capital supremely indifferent, 'not a trace of mourning . . . The regicide seemed to usher in peace and order, and brought justice instead of a savage despotism.' He noted the paradoxical consequence of hundreds being freed from prison, from which he concluded 'dictators do not suit our age. Nations which have once tasted liberty do not allow themselves to be deprived of it.'[87]

The Press played a significant role in Carlos's downfall. Faced with a more confident and critical intelligentsia, the Monarchy struggled to manage the new public opinion.[88] Satire, the serrated edge of popular journalism, was joined by the illustrated newspaper, extending imagery from cartoons to photo-journalism. 'Graphic reporting' gripped the public imagination, and shaped its reading of the Monarchy.[89] Carlos was stoic, continued to read the daily press uncomplainingly, give interviews and talk to editors.[90] By contrast, Franco wanted to take the fight to the Republican press. But, as Queen Amélie lamented, this put Carlos, not him, in the firing line, with tragic consequences. So, Carlos had already endured slow torture, as he fumbled to take the pulse of public opinion. Oliveria Martins[91] had urged him not to be 'a dummy king,' but to go out and embrace the new mass politics; to re-moralize a shamed Monarchy. Carlos took to unescorted walks around Lisbon. But ultimately taking Martins' advice led to death in an unguarded carriage in a public space. The Republican poet Guerra Junqueiro's black irony captured the mood when he said that Carlos had been 'ready for slaughter.' The journalist Fialho de Almeida compared the moral disconnect between Carlos and his people with the popularity of monarchs in new nations like Italy and Germany. Portugal had become 'a monarchy without monarchists.'[92] The estrangement of Monarchy from political parties led to the 'aggrandisement of royal power', a constitutional abuse that drove even some Monarchists to contemplate regicide as solution for tyranny.[93]

At only eighteen, the new king, Manuel, possessed sufficient maturity to sack Franco as the chief architect of disaster. He left office crying like a child, and retired from politics a broken man. The Queen Mother refused to spare him: 'You promised to release the monarchy from its tomb and all that you have done has been to dig the graves of my son and grandson.'[94] What Manuel found so hard to forgive was Franco's failure to set up proper security arrangements.[95] The new King's unforgiving priority was to reconcile the two main political parties. But the problems were structural and could not be solved by a mere change of personnel. Manuel was doomed to preside over six conflicting governments between 1908 and the 1910 Revolution.

Writing after the Revolution at the end of 1910, E. J. Dillon made some pertinent observations on the impossibility of Manuel's inheritance. Dillon practised an unrestrained journalism and practically accused members of the ruling elite of being political murderers. At the heart of the dysfunctional party system was the Monarchy's financial dependence upon the Monarchist Party for secret loans. In power, Monarchists lied about them; out of power, they leaked, even to Republican newspapers. Dillon saw a generation, illiterate, taxed to the hillt, and deceived, turning to 'subversive acts' out of desperation.[96]

He was an open Monarchist, and had some sympathy with Carlos' last resort to João Franco. But for Dillon, the King repented not out of contrition, but because he had been caught with his hands in the till. Dillon, however, dropped the bombshell that Progressives may have had a role in arming the regicides themselves. He detected a cover-up during which 'Influential politicians . . . had had a hand in killing their King '[97] but continued in government as if nothing had happened. And he named names: Prime Minister, Teixeira de Sousa; Luciano de Castro, who had Manuel proclaimed king as quickly as possible; and the opportunist Republican, José Maria de Alpoim. The Republican victory in the Lisbon municipal elections of 1910 just underlined how unpopular this shower had become.

Dillon was nobody's fool. Born in Dublin in 1855, his study of oriental languages led to a doctorate from Leipzig and a Chair at the University of Karkhov in 1884. Three years later he abandoned it for journalism, becoming the *Daily Telegraph's* Russian correspondent. The 'greyish little man with a stubby beard and soft voice'[98] only turned his attention to Portugal after reporting on a clutch of Europe's major crises in Armenia, Crete, China, and Bosnia. In 1914, the *Telegraph*, more or less, sacked him, for becoming too opinionated in his journalistic style. For a non-Portuguese specialist his appreciation of the internecine political rivalries of the final phase of monarchical constitutionalism is impressive. The fractured party system collapses and devours itself; the Monarchy fiddles while Rome burns.

Republican progress to 1910 was despite an ambivalent relationship with legality. In July 1907 Bernardino Machado told *Le Matin* that Portugal would be a republic in two to three years by 'direct action if it be opportune.'[99] The PRP's strength lay not in its seven MPs so much as in civic associations and shady links with the secretive *Carbonária*.[100] As the Monarchy rocked, Britain opportunistically decided the Alliance was between states not regimes. Strikes deepened, as students threatened to burn Coimbra University down.[101] The PRP decided to honour Machado's promise, with the armed forces and the *Carbonário* in the vanguard, and much of the urban middle class applauding from the sidelines. A regime whose only hope was reform fell like a pack of cards because it refused to relinquish the functionalism of closed privilege. Portugal was not on the verge of proletarian insurrection, not least because the working class was so small. Few, though, appreciated in October that the Republican revolution was to enact its own model of political closure.

4 Historians, the '5 October' and the emergence of civil society

The question of what type of revolution was made in 1910 has intrigued historians. One recent, influential view has been that it marked a maturation of civil society. Through the 1970s and 1980s, social scientists, particularly in America, thought they observed an historical process by which authoritarian states were giving way to greater democracy. Their evidence was drawn from places like Portugal (1974), Spain (1975), Argentina (1983), Brazil (1985), and Chile (1990). This fitted with a paradigm in American political science that conflated Iberian Europe with Latin America in a comparative history. The revolutions in Eastern Europe in 1989 opened debate around Fukuyama's question 'is this the End of History?': the culmination of the long march of liberal democracy towards world hegemony.[102] Communist dictatorships were overthrown by loosely organized civil action in peaceful transfers of power, in most cases.[103] Historians whose problematic was the state's authoritarian tendencies provoked a debate on its relationship to civil society. The 1990s were expected to bestow a history of active citizenship's triumph in making the state more democratic. The First Portuguese Republic lasted only sixteen years. It took the Eastern Europe of 1989 about the same timespan to deliver its false dawn, as it declined to mimic Western democracy. Admission to common institutions like the EU did not guarantee conformity. The aftermath of the financial crash of 2008 wrought havoc on old members and new. The return of the Far Right made a mockery of the hopes for a 'new democracy.' Social scientists rescued what they could of their shattered paradigms; historians turned towards a vicissitudinous history in which civic action played a more plural role in relation to the state.

The centenary of 5 October 1910 provided an opportunity for historians of Portugal to re-consider the history of citizenship.[104] It served to confirm what Costa Pinto and Almeida had already said: Portugal had developed a civil society that made a revolution, but not one strong enough to guarantee democratic development. 1910 delivered but a fragile promise of democracy that contained the dialectical seeds of its own destruction in 1926. The road to 1910 was a crooked line that meandered through Portugal's ambiguous relationship to modernity. The nineteenth century had seen constitutional monarchy win the battle against absolutism by the 1830s. By the end of the century Portugal had established a secular state with a representative government and a free press: a 'mimic democracy'[105] within western Europe. It was a pale shadow socially too, because a lack of urban development meant only Lisbon and Porto had sizeable middle classes. Civic action emanated from there. Association spread from friendly societies to trades unions, to shopkeepers, mostly outside of the Republican party who, 'with the backing of a militant press and with vigorous efforts to create and disseminate a popular political literature . . . worked hard to create an activist citizenry.'[106] Yet, Republicanism practised a 'clientalist liberalism' that mimicked 'oligarchic parliamentarianism.'[107] It was suspicious of mass citizenship and the threat it posed to the power of the Party.[108] Yet, the Revolution was still much more than 'a military coup in Lisbon which resulted in the abolition of the monarchy after one day of fighting in the streets.'[109] Behind it lay Lisbon municipalism and its long struggle against the oligarchic, centralized state. At a bourgeois level alone it was a revolt against the class of oligarchic rentiers who drew the capital's commercial elite close through family connections. Between them they leaked capital abroad in search of higher interest, damaging the domestic economy. Republicans beavered away to overthrow this, gaining recruits in the law, press and university to weld into broader political coalitions.[110]

Women played their part in the Revolution. From 1908 the Republican League of Portuguese Women had campaigned for the vote but the franchise reform of 1911 excluded them. This was challenged in the courts by a thirty-three-year-old widowed doctor, Carolina Beatrix Angelo, but the further revision of 1913 explicitly excluded on grounds of gender causing a deep breach between Republicanism and feminism.[111] However, many Republican women reluctantly acknowledged the fears of men that a general female franchise would produce an enormous conservative vote from the more Catholic peasantry.

The Lisbon municipality voted conclusively Republican from 1908. The PRP 'assembled under its policy umbrella a broad spectrum of political groups ranging from moderate electoralists to proponents of Jacobin authoritarianism.'[112] One new councillor, the architect Miguel Ventura Terra, typifies the modernism of this rainbow coalition. His plan of June 1911, for a bridge to cross the Tagus, 'would cost the City Council and the State nothing, as it would add value to the vast expanses of the southern bank, with revenues generated from cafés, restaurants, terrace bars, suitable retail outlets established . . . while the road toll could provide another source of income that would offset the expense of construction.'[113] Journalism reported civic modernisation enthusiastically but was also itself an agency of change. When Republican journalists like Basílio Teles wrote about 'The appearance of the democratic factor in Portuguese politics' that had finally broken with the 'subservient nation's apathy', it took on an air of reality. The new democratic journalism had undermined Carlos, but its origins went all the way back to the iconoclasm of the 'Generation of 1870'.

The new journalism was being read in Lisbon by a population that had roughly doubled in the three decades before 1910. Literacy had improved by 10 percent, even if less than a third of people could read; mostly males. Far more of them could vote than could read – approximately 70 percent of adult males after 1878. Basílio Teles felt that 'everyone was in the street' by 1905, an exaggeration of the urban male's new-found fondness for politicized public spaces. In those streets news vendors were multiplying like locusts. By 1900 the Portuguese were consuming far more newspapers per head than even the English and French. Journalism was emblematic of a maturing civil society, infused with a fervent sense of mission. This was embraced by the new intelligentsia anxious to be at the cutting edge of change. The old dilettante writers transformed themselves into self-ascribed professionals stepping out as the new agenda setters, or the 'fifth power.'[114] The 'chattering classes' were highly clubbable from the founding of the first Portuguese Association of Journalists and Writers in 1880. But all did not glisten in the new 'Golden Age' of mass circulation. The integrity of serious Republican journalism was compromised by a sensationalism that fed upon a raw mass audience.[115] Importantly, though, it was free to do so, in the death throes of a constitutional monarchy stripped of censorship powers. The locusts of Aubrey Bell's imagination were foreign invaders. But as they descended from 1908, they discovered an endemic Portuguese Republican variety had been feeding upon an emaciated monarchy for years.

CHAPTER

2

Reporting the Revolution

1 The Press, politics and Portugal in 1910

The Edwardian period has been described as 'the Golden Age of Editors.'[1] The privileged began to treat Downing Street like a second home, as the daily newspaper became essential consumption for an increasing number of inquisitively literate readers. However, news from Portugal only intruded when the Portuguese did something exceptional. The regicide of 1908 was an exception, though the '5 October', 1910, caught the British press with few correspondents in Lisbon. Still, it took the arrival of the deposed King at Portsmouth harbour, tail between his legs and seeking friends, to sustain front page coverage for long. Portugal competed for political space with budgets, the Lords, the Constitution, the Balkans, the Arms Race and Morocco. As Foreign Secretary, Sir Edward Grey, nuanced discretion so fondly that he turned procrastination into a diplomatic art form.[2] Grey's foreign policy towards Portugal was as fraught with uncertainty and ambiguity as any he conducted towards Germany and France.[3]

Since reluctantly assuming office in 1906 Grey had fended off a furore over 'Portuguese slavery'. From *The Spectator* and elsewhere demands escalated for an end to the Old Alliance. Grey stonewalled, just as he did over the next great Portuguese issue, political prisoners. He refused to be pushed into picking a fight with an ally.[4] He also shared with the Liberal press a desire not to turn the Alliance into a regime question. So, the Republic was accepted with an open mind, rather than welcomed. To Liberal Imperialists, empire mattered more than monarchy. With or without Manuel II, the Portuguese ruled an extensive African empire, over which the Germans cast a covetous eye. Its future hinged upon one dominant concern: Britain's national interest. Grey's dilemma was that Portuguese Republicans were perfectly wise to this,[5] and radicals like Afonso Costa reminded him of the 'true fanatics' in his own party. Once in power, radical Republicanism disestablished the Church, locked-up Royalist opponents without trial, and gave nothing over the 'slavery question'. If 'London decided to hold its nose and accept the Republic as the best that Portugal could do,'[6] then Grey's nasal control was matched only by his capacity for casting a blind eye. He tried not to think about Portugal unless he had to, but the critics would not leave him alone.

Liberalism was in retreat by 1910. The Conservatives gained over a hundred seats over two elections against a continuing fall in real wages. The 'golden age' had lost its glitter, Liberalism its majority.[7] The pro-German lobby within the Party favoured appeasing Germany's territorial ambitions in Portuguese Africa. Such pressures contrasted with the relatively easy ride Grey had enjoyed until then. 'Chinese slavery' – the exploitation of indentured labourers in the South African gold mines – had been dealt with. But it disqualified any British government from assuming the high moral ground over 'Portuguese slavery'. Not that Grey aspired to humanitarian altruism. The Foreign Office's function was to protect the national interest, not to change the world.[8]

For failing to stand up to the Belgians over the Congo, E. D. Morel reviled him as 'that weak-kneed invertebrate politician', and on the Middle East Professor Edward Browne of Cambridge thought him 'so ignorant that he hardly knows the Persian Gulf from the Red Sea.'[9] Field Marshall Sir Henry Wilson, an Irish Unionist assassinated by the IRA in 1922, dismissed Grey alongside the entire Portuguese nation as:

> An ignorant, vain, and weak man, quite unfit to be the Foreign Minister of any country larger than Portugal. A man who knows nothing of policy and strategy going hand in hand.[10]

Wilson unwittingly exposed a broader British condescension towards the Portuguese. In politics, the prime example was the willingness to trade away the Portuguese colonies as part of a German settlement. Churchill hoped it could be the 'external question upon which we could frankly co-operate.'[11] But, as Grey regretted, 'This agreement was left as I found it on entering office.'[12] Apart from its diplomatic leverage, he was largely disinterested in the country and certainly not pro-Republic from its outset, as some suspected.[13] Portugal, for Grey, was, at best, a distraction; at worst, an irritant. The Revolution's importance to him lay in narrow diplomacy – the threat it posed to the good relations between the two royal families.

In private, Grey was franker about his contempt for Portuguese colonialism. In December 1911 he described the colonies as 'sinks of iniquity.'[14] He thought it would be better for Portugal to sell the colonies, but the Alliance prevented Britain from openly supporting this. For all his disdain, though, Grey understood the national regeneration issue:

> Portugal won't part with her colonies... for when nations have gone downhill until they are at their last gasp, their pride remains undiminished if indeed it is not increased.[15]

Yet, a year later Grey got within a hair's breadth of signing an Anglo-German agreement to divide the Portuguese colonies. Sir Arthur Nicolson, Head of the Foreign Office, thought it a done deal. He expressed his shock that Grey could contemplate violating treaty obligations by entering such a 'discreditable transaction' with Germany.[16] But, Grey had influential Cabinet support from Churchill. Both appreciated, by 1912, that Republicanism's grip on empire was as firm as the Monarchy's. Despite their mutual problems with entrenched aristocratic privilege, there was little sense of fraternity between British and Portuguese liberals. Neither Grey nor Churchill, thought Afonso Costa a man to sit down to dinner with at the Reform Club.

2 'Fifths of October': The British Press and the 1910 Revolution

The Press presented the public with competing narratives about '5 October'. On the other hand, there was considerable agreement, particularly over its implications for Britain. The *Daily Chronicle*, *Daily Mail*, and *The Times* devoted some of the most detailed coverage of '5 October'. The *Manchester Guardian* and *The Observer* provide more occasional, but often insightful, reportage. Party affiliation was not that important, as '5 October' was as likely to be read as an anti-Monarchical threat by a Liberal newspaper as a Tory one. More importantly, newspapers contained a plurality of views. There were differences between the attitudes of reporters and editorial opinion. Context and site counted for a great deal. Editors mediated opinion between the front-line correspondent and domestic audience, blending the immediacy of events into the deeper, structural concerns of foreign policy. The relative tranquillity of Fleet Street contrasted sharply with the front-line reporter dodging bullets along the Avenida de Liberdade. Lisbon's central thoroughfare was built in the early 1880s like a Parisian boulevard. It is 1,100 metres long and 90 metres wide; so long that residents joked that by the time one walked from one end to the other a Ministry might have fallen. On 5 October 1910 no sensible person was strolling along the Avenida. It became a battleground that took the smiles off everybody's faces.

3 The grand narrator: M. H. Donohoe's '5 October' and the *Daily Chronicle*

The *Daily Chronicle* was edited by Robert Donald, a Liberal associate of Lloyd George, who had transformed it into a popular title selling over 100,000 copies per day in 1910. Donald recruited a group of talented journalists, including Philip Gibbs, who, in 1913, pioneered investigative reporting into political imprisonment in Portugal. The *Chronicle* agonised over the causes of the Revolution. It blamed the misrule of the oligarchy rather than the Monarchy. Franco's dictatorship was explained away as the last resort of Carlos; Republicanism as the gainer from a toxic mix of manipulated elections and high taxation. By 1910 the political capital of the House of Bragança was used up, and the Army joined the Navy in revolution.

But, the *Chronicle* probed more deeply than the failures of the political class for revolution's roots. The social base was decadence that came from race dilution:

> To this day there is large admixture of Negro blood among the lower classes, whilst amongst the aristocracy there is a considerable dash of Moorish blood. The result is that the Portuguese of today are not of the same pure race as were the Portuguese of the great age.[17]

Such views were commonly found in Liberal as well as Conservative publications. Amongst governing Liberals, pro-imperialism was a dominant voice. It was fuelled by widespread acceptance of eugenics amongst the educated classes. This pointed to dangers to the body politic of miscegenation and hybridity. Eugenics underpinned a racist world view and provided one vital cultural sinew of empire.[18] Many Portuguese adopted such views as a means of explaining decline into decadence. In the *Chronicle*, they implicitly delivered an ideological justification for 'semi-colonisation'.

The *Chronicle*'s Portugal had become so dysfunctional that it had thrust a boy king forward to do a man's job. There was sympathy for Manuel, who took the Crown almost before the family blood had dried on his clothes. A 'mother's boy' and Anglophile, with a family home in Twickenham, he had wanted to be a sailor not a king. Studious, sportsmanlike, all had seemed plain sailing until he found himself drowning prematurely in corrupt court politics. Despite keeping an open mind over the Revolution, the *Chronicle* suspected it might take another strong man like Franco to pull the country together again.

The *Chronicle* boasted that its correspondent, M.H. Donohoe, was the only journalist writing for a British newspaper in Lisbon on 5 October. However, because his wire had been cut by revolutionaries, he had to sail to Vigo in Spain, to transmit news of the Revolution. Assisted by the Eastern Telegraph Company, it did not go out until the middle of the afternoon of 6 October, via the company's station in Cornwall. Donohoe's fascinating eyewitness account appeared on 7 October, a day later than the *Chronicle* would have liked.

Donohoe was an experienced foreign and war correspondent by the time he arrived in Lisbon, in late September 1910. Born in Galway in 1869, he was traditionally educated at the Catholic, Marist Brothers' School. His first journalistic post was on the *Courier* in Sydney, but he soon moved to the *Evening News*, then to the *Town and Country Journal*. By 1900 he was reporting for the *Daily Chronicle* on the South African War,[19] then on the Russo-Japanese War and the Balkan Wars.[20] As a hardened war reporter Donohoe still saw 'some of the most desperate street fighting that it has ever been my lot to witness'[21] in Lisbon. Although delayed, his report from Vigo, is a detailed and gripping narrative that has the Revolution beginning late on Monday 3 October, then lasting about thirty hours through the fourth, until the Republicans finally claimed victory early on the fifth.

With hindsight, Donohoe claimed to have detected signs of imminent rebellion on his arrival three weeks before. But the catalyst was the murder of the anti-clerical, Republican MP and medical director at the Lisbon Asylum, Dr Miguel Bombarda. Bombarda struggled with conscience, feeling that political involvement contradicted medical ethics.[22] Nevertheless, he was one of fourteen Republicans elected to the Cortes in August 1910, against the grain.[23] The Lisbon Asylum treated about eight hundred patients. Against Bombarda's wishes, Lieutenant Rebello dos Santos, who was on the General Staff, had been released to recover.[24] On 3 October, he returned from Paris voluntarily, and shot Bombarda dead after an argument. Donohoe implied that the murder of a doctor by a mentally ill man would not usually have provoked more than public concern. But Bombarda's politics had returned to haunt him. Santos was a committed Royalist who had killed a prominent Republican. The subject of the argument is uncertain. Significant, for Donohoe, was that Republican newspapers exploited the murder to propagandize for the overthrow of the Monarchy. A riot ensued after two Royalist priests were stoned in the street. Some rioters were armed soldiers. Shots were exchanged, as they were eventually forced back up the Avenida de Liberdade to the artillery barracks. Soon they were back, with their officers, advancing upon the centre of the city, with four field guns in tow. Small arms were distributed amongst civilians. The northern part of the city around Pombal and the Edward VII Park became the rebels' stronghold. The showmen who had set up their stalls for the October Fair all along the northern end of the Avenida were disrupted, so they joined the Revolution, converting their stalls into barricades.[25]

Such spontaneous scenes contrast with evidence of revolutionary planning to disrupt communications. Telephone and telegraph cables were cut. The Military Commander of Lisbon arrived at Cascais station to find the tracks had been torn up, so he had to borrow a car from a British resident. More spontaneous was the shooting of three officers of the Sixteenth Infantry Regiment for refusing to join the Revolution. Police joined the Royalists, although the Chief suddenly went home with a fever. Lisbon's police force was one of only two in Portugal in 1910; the other was in Porto. After the Revolution a gendarmerie (GNR) was founded to republicanize the state. Landowners did not want to pay for policing, while liberals like Eça de Queirós feared creating an enemy of the people. Costa did turn the GNR against labour militancy but benefited from its tax collections. But in 1910, it was no match for the Navy and Army, emblematic of the weak civic culture of the state fractured by revolution.[26]

Donohoe's Royalists seemed remarkably unprepared. Several Cabinet members were caught dining out. The King was hosting the President-Elect of Brazil, Marshall Hermes de Fonseca, in the Necessidades Palace, just as the revolutionary sailors were flocking ashore in numbers. Anyone seeking a cab in Lisbon on the morning of 4 October was disappointed, as they were all commandeered by sailors on their way into action. Some without cabs were provided with trusty steeds by members of the public. The sailors used them for charging the Royalist ranks, as they took control from Republican infantry sergeants.

Into the early morning of 4 October, the Royalists retreated from the Republican offensive to defend the King with field and machine guns. A first assault on Necessidades Palace by Republican infantry was mown down by machine-gun fire. Shortly after sunrise a detachment from the Marine Barracks at Alcantara launched a more careful attack, as Royalist snipers fired from the hills above. At the same time, three warships, lying in the Tagus estuary, came out for the Revolution, while the remainder of the Fleet hesitated. Vicious hand-to-hand fighting was observed aboard one, the *Dom Fernando*.

Donohoe's describes Lisbon on the morning of 4 October as 'a city of the dead . . . I walked through the streets and, except on the quay side and in the parts of the city held by troops, did not encounter a living soul.'[27] All public transport and commerce ceased. But on reaching the waterfront he found a divided fleet at battle stations. A host of foreign vessels awaited the outcome, including the *San Paolo* that had brought the Brazilian President-Elect to Portugal. Up river, the Necessidades Palace was being shelled from only two hundred yards. Donohoe retreated to a bird's-eye view: the top of the Braganza Palace Hotel, the tallest in the city.

Inside, Donohoe imagined a King standing fearless under a Republican ultimatum to abdicate while 'many of his craven entourage fled.' Reluctantly 'the pluckiest man in Portugal'[28] was persuaded to leave, smiling and smoking in an automobile. Hostilities continued late into the day as several civil servants in the Ministries of War and Marine were killed by naval bombardment. Civilian spectators in the Praça de Comércio, some hanging from windows, also died in the process. Besieged Royalists defended the square with two field guns, fatally striking Republican warships.

The Republicans advanced south along the Avenida de Liberdade throughout the 4 October. Foreigners became accidental casualties. In the Hotel Inglaterra, C. T. Kaye from Huddersfield got an unexpected early morning call from gunfire at 5.30 a.m., as bullets came streaking through his room. He crawled out, terrified, to join other Englishmen seeking safety. They were trapped within the hotel until the evening, then escaped with other French, German and Portuguese guests. Using an 'improvised ladder' they reached the yard, from where they then had to climb a ten-foot wall to reach a stable below ground level. One Portuguese woman with a two-month-old child showed immense bravery. For the next two days they eked out a quasi-biblical existence, lying on straw with six mules. During breaks in the shelling a benevolent waiter ran from the hotel to supply them with bread and fruit.[29]

On the morning of the 5th, Kaye made a break for the river where he managed to get aboard the Royal Mail steamer *Asturias*, bound for Southampton via Vigo. He moved from doorway to doorway dodging stray bullets for a full two miles. Donohoe met him on the ship. He told him he never wanted to see another revolution as long as he lived, and could not wait to get back to Yorkshire. He brought souvenirs, though: three shrapnel bullets he had dug out of his bedroom wall.[30]

Until late into 4 October, Donohoe was still buying into the official Royalist narrative that the Monarchy had every chance of surviving.[31] He credits both sides for allowing him to move freely between them at his own risk. He visited the Republican leaders in the Rua Garrett, where they were masterminding revolution from a chemist's. He found anxious men with little confidence that, within twenty-four hours, they would be the Government. Nerves jangled as 'inky blackness settled down over the disturbed city, and the fitful gleam of the few street lamps that escaped destruction could not dissipate it.'[32] The Revolution seemed poised on a knife-edge, as Donohoe could still hear 'the sharp whirr of the machine guns . . . on the northern heights.'[33] He made his away along the Avenida, but could see little for lack of light, so returned to the roof of the Hotel Braganza. From there he could see two Republican warships trying to assert control of the riverside. On the *Dom Carlos*, where mutiny was now complete, he witnessed a gruesome execution:

> the warship's forward searchlight was turned on the quarter-deck, lighting up objects as if it were day. There stood a group of officers and a few sailors round a machine gun . . . a volley from their enemies, hidden by darkness, crashed into their midst, and I saw that the groups of men on the quarter-deck were using a machine gun . . . the tell-tale light flashed out anew. It held the victims in its grip, and as their dark uniforms were silhouetted against that beam of white light the hidden machine-gun whirred afresh, and the rest of that group, on the quarter-deck, went down . . . Once more the searchlight flashed out, but there was no need of fresh Republican volleys. Every man of that little body was lying dead around the gun.[34]

For Donohoe, treachery was committed by those on the *Dom Carlos* in coming over to the Republican side. Its defection completed Republican control of the Navy, and the Navy won the Revolution. Still, he thought it had been a close-run thing. He admired the Royalists' courage, and thought the King an honourable young man, who had been badly let down. Republicans had subjected him to a ham-fisted attack upon the Necessdades Palace, strategically planned from a pharmacy. Along the riverside their attacks had been indiscriminate and costly of civilian lives. The retribution of the Navy had been ruthless.

But the killing was not quite over. Royalists waved white flags throughout the 5th but the Municipal Guards 'fell in heaps rather than surrender.'[35] Donohoe personally witnessed one particularly pathetic endgame. A Royalist Infantry Brigade defended their position in Rossio Square against a Republican detachment whose devastating Maxim gun spread them like rabbits across a field. A Royalist captain tried to save the lives of his men. Wearing a bloodstained headband, his face blackened by gunpowder, he broke his sword in half and collapsed onto the pavement head in hands. It was like Custer's last stand in the Rossio.

It was not quite the last stand. Some enduring Royalists were holding out in the Observatory. Lisbon is built on seven hills, and the Republicans' route from the southern end of the Avenida de Liberdade to the Observatory had to go up the steep Calçada de Gloria. After many hours of exchanging artillery fire, the Republicans decided on another route of attack: down the Avenida Braancamp from their stronghold at the north of the Avenida, then up to the Botanical Gardens and the Observatory. The surprise attack detached the vanguard of the Municipal Guards from the rest of the Royalist forces. The outcome was serious for the ultra-loyalist Municipal Guards, who proceeded to be 'caught like rats in a trap, and shot down by the insurgents.'[36] With them went the last hopes of the Royalists holding the city centre. Desertions caused the Royalist commander in the Botanical Gardens to retreat to the square in front of the Church of São Roque.

São Roque was completed in 1619, originally designed by the Italian, Filipe Térzi (1520–97). Its renown dates from the middle of the eighteenth century because of the installation of the Chapel of St John the Baptist. It took the Italian architects Nicola Salvi and Luigi Vanvitelli most of the 1740s to construct it, not in Lisbon but Rome. It was then, remarkably, transported to Lisbon in sections by three separate ships.[37] Funded by Portuguese gold discoveries in Brazil, it was, at the time, the most expensive chapel in Europe. It was one of the few of Lisbon's buildings outside the Alfama to survive the 1755 earthquake.

In the square in front of this historic building whose chapel marks the hubris of the Portuguese Empire, the Royalists were cornered. Many surrendered, or ran away. 'The men refused to stand against the advancing Republicans,'[38] Donohoe lamented. São Roque, once the pride of the Portuguese Monarchy, looked down upon this debacle: the humiliation of the few remaining supporters of its last king. Down the hill they ran, into the arms of Portugal's greatest poet, whose statue has stood in the Praça Camões since 1867. No words could save them. The fleeing Royalists, armed only now with rifles, were shelled by the Maxim and a field gun. Desperate, they tried to break into houses, only to find them firmly barred. Bodies lay all along the street; white flags saved some. Donohoe estimates those Municipal Guards took twice the casualties of other Royalist troops.[39] Within half an hour of their final defeat the Republic was declared.

Donohoe has the Republicans controlling all the capital except the St George's Castle military barracks, as he shipped out of Lisbon late on 5 October. The Castle fell the next morning. Beyond Lisbon there was little revolutionary activity. In Porto, both regiments remained confined to barracks to the taunts of a Republican crowd. Braga and Guimarães remained loyal to the Monarchy, although Coimbra declared for the Republic early. Even in Lisbon, many simply hid in their houses until the armed forces stopped fighting.

'Donohoe's Revolution' compares closely with the *Chronicle*'s editorial analysis of a Monarchy consumed by the state's deep structural faults. Its '5 October' was a military overthrow without a trace of popular uprising. But that ignores the role of the *populares* – armed citizens who played a key role in the street fighting of 4–5 October.[40] 'Donohoe's Monarchy' is particularly tragic, defended by heroes like the Municipal Guards; the King, himself, undermined by 'treachery and treason.' The turncoats in the Navy emerge as the particular villains; the chancers in the chemist shop in Rua Garrett, the inheriting scoundrels. But for all its selective treatment of historical agency, it is a unique narrative; a captivating eye-witness account written with the verve of the practised story-teller, and laced with vignettes targeted at his British audience. He clearly exercised great courage in negotiating the dangerous streets of Lisbon to get his story. The reader is familiarized with the geography of the city through a guided tour of the conflict zone, street-by-street, district-by-district, across land and water.

The *Chronicle* declined modesty over its scoop:

> The long and detailed cables from "The Daily Chronicle" Special Correspondent, Mr M H Donohoe, have attracted world-wide attention ... and in this country the account was more extensively quoted by our contemporaries than perhaps any newspaper story of recent times.[41]

The London daily press, *Manchester Guardian* and *Glasgow Herald* used Donohoe's dispatches. The latter praised his insight in arriving In Lisbon three weeks before the Revolution. His reports filtered into the local press, too. The *Western Daily Mail* thought his life epitomized by romance combined with practicality.[42] The Positivist, Frederic Harrison, a friend of the new President Teófilo Braga, wrote, 'I can recall no more striking success of British journalism.'[43] Donohoe had almost become the subject of his own story; his journalism rivalling the Revolution as event. As the junior reporter during the Boer War, Donohoe learned much from Henry Nevinson, thirteen years his senior. Nevinson's three golden rules for a war correspondent were: be on the spot before the trouble starts; be as close to the lines as possible; never get killed.[44] In October 1910, Donohoe passed all three tests. He had reported what his newspaper liked to call 'the Battle of Lisbon', and lived to tell the tale.

4 Class, race and the 'othering' of Portugal: The *Daily Mail*'s '5 October'

The *Chronicle*'s rival the *Daily Mail* was an early acquisition (1896) of the greatest of early twentieth-century Fleet Street barons, Alfred Harmsworth, who turned it into a mass circulation title priced a halfpenny.[45] Its first full report of the Revolution came in the 6 October edition, following a brief mention the day before. The report from its correspondent, A. M. Oram, was timed at 3.45 p.m. on 5 October, which gives the lie to the *Chronicle*'s claim that Donohoe was the only British one there.[46] He confirms some of the detail of Donohoe's report such as the interruption of the Fair. However, Oram suffered from the same interruptions in communications. Like Donohoe, he was dependent on the good offices of the Eastern Telegraph Company.[47]

The *Mail* was ahead of the *Chronicle* in sending back eyewitness reports of what had happened in Lisbon. These came form its correspondent in Vigo, where the *Cap Blanco* berthed having escaped Lisbon amidst the Navy's bombardment of the Necessidades Palace. The testimony of the disembarked is, however, unreliably based on impression and rumour.

From 11.30 a.m. on the 5th, the *Mail* becomes reliant upon Reuters for its reports because Oram had departed, possibly on the *Cap Blanco*. Reuters' coverage contrasts with Donohoe's minimising of popular participation. From 8 a.m. a crowd gathered in Dom Pedro Square and to cries of 'long live the Republic' raised the Republican flag over the Arsenal and on the City Hall. Eusebio Leão, a member of the PRP's directorate, spoke just after midday. He 'entrusted the policing and maintenance of order in the city to the care of the citizens.'[48] He urged them to respect life and both public and private property, though, just to make absolutely sure, the banks were being guarded. The Bank of Portugal, itself, was flying the Republican flag by mid-afternoon. By 1.30 p.m., there had not been a single attack upon property in the city. The Spanish Ambassador paid an early visit to the Republican leaders, for which he was loudly cheered. They crowd sang *A Portuguesa*, soon to be adopted as the National Anthem. Originally, a nationalist response to the British ultimatum of 1890, it had become the battle cry of Portuguese Republicanism, providing the historical script for '5 October'.

Teófilo Braga, was President of the Provisional Government.[49] The *Mail* erroneously reported that he was the son of a Lisbon doctor, rather than of a teacher. Teófilo was born in Ponta Delgada, capital of the Azores, in 1843. He studied law at Coimbra, where he lodged with Antero de Quental's uncle. Quental, and Braga had pioneered the Generation of 1870's critique of the constitutional monarchy's conservatism. Through the 1870s, Braga moved towards Positivism applying Comtean sociology to the writing of literary history as the expression of a 'people emancipating itself.'[50] But his politics reflected the ambiguous nationalism of Republicanism, advocating national revival while sympathetic to Iberianism in the form of a confederation of penisular states. He was strongly anti-clerical, but felt a divine mission in Africa to restrict Islam.[51] He attacked Britain for 'fraudulent treaties' dismembering Portuguese territory abroad. When the American, Percival Phillips interviewed Braga for the *Daily Express*, a week after the Revolution (12 October 1910) he found him 'filled with sincerity and patriotism.' This included defending the African colonies. Blacks would be treated with humanity; servitude would be ameliorated, not ended; rather like the white management of Brazil.

Edgar Prestage thought Braga 'a voluminous writer more versatile than accurate.'[52] Aubrey Bell described him as 'one of the acutest and most unscholarly critics of our day,' hinting that he was a Jack of all trades and master of none.[53] Bragança-Cunha considered him to have 'immolated his literary faculties to secondhand free thought in religion and violent socialism.'[54] All three were conservative critics, apprehensive about Braga's liberalism, rationalism, anti-clericalism, Positivism, and, of course, Republicanism. During the tri-centenary celebrations of Camões 1880, Braga's Republicans tried to turn the marches into a national protest against the Monarchy. The experience was subsequently intellectualized into an argument for an imagined Portuguese community in which great historical figures would be ritually consecrated to synthesize the national character.[55]

Despite interest in the cultural sphere, Braga's Positivism prioritized scientific method in studying human society. Like Marxism it explained social stratification as determined by capitalist economic relations. Unlike Marxism, it defended nationalism and imperialism. Its critique of existing social hierachies was expressed in its Republicanism and anti-clericalism. In domestic politics, it supported franchise extension, public education, and administrative decentralisation. Braga's liberalism was sceptical of the *étatism* of the 'social contract'. Franco's dicatorship underlined the need to safeguard liberty by strengthening individual rights through contracts of association.[56] Braga had been active in the Republican Party for over a decade when he manned the barricades in Porto in 1891. Internal recrimination followed its failure, as Republicanism struggled to capitalize upon the disintegration of the other parties. The dictatorship was three-years old when he entered Parliament in August 1910, better known as a poet, literary historian, and Professor of Portuguese Literature at the High Literary College in Lisbon. Yet, as a national republican figure, he possessed the unifying credentials of a figurehead when the time came in October. The only serious doubt was his age – sixty-seven – though 'tall, thin and with a commanding presence,'[57] he still cut an impressive figure. Braga presided over a new Cabinet with an average age of fifty-two.[58] Younger men – middle-class lawyers and academics, like Afonso Costa – were to seize the initiative.

Braga declared the Provisional Government by telegram at five minutes to midnight on 5 October. It was in French, so the *Mail*'s claim that it was an exclusive is unlikely. The communique guaranteed the Royal family's safety, although its whereabouts was uncertain. Braga claimed popular support for the Revolution, even in the countryside. The Army were completely Republicanized and were restoring public order. The reaffirmation of the Alliance was about to be tested by the arrival of the royal yacht in Gibraltar, with the Governor's full hospitality.[59]

The *Daily Mail*'s reporting of the Revolution has to be read in the context of the scoop war it was conducting with the *Daily Chronicle*. It led to false claims such as the *Chronicle*'s that it had the only correspondent in Lisbon on 5 October.[60] A. M. Oram left earlier than Donohoe, arriving back in London by the same route, via Vigo. Once home, he concentrated on covering the King in exile. He was quickly replaced by G. Valentine Williams, who was able to get through by train a couple of days after the 5th. It was one of the many things he failed to remember accurately in his autobiography.[61] Williams was still ten days short of his twenty-seventh birthday on 5 October, and was to go on to have a distinguished journalistic career. His father, G. Douglas Williams, had been the Chief Editor of Reuters News Agency, and Valentine, too, joined it as a sub-editor in 1902, moving to the *Mail* in 1909. After Portugal, he covered the Balkan Wars (1912–13). During the First World War he received the Military Cross, having been seriously wounded covering the Somme (1916). After the War, he developed a second career as a prolific writer of detective fiction, of which he published twenty-eight volumes prior to his death in 1946.

Williams dismissed the Portuguese Revolution as 'pretty small beer,'[62] restricting the chapter in his autobiography about it to tales of the royal family, and anecdotal personal experience around the siege of the Quelhas Monastery. But, Williams' own fondness for royalty, did not blind him to its shortcomings: 'the Portuguese Monarchy was several centuries out of date and a pretext for supporting at the public expense a decadent and worthless autocracy.'[63]

The Lisbon Williams arrived in was silent and deserted, full of shell holes with dead bodies scattered along the 'Avenida de la Liberdade' [sic]. By 1938, after many years of writing fiction, he had forgotten the little Portuguese he had ever known and did not care to check street names. On arriving at the Avenida Palace Hotel there were no staff on duty, so he just went upstairs and chose a room. By morning, someone had appeared to tell him he had slept in the Royal suite. The night of the Revolution the King had slept in the Necessidades Palace. Williams was in his bedroom four days later. Manuel's French novel was still beside the bed, next to his eyeglass which Williams' guide presented to him as a souvenir. It lived a charmed life beyond royal command. Williams' girlfriend later wore it playing opposite Granville Barker in Arthur Schnitzler's 'The Wedding Morn' at the Palace Theatre in London. Williams claims that Queen Maria Pia pleaded with Manuel not to flee. Manuel was desperately hoping for an English warship to rescue him, but the Queen Mother told him not to rely on them.[64]

Williams' account of the siege of the Quelhas Monastery cannot compare with Donohoe's eyewitness reporting elsewhere in the city. He does capture the violent anti-clericalism that so disturbed Francis McCullagh. But too much of his account is inaccurate. He claims to have been sitting in the Café Martinho in Rossio Square,[65] when people came running from all directions shouting 'Los padres, los padres'. This was impossible as it has been located in the Praça de Comércio since 1782. It is also unlikely that the people were speaking in Spanish, not Portuguese.

Jumping a cab to the Quelhas Monastery, Wiiliams found a full-scale bombardment with armed defenders resisting cavalry and infantry.[66] During this cacophony, he claims to have fallen asleep whilst taking cover behind a car. The few hours in the royal suite had clearly not been enough for him to recover from the journey from Paris. On awakening, he was arrested as a Jesuit spy. He puts this down to being dressed in black (his father had recently died). But black was the colour of the cleric, several of whom were firing out of the windows of the Monastery. Producing his passport did not get him off because, he claimed, his interrogators were illiterate. They arrested him and he was only released when an officer who could speak English was found.[67]

Returning to Quelhas, the insatiable journalist found looting in full swing. Republican soldiers were pursuing inebriation in the

Monastery's brewery. 'Everything belongs to the people! Help yourself!'[68] they rejoiced. The Catholic in Williams was neither impressed, nor tempted. He hotfooted back to the city, to visit Bernardino Machado, from whom he got a chilly reception, perhaps because he had been brought to the door in his pyjamas.[69] Machado dismissed Williams' concerns for the 'monks' library' at Quelhas, which Williams was equally dismissive of as 'the ponderous pedantry of academic republicanism.'[70] Once the Republic was installed, the *Mail* and Williams retreated from Portugal, like most of the British Press. It regretted Portugal's disastrous loss of a Monarchy 'so closely bound up with the glories of the Portuguese past.'[71]

Covering the European reaction, the *Mail* reported reverberations across the Iberian Peninsula. In Spain, Prime Minister Canalejas shared Williams' regrets. He hoped that reinforcements from the provinces would swing the conflict the Monarchists' way. Ominously, a Spanish warship, the Numancia, was leaving for Lisbon.[72] The French Cabinet was concerned to protect French citizens in Portugal. Queen Amélie, herself was a daughter of the House of Orleans. The Portuguese Minister in Paris had been taken completely by surprise by the Revolution. Manuel had shown a little more foresight when he told a French actor in Lisbon,' I hope to see you again next year . . . That is if I am still here.'[73] Meanwhile, German fears that the Revolution might be a British conspiracy were dismissed in the *Mail* as a 'preposterous suggestion.'[74] Two British cruisers in Lisbon harbour did not mean that Britain was about to impose a military presence. Neither were the Portuguese royal family about to become virtual hostages in Britain.[75]

The *Mail* produced a similar structural analysis of the Revolution to the *Chronicle*: corruption, the 'spoils system', financial deficits, trade imbalances, even illiteracy. But it differed in blaming 'extortionate taxes such as might rejoice the heart of Mr Lloyd George.'[76] The Monarchy emerges relatively untarnished. Manuel intended to be a unifier in a state where Republicanism's penetration of the Army and Navy made its politics intractable. Manuel was a loss because 'Courage and fearlessness, indeed, is part of the royal training; it may even be said to be inherent in royal blood.'[77]

But there was no 'blood sin' for the *Mail*, as there was for the *Chronicle*. Its editorials do not resort to race as an explanation for the decline of the Portuguese nation state. Empire is not identified as a corroding influence. The *Chronicle*'s Liberal Imperialism resorted to the pseudo-scientific support of eugenics; the *Mail* preferred class and the breakdown of social hierarchy. The Monarchy personified the high moral qualities of *ancien régime* Europe: aristocratic paternalism, courage, public service. The fault lay with the stratum below which, self-serving, and dishonouring of national values, had succumbed to middle-class avarice.

The *Mail*'s diplomatic correspondent, however, struck his own path and succumbed to the blood analysis of the *Chronicle*. For him, the dilemma was to explain how, despite restoring parliamentary constitutionalism, Manuel was still overthrown. What was the subliminal causal link that turned reform into revolution? Put another way, why was Portuguese parliamentarianism unable to follow the 'English' model? In an obtuse piece of neo-colonialist chauvinism, the argument was that Portugal lacked 'temperament':

> The secret of representative government is not to be learned from text-books. The traditional and unwritten codes, the half-lights and compromises and silent understandings that direct its workings in England, are not things that can be manufactured. They are properties of the blood, elements of national character, the product of special conditions and distinctive experiences. To formulate and define them, to incorporate them in a Constitution, and to hope it will prove workable is to miss altogether their essential quality and to indulge in the vain dream that the slow processes of time can be eliminated and the centuries taken at a leap.[78]

The South Americans, Italians, French, even Americans, were dismissed on a global scale as all failing to imitate the British Constitution. Portugal's politics is compared to Boss Tweed's New York:[79] 'a few thousand professional politicians, with attendant cohorts of carpet-baggers, running the machine at Lisbon or flooding the country with their plundering nominees.'

There is just a hint of a theory of primitive under-development in the delineation of national specifics within patterns of general democratic development. But this was incidental to a journalism driven by ideology, not political science; emotional persuasion, not reflective contemplation of the past. Ironically, the insistence upon historical stages that cannot be jumped, resembles crude Marxism. Portugal's revolution is explained by a premature lunge wrenching the body politic apart. This ostensible historical error was the result of 'temperament', a subliminal discourse on racial determinants of 'national character.'

This was a neo-colonialist discourse addressed to an imperial subaltern. Said originally applied 'othering' to Western reconstructions of the East, and mainly through literature not journalism.[80] But, through journalism the audience for 'othering' was even wider. Cultural constructs could dispose mass public opinion towards neo-colonialist subordination. Eugenicist discourse provided a racial ideology that validated the inferiority of allies, as well as colonial subjects. Within British politics, cultural condescension underwrote the expendability of the Portuguese Empire in negotiations with Germany. Cabral thought the 'semi-colonisation' of Portugal dated from 1703. If so, the 1890 Ultimatum was an embarrassing confirmation. For British neo-colonialism, '1910' became the next watershed for teaching the Portuguese a history lesson. Portugal had failed as a nation. The blood deficit ran through social classes making it incapable of stable monarchical government. The enlightened despotism of Carlos and Franco had been rejected as the least bad option. The problem then was to shape an unfortunate revolution according to neo-colonial requirements.

5 From a distance: *The Times*' '5th October'

The Times, like the *Mail*, was owned by Alfred Harmsworth from 1908. In 1910, it was edited by George Buckle who cemented its reputation as a newspaper of record, supportive of government rather than party. It had been concerned about Portugal from at least the spring of 1910, warning of the imminent collapse of the other parties in the face of the Republican threat to Church and Throne.[81]

On the 4 October 1910 *The Times* was not expecting a revolution in Portugal. It was more concerned with looking back, to commemorate an important war centenary: the Battle of Busaco, on 27 September. The occasion was spoiled by a handful of ruffians from Lisbon who turned up to shout 'Long live the Republic!' and were promptly beaten up.[82] The Busaco commemorations were the last imaginary of Portuguese Royalism. Within the week the Monarchy was gone. As the bullets whizzed around the head of that most twentieth-century of journalists, M. H. Donohoe, *The Times*, like Portuguese Royalism, was left wallowing in nostalgia. Shaken out of it as the shock waves reached Madrid, its Portuguese correspondent found himself, reliant upon Reuters, or announcements by the Spanish Government, for news to wire home. With the hard news flooding onto the pages of the *Chronicle* and the *Mail*, *The Times* had to scout around European capitals for reactions. With no-one in Lisbon, it fell back on the past and ran a long, historical leader on the reasons for the 'Decline of Portugal'. The nineteenth century is read as one of internecine conflicts, leading to shorter-term expediency of a corrupt party system that plastered over the wounds. *Rotativismo* was the final hospice of a Monarchy sick with corruption.

Having looked back, and unable to sight the present for lack of a reporter, *The Times* looked forward. It concerned itself with the possible outcomes of the Revolution for international relations and the balance of power. Its Berlin correspondent repeated the claims made elsewhere that the mouthpiece of the German foreign ministry, *Lokalanzeiger*, was irresponsibly spreading the rumour that the British government was cognisant of the revolutionaries' plans. At the same time it denies any possibility that Germany will intervene in favour of restoring the Monarchy. More pertinently, the *Berlin Post* flagged up the possibility of 'England' and Germany dividing Portugal's colonies between them: 'it would be a blessing for the African.'[83] In Vienna, The Portuguese *Chargé d'Affaires* speculated that the Miguelists might have joined an unlikely alliance with the Republicans to overthrow the Monarchy. Their exiled leader Dom Miguel, a resident of Lower Austria, watched, enthralled, whilst visiting his brother-in-law in Bavaria.[84]

The Pope was reported as being exceedingly distressed at the unexpected turn of events in Portugal and understandably concerned for the safety of the King. The Vatican had a very simple explanation of the Revolution. It was entirely the work of the Freemasons who organised the whole thing from Sebastião Magalhães Lima's flat in Paris.

The Spanish were embarrassing themselves. The Ambassador in Lisbon had gone in full uniform to pay his respects to the new Republican Government, while Madrid was still stressing the loyalty of the North and the countryside to the Monarchy. He complained that he had the welfare of 7,000 Spaniards in Lisbon to protect. Furthermore, *The Times* was getting as much information from the Spanish Ambassador in Paris, as it was from Madrid. For a former Foreign Minister, Perez Caballero was leaking like a sieve. He dismissed the idea of a replicated '5 October' in Spain. The people and the armed forces were much more loyal. He looked forward to continued good relations between a Republican Portugal and a Liberal Spain. Then, a French journalist put him on the spot:

> In reply to a reminder that Portuguese Republicans and in particular certain members of the new Provisional Government cherished the more ambitious dream of an Iberian Federation, the Ambassador pointed out that these were very distant prospects, and that Portuguese Chauvinism would be the prime obstacle in the way of their realisation.[85]

The French Republic, reported *The Times'* Paris office, would not welcome the revolutionary Portuguese regime with unqualified fraternal enthusiasm. French Republicanism was conservative and no admirer of Portuguese Jacobinism. 'The Manifesto of the Provisional Government' took minds back to 1848.[86]

The British government acted swiftly, dispatching Ambassador, Sir Francis Villiers, to meet President Braga on the afternoon of 6 October.[87] Villiers held Portuguese politics in low esteem. In 1907, after a year there, he conjectured 'if elections were held, the Republicans would carry every constituency in Lisbon and Porto.'[88] Villiers was a liberal monarchist but his reports to the FO deplored its corrupt judiciary, high illiteracy rates, and parlous finances. Like Finot, he noted the public indifference to King Carlos's death shown at his funeral. Manuel impressed him only a little more than his father. On 4 October:

> The politicians who had brought the monarchy to destruction crowned their career of selfish mediocrity by rapid disappearance at the hour of danger . . . Not a single officer of the army or navy came to the palace.[89]

Villiers assessed that Manuel had brought the Revolution upon himself through personal character flaws. Dominated by his avaricious mother, conceited and narrow-minded, he closeted himself away in the Court. He was not a national leader, confirmed by the manner of his departing the country.[90] Hence, Villiers felt no disloyalty in meeting Braga. A band was playing the British and Portuguese national anthems, to a crowd of around 30,000 gathered in the Terreiro do Paço. Villiers made a short speech in English, unembarrassed by his lack of Portuguese. British diplomacy had seen through the regime change with a stiff upper lip.

Readers of *The Times* might have felt short-changed by their Portuguese news coverage. Absence of foresight (and a reporter) caused it to reinvent itself as the vehicle of foreign opinion; a distant voice from other capitals where it was represented. Its reporting compares poorly with the kind of bulldogs its rivals had sniffing around Lisbon on 5 October. In its favour, however, it allows us to see the Revolution played out within the vital context of European diplomacy. But, at the same time, this marginalizes the nation and robs the event of autonomy. In comparison, the *Chronicle* gives us revolution as war reporting, as the Portuguese make their own history. The *Mail* compensates for its frailty in the war zone by seeking the roots of revolution in the *longue durée* of Portugal's history of miscegenation. But the distant outsider, *The Times*, could only gaze opaquely through the windows of Lisbon's neighbours. To its readers, Portugal seemed, as ever, marginalized. Despite an event of fundamental historical autonomy, it remained confined to the periphery of Europe.

6 The *Credito Predial* Scandal and Luciano de Castro's Revenge

The financial crisis that contributed to the Monarchy's fall was comparatively overlooked by the Press in Britain. Fortunately, *The Observer*, a poorly produced Sunday then, was the exception. *Credito Predial* was a state protected financial institution that temporarily 'pensioned' former ministers, until their time to return to office came again, with rotation. The leader of the Progressives, Luciano de Castro, was effectively joint guardian of the *rotativismo* system and he was *The Observer*'s villain of the piece. Having lost office as the prime minister responsible for the 1890 Ultimatum, he clawed his way back to power, in rotation, between 1897–1900 and 1904–6.[91] From the early 1890s to the crisis of 1909–10, *rotativismo* rested on the consensus between the two parties that, when one was in office, the other occupied key positions at the bank. De Castro, however, had upset this fine balance by claiming too many banking spoils for his minions while in office. Carlos had suspended the self-serving Cortes in 1907, but Manuel was intent upon restoring it. In December 1909 he appointed Veiga Berão, a Regenerator, as prime minister. De Castro, as Progressive leader, turned against it. Drip upon drip of information through the first part of 1910 revealed a web of corruption around the bank. It was deeply in debt. Dividends had been paid out of capital for fifteen years, and even the Monarchy had enjoyed generous loans from it.[92] De Castro had known all about it, but so, too, had the Regenerators who had also pocketed their share. Both parties had bled the country dry. The difference, by 1910, was that Republicans and the public knew about it. When De Castro withdrew support for the system that underpinned the Monarchy, he let Republicanism in.[93] The elections of August 1910 took place against a background of revelations about the financial scandal at *Credito Predial*. De Castro was a sick man, but still capable of manipulating politics from behind the scenes. E. J. Dillon tried to be generous, attributing to De Castro some attempt to rescue the stability of the system from his sick bed. But he concurred over *Credito Predial*: De Castro had to share the blame with all the Progessives who had conspired to wreck lives. The collapse of the bank meant that 'hundreds of petty tradesmen in retirement were ruined.'[94]

7 E.J. Dillon's 'close shave'

Credito Predial had already influenced Dillon's view of the constitutional monarchy by September, 1910, when he gives us a rare glimpse of the Revolution (in the *Daily Telegraph*) from Porto, not Lisbon. Like the experiences of Donohoe and Valentine Williams, his experiences demonstrate the precariousness of the foreign journalist during the Revolution. Like Williams, he was leaving a monastery, when he was confronted by an armed mob that took him for a priest. Spotting fingers on triggers he quickly cried out in Spanish 'long live the Republic', and was allowed to pass.[95] From this, we may assume that Portuguese was not one of the twenty-six languages he claimed mastery of.[96] His 'close shave' combined with communications blockages seems to have encouraged him to sail back to England.[97]

It left him with a more balanced view of militant, anti-clerical Republicanism. For a Monarchist, he remained more critical of the outgoing than the incoming regime. The former had presided over 'an utterly rotten fabric' that 'had lost all moral force and energy' whereas the Republicans, for all their hopeless idealism, behaved with moderation and patriotism. They were foolish to put arms in the hands of citizens but, when this led to 'representatives of urban rascality' storming the Bank of Lisbon and the Azores, it was loyally defended by 'poor ragamuffins without boots to their feet.'[98]

Dillon was contemptuous of those who had abandoned the King in his hour of need. Teixeira de Sousa's[99] treacherous retreat is contrasted with Paiva Couceiro's gallant defence of the monarchy.[100] He was in Lisbon very shortly after his close shave seeking interviews with dignitaries. This may have influenced his orderly depiction of society in early Republican Portugal. Bernardino Machado, the new Foreign Minister, was content to use him as a conduit to the British Government. Machado lauded the high ethical standards of British politics whenever Dillon was near. The new War Minister, Correira Barreto, talked-up the value for the Alliance of the Republic's conscripted army. In an effort to validate the Revolution as a popular one, he extolled its moral purpose, carried out by enthusiastic civilians, as well as marines, bluejackets, and even telegraphists. A contemporary joke sent up the new regime as one established in Lisbon then announced to the rest of the country by telegraph.[101] Dillon became such a revisionist friend of Republicanism that Bragança-Cunha later condemned him as an apologist.[102] But, in October 1910, the journalist was freer to take an optimistic view than later. It was necessary to co-exist with it and, as Francis Villiers had shown, pragmatism was the only eternal British policy. Dillon shared his search for compromise. A man who had just survived a close shave had inclined towards playing it safe.

8 William Archer's soliloquy

Dillon's compromise with the Republic moved him close to a select band of 'anti-Locusts': public supporters who defended it in print.[103] William Archer bolstered this group a couple of months after Dillon. In other respects they could hardly have been more different, illustrating the socio-political diversity that characterized both pro and anti-Republican camps. Dillon's Irish Catholic, theological background was a world away from Archer's. Archer was born into the small Glasite sect in Perth, Scotland – a fringe Presbyterian group founded in the early eighteenth century by Robert Glas. Its strong discipline remained with Archer into later life, turning him away from religious belief, towards rationalism and anti-clericalism. A veteran of five schools by the time he reached Edinburgh University, he graduated in literature in 1876.[104] Archer qualified for the bar in London, but never practised. Instead, he became a theatre critic. Family connections in Norway enabled him to become fluent in Norwegian and an expert on Ibsen. He went on to work personally with both Ibsen and George Bernard Shaw. Archer's writing was far from restricted to drama. In 1910, he published a study of race relations in the USA. Later (1917) he turned his attentions to India. In the same year he declared for the Portuguese Republic (1911), he produced a larger tome which blamed state-church collusion for the execution of the anarchist Francisco Ferrer in Spain. A Liberal Imperialist at the time of the Boer War (1899–1902), by the First World War he had placed his hopes for Europe in the advance of Socialism.[105]

Archer recycled Bernardino Machado's picture of the collapsed party system leaving a small clientele feeding off the Monarchy. Revelling in medical metaphor Archer pronounced: 'The Portuguese monarchy was dead; and the causes of death as disclosed by the autopsy, were moral bankruptcy and intellectual inanition.'[106] Archer echoes Dillon in attributing a higher sense of moral purpose to the new Republican leaders. Braga was not just 'a delightful old man' but also a learned scholar. Machado's immense popularity was explained by his great intelligence, vitality, eloquence, wit, and charm. These men brought a sense of fairness that contrasted with their opponents. Archer is in awe of the initial rush of radical legislation. He welcomes both the restoration of press liberty (shortly to be curtailed) and the divorce law. Above all, the Church deserved its disestablishment because it was so exclusionary. Churches were either locked or accommodating tiny congregations.[107] Jesuits deserved to be expelled because, doctrinally obsessed, they had failed to improve literacy. The state would hugely increase investment in education through savings made from abolishing the Monarchy. Archer predicted there would be no *Vendée* in Portugal as a result of Republican radicalism. Relieving taxation on the poor, and reforming landlord-tenant relations would prevent it. But he badly misjudged Royalism's residual power for counter-revolution. Couceiro's first rising occurred eight months later. Neither was there any significant re-distributive taxation in the period to 1914, although there was educational reform.

For his British audience Archer addressed the Alliance with greater prescience. He understood why Republicans saw it as one between two monarchies, rather than peoples. He also urged respect for Republican commitment to empire. As a polemic against the grain of anti-Republicanism in Britain, Archer's is a stout and singular defence. As a strategic prediction of the trajectory of Republican politics from 1911, it suffered from naive optimism.

The Revolution is principally debated these days by historians. At the time, optimists like Archer hoped it would inject a short, sharp shock towards modernization. But what the optimists struggled to foresee was that modern politics did not necessarily mean greater democracy. The PRP's dominant party politics has been depicted as bound to generate factional conflict because it was so exclusionary and cadre-driven.[108] But this has to be seen against its exclusion, 1878–1910, from ever having more than five percent of the elected deputies despite overwhelming municipal support. The Republic brought a more active parliamentary democracy, one that proved a law-making regime far in excess of the Monarchy.[109] Other historians have breathed life into the Jacobin model popular at the time.[110] Another is fascinated by the Catholic origins and imagery of a failed 'revitalization moment'; a revolution rooted in Portugal's 'tortured relationship to modernity.'[111] In 1911, William Archer thought he sensed that Portugal was changing rapidly. He was right about that; it was, but not in the way that he expected. The path through the Republic was not linear; it was a crooked line.

CHAPTER
3

Changing Places: King Manuel into Exile

The King's '5 October' began when he was awakened early on the morning of the 4th by the sound of bombardment. By the afternoon, revolution was at his doorstep and he was persuaded, by his prime minister and the Spanish Ambassador, to leave. The chief officer of the Royal police, Teixeira de Sousa, gave an account to a special correspondent working for the Press Association shortly after the royal family had left the Necessidades Palace. As the fighting broke out about three o'clock on the afternoon of 4 October, Teixeira escorted the King, the Marquis de Fayal, Captain of the Royal Guard, and Count Pabugosa, through the palace gardens and into the motor car. An overland escape was the only feasible one as the river was lit by searchlights from revolutionary cruisers. Relaxed and smoking a cigarette, the King was taken to the royal palace at Sintra, to meet up with his mother and grandmother – an inglorious exit said one correspondent.[1] After a few hours, Manuel left for Mafra, the women following later. Mafra was strategically placed for Ericeira, and the move was probably made on the advice of the Duke of Oporto. Meanwhile, the King's uncle was living a charmed life. He had been leading the Royalist resistance in Lisbon until the morning of the 5th, but, once all was lost, escaped to Cascais, where the royal yacht was moored. In tears, he sailed for Ericeira, blaming Queen Amélie's resistance to advice for the catastrophe.[2]

The King was joined in Mafra Palace by Queen Amélie and Queen Maria Pia, who had arrived in haste from Sintra. Although a Royal Guard had greeted them, the Palace was without servants. A local doctor was summoned to act as a substitute chef, presumably because he could be trusted not to poison the royal party. Other local loyalists arrived to comprise a makeshift guard outside the King's bedroom. He retired on the night of the 4th sounding as if he was reconciled to his fate: 'Let us take some sleep for the Virgin is watching over us.'³ He awoke early. At 4 a.m., a telegram arrived expressing optimism that all might not be lost. By 10 o'clock, it was. An officer, who had been sent by motorcar to Lisbon in the early hours to monitor the situation first hand, reported it was hopeless. At about two o'clock the next day, the hoisting of the Republican flag in Mafra pronounced the success of the Revolution. It was also the signal for the royal family to leave, which they did in style in an entourage of three cars. Queen Amélie took the first one, intended for the King, declaring: 'No, I go in that one. The King can take the other one. He still does what I tell him.'[4]

The Portuguese royal family that had departed Mafra in such high dudgeon exited their limousines and walked towards the beach with just three trunks and the clothes they stood up in. There were few fond farewells from the people of Ericeira. Only about forty civilians turned up. There was little need of the cavalry's royal guard to keep them in order. A single woman kissed Queen Amélie's hand, who reacted to this indifference by declaring: 'How horrible! I never imagined the Portuguese would treat me like this.' She nervously boarded the small boat which took the party to the yacht, while the older Queen Maria Pia was reported as being 'almost in a fainting condition.'[5] The two women had never got on. The dignified Amélie – 'without doubt the most beautiful woman who has ever reigned in Portugal'[6] – was more frugal than her mother-in-law, whom she thought far too fond of hats.

Above the harbour of Ericeira, looking out to the Atlantic, is the small Capela de São Antonio. The chapel was erected in 1645 to bless the seamen who set out from the jetty below. Long after the painful departure of the royal family a plaque was placed on the south side that reads:

Foi nesta praia que no dia 5 de Outubro de 1910, embarcou para o exílo a família real Portuguesa perante a respeitosa attitude de toda populacão de Ericeira
It was on this beach on the day of 5 October 1910 that the Portuguese royal family embarked for exile before a respectful attitude of all the population of Ericeira

St Antony is the patron saint of Lisbon. The church named after him there lies in the shadow of the Cathedral. Canonised in the thirteenth century, his feast brings the narrow streets that surround it to a stop every 13 June. The plaque in Ericeira faces not towards the sea, but south, across the rolling Estremaduran coastline, towards Lisbon. It is as if St Antony has cast the monarchy to the seas, to share the historic fate of so many Portuguese sailors through the ages. But the plaque commemorating the memory of these events points not in their direction, but to Lisbon, towards the future. In truth, the people of Ericeira had not been respectful. Their Queen had thought them quite horrible. Had she been in the capital she would have experienced the real meaning of horror. The scornful farewell of the fisher people of Ericeira was a gentle ending by comparison.

Beyond, the royal yacht *Amélie* had been ready to receive the refugees into its bosom since early in the day. Across the narrow beach towards the white-walled fishermen's cottages beyond, the royal family looked back on a Portugal to which they would never return. If Manuel retained any sense of irony, he might have pondered that, while Portuguese kings since 1139 had vacated the throne in diverse ways, he was the first to be scuttled in a rowing boat. This was not a good end for the naval cadet who had enrolled in 1904 expecting a brighter future.

From Ericeira, the royal family went missing for a while. False sightings ranged from Mafra, Cascais, the Brazilian battleship in the Tagus, to the Necessidades Palace in Lisbon. It was even suggested the King might be a prisoner, but the Republican provisional government knew that was not true. Neither was he taking refuge in the British Legation. The Spanish government were equally in the dark, waiting for British sources to inform them. This was unwise as even the usually reliable *Times* was re-cycling unconfirmed reports, such as that King Manuel was heading for Rio de Janeiro with the President-Elect.[7]

The Duke of Oporto knew better. Already on board as the royal family boarded the Amélie, he had made sure that it was prepared for a swift departure for Porto. But there was insufficient fuel, so the Old Alliance was called upon to pick up the pieces of the debacle. The Amélie reached Gibraltar on the evening of the 6th escorted by two British cruisers, HMS *Newcastle* and HMS *Minerva*. Fayal and the *Infante* Miguel Bragança were allowed to disembark and given free use of the telegraph office. The King and his mother remained on board, very depressed, having run out of both coffee and sugar.[8] Manuel eventually telegrammed the Government in London indicating he would remain in Gibraltar for the present. He behaved for all the world as if he had just taken a cruise, not mentioning the Revolution. In London, Soveral's story was that Manuel was biding his time, awaiting the revival of Royalist resistance. In fact, his expectations were low, so he met with his uncle (Queen Amélie's brother) the Duke of Orleans, to prepare Wood Norton, their family home in England, for the arrival of the exiles.[9]

As Manuel sailed into exile he could have done without the waves created by the beautiful French actress, singer and dancer,

Mademoiselle Gabrielle Deslys. But the Press loved her. From Milan, where she was playing, she gave *O Seculo* a scandalously self-referential interview, admitting her 'friendship' with Manuel. Apparently, the young king shared his uncle's partiality for actresses and had been smitten after seeing her in Paris. Gaby, at twenty-eight, was eight years older than Manuel. Their attraction had 'matured' from Paris to Lisbon which she so adored that she agreed to perform in a charity concert there, in February 1910. She hints at Queen Amélie's disapproval of her relationship with Manuel: 'I had opportunities for observing the immense influence she wields over her son. . . . He is such a good boy, intelligent and religious.' Only now had she come out about her relationship with the King, to deny accusations that she was a gold-digger. She really had little need of the many presents he bought her (she denies they were 'luxurious') because she commanded enormous fees on the European stage. She was in such demand that she could afford to turn down an offer to play King Manuel's fiancée in a comedy revue about to be launched in Lisbon. So affronted were temperamental impresarios in the capital that they spread malicious rumours she had actually entered into a morganatic marriage with the King. Gabby exited stage right with the declaration that she would rather be Queen in the great world of art, than of a petty state like Portugal.

Republicanism turned Gaby into a *bête noire* who was, at least, Manuel's ruin and, at worst a foreign spy. For a Republican journal like *O Seculo*, in the days after exile, the image of a wastrel philanderer was meat and drink. It was competing for readers with nineteen other dailies in a population of 250,000.[10] The *Daily Chronicle* fed at a parallel trough. For the King, they rubbed salt into the wounds of Cupid's arrow. Manuel continued to see Gaby in exile, until she moved to New York in the middle of 1911, where she began a relationship with fellow actor Harry Pilcer. She died in 1920, aged only 39, after multiple operations for a throat infection. It was said to have been brought on by influenza. Manuel died prematurely young and childless, aged 42, also of a throat infection, in 1932. It was reported as sudden but it was noted that he had been under the regular care of a laryngologist.[11] The immediate cause of death seems to have been a burst abcess that caused him to choke before the doctor arrived.[12] His doctor, Thomaz de Mello Breyner confided to his diary, unpublished until 1992, that Gaby had given him syphilis.[13]

An Italian warship conveyed Queen Maria Pia and the Duke of Oporto from Gibraltar to the Queen Mother's homeland on the 9th. The Republic refused permission for her ever to return, but did grant her a comfortable annuity despite the fact that she left in Portugal an unpaid gas bill for 12,000 pounds.[14] Manuel's intentions were the subject of rumour. The Spanish Government denied he was heading there, and the Foreign Office knew nothing of his plans. The *Chronicle*, however, would have none of this. Convinced he and his mother were on their way to his uncle's house, Wood Norton, near Evesham, its special correspondent door-stepped the Duke of Orleans, on the evening of the 10th. The Duke had scarcely lived at Wood Norton since 1900. He had offended Queen Victoria by writing a letter supporting the Boers to a French caricaturist. Unperturbed, when he was not at his Belgian residence, he spent a lot of time yachting around Europe, or on his estates in Spain, Sicily and Hungary. He was a colourful character. Born the great, grandson of Louis Philippe (King of France 1830–48) in Twickenham in 1869, he was forced to return to Britain in exile with his family in 1886.[15] Educated at Sandhurst, he was attached to the King's Rifles with whom he served in India. Subsequently, he took time away from military studies to father a child by an actress he had met in a casino in Lausanne in 1889, at a time when he was expected to marry his first cousin, Princess Marguerite. Early in 1890 he left Switzerland to enter France illegally, for which he served two months in prison before returning, via Switzerland again, under the English patronage of the Duke of Cambridge. The Duke arranged for him to be sent on an expedition to the Himalayas. The trip did not cool the young Duke's ardours for in 1891 he was forced to break off the relationship with Marguerite when his liaison with the Australian opera singer, Nellie Melba, led to a divorce case. On the death of his father in 1894, he became the official *Orleanist* claimant, which he pursued with deadly seriousness. The next year he was named as co-respondent in another divorce case. In 1896 he entered a loveless and childless marriage with Archduchess Maria Dorothea of Austria, from whom he separated.[16] Eventually, in 1917, aged 52, he married a third time to a woman twenty years younger.[17] This was the American millionairess, Nevada Stoody Hayes, who had lost three previous husbands, herself: one by death, one by divorce, the other by annulment. The Duke died two years later leaving everything to his wife.[18]

So, it was in deferential apprehension at this life well-lived that the *Chronicle*'s special correspondent arrived at the Duke's beautiful domain. 'The house of kings in exile, Wood Norton, has long been the home of . . . the heir – by Blood Royal – of an ancient crown,'[19] he purred. Impressed by the great iron gates adorned with the symbol of the crown of France and the *Fleur de Lys*, he approached the house along an avenue of trees of autumnal scarlet to be greeted by a doorman dressed in the rich livery of old France. It made it impossible to forget this was the house of an exiled king with Bourbon blood running through his veins. It was rumoured that it was to become the home of a second king in exile. Was Manuel aware that the Duke's old-fashioned demand for deference made the estate friendless? The Duke only deemed to smile at those who doffed their hats, and even then they should not think of visiting.

Our correspondent is greeted with charm and courtesy, but only to lull him into a sense of false security. At six feet two inches, soft beard still blonde, soft white hands, the Duke was the very figure of a French nobleman of the old school. His pedigree gave off an air of dignified plausibility, while denying he knew anything of rumour. Yet, it had already been reported that he met the Marquis of Soveral in London on 7 October. Soveral also denied everything.[20] The Duke was prepared to admit that Queen Amélie had declined his offer to go out to Gibraltar. She told him the King was in good health and that rumours to the contrary were put out for political purposes. Otherwise, keen to keep the Press away from Wood Norton, the Duke deflected attention from Manuel and his mother's imminent arrival. The *Chronicle*'s correspondent was sent packing beyond the iron gates that jealously guarded Wood Norton's solitude.

The day after the Duke of Orleans' pantomime of disinformation, the *Daily Chronicle* announced that the royal yacht *Victoria and Albert* was on its way to Gibraltar. The Duke claimed he had only received a telegram to this effect from Queen Amélie after the interview. George V was in a delicate situation. He wanted to assist a friend in need without offending the new Portuguese Government, which showed no vindictiveness towards Manuel.[21] Manuel was reported to be 'completely recovered from his nervous breakdown,'[22] but concern traversed *ancien régime* Europe. Tsar Nicholas I received a letter from his mother deploring the way the Braganças had been driven out. 'The Portuguese must be disgusting . . . It is revolting especially to see with what ease revolutionaries upset everything.' She hoped no other countries would recognise 'this wretched republic.'[23] The Governor's residence in Gibraltar was crowded with foreign guests. Queen Amélie's sister, the Duchess of Guise, had also arrived, along with the Italian Ambassador to the Court of Spain. They were joined by the fleeing ex-Governor of the Azores. Large numbers of armed police surrounded the residence.

The Republican Government in Portugal was not entirely unforgiving over the King's departure. When the Amélie returned, its captain, Mareira Desa, and all the other officers were stripped of their commands. This was just the moment for M. H. Donohoe to be back in Lisbon for another scoop. He was on the spot to interview the chagrined Desa, who recounted how they had left Ericeira in such a hurry with only the barest of provisions. Desa passes over Manuel's health to emphasize that the greatest emotional distress lay with the Queen and her mother. Manuel smoked a lot, while the Duke of Oporto paced the deck incessantly. Dinner during the twenty-four-hour trip consisted of sardines, cheese and fruit. There was no champagne, so a green wine was all that was available.[24] But the King bore up and drank it without complaint. The royal ladies however could not stomach it, preferring water. Thankfully, some Brazilian coffee was found and gratefully consumed. Contrary to the image of a man teetering on the edge of a nervous breakdown, Manuel was the most optimistic of a depressed party. He was even relieved at shedding the burden of the Crown:

> His majesty spoke in strong terms of the disgust he felt with the army of sycophants and corrupt place hunters who had surrounded the throne, and he did not hesitate to express his admiration for some of the Republican leaders, who, at all events . . . had shown courage and energy, whereas the warring sections of the Monarchist party had shown neither resolution nor ordinary pluck.[25]

Manuel claimed he had not seen a single member of his Cabinet during his last day in Lisbon. They were too busy fleeing or going into hiding. As he left Gibraltar, he thanked all those who had helped him, and wished them and Portugal under the Republic well. Some of the Royal Navy sailors, whose ships had ringed the *Amélie* in Gibraltar harbour, were reduced to tears.[26]

Manuel and Queen Amélie arrived in Plymouth on 18 October to careful security arrangements. Their ship had been moored off the Sound for hours to ensure they could arrive under cover of darkness. Only as dusk fell around 5.30 p.m. did they disembark. Their reception was low-key: lesser representatives of the British Crown, the Duke of Orleans, the Marquis of Soveral, and, significantly, the Spanish Ambassador, ordered to attend by King Alfonso in one of those rare historical moments of Iberian monarchical solidarity. A strong police presence prevented all but officials and representatives of the Press from getting near the landing pier. Manuel was looking 'careworn and worried' as he stepped ashore. The full realisation of how far he had fallen must have hit home as he was received by the superintendents of Plymouth Docks and the Great Western Railway. There was no ceremony, no troops, no guard of honour. Royalty had been reduced to the ranks. But the exiles did not linger in Plymouth, taking the 6.33 p.m. Great Western special service to Evesham. It was not every day that Mr Grant, its divisional superintendent, got to open a carriage door for the ex-King of Portugal.

It was as well that the royal party had the carriage to themselves because Manuel had an enormous pile of correspondence to deal with. At Evesham, virtually all security had lapsed. The town had gone to bed but for a small band of yokels who had gathered at the station to cheer. Possibly they were drunk, as it was around 11.30 p.m. and throwing-out time. A couple of porters emerged from the shadows to join the handful of detectives and journalists. The tall figure of the Duke of Orleans stepped out of the train with his sister on his arm; then the ex-King, much younger, but serious and sorrowful. Our special correspondent detects a haunted look as he moved along the desolate station. 'It stirred one to pity for the boy who had lost his country. This new home of his, this English retreat, was not inviting to him as he drove to it through the darkness of night in Worcestershire.'[27]

Evesham's 'dim and silent' high street was briefly lit up by the glaring headlights of the three motorcars that swept the royals away, on the short road journey to Wood Norton. Arriving about midnight, they were followed to the gates by the media pack that refused to let go of their story. There, they were forced to halt, as the Duke disappeared holding Amélie's hand, followed by Manuel. The flag of the Braganças already flew above the chimneys and gables of the house. The servants, who had been hard at work all day preparing for the arrival of 'the boy king', transforming Wood Norton into little Portugal, greeted them. It was as well that the royal party was late because the new French chef had not arrived. The fully liveried, white silk-stockinged, blue coated, buckle-shoed, hair-powdered footmen were at their wits end. But someone, somehow produced a feast fit for the belated royals. It was, of course, fairy-tale journalism to quench the insatiable royalist appetite of the consuming public; journalism that was a world away from M. H. Donohoe's war zone of a fortnight before.

Valentine Williams got a few things wrong, but he clearly recognized that Manuel was an exile in England because of the unreliable Portuguese aristocracy 'who however much they might conspire in the Lisbon bars, were mainly concerned in conserving their personal fortunes and continuing to live without working.'[28] No wonder that Manuel had little heart for actively pursuing a restoration. The Marquis of Soveral,[29] now confidante to the ex-King in England, was the exception. He too was now destined to live out his life in English exile. Williams has left us a delightful sketch of the Monarchy's Portuguese Minister in London, loyalist and friend of Edward VII. He was lampooned in London as 'The Blue Monkey' because of his partiality for bright blue frock coats, set off by his dyed black hair and prominent moustache. Behind the man of fashion lay a highly intelligent diplomat who had played a prominent part over the partition of the African colonies in the 1880s. The Revolution cost him his post in London and most of his prestige. Bernardino Machado paid him a generous tribute, even as he sacked him. He was a charming and sympathetic character who inspired confidence but national opinion demanded the removal of all functionaries of the Monarchy. 'The attentions which he has received in England are great recommendations for him and proof that he has always shown tact and ... enjoyed consideration at the Court of St James's.'[30]

Soveral carried the decline of his reputation with the style of the gentleman that he was. Despite being confined to a small bachelor flat off Manchester Square, never a day passed without him being seen strolling along Bond Street. Through the heart of the West End he perambulated 'perfumed and corseted, with a flower in the buttonhole of his bright blue coat and the shiniest of toppers, and always a pair of spotless white gloves,'[31] for all the world evidence that fortune was temporary, but class permanent. Equally enduring was the Old Alliance. Several counted Edgar Prestage, with whom he had helped found the Portuguese Chamber of Commerce in 1906,[32] as a friend. But greatest of all was the King, himself: Edward VII. Edward died in May 1910, a few months before the Revolution. Afterwards, George V kept him close. Soveral's old age was eased by frequent invitations to shooting parties at Sandringham that helped the painful memories of enforced early retirement to fade.

The churches in Britain welcomed the exiled royal family. At a service in Manchester the Archbishop of York, Dr Cosmo Lang,[33] even managed to work them into a sermon that was supposed to be about conciliating the striking railway workers. He extolled, 'a great measure of sympathy goes out from us to the young king and his mother – the King called to the throne in circumstances of such profound and memorable pathos and now called to abandon it under circumstances so bitter to any young man of bravery and spirit.'[34]

Not to be out-compassioned, the Catholic priest of the Church of the Holy Name in the same city added a word of warning: 'a Catholic throne has been overturned and, the Royal Crown of Catholic Portugal, which for the past two years has been mostly of thorns, has been snatched from the brow of its boy king.' Without a hint of contradiction, Father Day was at pains to stress that the Church welcomed all forms of government: monarchies and republics alike. 'Yet, it is inconceivable that the Church can possibly be indifferent to the sudden creation in the heart of a Catholic country of an infidel government of doctrinaire philosophers and intellectuals of the type of the French Revolutionaries.'[35]

Manuel may have lost his country to a party of secular, Francophile Republicans, but at least he had no financial worries. In January 1911, the Republic granted him a monthly pension of 1,180 pounds to help cushion his English exile. The Braganças had also protected their family fortune astutely. Their state properties were confiscated but they were allowed to keep three palaces and the revenues accruing from their estates. Capital investments and art treasures were safe. It was estimated Manuel would have a comfortable income of 20,000 pounds a year. On death in 1932 his personal fortune had grown to be one of the largest of the growing band of exiled European monarchs. He left all his property in Portugal to the nation, save only the revenues from them for his wife to live on.[36]

Much of Queen Amélie's wealth had always been invested in Paris; much of Manuel's was swiftly exported from Lisbon to London. In Whitehall, it was no doubt comforting to know that 'The Royal House . . . will not be in any sense poor refugees.'[37] For all this, there was much nostalgia expressed over the Monarchy. The *Daily Mail*'s eulogy was representative: 'Another historic dynasty appears to have vanished. Nothing can disguise the great loss which Portugal has suffered. The fall of the royal house so closely bound up with the glories of the Portuguese past is in itself a disaster.'[38] But the black coats of British diplomacy had little time for sitting on the ground, telling sad stories of the death of kings. The undertakers of the Monarchy deftly turned their backs to face the Republic.

Manuel and his entourage of exiles moved from Evesham to Abercorn House in Richmond, in 1911. The owner, Sir Harry Maclean, a colourful army officer, had retired twice: first aged twenty-eight to work for the Sultan of Morocco, then more permanently in Tangiers in 1909.[39] In 1913, Manuel moved to Fulwell Park in Twickenham, smoothed by the backstage efforts of George V to have his furniture released from the former royal palace.[40] He forgot to take from Maclean's house a substantial set of personal papers that were tucked behind a heavy piece of furniture. The cleaners found them and informed Maclean but, living in Tangiers, he seems to have neglected the information. His granddaughter was more cognisant of their historical value and donated them to Kings College, London in 1984.[41]

Discretion was never Manuel's best accomplishment. He had told Churchill as early as June 1911 that he hoped to return to Portugal by way of a *coup d'état*.[42] His personal correspondence for the year 1912, in particular, reveals that he was an active plotter. He was directly involved in planning the overthrow of the Republican Government to restore the Monarchy. In this he had to tread carefully because the leader of the July 1912 rising in the North, Couceiro, was a Miguelist. His master, the Pretender, is revealed to have been bankrolled to the tune of 800,000 marks by his sister, Princess Charles of Bavaria. Germanic connections did not end there. Another vague letter saw Manuel solicit help from the banker Ernesto Driesel Schroetter. Tensions between the two camps deepened after the expensive failure of the rising. Letters to Aires de Ornelas, former Governor of Mozambique and Manuel's intermediary with the Republic, confirm an uneasy co-ordination between Lisbon and England.[43] Manuel refused demands for money he claimed he did not have. Ornelas seems to have been planning the purchase of a warship.[44]

More incriminating was the fifty-two-page plan Manuel had clearly helped draw up to overthrow the Republic and restore the Monarchy. It seems incredible that he could leave such a document behind when he moved in 1913. It outlines the political and philosophical principles the restoration would be based on. It denies the legitimacy of the Revolution, which is to be replaced by a representative monarchy. Without a hint of contradiction, it then sanctions armed action and a mass civil movement to achieve this. There seems to have been a naïve confidence in popular support. More realistically, the plan shows awareness that to ensure success it was necessary to bridge the divisions among the Royalists. It identifies three key stages in the counter-revolutionary transition. Firstly, the Republic would be overthrown, and Lisbon occupied, even at the cost of civil war. Secondly, the King would appoint a Junta and Cabinet of national reconciliation. This would restore the pre-5 October Constitution. Thirdly, an election would take place under the Electoral Law of 1910, but only once a mass Conservative Liberal Party had been formed that could deliver a Monarchist victory. There is a naive belief that a restoration was possible because voters had become aware that the Revolution was a conspiracy against the masses. The plan is not so much a blueprint for change as a replica of the old manipulative political system.[45]

The first rising in October 1911 proved little more than a farce. The Republican press had alerted the Government to it well in advance and prepared the public with propaganda. The rebels got no further than a temporary occupation of the border town of Vinhais. Photographs of imprisoned female villagers stared out at the reader captioned, 'the bread's not too hard in here.' Photographed too was the local priest, Buiça, father of the assassin, beside his orphaned granddaughter Elvira and a band of obdurate Republicans. Over two hundred were imprisoned after these events, as the Republic's insecurity deepened. The *Carbonário* came into its own attracting the ambitious workman keen to earn a day rate far above that prevalent in his trade.[46]

Couceiro's Royalists retreated into Spain. He, himself, turned up at the unlikely venue of the Lord Warden Hotel in Dover on 30 January 1912. Accompanied by Miguel, the Pretender, they were there to make their peace with Manuel. The 'Pact of Dover' agreed that a Miguelist would succeed Manuel should a restoration ever be effected. Shameless over plotting on British soil they issued a suitably vague press release in several languages: 'the two Senhors promised to employ their forces in common to free the beloved homeland from the very sad situation in which it found itself.'[47] They had another crack in July 1912, and made a deeper impact. This time much of the fighting took place around Chaves, without Republican troops who had been diverted to Montalegre. The local milk-boy achieved heroic status in the Republican narrative when, on his early morning rounds, he raised the alarm. The town's citizens-in-arms leapt out of their beds to fend off the Royalists.[48]

Manuel had never been the luckiest of Portuguese monarchs. But for the Regicide he would never have been King at all. In 1909, his grand tour of the country to 'get to know the people' turned into a disaster when a wave of earthquakes struck villages along the Tagus estuary.[49] A visit to England in November of the same year took him out of the seismic zone, to the Guildhall, where his speech on the Old Alliance made a good impression, despite being delivered in broken English. There were hopes that he might find an English Queen to take back to Portugal, but these proved premature.

So, by 1913, the exiled Manuel decided to make a fresh start. Without hope in his own country, with Gaby long gone to live the high life on the American and European stage, he moved from Richmond to Twickenham, and decided to marry a German princess. She was Princess Augustina Victoria of Hohenzollern, Manuel's second cousin. The wedding took place on 4 September in the castle that was the bride's family seat.[50] Manuel had taken great pains to secure his wife, even soliciting Kaiser Wilhelm II's support during a visit in November, 1912. This was in spite of the fact that she was said to be worth as little as he was.[51] This was not quite true of a young woman who brought a dowry of 200,000 dollars.[52] The morning service began at 10 a.m. The weather was cloudy, although dry; not much better than in Twickenham, where a light to moderate easterly breeze kept temperatures cool at around 60F. The widowed Queen Amélie was present to see her surviving son married. The Prince of Wales was also amongst the guests. Reuters, doing its bit to warm Anglo-German relations at a chilly time, noted that he was well received in the German town. Cardinal Neto, former patriarch of Lisbon, officiated. He had time on his hands since Afonso Costa had made him redundant. At 2.30 p.m. the happy couple left for their honeymoon in Bavaria,[53] but the chill of the mountain air did not agree with the newest member of the Bragança dynasty. She caught influenza and had to return to Sigmaringen.[54] Her recovery there delayed the couple's return to Fulwell Park, Twickenham, which had been regally furnished from the trappings of the Royal Palace in Portugal.[55] Royalists all over Portugal collected for a wedding present in the face of official disapproval and *Carbonária* harassment. Those in Lisbon deposited a gift at the British Legation, which tried to smuggle it out on a ship transporting correspondence. But customs' officials were alert and impounded the politically-charged cargo. A full-scale press row ensued. *O Mundo* condemned the British Legation for neo-colonialist abuse of Portuguese hospitality: 'the Republic is not disposed to allow England's representatives to come and lord it at Lisbon.'[56] It was a reminder that the last King of Portugal retained the capacity to inflame Republican patriotism. Anglo-Portuguese relations had descended from icy into the permafrost.

CHAPTER

4

The Catholic

1 Resurrecting McCullagh

But for the work of John Horgan, Francis McCullagh would have been largely forgotten today. He deserves to be remembered as one of the leading foreign and war correspondents of the early twentieth century. Horgan, however, deals little with McCullagh's journalism on the early years of the Republic, which presented a distinctively Catholic view in a number of different publications. McCullagh never forget he was a Catholic writing about an anti-clerical republic, and that imparted a significant bias. As a journalist with a growing international reputation, he communicated those criticisms via publications that reached far beyond a Catholic audience. To his credit he invariably got the balance right: journalist first; Catholic second; but always a Catholic journalist, critical of the Republic.

He was born the son of a publican, in Omagh, County Tyrone in 1874. Educated in a seminary, St Columb's College, Derry, he set aside early vocational thoughts of the priesthood for a career in journalism. As a young man, he was remembered as conservatively well dressed, short, quiet, and famed for never losing his temper.[1] This contrasts with the polemical, thirty-six year-old anti-Republican of 1910. In the 1880s, he wrote, off and on, for the *Scottish Catholic Observer*. Through the 1890s, he worked his passage through Columbo, to Bangkok, ending up as the correspondent of the *Japan Times*, from where he controversialized about Japan needing Christianisation to liberate its women. He reported on the Russo-Japanese War (1904–5) for the *New York Herald*, his reports becoming world exclusives. Much in demand, he began to freelance out. Before Portugal, he reported from Turkey (1909). After, he was very critical of the Italians during the Libyan War (1911–12), condemning its imperialism for being backed by bankers. As an observant Catholic, it is evidence of openness of mind. He was not open to taking up the Italian nationalist Marinetti's challenge to a duel, however.[2] This was the least of

McCullagh's worries when later in 1912 he was taken prisoner by the Bulgarians. On liberation, he went to Morocco to report for the *Pall Mall Gazette* of W. T. Stead.[3] Again, his critical attitude towards capitalism surfaced over the role of arms dealing in inciting violence in Africa. Pieces in the *New York Evening Post*, as well as the *New York Tribune* placed the atrocities of European imperialism before the American public.[4]

McCullagh became a major polemicist against the Republic in its early years. He dismissed as simplistic the Republican view that the Church was a main cause of revolution. Against this he charged Republicans with false propaganda in order to incite anti-clericalism and overthrow the Monarchy. His Catholic criticisms appeared widely across publications in several countries, notably in Britain.

2 The testing of Father Torrend

The Jesuit College of Campolide had been founded in 1858 and by 1910 was renowned as one of the finest boys' schools in Portugal.[5] Its curriculum extended well beyond religion, to science, commerce and European languages. For half a century it had helped broaden a Portuguese curriculum dominated by law, literature, and medicine. The Jesuits first gained a reputation for mathematics teaching in Portugal in the sixteenth century. But the Society was closed down by Pombal in 1759, and was not restored until 1848, from when it enjoyed a renaissance. The jewel in Campolide's academic crown was the science journal *Brotéria*.[6] Originally founded in 1902, by three Jesuit scholars at São Fiel College, it was part of the Catholic response to Comtist anti-clericalism. Its mission statement refused the new Republicanism's insistence that science was incompatible with faith. *Brotéria* attained an international reputation and, from 1907, actually published three discrete periodicals, for popular science, Botany and Zoology. *Brotéria* was a unique journal, but also part of a European Jesuit academic revival in the early twentieth century.[7]

The distinguished academic Father Camille Torrend, principal at Campolide, edited *Brotéria* in 1910. The College's natural history curation, run jointly by Father Torrend and his Swiss colleague, Father Luisier, had a reputation for being second only to the British Museum's. McCullagh describes Torrend as short, with a broad face and curly hair, youthful in appearance and aged about forty. In fact, he was a very youthful forty for he was only thirty-four, remarkably vivacious, with a bright and clever face, according to another source.[8] He had been born in 1875 at Le Puy, Haute-Loire, in the Auvergne.

Its twelfth-century Cathedral became a place of pilgrimage as legend had it that it was built upon a shrine to the Virgin Mary. This proved a fortuitous beginning for a devout Jesuit like Torrend. But he was also a distinguished mycologist (the study of fungi) who had published on myxomycetes (slime moulds). In the month of his expulsion, *The Philosophical Review* published a paper on the transformation of vegetables that he had contributed to a progressive Catholic symposium on Darwinism.[9]

Camille Torrend's '5 October' began not in Lisbon, but in Barro College for novitiates, near Torres Vedras, where, he told the French journalist, Maurice Muret, the college was attacked by a mob. The vineyard watchman panicked and killed one of them. The next day about three hundred troops arrived to investigate the Jesuit population of eighty-six. The watchman had long fled, and the Superior immediately surrendered, surprising the Republican troops who expected 'a shower of grapeshot.' The fathers were taken to the local railway station and dispatched for Lisbon. During the trip, their guards treated the priests very well. But as they entered the capital from the north-west, the stationmaster at Amadora broke through the cordon hitting an old Jesuit on the head with the butt of his red flagstaff. On reaching Campolide 'a great rabble' hurled insults urging the priests be shot. The train was halted again in the docks area of Alcantara because the line had been severed in three places. Local Republicans had spread a great fear that a Jesuit army was advancing on Lisbon from the North, complete with field artillery. The train was prevented from reaching central Lisbon, and all eighty-six Jesuits had to be evacuated and brought to Caxias fortress, nearby.

The French Legation, had been alerted to Torrend's detention by a friend. It intervened for his release and he was sheltered in the Church of St Louis, by the chaplain, Father Caullet. Torrend was ready to leave for England when the Minister of Justice, Afonso Costa, offered him an extraordinary bribe. If Torrend would cease being a Jesuit he could have a Chair at a Portuguese University – an offer that was hardly within Costa's gift. Torrend refused Costa's attempt to remove him from politics, insisting on the right of Jesuits to speak freely to the press.

Torrend gave Maurice Muret further evidence of Republican ideological warfare against Jesuits. The idea that Jesuits had built a network of subterranean tunnels beneath their institutions was laughable. Campolide was built on a hill made of basalt rock. Although there had been some excavations over the centuries, these only provided for functional rooms, cisterns and sewers; all unfit for any human to pass through.[10] Torrend provided a detailed enteric map of the bowels of Campolide with the further promise of photographic evidence.

When McCullagh read Muret's interview, he weighed into the conflict of competing narratives. Superstition in Portugal was worse than in China he declaimed: 'the Jesuits had ceased to be men. They had become hobgoblins, malignant sprites whose secret passages ran underground from one end of Portugal to another.'[11] Local peasants near Barro apparently believed that the proliferation of scientific instruments at the college was 'the work of the Evil One.' At Campolide massive destruction took place and its valuable scientific instruments 'roughly handled and thrown about by soldiers who care as little about science as a swarm of orang-outangs.'[12] Myth was even distorting the narratives of foreign correspondents. One American had reported that firing was still coming from 'subterranean passages' a week after the Revolution, and that twenty nuns had been brought up after a five-day submersion. Another narrative circulating had a handful of Jesuits hiding in the tunnels below Campolide from where they launched nocturnal armed raids against soldiers. The Government were said to be taking it so seriously that they planned to smoke them out with sulphur fumes.

Three days after the Revolution, the Society of Jesus and its colleges were closed down. It was too late to prevent Camopolide's great library of over twenty-five thousand volumes from being ransacked. Priceless scholarly treasures disappeared at a rate of knots: a 1498 edition of the works of Horace, a first edition of a 1600 Life of St Francis, rare editions of Camões, and even one by the fourteenth-century Persian poet Hafez. If the Republican guards were not stealing things themselves, they were giving them away as souvenirs. Roman coins were redistributed like a perverse act of charity. McCullagh did not spare the philistines: 'the republican apostles of progress and enlightenment . . . are little better than Huns.'[13] Not satisfied with the Library, the mob looted the chapel. Anything of gold or silver disappeared out of the door. When all had gone 'the Huns' returned to desecrate the images on the walls. As this travesty unfolded, the Jesuits were hustled off to prison by armed civilians (*populares*) who lacked legal authority of arrest. The sacking of Campolide seems to have been conducted in a spirit of hysterical fear. The invading mob had expected resistance from large numbers of armed Jesuits holding out in a catacomb of tunnels. All they found were seven unarmed, rather frightened priests.

Several of the leading Jesuits had already escaped abroad; others like Torrend were swiftly released, often into agreed exile. Torrend sailed to an unlikely destination for a Catholic: Fishguard. Landing on

21 October 1910, he stayed with the Jesuits at Farm Street, nearby. He had studied at the Jesuit House at Milltown Park, near Dublin, as a young man, but this was probably his first visit to Wales. By contrast, he spent most of the rest of his life in Brazil, where he continued as a priest, and with his academic work as a professor in a college in Bahia. He died there in 1961, aged eighty-six.

By 13 November, Torrend, the French refugee from Portugal, was at Stonyhurst College, the Jesuit public school near Clitheroe in Lancashire. Even there, he could not escape the competing narratives of Portuguese Jesuitry. His ire was raised by a letter, from Stuart E. McNair from Coimbra, in *The Scotsman* for 9 November. McNair had become involved in a bitter exchange through October with Father M. J. Power. The latter singled out soldiers' persecution of nuns as 'being true to the reputation they had acquired during the Peninsular War, of being the biggest cowards in Europe.'[14] Power's rugged masculinity omitted to say that the monks of the English College and the Irish Dominicans in Lisbon were left alone. He complained of the treatment of a former mill girl from Preston, and two sisters from Liverpool, who were denied proper food and a change of clothing in prison.

McNair presented an alternative narrative, robustly. Power did not understand 'the execration with which the Order is held by the common people.'[15] Dynamite was thrown out of the Quelhas windows at the military that had come to protect the Convent. Arms were found after the siege. The authorities had still done their best to prevent looting such as of the Library. The girl from Preston had, regrettably, died, but McNair thought those who persuaded her to enrol in an unpopular foreign religious order had some responsibility. He also regretted the reduction of the detained nuns to a vegetarian diet, but 'they had left behind them in the Quelhas convent a great abundance of bread, eggs, preserved fruits, wine, champagne, and liquers.'[16] Readers of *The Scotsman*'s letters' page were left wondering whether the convent was more plentiful in arms or foodstuffs. McNair's Evangelicalism had elided with Republicanism through a shared contempt for Jesuitry.

McNair had first gone to Portugal in 1891 as an engineering draughtsman, aged twenty-four. He came under the influence of his landlady, the widow of the hymn writer, and Brethren Bible teacher, Richard Holden. She was renowned for dispensing charity to the ragged children of the local neighbourhood. Richard Holden had founded The Brethren in Brazil in 1878, before returning to Portugal the next year. The Brethren was originally founded in Ireland in the 1820s as a rejection of both perceived spiritual distortions of

Anglicanism and the sectarian practice of much Nonconformity. Consequently, the Anglican authorities at the English Cemetery in Lisbon refused to bury Holden after his death in August 1886. McNair's first spell in Portugal lasted five years, before he departed for Brazil in 1896 to continue the missionary work begun by Holden.[17] It is unclear when he returned to Portugal, but he was evidently there in 1910.

Torrend counter-attacked with satire. As McNair had substituted imagination for evidence he – Torrend – might as well confess to being a dynamiter and a bomb thrower. Torrend challenged the objectivity of a man prepared to believe that Jesuits escaped from Campolide through eight-inch bore sewers. McNair admitted his evidence was circumstantial, although he denied it was from the Republican press, which he claimed never to read. Instead, he forwarded the official Government statement on the Quelhas siege, which, as evidence, was rather like asking the *Carbonária* to investigate itself. But Torrend was no more objective. He dismissed McNair's view that the common people rejected Jesuitry, in favour of a conspiracy theory that anti-clericalism was all the work of anarchists and hooligans at the mercy of the cheap press.[18]

In supporting Torrend and the Jesuits against secular attack, McCullagh challenged the confiscation of religious property as a mixture of ignorance and confusion. Firstly, a lot of the confiscated property was not owned by the Orders at all, but loaned to them by Catholic laymen. Secondly, some was owned by foreign Jesuit Orders over which the Portuguese Government had no legal rights. A third consequence of closing down the Orders would be the disappearance of the charitable work for the poor performed by nuns.

3 Vices of national character: The social origins of betrayal

In search of the destructive roots of revolution, McCullagh differentiated the religious from the corrupt political life of Portugal. His superficial analysis blamed the fall of the Government on personal failings. King Manuel had been betrayed by his Prime Minister, Teixeira de Sousa, a self-interested turncoat who allowed the Republicans to take over, leaving the loyal, monarchist Army hopelessly exposed. However, the King deserved nothing more as he tailed and ran to Gibraltar like a coward. However, McCullagh did recognize the limits of individual agency and examined some structural issues. The Army had been de-Christianized and corrupted by Freemasonry. The *Carbonária*'s terrorism discredited it as an institution. Anarchism lingered in the wings ready to exploit revolutionary chaos by destroying state and family, alike.

McCullagh was influenced by Francisco Manuel Homem Cristo who, as a Republican Army officer, had taken a prominent role in the crisis of 1891. But, he had drawn back from supporting the Porto revolt of 1891, then did the same on 5 October 1910, going into exile in France. He was a long-standing critic of Afonso Costa in the pages of the newspaper he edited, *O Povo de Aveiro*.[19] Homem Cristo proffered a conflated racial theory about the leadership of the Revolution that resonated with McCullagh: 'Is it not rather the work of the Positivists, the Comtists, of Teófilo Braga and his friends? Indiscipline . . . [was] . . . the peculiar possession of this semi-African race which we call Portuguese.'[20]

An equally important influence was the French sociologist, Léon Poinsard. Poinsard had been invited by Manuel in 1909 to investigate the 'social question.' His conclusions were published in two volumes in 1910 as *Le Portugal Inconnu (Unknown Portugal)*.[21] He identified reform of the clientalist system of *rotativismo* as key, advocating its removal through reorganisation of local government. McCullagh prioritizes Poinsard's more primitive social analysis, which he presents as the Catholic riposte to the Positivism of the 'Generation of 1870.' Portugal's decline was rooted in the parasitism of a ruling class that had luxuriated in the riches of empire since the sixteenth century. It had neglected commercial and moral education and allowed Portugal to drift into moral decline through the nineteenth. Portugal's young men should have been the coming generation of thrusting entrepreneurs; instead, they avoided hard work in favour of a life of foppery and literary leisure.

McCullagh thought that the social failure of empire had left a ruling class better at glory hunting than book keeping. Portugal had, for a generation, needed a dictator like João Franco to pull it together. But the regicide ended any hope of strong government as the immature Manuel showed himself incapable of staving off a revolution made only by a small group of urban malcontents. Abandoning structural analysis for conspiracy theory once more, McCullagh's '5 October' becomes the work of the street loafers of Lisbon: 'the rag, tag and bobtail of the city.' They behaved 'like cattle, like savage Negroes, like blind men . . . stagnant barbarians,'[22] Brito Camacho's newspaper *A Lucta* howled to McCullagh's approval. Ninety-three percent of them were illiterate, ignorant animals unable to read voting papers, he added, well aware that such calculations were impossible.

McCullagh's mob theory posited conspiratorial leadership – a secret society of anti-clerical freemasons – whose primary target was the Church. McCullagh resorted to pseudo-theory to explain the seductive influence of politicized Freemasonry to his English-speaking audience:

> The Southern European is . . . peculiarly liable to fall into the net of some occult association. It may be on account of his weakness and of that love for vague, high-sounding generalities to which M Poinsard refers . . . Returning recently to England from Portugal, I met on the steamer a Portuguese youth who belonged to so many different secret societies that he could not remember all their names. His case was typical. So far as I can make out, the sole object of those societies is to overthrow things established, whether these things are good or bad. They have no definite constructive programme, as will be seen from an examination of their activity in Portugal.[23]

It was possible that Poinsard would have refused this crudely reductionist view of the Portuguese character. His own social anthropology was derived from Frédéric Le Play and his social catholic journal *La Science Sociale*, which had originally published *Unknown Portugal*.[24] Formerly an atheist and much respected social reformer, Le Play had converted in 1879. After that, he defended Catholic education against the secular reforms of Jules Ferry. For Le Play, the rot had set in with Rousseau, whom he held most responsible for the deplorable social values enacted by the French Revolution. Before 1910, sociology had made a limited impact on the Portuguese curriculum. Teófilo Braga's Positivism emerged in the 1880s, but it was contained within the Law faculty at Coimbra. Poinsard's Catholic, corporatist reformism, and that of his fellow Frenchman Paul Descamps, challenged Positivism, and laid the theoretical foundations for the later Salazar dictatorship.[25]

Poinsard studied the history of property law and its effects on social relations. His field research exhibited a thoroughly modern methodology, travelling the nation to draw ethnographical evidence in search of the material conditions of economic decay. For example, his study of Algarve peasant farmers was based on family monographs. He observed the destructive effects of the constant labour migration of males trying to sustain the family economy.[26]

But, for Poinsard, the problem ran deeper than economics. The Portuguese family was suffering from a social and spiritual malaise spread by secularization. The ruling classes were also socially diseased; indolent, fat and lazy, they had lived off the profits of empire. Neglect of religion had corroded their value system, leaving them incapable of spiritual remorse. The political expression of this complacency was *rotativismo*: power sharing by the degenerate. Political reform alone could not heal the nation. Poinsard's regeneration started at the bottom with the moral reconstitution of the family.

4 'Dechristianisation': Freemasonry and anti-clerical violence

McCullagh, the journalist, was convinced that Freemasonry was the immediate danger. He had read an interview with an Army officer, Captain Palla, in *0 Seculo*, in which Palla confessed he had been setting up lodges since the 1890s. Palla shed important light on the nature of the Army revolt in October. Having limited success with the General Staff, he had concentrated on subverting non-commissioned officers and rank and file soldiers. On '5 October' they had actually managed to load the rifles of many Royalists with blank bullets. Extraordinarily, Palla claimed the Government knew of his sabotage and stood by. It led to officers of the First Artillery regiment being butchered by the rank and file. McCullagh predicted that military backing for *Carbonária* anti-clericalism could only make it more violent. Alongside the *Carbonária*, the Anarchists were quite prepared to dynamite their way to power. A cork workers' strike threatened to spill over into other sections of the labour movement.

Republican ineptitude proceeded to deliver McCullagh's Catholic cause an ideal heroine: the English nun, Mother Mary Tipping. Anti-clerical mobs had twice besieged the Dorothean Convent, Mother Tipping having to bribe them with wine and cigarettes to leave. After the second occasion, regular troops kept order. However, the General Staff swiftly replaced them with a unit of unruly, anti-clerical sailors. The Convent was fired on and looted. The Government blamed the returning mob, but McCullagh claimed it was the 'bluejackets' (sailors), themselves. The nuns were either arrested or taken away for their own protection. A distressed Mother Tipping was released into the care of Hugh Gaisford, the First Consul to the British Embassy, and his wife. The Gaisfords' compassion was fatally rewarded. The deeply disturbed Mother Tipping awoke in the middle of the night and, according to McCullagh, believing herself to be pursued by a mob of phantom sailors fell from a window to her death. But he floated the alternative explanation of suicide under extreme stress. The doctrinally correct *Tablet* fiercely denounced such a possibility, leaving McCulllagh embarrassed.[27]

He drew two connected lessons from the tragedy. The Government's scapegoating of the Church provoked a violent anti-clericalism it lacked both the will and capacity to control. Presiding over this chaos as Minister of Justice, was Afonso Costa, architect of the Law of Separation of 20 April 1911. McCullagh complained bitterly[28] about what one authority has described as 'the most extraordinary and severe anti-clerical action taken by a government in Europe up to that time.'[29] However, it appears less exceptional when seen as the culmination of a secularisation of Portuguese society stretching back a century. But, the Republican Government wasted no time. The laicisation of society began just three days after the Revolution and was rushed through in Portugal in less than eight months. Its French model had taken a quarter of a century. The historian of the Azores has seen this as 'the crippling of the Catholic Church' because:

> Republicans expelled religious orders from Portugal and nationalized their property . . . secularized religious holidays; permitted divorce; abolished the teaching of Christian doctrine in primary schools; mandated the civil registry of births, marriages, and deaths; enforced legislation prohibiting church burials; and banned the wearing of religious vestments outside church buildings . . . Catholicism ceased to be the religion of the state, religious freedom was guaranteed to all, and other religions were accepted in Portugal . . . The administration of churches and chapels, once under local parishes, became dependent on Cultuais, lay associations without members of the Church that oversaw all religious services and property. Bishops and priests were no longer dependent on the state for their upkeep but relied directly upon the generosity of the faithful, although the Republic was willing to award a lifelong pension to all clergy who submitted a written request. This would lead to a breach between priests receiving pensions, who sympathized with the Republican regime, and more traditional clergy, who remained faithful to the monarchy.[30]

A discourse of 'crippling the Catholic Church' echoes contemporary rhetoric such as McCullagh's. At times, this extended into a narrative of 'religious war' and 'terrorism'. Positivism had added a scientist edge to anti-clericalism, but even Costa negotiated with the Church in hope of a settlement between October 1910 and February 1911. Privileging ideology over structure in Republican policy confirms the picture of a state driven by fanaticism, and mirrors contemporary Catholic opinion. In contrast, the continuity argument explains the Laws as the culmination of a process of laicisation stretching back to at least 1834, and even to the Pombaline Enlightenment. Because Separation was paralleled in other European states, it was unexceptional.

Laicisation needs to be read down, through social stratification, as well as across historical time. Anti-clericalism is open to a pluralist interpretation. It was most visible at the political level of institutions, but it also seeped deep into popular culture. Even at the top of the Republican Party, it ranged from ideological atheism, to a gentler, *étatist* laicisation. Its meaning within popular culture was equally ambivalent. The ideological fervour that burned down churches was rare (although some were ransacked). More common was a seething resentment of the quasi-taxation that went to support the Church. Sometimes, it was more personal – dislike or opposition to a particular priest, rather than the Church as an institution.[31] One historian detects a 'moral economy of the crowd' at work in the protests against the Laws, in that attacks on the Church were seen as against the community. This conceptualisation might be extended to encompass the defence of 'customs in common.'[32] This process is shrouded in ambiguity in that it conservatively reaches back to a paternalist past to oppose a modern authoritarianism. But in 1911, Portuguese 'plebeian culture' stood at a frontier between the traditional and the modern. Those who feared the modern clung to the known in the face of the unknown; to the rituals and customs that had always defined Portuguese collective identity in the rural, Catholic areas.

When McCullagh sensationalized the Separation Law as 'a law of Extermination'[33] he chose to ignore the Church's history of surviving anti-clericalism stretching back to the eighteenth century. In 1759, Pombal had expelled most Jesuit orders as unable to keep pace with the educational and scientific progress the modernisation of Portugal required. The more progressive orders were allowed to continue, however, both in their educational and charitable work, and as property owners. But, they suffered as a result of Portugal's civil conflict in the 1820s and 1830s when Liberal governments either taxed or confiscated properties, and excluded the clergy from politics. In 1834 the orders were closed altogether. From the 1850s, however, they began to creep back under the guise of charitable organisations. Fifty orders had legal recognition restored in 1901. Ordinary clergy continued to be paid by the state as *de facto* civil servants throughout the nineteenth century. So moribund was the Church, however, that recruitment levels to the priesthood fell consistently.[34]

McCullagh admired the light touch with which the liberal monarchy handled the Church through the later nineteenth century. By an informal concordat the state exercised a clear control over the operations of the Church – over appointments, for example – but there was no attempt at the 'dechristianisation' imposed by the Republic.[35] By the turn of the century, the effects of the First Vatican Council's crusade against the evils of modernism (1869–70) had led to a religious revival in Portugal. The *Ralliement* in France pointed the way towards reconciliation with republican states. Pope Leo XIII taught compromise and co-existence with the political realm provided God was allowed to remain active within it. Some Portuguese Catholics hoped for a similar compromise after 1910, but others regarded their Catholicism as inseparable from their Monarchism.[36] A few even supported insurrection. In the years before 1910, the Jesuits were in the vanguard of Catholic revival, boasting a dozen monasteries and as many schools, two million members of their lay association *Apostolado da Oração*, in addition to the prestigious *Brotéria*. A Nationalist Party representing politicized Catholicism won a handful of seats in 1904.[37] This restored influence was crushed by Separation which even survived into the *Estado Novo*.[38]

McCullagh saw the Separation Laws as a co-opting of the Brazilian model rather than the French. But in neither state did he think that separation had been characterized by the overt repression that was seen in Portugal.[39] He accused the Portuguese Republic of being driven by a singular spirit of persecution. Costa had publicly announced his intention to eliminate Christianity within two generations, an aspiration that encouraged violence:

> In Buarcos, near Figueira da Foz, a procession was recently authorized by the administrator of the Council, but the local Republicans stoned the procession, broke it up, and destroyed some of the images that were carried in it. The same thing happened in Guimarães.[40]

Pensions came in for particular criticism. They were granted to the conforming as a means of short-term, social control but turned dissenters into rebels. Furthermore, the state tempts priests to marry by allowing them to leave their pensions to wives and families, 'a real incitement to clerical corruption and to desertions, which have up to the present been rare.'[41] Worse than despotism was the passing to local commissions (*cultuais*) power to decide on pension levels according to a priest's personal wealth and outside income.[42]

McCullagh expected the banning of all Portuguese clergy educated abroad and visiting foreign clergy, to have a serious impact on the Church's functioning. He suggested the Republican state only retained diplomatic relations with the Vatican to protect the empire in the Orient and India. Overall, he considered expropriation of property, policing of finances, regulation of operational hours, and banning of religious processions amounted to state co-option, not mere separation.

McCullagh identified three insidious consequences of the new anti-clerical laws. Firstly, religion was reduced to the status of a 'cult', being allowed no religious practice outside of the church. Income was controlled, for example one third had to be publicly declared for charitable sources. Secondly, the Church's rights as a property holder were attacked with damaging social consequences. Good works were endangered. 'Unnecessary' parts of Bishop's palaces were being sub-let. Relations with foreign governments were threatened, for example properties owned by the British Protestant community in Porto had been confiscated.

Thirdly, the priest's status and authority was all but removed. He would only be paid if he abided by the new laws, something most would not. Article 181, which banned unauthorised pastorals, was to become a central bone of contention between church and state. McCullagh condemned it as an attack upon free expression, as were measures to gag the Catholic press into 'the silence of the church yard.' Costa was on public record as saying 'the religious sentiment is a lie and every kind of church is a farce.' The Jesuits were 'an association for robbing and killing.'[43] McCullagh reverses the charges. It was 'republican heroes ... [who] . . . broke into a Lisbon schoolroom where two priests were teaching a number of boys and, after murdering these priests – one of whom was a very aged man – mutilated them before the schoolboys in a manner worthy of "Jack the Ripper"'.[44] He thought this an exceptional regime that made vindictiveness the norm in state-church relations. Another victim was the Rev. Augusto Carlos Ferreira Coimbra, Professor of Mathematics in the seminary of Cabo Verde, who was suspended for preaching against the new divorce law.[45] Others included the majority of Portuguese bishops, banished for non-compliance. One of these, Bishop José Alves Correia da Silva, lost his post as Professor of Theology, went to prison several times for resisting the laws before finally opting for exile. He did not return to Portugal until 1920, from when he became Bishop of Leiria, responsible for constructing the cult of Fátima.[46]

5 Counter-revolution and the Catholic revival

The Papacy urged peaceful resistance, but militant Catholic Monarchists rebelled. Captain Henrique Paiva Couceiro, a former Governor of Angola and empire loyalist, had been one of the Monarchy's staunchest defenders in 1910. In March, 1911 he offered an olive branch to the Republic by requesting a plebiscite on the Monarchy. When it was predictably rejected, he joined a motley crew of dissident Monarchists (Miguelists and Manuelists), priests and peasants, across the Spanish frontier in Galicia, and plotted. A first rising was easily repelled in October, 1911, then a more serious one, in June 1912.[47] After that, McCullagh's hopes that the Church might be saved by a Royalist uprising faded.

But he need not have been so apprehensive. The Separation Law was so badly administered that many areas had no *cultuais* to impose lay authority on the religious. In the isolated Azores, 'religious processions were held annually as if the Fifth of October of 1910 had never happened.'[48] Religious festivals continued in the Catholic North, particularly, where the Separation Laws offended popular morality. Banning the chiming of bells was an offence against the 'acoustic landscape'. Confiscation of Church property, and goods, was theft from the community. As Church buildings performed more than religious functions, any attack upon them was upon customs in common.[49]

Catholics were prepared to let *União Nacional* lie dormant, only to see the Government close its leading newspaper, *A Palavra (The Word)*. Republicanism was better at repressing Catholicism's organisation than its ideas. Historians have even suggested that Republican repression added fuel to the Catholic revival.[50] Camille Torrend is a fine example of that revival. After escaping the clutches of the Republic, he had hardly rested. In a French publication he called for absolute obedience to Rome on the religious question as the only hope of saving the Church in Portugal. There was no room for the kind of compromises that had been made in his native France. His most vehement *pièce de la résistance* was published in one of McCullagh's favourite journals.[51] Torrend thanks 'The English Lady' who helped get him released. This may have been the Duchess of Bedford, although she did not begin campaigning on behalf of political prisoners until early 1913. Afonso Costa is castigated for his duplicity and misunderstanding of the causes of the Portuguese crisis. Torrend was nursing a grievance against him for not rescuing his personal, mycological library from the mob in October 1910. Costa is cast as 'the Pombal of the twentieth century'[52] for turning Jesuits into whipping boys. His lies provide the new currency of politics, spread by Freemasons. Jesuits are bomb throwers, pluck out children's eyes to make oil, bribe the Press and control the Vatican. Tales about secret tunnels below monasteries, might have come straight out of Edgar Allan Poe. For Torrend, the tragedy was that Costa's 'paganism' had raised the expectations of the working class so high they were no longer content to wait for paradise. Costa should have left the religious question alone and concentrated on raising peasant living standards. The ladder out of poverty was not atheism but more religious education, Torrend preached.

He turned to the damage done by anti-clericalism to foreign relations. Neither the French, Italians, Germans, nor English trusted Republican assurances that the religious laws only affected Portuguese. All were intent on saving the property of their religious congregations from 'the apaches of Lisbon' – looters. Torrend predicted a slippery slope to anarchy as churches were pillaged, factories burned, vineyards ravaged. As English insurance companies disliked anarchy, it would be better to restore English property rights as a statement of shared values. Torrend feared the effects of social instability on a volatile Portugal:

> The Latin races of Southern Europe have special need of strong religious feeling, so as to develop the consciousness of duty in all classes of society (particularly the uneducated classes), and so as to restrain them from the excesses to which their hot temper is bound to give rise unless kept under a firm control.[53]

A further example of the Catholic revival, and a McCullagh fellow-traveller, is the mysterious 'Sylva Doria', a pseudonym put to a vitriolic attack upon Costa in the wake of the Separation Laws. Costa received widespread criticism, but this was perhaps the most uncompromising piece of invective to be found in an English-language publication around 1911. It amounts to a character assassination within a pretence of examining church–state relations.

The author is particularly incensed by Costa's treatment of the Portuguese episcopate. The Archbishop of Lisbon, three Archbishops, and nine Bishops had sent out a pastoral letter urging their flock to obey the Republican Government in all matters except those of conscience. This was enough for Costa to go to war. He banned the reading of it in all churches, and closed down printers who did not comply. All but the Bishop of Porto, Dr Antonio Barroso, obeyed, and he was summoned to Lisbon. Rumour had it a hostile crowd of 'nun beaters' had gathered at Rossio to murder him, so the Bishop's train was stopped at Campolide and a government car laid on. His secular arraignment lasted for five hours, after which Barroso was deprived of his See, although allowed to keep his pension. Officially, this was out of recognition for his missionary service in Africa (he had been Bishop of Mozambique). However, our author suggests it was to prevent the raising of huge amounts of money from his supporters. Barroso was tough and fearless, 'a big, loose-jointed, long-bearded old man with a halo of white hair crowning a massive brow, and with the rugged and commanding presence of a Biblical patriarch.'[54] He had not flinched when soldiers and Republican guards invaded his

78 | *The Catholic*

episcopal palace. Even the dreadful Costa admitted he was proud to have him as an opponent.

Our author seeks to turn Barroso's case into a stand-off with Costa. Rome was incensed by Costa's provocation, and the diocese of Porto up in arms. Costa is accused of bringing his corrupt legal practises into government. His ministry was run like Tammany Hall, filled with 'insatiable republican office-hunters.' In the provinces, he had turned local government over to 'village loafers and pothouse politicians.' With cannibalistic bad taste, 'Doria' implies that the British were revelling in the Portuguese Church's ordeal: 'Rev John Bull has a warm corner in his heart for any who quarrels with the followers of Loyola, even for the South Sea Islander who dines on Jesuit.'[55] 'Doria' warns that, unrestrained by a monarchy, Costa is even more dangerous than Lloyd George. Vain, ambitious, narrow minded, freethinking and anti-free press, only a man such as Costa could have so mishandled the liberal, democratically-minded Bishop of Porto.

'Doria' accuses Costa of attacking the independence of the judiciary after it failed to convict João Franco. Having pointed out these limits on the Justice Minister's power, 'Doria' incongruously goes on to accuse him of greater autocracy than the Tsar. Twenty-seven of the thirty priests arrested by an anarchist-led mob in Porto had to be released. He misjudged how strongly people in the North were prepared to defend their priests from persecution.

The flagellation of Costa continued unabated with a venture into futurology. He is delivering the country to the old enemy, as Couceiro's forces gather on the border with Spanish approval. There will be a repeat of 1873: a Spanish Republic that lasted only two years. The prediction was inaccurate; the Portuguese lasted sixteen. But his conclusion was remarkably prescient: 'It is more probable, however, that Lisbon will see several republican administrations, each worse than its predecessor, until finally the country falls under the iron rule of a military dictator. I do not think there will be more than one dictator.'[56] This 1911 text can be read as a sniping piece of Jesuitical defence, but this vision of Salazar resonates of Nostrodamus.

6 The new constitutionalism: A *Carbonária* Republic

The Separation Laws in place, McCullagh turned to the pending constitution. McCullagh's criticisms were not limited to obscure Catholic journals, nor even to the mainstream British periodical press, where most of his lengthier writing had appeared. In May, he published a detailed critique of the proposed Republican constitution in one of the world's most influential newspapers, the *New York Times*. It was one of several newspapers that McCullagh worked for as a special correspondent. In 1909 his reporting of the Turkish Revolution and expulsion of Abdul Hamid launched him into the club of what the Portuguese increasingly referred to as 'graphic reporters.'[57]

The architect of the constitutional proposals was Teófilo Braga. At 71, McCullagh implied he was past it and entering the gentle decadence of old age. No wonder the proposals were so bad. McCullagh hardly knew where to start. A single chamber would prevent any revising power, inviting oligarchical rule and even absolute power. Excessive decentralisation would obstruct implementation of central legislation. It was a concoction of the worst aspects of the French, Swiss and Greek systems. There were no clear proposals for a foreign ministry, nor for a diplomatic body in a Constitution designed to govern the state with the fourth largest empire in the world. Portugal would be reduced 'to the category of those minute States San Marino or Andorra.'[58] McCullagh accused the Republicans of poor planning. They had made a revolution without a blueprint because they were short-term fixers who could not see beyond the forthcoming elections on 28 May. Significantly, McCullagh's criticisms were directed at Republican incompetence, not at Portuguese incapacity for constitutionalism. He does not align himself with those Portuguese who warned against importing unsuitable 'English' ideas.[59] Journalistic vanity left McCullagh puzzled as to how many Republicans, who had been distinguished writers in their previous lives, could become 'ungrammatical, impolite, tactless and curiously unfit.'[60] As politicians they were making schoolboy errors in drafting legislation. The wrong religious buildings were being confiscated; absurd debates were had as to whether priests habits were long enough to be arrested for; then, journalists were arrested for criticising absurdity. Republicans were shooting themselves in the feet through incompetence. They were alienating even non-Catholic opinion that might be expected to sympathize with anti-clericalism.

Typical of their incompetence, for McCullagh, was the mess the new government got itself into over the appointment of its diplomatic representative in London. Sebastião de Magalhães Lima was the desired choice. McCullagh describes him as 'a peripatetic revolutionary' who behaved pompously on arrival. Grey refused him and he returned home with his tail between his legs. Magalhães Lima had been a convinced Republican since his student days as a member of the 'Generation of 1870.' In 1881, he helped found the Republican newspaper, *O Seculo*. He took a prominent role in criticising British policy over the 1890 Ultimatum and also its support for the constitutional monarchy. During the Franco dictatorship, he opted for exile rather than be arrested. Even on 5 October 1910 he was still in Paris. He was the epitome of Republican Freemasonry, elected as the tenth Grand Master of the Grand Orient Lusitano Kingdom in 1907.[61] He was also, as head of *Sociedade Propaganda de Portugal*, one of the pioneers of modern public relations.[62]

He was replaced by the more acceptable Manuel Teixeira Gomes, but even he was not treated with customary diplomatic respect. McCullagh observed that *The Times* was deliberately scornful of his diplomatic status.[63] So, Teixeira Gomes wrote to the Editor complaining about its disdain and in defence of the Separation Laws. He signed it, M. Teixeira Gomes, Portuguese Minister, 12 Gloucester-place, Portman-square, W.[64] This was the official residence of what the Republican government was now proud to call the Envoy Extraordinary and Plenipotentiary to the Court of St James's.

Between the summers of 1911 and 1912 McCullagh spent time embedded with the Royalist forces on the Spanish side of the Portuguese border. He spoke some Portuguese in addition to seven other languages.[65] His analysis of Royalist failures compares unfavourably with the judgement of modern historiography. This puts defeat down to a combination of the Army remaining pro-Republican, lack of arms, poor leadership and peasant indifference to the cause.[66]

McCullagh had a simpler explanation. As the 1912 rising had considerable peasant support led by the priests, it was foiled only by the *Carbonária*, and last-minute Government arrests in Catholic strongholds like Braga. He reports the Army as widely disaffected in a number of barracks and the peasantry as only awaiting a successful lead from them.[67] Couceiro planned to seize control of the North's communications and then to impose a blackout on Lisbon. But the *Carbonária* sabotaged this strategy. Intercepting messages between plotters, it kept the railways, telegraph wires and bridges intact, much as it had done during the revolt of the year before. In 1912, they also assumed a policing role, with state approved powers of arrest. The *Carbonária* had been transformed into a pluralist, sub-state, agency, acting as soldiers, police and spies. In the Army they rooted out subversives, causing tension with officers and rank and file. In the villages, Royalists were shown no mercy and peasant myth had it that they carried enough dynamite on their persons to destroy the entire community at a stroke.

McCullagh's critique of the *Carbonária*'s role in the risings of 1911–12 is contradictory and ambivalent. He criticizes their extra-legal behaviour but never the illegality of the coup attempts, themselves. On the other hand, he admires the Government's use of modern technology, such as wireless telegraphy or requisitioning of motor cars, to consolidate state power.

7 Press Freedom

> The present treatment of the Royalist and Independent press of Portugal is a curious commentary on some of the frenzied oratory we heard on the establishment of the Republic about freedom rising in her virgin essence.[68]

As political prisoners were about to be amnestied in early 1914, McCullagh published a timely warning about continuing press repression. Three years earlier he had published a shorter piece which had probably fallen upon the relatively stony ground of Boston Catholics in the USA.[69] In the later piece,[70] McCullagh piloted an abysmal comparative analysis of press repression. He compared the threat presented by Portuguese Republicans with that of Indian Nationalists. He compounded this misjudgement by arguing the press was freer in Russia than Portugal, and political prisoners treated less harshly.[71] Possibly he was giddy with the success of the amnesty in spring 1914. He triumphally cited the release of the Editor of *O Dia*, Moreira de Almeida who 'would have had no prospect of being released or even of being tried were it not for the action of the British Protest Committee in forcing the Lisbon Government to grant an amnesty.'[72] McCullagh had been put in touch with E. M. Tenison, in early 1913, by Edgar Prestage, his fellow Catholic and scholar, who lived in Lisbon. Mabel Tenison's brother, Julian, had also been impressed by McCullagh's reporting of the Russo-Japanese War.

Almeida's release, however, probably had as much to do with journalists on the spot, like the Frenchman, Paul Vergnet. He told McCullagh and anyone who would listen about the insidious tactics of press repression. Editors like Almeida were messed about. They would be denied permission to publish until very late, forcing them to print; then they were refused permission to sell, so that the whole day's production was wasted.[73] McCullagh explained Republican harassment as the simple need to suppress the truth about Republicans' broken promises. He compared the situation unfavourably with the Monarchy, when Republican 'papers were allowed to publish:

> For years their great papers in Lisbon poured forth an almost uninterrupted stream of lies and filth ... [that] ... not only injured the prestige of the Portuguese monarchy abroad, but did infinite mischief

at home by debauching the minds of the half-educated workmen, soldiers and sailors.[74]

Even foreign journalists were now being threatened, and Aubrey Bell had actually been imprisoned for a short time. McCullagh knew Bell very well, having shared digs with him, and had the greatest respect for his impartiality. Bell lived under constant threat of expulsion because he refused the British Legation's advice to self-censor. For McCullagh, the irony of Bell's predicament was that he had never assisted Monarchists, as he was convinced they could never return to power. On the contrary, he had bent over backwards to praise Costa, to facilitate the release of political prisoners. His reward was to be imprisoned, himself. McCullagh reminded that press repression extended to the perimeters of empire in the Far East. During 1913 he had contributed to *The North China Daily News*. Local Republicans of Portuguese extraction had tried to organise a boycott of it in response to his pieces about the Republic.[75] McCullagh had a weakness for what Horgan has fittingly termed 'enragement journalism'. In its vulgarization of history it was capable of constructing the crudest of analogies, and there is no worse example than the one drawn below:

> The conduct of the Republicans towards the Royalist Press would befit a gladiatorial bully of decadent Rome who, having treacherously blinded a better and more skilful opponent, should make a great display, flourishing his sword against the unhappy man in the amphitheatre before giving him the finishing blow.[76]

The critical reader of Portuguese news was entitled to despair at what the blarney had come to.

8 The penance of indulgence: History as nightmare

McCullagh's journalism became a crusade against Portuguese Republicanism's perceived vendetta against Catholicism. In the service of the cause he recruited history as propaganda. He was not alone in calling out Republicans as Jacobins preying upon an illiterate peasantry. Also like many contemporaries, he claimed similarities between the *Carbonária* and the role of secret societies in the Young Turk Revolution of 1908–9. In both cases, 1908 and 1910, he detected internecine divisions creating ideal conditions for secret conspiracies to practice persecution.

At the beginning of 1914 McCullagh published what became his most influential and much cited piece on the 'nightmare republic.' It was a long retrospective on its nature and causes.[77] In the short-term, he argued that Republicanism had been allowed to destroy traditional Portugal through Royalist inertia. But he also returned to Homem Cristo to propound ideas about the decline of the Portuguese character being caused by long-term racial miscegenation. By 1914, the earlier pseudo-social science had festered into an inflamed racism.

McCullagh's Revolution of 1910 is an accident of negatives. The Republicans had more cunning; the Royalists more cowardice. Consequently, power fell into the laps of the corrupt middle classes – predominantly mendacious lawyers without ideals; kleptocrats, who proceeded to empty governmental coffers into their own pockets. McCullagh's Revolution is a farce that begins with a lunatic sex scandal in a Jesuitical asylum. Dr Bombarda is murdered because he was having an affair with his patient's lover. The Republican press is accused of a three-year cover-up in order to accuse the Jesuits, themselves, of the murder. This was just one example of the Government's propaganda machine running out of control. Other distortions included bomb-throwing nuns and marksmen monks shooting from their tunnels beneath Campolide College. With typical cultural condescension, McCullagh accuses Afonso Costa of governing like a Central American republic.

McCullagh launched an avalanche of invective upon the 'nightmare republic' of his imagination. The new Museum of the Revolution honoured the murderers of King Carlos. In the streets, schoolchildren proudly displayed badges proclaiming 'No God. No Religion'. If they progressed to the new University of Lisbon, the curriculum enforced secular republicanism. Congregations showed indifference to the imprisonment of their priests. Nursing nuns were dismissed because *Carbonária* spies caught them praying whilst on duty. Diplomats lost their jobs because they were not Republicans. Soldiers applauded their generals' incarcerations. Anti-republican naval officers were murdered as jeering crowds looked on.

Returning to the Church, McCullagh accused Costa of ransacking it and justifying the confiscation of monastic property with lies about financial corruption. Costa had produced no evidence. The state's severing of the link with Rome had restricted bishops' choice of priests, causing the appointment of countless incompetents. Worse, several hundred priests known to be living with women, had broken away to set up schismatic churches.

By 1914, McCullagh thought the Government's problem was that it had no programme beyond separation. Its only policy was staying in power. This was the root cause of locking up political prisoners that led to the slandering of British protestors like Conan Doyle and the Duchess of Bedford. To cling to power, Government gerrymandered the electoral register and inflicted press censorship. Complaining judges were packed off to Goa, while the prime minister's brother corruptly profited from selling state lands in São Tomé. As the working classes experienced falling living standards, education deteriorated. In contrast, the parasitic state bureaucracy expanded, and the *Carbonária* became a paramilitary law unto themselves.

All this had been allowed to happen, McCullagh regretted, because of the weaknesses of the Royalist class. The worst of them made their peace with Republicanism and dipped their snouts into the trough. Others fled into a comfortable exile in Spain. There, they were financed for arms by the exiled King in Britain, nobles in Portugal, and Brazilian sympathizers. But, by 1914, McCullagh realized the hopes of 1911–12 had gone. He accused the Royalist bosses of no longer wanting the inconvenience of organising an invasion. They pocketed the cash and, worse, informed Republican spies how to intercept the arms shipments. Serious conspirators like Couceiro were left with the hopeless task of employing young peasants to do the work of men in arms. And all for what? The King was so incompetent he would not know how to stay in power if restored. The real threat to the government existed on the Left. Here, he foresaw the ultimate nightmare scenario: a left-wing revolution that would provoke Spanish military intervention and an end to Portuguese independence.

The core of the Portuguese problem, for McCullagh, was the lack of a shared perception of the national interest. In the vocabulary of modern historiography, he felt the Royalist class, the natural leaders, had failed to impose a top-down nationalism. That failure could be traced back to the economic origins of national decline with the loss of the gold-bearing colonies. Subsequently, resources were drained in a fruitless search for imperial substitution. This struggle to sustain empire had bred the historical vice of the Portuguese, racial miscegenation, 'the adulteration of the race by East Indian, Brazilian, and especially by negro blood.'[78]

It was a theory shared by many contemporary thinkers about national decline. McCullagh rooted it in slavery spreading Africans across the empire. Even in the Algarve, they merged with the local population as a result of the annual African slave market. This was typical of a kind of racial negligence:

> unlike the English or the Americans, the Portuguese never seem to have had what I may call a colour sense. Ceylon and India swarm

with the descendants of the old Portuguese, who are darker in hue as well as lower in the social scale than any of the natives. The same phenomenon is to be noticed in Macâu and again in all the other colonies of Portugal. Even on the mother country the effect was bad. Explorers, soldiers, sailors, planters, and colonists of all kinds seem to have had a mania for bringing home with them children of every colour of the rainbow. Even today in Portugal one sees, in the families of returned colonials, the most curious mixtures of black, white, grey, and yellow – all on a footing of perfect equality.

Neither did McCullagh excuse the Church. The Inquisition adulterated the national blood by forcibly Christianising Moors, Jews, and other Asiatics. The result was moral and religious decline because 'Portuguese blood – itself as good as any in Europe – never mixes well with any Asiatic or African blood.' Such statements make John Horgan's judgment that 'McCullagh . . . was not immune from attitudes that can only be described as racist'[79] something of an understatement. But the passages cited constitute only the tip of an iceberg, as he linked imperialism and racial miscegenation to the crisis of 1914:

The contamination of the lower orders by Negro blood took place centuries ago, but the contamination of the upper classes still goes on. During the past century there has been a steady stream homewards of Brazilian capitalists with woolly hair and a suspiciously dark complexion but also with plenty of money. These returned exiles had never any difficulty in buying titles of nobility from an impoverished Government, and in allying themselves by marriage with the old aristocracy. The ruin of that old aristocracy was completed by the abolition of the principle of primogeniture about the middle of the last century as a result of the premature and unfortunate Constitution, for the introduction of which England is solely to blame.[80]

For McCullagh, a negligent Portuguese imperialism, permitting racial miscegenation, had come home to roost in the metropole. Postcolonial migration from Brazil had further diluted the purity of Portuguese class society. Capitalism had become adulterated by colonial money and, without strong legal protection, property rights diluted. McCullagh blames the abolition of primogeniture in 1864 (and British neo-colonialism, indirectly) for this. But for him, bad blood was the base contaminant of the Portuguese character, with all its social implications of moral decline. Its civic offspring was an hysterical politics, orchestrated surreptitiously by secret societies. By then, it was too late for Portugal to benefit from what McCullagh describes as Palmerston's 'Peninsular Liberalism.'[81] Portugal's volatile racial mix repelled the civilising influence of British constitutionalism. The result was the overthrow of its immanent stabilising forces: altar and throne.

McCullagh spent most of the First World War in military intelligence. He was sent back from Russia in 1919 having failed to convince the Bolsheviks that he was only a journalist. Allowed to return later, he interviewed Trotsky, but before that, the head of the Ekatarinburg firing squad that executed the Romanov family. During the Spanish Civil War, his Francoist sympathies saw him line up with the Irish Volunteers, supporting the Nationalists. After its conclusion, he went to work and live in New York, where he remained for the rest of his life. In April 1953, he was found wandering, confused, in the financial district. Diagnosed with dementia, he died in the state mental hospital at Bellevue in November 1956, aged 82. By then, the impassioned journalist whose old fashioned, *enragé* reporting had offended states all over the globe had entirely lost touch with the world.[82] If by that time he could remember he was a Catholic, his faith may have left him with an untroubled conscience as he prepared to meet his maker. Between 1910 and 1914 he never forgot his Catholicism, and he leaves us a First Portuguese Republic deeply in need of redemption.

CHAPTER

5

The Disgruntled Royalist

1 The invisible Goan

António Vicente Valente de Bragança-Cunha seems to have come to England from Goa, around the beginning of 1911. Almost from the moment of his arrival in London, Vicente deluged the Republic in a torrent of criticism. An historian, who published a grand narrative of the Portuguese Monarchy shortly after its demise,[1] he made a living for a while as a Lecturer in Portuguese Literature at University College, London.[2] In the spring of 1913 he was living at 24, Little Russell Street, just around the corner from the British Museum and Library.[3] A prolific critic, he furnished learned periodicals, like *The New Age* in particular, with regular commentary on Portuguese affairs. In print, he shied away from no opponent; on the Left or Right; British or Portuguese. His analysis of the Monarchy's fall had much in common with McCullagh's racial explanation. As Catholics, both came from colonized backgrounds. But, Bragança-Cunha's Catholicism signified incorporation; McCullagh's remained a creed of contrariety.

Bragança-Cunha arrived from the Portuguese empire a fully-fledged Lusophone, but critical Royalist. He had absorbed a good deal of German and Dutch anthropology, which sharpened his polemical appetite to the detriment of his historical judgement. Both his historical narratives are driven by grievance, dispossession, and lost entitlement. Yet, as a colonial Portuguese publishing in English, he remains a unique voice through this period. As a journalist, he was capacious. His output on Portugal exceeded even that of McCullagh, and, unlike the Irishman, he had no obligation to write about anything else.

The Goan Bragnaças[4] had been called Desai when the Portuguese first arrived in Salcette, South Goa. The Jesuit mission of St Francis Xavier forcibly converted them from Hinduism in the 1540s. They earned the royal name after three centuries of co-operation with the Portuguese. Francis Xavier Bragança was knighted in 1842. The original sixteenth-century house at Chandor became the expression of *India Portuguesa* – 'the corner of Europe'[5] – a colonial palace in cream with the largest private library in Goa. In 1910, the head of the family was Luís de Menezes Bragança. Against family tradition, he was a critic of Portuguese colonialism, and a pioneer of modern Goan journalism. He helped make *O Heraldo* (founded 1900) a voice of social reform that trained up the next generation of progressive Goan journalists.[6]

Luís was married to Vicente's sister, Ana, and was cousin to both. Born in 1878, Luís was older than Vicente. His younger brother Tristão was born in 1891. Vicente was in his twenties when he arrived in London. The only likeness we have of him is from a 1911 drawing in *The New Age*. He rejected Luís's politics and, as a journalist, followed more in his father's footsteps.

Vicente inherited his wealthy status through the maternal line. His maternal grandfather was Francis Xavier Bragança, family patriarch and owner of the Chandor estate. Privilege had not made Francis Xavier a conservative. A liberal, he had shed his seminary education to marry out of caste,[7] contrary to the endogamous tradition of Chardos, as converts to Catholicism from the Kshatriya caste were known. Caste society in Goa did not fit the inflexible patterns found elsewhere. Brahmins were not always dominant and greater social mobility was possible.[8] As Chardos, the Braganças regarded themselves as the equals of Brahmins. At the same time, as Chardos, they evidence the way in which religion bisected caste in Goa. Chardos, gravitated towards the Portuguese administration winning preferment for loyalty.

Vicente was very much his father's son.[9] He was the eldest of four, of Dr Ligorio da Cunha and Filomena de Bragança Cunha. With Vicente's uncle, Ligorio set up *O Nacionalista* in 1904 as a progressive conservative newspaper supportive of modern monarchy. Both Ligorio and his brother Isidoro were members of the Nationalist Party of Portugal, in Goa.[10] Goan journalism emerged out of a divided civic culture. Portuguese colonialism splintered identity, dividing families like the Braganças. Vicente, his father and uncle represented the loyalist wing; Vicente's cousin, Luís de Meneses Bragança, the liberal, republican wing. Vicente's younger brother, Tristão, leaned towards Marxism in opposing colonialism and was the real 'father of Goan nationalism' for Socialists.

But Luís set the standard for nationalist journalism. He was born into a Goa in which even the privileged like himself were denied education beyond the seminary or lyceum. Luís required neither because of the family's private library. Vicente and Tristão were of the first generation educated abroad; at University College, London and the Sorbonne, respectively. Although Goa had three token MPs in the *Cortes* from as early as 1822, their function was to collaborate with Portuguese interests against intrusions from British India.[11] The new constitution of 1911, as extended to Goa, created civic equality and secularism for the first time. For example, Hindus as well as Catholics, became entitled to basic education.

In *O Debate* Luís firmly supported the new Republic's values.[12] But he did not argue for an independent Goa because he saw a Republican, greater Portugal as a defence against the claims of British India. The Bragança family shaped Goan public discourse but it wrote for a small, Portuguese speaking, elite constituting only about three per cent of all Goans.[13] Political parties emulated the metropole. The *Centro Democrático* was the Goan arm of the Portuguese Republican Party. It welcomed greater autonomy granted by the 1911 Constitution, but Luís de Meneses Bragança was naive in believing it 'organized the Portuguese Nation into a United States, placing the continent and the colonies on a footing of political equality.'[14] Africans in the Empire, for example, were denied equality as too 'non-civilised' to qualify for *assimilado* (assimulated) status.[15]

However, the Revolution did lead to an explosion of publications in local languages. Hindus, in particular, entered civic life properly for the first time as the initial generation of non-Catholic recipients of public schooling became professionalized.[16] But, secularization caused Goan Christians to emigrate in increasing numbers.[17] Much else disappointed, especially franchise reform only for those taxpayers literate in Portuguese, alongside interference with historic forms of landholding rights.

As Vicente de Bragança-Cunha fled Republican Goa for England, provincial congresses were springing up in optimism, voices of a new civic conscience.[18] But their professionalized Portuguese speakers were dismissed by Tristão de Bragança Cunha as 'denationalized', or a simulacrum of Portuguese identity. They constructed a narrative that built an imaginary bridge from Goa to Coimbra's 'Generation of 1870'. The Republic had not produced a Goan national identity, just a subaltern Lusitanian Republicanism in the periphery; one still defined by the dominant ideology of colonialism. Immaculately dressed in a western suit, communicating in Portuguese, Luís De Menezes Bragança pioneered this imagined community: the 'Lusitanisation' of Goan society.[19] But Luís has also been seen not as collaborator but as radical agent, a passive resister of the Portuguese project in 'lusophony'[20] in its failure to maintain a cultural dialogue of mutual respect.[21]

Vicente's brother Tristão rejected lusitanization as mystification. Once, *assimilado* status had bound families like his through privilege, as part of 'a unique syncretic culture.'[22] Now, that power of acculturation through the 'othering' of *indígenas* (indigenous Goans) had waned. Vicente was an invisible Goan who passed himself off as Portuguese; Luís was a Lusitanian, Republican Goan; Tristão, an irredentist, favouring unity with India. In *The Denationalisation of Goans* (1944), Tristão deconstructed the Portuguese colonial narrative of civilising conferment. Like Charles Boxer, later,[23] Tristão insisted on its racism. Like Luís, he blamed the Church as mediating agent of the imperial state. It had imposed a 'crisis of self-representation' – 'mental slavery, political subjection, unnatural manners, cultural stagnation and decay, lack of character and personality, physical degeneration and economic ruin.'[24]

Tristão argued that those who responded by emigrating were victims of a 'double colonialism', hybridizsed once by Portuguese colonialism, twice by emigrating from it.[25] He might have been thinking of his own brother who had done precisely that. Subaltern studies' historians contend that Portuguese colonialism 'occidentalized' Goa. It treated religion as more important than race in social classification, facilitating the Lusitanization of families like the Braganças.[26] For them, language was the other great signifier of Lusitanization and it set up a conflict with those Konkani speakers who contested the Portuguese discourse of 'Lusophony.'[27] However, Lusitanization itself came under pressure as Portugal took on the ambivalent identity of 'colonised coloniser.' Goa developed a transimperial dependency upon British India. In 1878 the British obtained privileged access to the Goan market; Portugal suffered and raised taxes; and, Goans left. From India, Congress' nationalism soon intersected Goan with an alternative national identity.

Since Goa's liberation in 1961, its history has become fully incorporated within South Asian subaltern studies. Some historians have compared Tristão de Bragança-Cunha's contribution in combining the history of identity with resistance to that of Franz Fanon or Amílcar Cabral. By comparison, earlier Lusitanized liberals like Luís de Meneses Bragança have struggled to maintain their place in the historical canon, and have even been dismissed as 'submissive servants.'[28]

Vicente de Bragança-Cunha brought Lusitanization to London. The smart money was on him being as immaculately dressed as cousin Luís. But, as a Monarchist not a Republican, he was even more Lusitanized than Luís. A key, sub-textual signifier of his denationalized status is that his writing sublimates his Goan identity. The Goan stands invisibly behind a Portuguese. This extreme Lusitanization contrasts with Luís and Tristão. In Vicente, any trace of Goan national consciousness is absent. He disguises by omission.

Vicente arrived from Goa into another contested space – a metropole that acted as a 'junction box of anti-imperialism.'[29] Indian nationalists even plotted assassination,[30] but that was exceptional. Most slotted seamlessly into public life with sartorial elegance. Liberal imperialism prided itself on its pluralism in accommodating diverse points of view. London's cultural magnetism saw Indian nationalists come to live cheek by jowl with at least one Lusitanized Goan.

The brother and cousin he left behind continued to disagree. Luís celebrated Republican colonialism's wider embrace of citizenship. Tristão was unconvinced. His imagined India of the future contained neither Portugal nor Britain. Along with the departed Vicente, the conflicted discourses of the Braganças illustrate the 'crisis of self-representation'[31] of early twentieth-century Goans. Nationalist historians, since, have privileged the stories of Luís and Tristão. By contrast, Vicente became an almost forgotten figure. Yet, his denationalized identity was no less typical. Historians of the Portuguese diaspora have emphasized the complexity and ambivalence of hybrid identities resulting from colonial experience.[32] The Goan Braganças epitomize that complex ambivalence. Colonialism fractured their family identity, and one splintered progeny was Vicente de Bragança-Cunha. As enraged as Francis McCullagh by the overthrow of the Monarchy, he raised his pen in anger in the capital of an alien empire.

2 The Historian

Just before he took to journalism critical of the First Republic in 1911, Bragança-Cunha established himself as an historian with *Eight Centuries of Portuguese Monarchy*. The title disguises an uneven narrative in which the first seven centuries are accelerated through in about the first one hundred pages. This occurs because the author's principal interest is the decline and fall of the constitutional monarchy through the nineteenth century. So pessimistic is the tone that one reviewer commented, 'Every page . . . breathes a spirit of hopelessness so deep as to make even the present as of little account beside the fatal and unalterable deeds of the past.'[33] The same reviewer conceded, however, that the author managed to hoist the Republic on its own millenarian petard. There was too much freedom, too many strikes that led to too much repression. There was also too much divorce, and too much free love. *Eight Centuries* remains worth reading largely for its contemporary commentary on the crisis of 1910–14. As a general introduction to Portuguese history it is a thinly-veiled requiem for the Monarchy.

It was a quarter of a century before the historian, Bragança-Cunha, returned to the First Republic. After completing his studies at London University and teaching Portuguese literature for a while, he travelled to Bombay in 1915, and organized a series of conferences on Portuguese literature. *Revolutionary Portugal* was published in 1937 (six years before he died), from London whilst he was in Paris. It is unclear how long he had been in France. From his home region of Salcette in South Goa, he had edited the journal *India Portuguesa* (Portuguese India) from 1919 to 1922. It was wound up in 1937, ending a continuous publication since 1861. He published another book, *Indo-Portuguese Literature*, in 1926. It is uncertain, but likely, that he was working as a journalist in Goa beyond its publication in 1926.

Eight Centuries reveres the first two-thirds of the sixteenth century as the high point of Portuguese nationalism whose greatest hero was Camões. It peddles the traditional narrative that Portuguese history went downhill from Sebastian's defeat at Al-Kebir in Morocco in 1578. The Portuguese failed to build the empire after the example of Albuquerque into a compassionate Christianity recognizing no impediment to racial inter-marriage. The sixty years under Spanish occupation (1580–1640) is imagined as a punishment for a vain Portuguese people mistaking themselves for a chosen people,[34] he opined twenty-six years later.

Braganca-Cunha convinced himself that imperial decline revealed an historical fault line in the Portuguese race. He constructed a theory of decay from personal correspondence with the Dutch anthropologist, H. M. Bernelot Moens. Moens was a Social Darwinist, and close to Ernst Haeckel, the German zoologist responsible for 'Monism' – a philosophy that distorted Darwin's teachings to 'open up a new path to moral perfection.'[35] Haeckel placed the 'indogermanic central peoples' at the top of a racial hierarchy. He advocated selective breeding including the killing of the sick; ideas that influenced Nazism.

Moens reduced Mankind to five types: uncivilized, civilized, humanized, cultured and perfect.[36] He did not believe it was racial mixing that was problematic; it was more the Portuguese had not mixed with 'quality'. Moens had perfected this typology after an interesting life. He failed at school due to hearing and other impediments, and was sent away to a Forestry Academy near Berlin, in his early twenties. There, he was educated by Social Darwinists of the Haeckel school, alongside the sons of Prussian, Baltic and Russian aristocrats.

Returning to the Netherlands as a schoolteacher, he advocated a test for Darwin's evolutionism by artificially inseminating female apes with the sperm of 'negroes' to see if they became pregnant. Supported by Haeckel, he started fund-raising publications that were shunned in Holland. He modified his ideas during the First World War, but clung to the ideal of perfect human procreation through mixing the best specimens from each race.

In the course of anthropological research amongst the black American population in 1917, he photographed some young females. In the heightened security climate as the USA entered the War, he was arrested. Suspected of espionage, of which there was no evidence, he was found guilty of possessing pornographic pictures. Sentenced to gaol, he was released on bail, and detained in the USA until 1923, when the case was dropped. He returned to live in France from where he warned of an international racial war. But he did not advocate this, and to his death in 1938 championed tolerance, peace and inter-racial harmony against nationalism and racism. He has been accused of being a catastrophist, possessed of a polarized and apocalyptic view of civilisation; and of misunderstanding Darwinism and the nature versus nurture debate.[37] Moens led Bragança-Cunha to some dangerously false conclusions about the Portuguese, such as explaining the inadequacies of Republicans through their having 'features . . . of Negroid origin.'[38]

Such racist views on miscegenation shared ideological space with mythologies about the 'pure origins' of the Portuguese race. These underpinned Lusitanian nationalism's refusal of any blood mixing, whatsoever. Against this was an established liberalism that welcomed miscegenation as an historical strength. But even some Republicans flirted with a Social Darwinism whose influence spread way beyond the European Right.[39] Within nationalism there was a strand that tolerated miscegenation, but which focused on not allowing it to dilute Portuguese essence.[40] Bragança-Cunha had long been interested in searching for perfect historical human beings. Against these he posed anti-heroes, like João V (1707–50) who undermined national character by abdicating governance to a superstitious Church. Pombal was another: a statesman who 'sinned outrageously against the Portuguese virtue of liberty,' whose reputation 'rests on racks, gibbets and dungeons.'[41] This construct erases the great centralizer, or the rebuilder of Lisbon after the earthquake, leaving just a dictator without civic contribution.

Bragança-Cunha also constructed watersheds, like the Peninsular War that turned Portugal into a distressed nation dependent upon the Old Alliance. But in his priority of causation Portugal's own weakness is responsible not British neo-colonialism, hidden away as 'the English' pursuing their national interest. The liberal interventionism of Canning in the 1820s is cited admiringly:

> Let us fly to the aid of Portugal, by whomsoever attacked, because it is our duty to do so, and let us cease that interference where that duty ends. We go to Portugal not to rule, not to dictate, not to prescribe constitutions, but to preserve the independence of our ally.[42]

But the historian is short of context, here. Canning had made that speech in December, 1826, to smooth over intervention in Portugal's constitutional crisis. Five thousand troops were sent to Lisbon to defend Pedro's constitution against the Spanish backed invasion of his brother, Miguel. But Britain was anxious to avoid charges of hypocrisy at a time of intervention against liberal regimes by the absolutist Holy Alliance. Canning was effectively 'spinning' a liberal intervention whilst preferring to use the concert of Europe to defend British commercial interests.[43] Bragança-Cunha's selected passage also omits other crucial sentiments. Canning had added, 'We go to plant the standard of England on the well known heights of Lisbon. Where that standard is planted, foreign dominion shall not come.'[44] For Canning, British predominance in Lisbon was an essential element for a favourable European balance of power. A pragmatist, he committed neither to isolationism, nor intervention.[45]

Bragança-Cunha was a consistent defender of liberal constitutionalism. Miguel's Constitutional Charter of 1826, he dismissed as perfidy – a fraudulent national vote to obtain absolutism tantamount to political pimping. Miguelists had gone out to register even harlots to vote,[46] making the Constitution 'a blank parchment' without moral foundation.[47] The Miguelists were expelled by the early 1830s, continuing to plot abroad assisted by the Spanish King, Ferdinand VII. By the time *Eight Centuries* was finished, shortly after 5 October 1910 for publication the following year, another Spanish King was supporting new Miguelist usurpers from across the frontier. This time their joint enterprise was against Republicanism.

The triumph of Portuguese Liberalism after the 1830s was illusory, in Bragança-Cunha's history. The Civil War taught repression and bred a competitive factionalism that led to Rotativism. The best of the parties – Fontes Pereira de Mello's Regenerators – tried but failed to arrest a declining economy and empire. In this Portugal, constitutional monarchs are failed by factious politicians who prevent them from realising the best of all political worlds.

He was also an unapologetic imperialist, and disingenuous over the abolition of slavery (1875) which he accepts at face value. Making a virtue out of necessity, he argues it forced Portugal into a moral justification of empire. Yet the only 'morality' he cites behind Portuguese occupation of its African territories is that of prior occupation. He glosses over the neo-colonialism of the1890 Ultimatum, pragmatically clinging to the Old Alliance. The British Navy had Delagoa Bay, the Cape Verde Islands, and even the Tagus estuary, itself, in its sights. It is difficult to find a clearer acceptance of Portugal's subaltern status in the historical literature than this. The compliant Portuguese Goan even tries to deflect responsibility from Salisbury by selecting a soft target: 'the influence of the Scottish Universities' Mission.' Salisbury is let off the hook because he was only trying to juggle diplomacy between investment and religious interests.[48]

In Bragança-Cunha's unlikely Africa we have Salisbury, an Anglican Conservative, falling under the sway of freethinking Scottish Presbyterian missionaries. Scottish ministries were active in Southern Africa from 1821, extending into West Africa from the 1840s. Bragança-Cunha's allusions target the free church Livingstonia, established on the southern shores of Lake Malawi from 1875. It was backed, from 1878, by the Glasgow-based Central African Trading Company, in an alliance of commerce and Christianity. Livingstonia was directed by Dr Robert Laws, an ordained medical doctor, who worked there for fifty-two years, also helping bring trade to the region. Laws established a Church of Central Africa Presbyterian which led the improvements in local education and water supplies. The Church provided an alternative Christian discourse to that of (Portuguese) Catholicism, helping to raise levels of African self-consciousness. It sent forth several leaders of trade unionism in Nyasaland and Northern Rhodesia, and also the father of the first President of Zambia.[49] This was a powerful achievement, but not one that suggests Scottish Presbyterianism controlled British African policy.

For Bragança-Cunha, 1890 is the tipping point for Portuguese constitutionalism. The end of African expansion was symptomatic of the imperial monarchy's inability to deal with national decline. A chronic budget deficit saw dishonest politicians sell off monopoly rights to the highest bidder. Foreign bondholders took fright at abandoning the silver standard and demanded a special European Commission to oversee Portugal's national revenues. Industry and agriculture were in a race to the bottom with technical education. But Bragança-Cunha always looks to the moral failings of politicians before systemic analysis. He was right that neither the Regenerators nor the Progessives were capable of either regenerating or progressing.[50] The question was, why?

Republicanism, he sees, as growing dialectically in the face of dictatorship. Both were terminal symptoms of an unreformable system. Republican propaganda flogged a traitorous monarchy for selling out to 'England' in 1890.[51] In its weakness, it closed off the political system to all but sycophants; in power, but incapable of governing.[52] João Franco had offered an initial glimpse of hope in tackling some of the worst sinecure abuses, but he could be gratuitously offensive in achieving so little. Worse, he practised double standards in dealing with the King's debts by effectively cancelling them. In *Eight Centuries* (1911), Bragança-Cunha still seems bemused by how a well-intentioned dictatorship had got out of hand. By 1937, he rewrote this history through elevating Carlos to lost saviour. A supreme intellect and master of foreign relations 'was condemned to death because he spoke truths unpalatable to Portuguese politicians.'[53] There is no criticism of his asset-stripping the state, just regret at the loss of an honest constitutional reformer, assassinated by a conspiracy of devious politicians.

For Bragança-Cunha, the failure of politics lies in personal agency. *Eight Centuries* ends with a hapless Manuel II, overcome by morally flawed, self-interested politicians undermining public spirit and patriotism. Despite his proclivity for heroic/anti-heroic polarisation, Bragança-Cunha does pay lip service to the economic determinism behind Rotativism's collapse. He acknowledges the destabilising effects of the *Credito Predial* scandal, causing five ministries to topple in two years and five months. In a country habituated to scandal, this one knew no precedent. He predicted that Republicanism would be the victor from this.[54] The scandal authenticated its teleological view of history through which it was destined to come to power. Bragança-Cunha even comes close to accepting it. But, in his frustrations with the present, he again reaches out for a nostalgic past. The constitutional monarchists had not learned the eternal lesson of the national hero, Camões: any king is only as good as the advice his ministers give him. But this was a lazy analogy. The self-serving state of 1572 had ossified into a self-perpetuating one by 1910. Resuscitating Portuguese nationalism whose greatest hero was Camões skated around the real issue. The state of 1910 was thoroughly rotten and the Monarchy was not misled nor ignorant, but complaisant.

Revolutionary Portugal rescripts this disastrous narrative twenty-six years after *Eight Centuries*. The author had moved from relative youth to middle age, from London back to Goa, then to Paris. His second history is a curse upon all houses. It begins with a renewed polemic against the sixteen years of 'chaotic' democratic rule (1910–26), but this is not because it has any time for the decade of military, and then 'fascist', dictatorship that followed. Bragança-Cunha's return to '5 October' from 1937 is a pathetic history. Loyal Royalist troops are let down by poor leadership, snatching defeat from the jaws of victory. Fear, ignorance, rumour, and panic, induce chaos. He has learned no lessons about the limitations of personal agency since 1910–11. Interpreting the Revolution as chaos abandons any serious determinism. It enables him to see the outcome as one of chance, except that the Monarchists had more apathy and less heroism than Republicans. It was a revolution by default.

Michael Derrick aptly described Bragança-Cunha as 'a disgruntled royalist.'[55] The Royalist lay in tormented dialogue with the disgruntled Catholic. As Derrick also noted, a whole chapter of *Revolutionary Portugal* is devoted to the religious question around the Separation Laws of 1911. Like all his history, Bragança-Cunha's religious history is peopled by heroes and villains. Afonso Costa is the Devil incarnate, and the Bishops of Braga and Coimbra, saintly defenders of the Church against its annihilators. However, he is not uncritical of the Church. The clergy was in moral decline, abasing itself to politicians and behaving like the election agents of the *rotativismo* parties.[56]

Afonso Costa is *l'enfant terrible*, the anti-hero persecuting the Congregations who fed thousands of Portuguese for free every day. His Republican press besmirched the moral reputation of nuns and drove them through the streets. Costa had turned Portugal into 'a detached fragment of Africa.'[57] He sacked Bishops, bribed priests with state pensions and generally placed Catholics in an inferior civic position to anarchists. No wonder the Archbishop of Guarda could ask: 'Is everyone to be allowed freedom of speech except the Bishops?'[58]

In the face of injustice arose a Catholic revival, which inched forwards with every crucifix destroyed, every priest deprived, every nun abused. Prodigal sons returned to the persecuted Church out of conscience. Ramalho Ortigão, who had taken his first step backwards from Republicanism over the regicide in 1908, satirized the Republic. *Ultimas Farpas* (Latest Barbs, 1913–15) was his last retort as cancer struck him down. For, Bragança-Cunha he exampled the qualitative failure of Republican democracy. Once, the 'Generation of 1870' had been the champions of the Republican alternative, only for leading figures like Ortigão to abandon it, disillusioned. Unmentioned, is Ortigão's flirtation with nascent fascism towards his end. That, exampled a life of political vacillation.

The Republic's treatment of the working class was next in the catalogue of failure. Bragança-Cunha acknowledged the Revolution had not been made solely in their name, but they had a right to expect improvement. Yet, this came from a critic contemptuous of a working class that had 'wallowed in a surfeit of idleness and drinking in the wake of '5 October.' Give them a statutory six-day week, rent laws, people's banks, and the right to strike, he bemoaned, and they reply with violent strikes that culminate in bombs thrown at Republican Guards tasked with protecting them. The Revolution had brought regress: 'the saturnalia of anarchy and confusion under a regime founded upon irresponsible public opinion.'[59] The ideological bedrock of this view was a fundamental conservative, Catholic belief in the futility of revolutions. They were a consequence of original sin, inherently destructive, designed to turn even good intentions into bad outcomes. Passing power to the irresponsible produced bombings of innocents by the ignorant.

3 The Journalist

Bragança-Cunha arrived in London, ostensibly to study, sometime between the end of 1910 and the beginning of 1911, in circumstances that are unclear. He may have fled the establishment of a Republican colonial government in Goa. From London, he was free to comment. More certain is that before returning to Goa in 1915, he earned some kind of living from lecturing and periodical journalism.

From the beginning, Bragança-Cunha did not give the regime a prayer.[60] In that, he was in tandem with 'S. Verdad', the pseudonym of *The New Age's* foreign affairs commentator, J. M. Kennedy,[61] who also passed himself off as 'a disgruntled royalist.'[62] *The New Age*, founded in 1907 by A. R. Orage, became Bragança-Cunha's periodical of choice. It was 'a political weekly that performed some functions traditionally associated with the literary review.'[63] Shaw, Wells, Belloc and Chesterton were all regular contributors. Although Orage described it as 'an independent socialist review of politics, literature and art,'[64] it also attracted a readership from the radical Right. Villis categorises it as proto-fascist, selling about four and a half thousand copies by August 1913. Orage, himself, moved from early Fabianism towards an elitist Nietzscheanism.[65] He, like other *New Age* contributors, veered between a modernist labour violence and a mythical return to medieval order, to solve class-conflicted, pre-war Britain's problems. Leaning Left, it flirted with Guild Socialism, which attracted people like George Lansbury, G. D. H..Cole and R. H. Tawney. On the other hand, Orage's racism may have attracted contributors like Bragança-Cunha. Orage editorialized that, 'The colour prejudice is real and in our opinion properly so. Miscegenation is one of the worst fates that can befall any nation.'[66]

When Bragança-Cunha first met John McFarland Kennedy they were near neighbours. Kennedy's flat in Hart Street, Bloomsbury, was a stone's throw from Little Russell Street. At twenty five, Kennedy was a prodigy, a Londonderry Catholic on the staff at *The New Age* since 1908. He led a life so reclusive that it was rumoured he was connected to British intelligence.[67] He also worked on the *Daily Telegraph* with illustrious colleagues such as E. J. Dillon and Rebecca West. His meteoric rise was snuffed out by a premature death, aged 32, a couple of weeks before the end of the War. Kennedy's short but brilliant career took him beyond journalism into translation and political theory. His *Tory Democracy* (1911) was an attempt to think a way out of successive electoral defeats in 1906 and 1910. It argued for a return to Burke's 'order and stability' to combat the 'anarchy and disunion' of Mill and Liberalism. He shared Orage's Nietzscheanism and its conviction that the strong must rule over the weak. For Kennedy, Tory aristocracy remained the best defence against the rot rooted in the Reformation and spread by the French Revolution, Liberalism and Socialism. The 'democracy' in Kennedy's thought was little more than sympathy for Guild Socialism. He was not attracted to its egalitarianism, but he did harbour a nostalgia for the feudal organisation of labour as a panacea for freeing the worker from modern state dependency.[68]

Bragança-Cunha's early critique advised the Republic to stop trying 'to alter the foundation of mankind.'[69] Proclaiming the elimination of the national debt was incompatible with ruinous borrowing, he overlooked the approval given by the middle classes for Costa's balancing of the budget at the expense of the poor.[70] Later, he conceded that 'the people were paying to the State more than their due.'[71] Bragança-Cunha denounced counter-productive attacks upon freedom of the press that were only driving moderate Republicans into opposition. Religious fanaticism even erased Lisbon's saintly street names, the Catholic complained. But there was a contradiction in his condemning the Government for this repression and for extending too much liberty.[72]

Ten months after the Revolution Ramsay MacDonald finally asked the Foreign Secretary why the British Government had not yet recognized the Portuguese Republic. Grey replied it awaited the full implementation of the new Constitution.[73] It was eventually recognized two months later (11 September). In between, Bragança-Cunha, who revelled in confronting socialists over the Republic, drove Ramsay MacDonald into silence. He reminded the new

Labour Leader that the Republic was a diseased body politic. Echoing Portuguese conservatives, he also criticized MacDonald's poor grasp of historical development in wishing foreign institutions upon an 'unhappy Portugal.' Liberal and socialist 'do-gooders' had made the same mistake in respect of the Young Turks.[74] *The New Age* was a publication open to socialist contributions but MacDonald never bothered to reply. The Republic's few Socialist sympathisers came from outside of the Labour Party. Bragança-Cunha refrained from gloating for a quarter of a century. Finally, the obligations of history persuaded him to break his silence on the former Prime Minister: 'the sudden retreat of the Labour member gave one the impression that he had introduced a subject with whose conditions and environment he was but imperfectly acquainted.'[75] He may not have intended to hit the man when he was down, but 1937 proved the most unfortunate of moments.[76]

Bragança-Cunha won that battle but not the war as the Republic was steadily recognized across Europe. He predicted civil war, whilst recommending the anti-Republican forces select the battlefield carefully. Politics under the Republican Government had been reduced to faction fighting and mob rule. For Bragança-Cunha, this was rough justice for a regime that venerated regicide. Only in Portugal could there be published an article entitled 'The Bomb in the Service of the Republic' without anybody turning a hair. He cites *The Times* in support of his view that the Republic accepted bombs as a feature of everyday life.[77] But he cannot be trusted with the evidence. The edition cited contained no such phrase, or interpretation. The closest approximation was in a short report on 'The Alleged Regicide Hall' that stated:

> the Government denies that there is a room in the "Revolution Museum" which is designed to glorify regicide. The cloaks and arms of Buiça and Costa – the murderers of King Carlos and the Crown Prince – are only exhibited in the same way as other objects which have an historical character.[78]

The Times was presenting the Government's justification objectively. It did report, in the same article, the continued suppression of the Monarchical newspaper *Correio da Manha*. But this was balanced by acknowledging several recent 'popular manifestations of Republican sentiment.' One was the turnout of a thousand Republican cyclists in Lisbon on Sunday, 8 January that must have warmed the hearts of any *Clarion* readers.[79] But they do not pedal into Bragança-Cunha's journalism. Neither does Manuel Borges Grainha, the

Director of the Museum, a lapsed Jesuit who made a remarkable transition to anti-clerical Republicanism. He had published widely on Jesuitry, Freemasonry and education, from his prior experience as a schoolteacher.[80]

Belfort Bax was perhaps Bragança-Cunha's most vehement critic and he stepped into the socialist space vacated by Ramsay MacDonald six months before. Bax was born into the very type of oppressive, bourgeois family he came to detest. He abandoned music criticism early for the law, combining a career as a barrister with socialist journalism. Although drawn to Marxism through the 1880s, he never committed to economic determinism, ethical socialism holding more attractions. It caused him to leave the Social Democratic Federation in 1884 and join the Socialist League, where he collaborated with William Morris. By 1889 he was back in the SDF after splits in the SL. In *The Religion of Socialism* (1885) Bax attacked Christianity as incompatible with socialism, and the modern family as a sham. The earlier generation of Bax scholars tended to see him as irrational.[81] He saw himself as making a consistent ethical and historical link from the French Revolution to the Commune, Positivism and modern Republicanism.

Bax saluted the bravery of the Republican assassins at the sacrifice of their own lives. But he made the extraordinary claim that they executed 'vengeance on one whom most democrats would regard as having richly deserved their fate.'[82] While he declined 'to shed very many salt tears over the fate of the late lamented King Carlos', it is unlikely many democrats amongst his readership shared this endorsement of assassination. He attacked Bragança-Cunha's hypocrisy for showing no outrage at the Spanish state's execution of the anarchist Francisco Ferrer in 1909. He had been judicially murdered, just like Buiça and Costa. Neither did he have anything to say about 'the cowardly monarchical conspirators,' who intermittently raided across the Spanish border. 'The *Senhor*' would be better 'keeping his hair on'. Bax drew breath to set down a more measured statement of English Marxism's position:

> The present Portuguese Republic does not profess to be a social democratic commonwealth, and hence it is no special concern of we Socialists to defend it; but in any case it represents such a great advance on the corrupt reaction it has superseded that no progressive man can fail to have a respect for it and its leaders, and to feel correspondingly indignant at the paltry attempts to besmirch it and them made in the Royalist interest.[83]

Bragança-Cunha remained calm and cleverly invoked characters from the Republicans' own pantheon of heroes to turn the screw. Brito de Camacho had urged Parliament not to honour murderers who drew upon the people's worst instincts. Almeida had regretted 'negative work, causing revolution and indiscipline everywhere.' Both followed Ortigão who had tried to steer Republicanism away from French tastes for martyrdom.[84] Bax was unimpressed by his opponent's selective use of evidence; even less by his conflation of the Portuguese Parliament and people with 'raving maniacs.'[85]

Perhaps Bragança-Cunha was queuing at the editorial desk with his latest reply to Bax's latest reply, when Orage decided to free-up the letter's column. We cannot know, but that was the end of it. S. Verdad (Kennedy) turned attention to a pressing British interest: the future of the Empire. The Republic's credibility depended upon defending it, he argued, just as the German Colonial Minister visited London. Kennedy favoured a compromise – the shelving of both German designs upon Angola and British ones on East Africa.[86] Kennedy was concerned this imperial crisis was about to fuse with mounting Portuguese opposition into a perfect storm. An unlikely coalition of reconciled Monarchist parties and labour promised a volatile cocktail of unrest over imprisonment without trial, which both decried as unconstitutional.[87]

Bragança-Cunha shared Kennedy's concerns about the regime's treatment of labour problems. He had always viewed the working class as self-interested and susceptible to demagogy, but admitted that its living standards were being attacked by an avaricious government. The labour movement was responding by comparing the present government to the corrupt Monarchy. As strikes mounted, repressive labour laws were passed, making protest more difficult or even illegal. Bragança-Cunha warned of the dangers of a multitude of unused bombs from the Revolution still in circulation. Republicanism's ideal of 'government of the people by the people' had collapsed into naked class struggle.[88]

For Bragança-Cunha, as for McCullagh, the degeneration of the Portuguese Revolution and the Turkish of 1908 were parallel narratives. Both liberal revolutions degenerated into repression. In Portugal, he presented Braga's claim of Positivist inspiration as pretence. It was not intellectual but coercive, dependent on militarising society. The *Carbonária* was 'committing atrocities that would put Morocco to shame.'[89] Even Sir Arthur Hardinge, the British Ambassador, had been arrested for 'conspiring against the institutions of the country.' He had asked a policeman the way to a church.[90]

Bragança-Cunha was making political imprisonment a

campaigning issue before the BPC was formed. He first echoed the spurious claims of the *The Times* that it was a departure from the practices of the Monarchy (which *had* politically imprisoned Republicans under Franco). Guilty prisoners now received extortionate sentences and degrading treatment, but the Republican Government covered this up. A special state organisation, *Propaganda de Portugal*, organized this, masquerading as a tourist agency. Bragança-Cunha claimed it was prompted by journalists' exposures.[91]

He also shared Kennedy's concerns about the Empire. But Bragança-Cunha's fears that it was not safe with the Republic were misplaced as it proved resolutely defensive. Like Kennedy, he detected 'ambitious eyes' turned towards an Empire that had foundered with the decline of aristocracy:

> The Portuguese were once a nation of gentlemen, high bred, courteous and chivalrous. As a colonising nation they were a small minority in the midst of a teeming population which possessed an ancient civilisation. But, nevertheless, they initiated a movement of mankind on the whole towards a higher level of excellence.[92]

Bragança-Cunha's thesis was that imperial decline was caused by class degeneration. The Republic was led by the low bred, venal, urban middle class, supported by its allies, a compliant press and the criminal *Carbonária* . It might have been Francis McCullagh speaking. Bragança-Cunha knew him professionally. In 1912, he turned down McCullagh's invitation to contribute a series of critical articles on Portugal in the journal *Outlook*. Bragança-Cunha told him they would be better coming from an 'Englishman.' McCullagh was possibly unimpressed by Bragança-Cunha's inability to spot an Irishman.

Bragança-Cunha was better on comparative political economy than race or class. He did address the future of the colonies through the more realistic lens of Portugal's economic underdevelopment within the international economy. He argued that national income was too low to sustain import demand from even cheaply-priced colonial exports. Neither was there sufficient export income to create purchasing power. Colonial administration was another Republican farce. Ministers treated their ministries like fiefdoms. He understood the imperial vulnerability opened up in Africa by the Anglo-German agreement of 1898. Only good government could avert the transfer of the Portuguese colonies to Germany. He warned against relying on the Old Alliance, his realism acknowledging Britain's prioritisation of its national interests. But without an ally Portugal lacked the armed forces to defend the colonies.[93] The Government had no constructive plan for colonisation or emigration.[94]

But this was a calm interlude upon Bragança-Cunha's troubled intellectual waters. The Nietzschean in him continually resurfaces. 'Insane Portugal' is a country caught up in acts of 'national madness', one as incoherent as McCullagh's 'nightmare republic', later. The Republic is presented as self-destructive, through raising a people's optimism before beating them into apathy. Republicanism had killed optimism by subverting Portugal's parliamentary system. Costa abused his position in order to ensure his close friend, Bernardino Machado, became President.[95] The Constituent Assembly delayed elections. One member condemned them as a bunch of ignorant agitators incapable of understanding national problems. Another proposed a blackboard in the Chamber for the purpose of explaining finance measures.

He has retreated again into personal agency and moral polarisation. Douglas Wheeler has argued that Republicanism exploited Sebastianism through presenting itself as a political millenarianism for Portugal's twentieth century.[96] Within the Republican narrative of 1912–13, Afonso Costa was the Sebastian to secure the '5 October.' Bragança-Cunha turns the Sebastianized Costa on his head. He is a false saviour without palingenetic power; an anti-Christ.[97] For Bragança-Cunha, Costa is Wheeler's first 'tension' in Portuguese history – *personalismo* (the 'vice of egotism').[98]

Bragança-Cunha had no time for Teófilo Braga's politics, but seconded his criticisms of the diplomatic mess Portugal found itself in. He shared Braga's doubts as to whether Britain could be trusted to preserve Portuguese integrity, because an Anglo-Spanish entente had opened Portugal up to intervention. The Old Alliance lay in ruins: 'Englishmen have grown indifferent to the fate of their ancient ally.'[99] And who could blame them when Sir Arthur Hardinge was practically driven out of Lisbon to Madrid? Portugal's neighbours sensed a threat to European stability when they saw religion being attacked by a vulgar populist exploitation of public opinion.

Even the amnesty for political prisoners was interpreted as an expedient measure to get Costa off the hook of a failed foreign policy.[100] Bragança-Cunha dismissed the Government's insistence that the Bill brought conciliation and closure. Into the Amnesty Bill, was slipped a clause providing for the banishment of 'instigators of anti-Republican movements'.[101] This ensured no amnesty for turncoat Republicans, like the journalist Homem Cristo, who was exiled despite having sat alongside Costa on the First Revolutionary Directorate of 1910.

Just before the amnesty, Bragança-Cunha reflected at length on the Republic's first four years. The historian resurfaced to explain how the *longue durée* had led to national decline, this 'dance of fools and of madmen.'[102] The Republic treated national decay as a superficial problem that could be solved by importing constitutional government it was not fitted for. But Portugal could not be simply regenerated by a new elite that closed its eyes to its own, equally narrow, social base – Lisbon and the armed forces. Nor, by one that lacked a strategy of national reconstruction. Bragança-Cunha's lens looked through a Revolution with no depth and without focus. Increasingly insecure, it repressed and propagandized to disguise a one-party state that was never Republicanism's objective. So, it reconfigured political discourse as the nation under siege as the Republican state turned in upon itself. This was the 'insanity' that Bragança-Cunha loathed, and about which McCullagh had nightmares. Everything they had taken for granted had been snatched away and all they had left was writing as therapeutic resistance.

4 Bragança-Cunha and the British Campaign

Bragança-Cunha occupied a unique position amongst 'The Locusts.' He was an exception in not being a British critic, but also because he asserted such independence. There is no evidence that he ever met any of the members of the BPC, although it must be counted likely as they were agitating in the same city. They contributed to the same publications. Nor does he seem to have been at either of the BPC's Aeolian Hall meetings,[103] otherwise he would surely have spoken. Yet, there is no doubting his support of the campaign to free political prisoners. He praised E. M. Tenison's championing of Dona Constança Telles da Gama,[104] through publicising her seven-month imprisonment for the twin offences of charitable dispensation and aristocracy![105] He also praised the Committee of British Residents in Portugal who had alerted Dom Miguel (the Pretender) to the dreadful conditions endured by Portuguese political prisoners. The British Residents wrote also to the *Morning Post*, Aubrey Bell's newspaper.[106] Bragança-Cunha admired Bell and other independent-minded journalists, such as Philip Gibbs, who voiced similar grievances.[107]

The question is, therefore, why did he not fraternise with the BPC in what was a common struggle? The answer must remain conjecture, but the clue may lie in a letter that he wrote to *The Nation* in August 1913, the origins of which lie in a heated exchange that had developed in that journal. S. H. Swinny (editor of the *Positivist Review*) and

E. M. Tenison (secretary of the BPC) contested the treatment of political prisoners in Portugal. It first drew in Homem Cristo, and later, Bragança-Cunha. In early 1913, Swinny had defended Portuguese prisons in *The Daily News*. This led to the Duchess of Bedford debating the comparative merits of Portuguese and English prisons with him in *The Nation*. The spat spread to the letters column of the *Daily Chronicle* when Sir Arthur Conan Doyle, citing Aubrey Bell's reports, suggested that Swinny 'has been shown what the authorities desired him to see.'[108] Gullible or not, Swinny shifted his defence to the Republic's egalitarianism: they were arresting all conspirators, Royalist or Republican.[109]

Tenison tried to expose Swinny's naivety by making public portions of a letter written to her by the exiled Republican, Homem Cristo, from Paris. He told her the regime was spreading disinformation, and that England should once again intervene in Portugal because 'humbug and hypocrisy have joined forces with tyranny and mendacity for the ruin of a once great nation.'[110] This was manna from heaven for Tenison, who told Swinny he had been duped on his recent visit to Portugal.

Swinny was unimpressed by Tenison's choice of friends. He had little time for 'patriots' who called for foreign intervention.[111] Tenison wondered how the Positivist Society might feel if he got six years solitary confinement and ten years deportation 'merely because he is a Positivist, and Positivism is contrary to the beliefs of the Archbishop of Canterbury.'[112] But Swinny continued to defend Republican justice by minimising its repressions. Strategically better-aimed – at British imperialism – was his sarcastic reply that Michael Davitt (his fellow countryman) would have appreciated the liberalism of Portuguese prisons, where he might have seen his family.[113] Homem Cristo retreated. He only urged 'moral criticism' of the regime, not armed intervention. In comparing the Duchess of Bedford's efforts with Canning and Palmerston, he wanted to dispel rumours that her campaign threatened Portuguese independence.[114] Tenison dragged in fallen hero Machado Santos, who justified a rising against the Government as long as a single political prisoner remained behind bars. Swinny considered it totally irresponsible to encourage intervention, but expected such behaviour from a turncoat.

At this point Bragança-Cunha exploded at the sound of foreigners debating the infringement of Portuguese sovereignty. They needed a history lesson in Teófilo Braga's four great causes of Portuguese decadence, 'the Inquisition, the Jesuits, the Braganças, and the English alliance.'[115] He had further lessons for Miss Tenison. The British played a double game and had prepared for the Revolution well in advance, assuring Republicans the Alliance would remain in place. Bragança-Cunha did not like Republicans but he liked attacks on Portuguese sovereignty even less. The subtext of this was that the invisible Goan had still not come out from behind his Portuguese nationalism.

5 Bragança-Cunha and modern civil society

The Britain into which Bragança-Cunha arrived hosted the recent emergence of an educated, professional public, consuming a journalism that shaped a new civic culture. He intruded upon a new profession of opinion formers. He had just escaped an insurgent, republicanized Goa that mirrored what was happening in Lisbon, and had reason to feel more comfortable in London. There, the 'new journalism' shared with Portugal a sensationalism driving a materialist cultural industry. As in Portugal, it did not refrain from speaking truth to power and criticising the state. It proclaimed a social conscience and appealed to the less advantaged through pricing its commodity low. But there was one crucial difference. The British Press was overwhelmingly Royalist, leaving little space for Republican views. A Portuguese Royalist like Bragança-Cunha could expect to work within a compatible culture.

Had he been in Lisbon, his situation would have been very different. Royalist hell-raisers were either behind bars or in exile. But, as Sardica has argued, even before 1910 progress towards civic consciousness was contained. Journalism never freed itself from *rotativismo* politics to become an autonomous voice. The promise of renewal generated by the intelligentsia after 1870 lapsed into avarice. The Press did not become the vehicle of regeneration.[116]

Bragança-Cunha was no admirer of this new culture of competitive citizenship, for it was destroying the Portugal of his imagination. When the Monarchy fell, he re-sited, claiming a space within a British culture of complaint about the new civic society that had dethroned his King. Although critical of it, he was, himself, a product of that Lusophone civic awareness that had grown in his own colonial Goa. Unacknowledged, he inherited some of its values: outspoken to the point of polemical, undeferential, and disrespectful of authority. He was the antonym of Magalhães Lima's 'uprising of the public spirit,'[117] but Bragança-Cunha made private noise in decibels. Like his Republican opponents writing up their gospel of national regeneration, he saw himself as an apostle of a true priesthood penning an alternative truth.

108 | *The Disgruntled Royalist*

Republican writers had created a cult of victimisation before 1910. From London, Bragança-Cunha turned their complaint on its head, and sent it straight back to Lisbon. With other 'Locusts', he pioneered a journalism of counter-victimisation, imagined through a nostalgic history. He flared across the printed page, a beacon of hope that a lost world might some day be restored. While Manuel and his entourage in Twickenham considered every careful step, Bragança-Cunha was the only Royalist in Britain kicking up a storm. There, he could make full use of a free press in a mature civic society, permissive of his polemics. He embraced it, but turned it back upon the liberal culture from which it sprang. Bragança-Cunha may have dressed like a dandy, but he wrote like a pugilist. He was Paiva Couceiro[118] in spats.

CHAPTER
6

The Lusophile

'Although I have as yet seen no reason whatever to be a friend of the republic, I write as a sincere friend of Portugal.' (Aubrey Bell, *The Spectator*, 26 April 1913)

1 The road to Santiago

Aubrey Fitz Gerald Bell was twenty-nine when he began working as *The Morning Post*'s correspondent in Portugal in 1911. He had been wandering around Iberia since leaving the British Museum as assistant keeper of printed books in 1908. He left Portugal for Canada in 1940 with the Order of Santiago and as one of the most distinguished scholars of Iberian studies of his generation. This was not predictable when he was arrested in October 1913 on charges of conspiracy. The coiner of the locust metaphor had become such a critic of the First Republic it felt the need to clip his wings. Bell's reports in *The Morning Post* were the major threat, but they were accompanied by critiques in *The Spectator*, *Contemporary Review* and *National Review*. He also wrote two books, *In Portugal* (1912) and *Portugal of the Portuguese* (1915), during this period.

In Portugal was completed in July 1911, in Mirandela, not Estoril where Bell was living. He described it as a travel guide but he was too modest. It is the twentieth-century's first great sweeping cultural commentary on Portugal, a predecessor of Rose Macaulay[1] and José Saramago.[2] It was researched during the first ten months of the Republic's existence, providing valuable insights into its reception by rural Portuguese society, in particular. As a snapshot of a transitional historical moment the reader is struck by evidence of continuity not change. The Republic intrudes only occasionally upon a narrative of the timeless Portugal of the *longue durée*. Bell's construct is a peasant Portugal capable of absorbing change within its natural rhythms of life. Politics is neutralized, so that great questions like Monarchy or

Republic float ethereally, like an urban intrusion upon the *mentalité* of the countryside: 'The Portuguese peasant preserves a noble independence . . . and considers the result of an election to be quite immaterial to his affairs.'[3]

The peasant's 'quiet human thoughtfulness' grows out of religious *mores* indelibly resistant to anti-clerical legislation. By contrast Republicanism is brash, urban and modern. The Catholic peasant is:

> of liberal mind, tolerant, fond of progress, and possesses much good practical common-sense . . . eyes turn willingly to the past . . . it is difficult to reconcile their humaneness with the barbaric neglect of prisons and prisoners that has been so often noted in Portugal.[4]

Does Bell's 1911 journey evidence the idea of a growing authoritarian state? The reader encounters a relative absence of the state, often where most needed: in the Beira Baixa, to educate the four-fifths of illiterate adults; in the Alentejo, where there was virtually no policing. In Redondo, two nightwatchmen in long cloaks concealing small arms beneath them passed as policemen. They reminded Bell of herdsmen. In the bucolic idyll of Elvas, there is no sign of Forte da Graça housing political prisoners, yet, just the seductive charms of the wide cobbled main street delightfully lined with white and yellow-washed houses, abundant with acacias. Elvas is the 'real Portugal' where the Republic evaporates amidst the raptures of tradition.

But in Lisbon it was a different story. Between the Cathedral and St George's Castle, men were doing time they did not deserve, in that dark symbol of the Republic, the *Limoeiro* prison.[5] But it had housed distinguished guests before the Republic, like Almeida Garrett who had slummed it with 'low miscreants' he detested. He survived to become Minister of Foreign Affairs in 1851.[6]

Sintra was the most loved of Portuguese towns by the English – Gil Vicente's 'paradise garden', and Byron's 'glorious Eden.' But the Revolution had shaken its golden boughs. Bell thought a few zealous Republicans there deserved to have their heads chopped off for erecting a street sign where there was no street. Avenida de Candido dos Reis commemorated the admiral who committed suicide because he believed the Revolution had failed. Bell fails to mention that legislation had been passed in 1911 allowing the renaming of streets after heroes of the Revolution.[7]

Revolutionary Republicanism reverberated through Coimbra, too. Santa Clara Convent had been emptied of its nuns, leaving only a lonely sexton to keep the light over Saint Elizabeth's shrine burning. But, as a Catholic and royalist city containing the *Aljube* political prison, Porto is the great anomaly of *In Portugal*. Bell has nothing to say of its politics, yearning only for the countryside beyond its dinginess. He was one Englishman who harboured no affection for the home of the port wine trade.

The poet Abílio Guerra Junqueiro is Bell's exemplary ex-Republican convert. In 1911, he was the Portuguese Minister in Switzerland. But, as a young member of the 'Generation of 1870', he advocated burning down Coimbra University as a first step to reform.[8] In 1907, he was fined for describing the King as a pig who tyrannized his people.[9] So, Junqueiro welcomed in the Republic, but withdrew, alienated by Costa's political manipulating.[10] The 'singer of revolution' had been lost to Republicanism but not to patriotism, continuing to be critical of 'cynical, shameless, drunken England.'[11]

As a text, *In PortugaL* was made as a culturally sophisticated travel guide. The tone is nostalgic, attractive to prospective travellers undesirous of visiting a Portugal of the anti-Christ and political prisons. But sources can be read against the grain and the Republic's troubles seep through. Modernisation had not brought the pollution of an industrial revolution but an effluence of toxic ideas, as revolution finally reached marginalized Portugal. No overt lesson is spelled out, but the subtext advises: visit traditional Portugal before it is too late. In 1911 there still seemed time, the fresh footprints of the authoritarian state are scarcely dry. *In Portugal* is a cultural history of the *longue durée* at risk.

2 'Thinking against the Republic' in the periodical press (1912–14)

On 2 April 1913 Aubrey Bell wrote a letter to *The Spectator* about Sabino José Costa who had died whilst imprisoned without trial in the *Limoeiro*. Bell implied that Costa's only offence, like that of many political prisoners, was 'thinking against the Republic.'[12] Bell had been thinking against the Republic in *The Morning Post* since 1911, but between 1912 and 1914 joined other 'Locusts' in trying to mobilize British public opinion in the periodical press. In two influential pieces, about a year apart, he stood back and offered a detailed dissection of the Republic's infancy.[13]

In the first of these, Bell argues that the euphoria that greeted the Republic glossed over its structural defects. Excessive centralism was not likely to overcome the political apathy inherited from the *rotativismo* period. As Eça de Queirós had said:

if a group at Lisbon decreed tomorrow that Portugal should turn Turk, you would find all the hats throughout the country taking turban shape.[14]

In the second, Bell focuses on the new Constitution and the parliamentary elections of 1911. The first inaugurated a weak presidency and a National Assembly dominated by middle-class males. The Electoral Law of 1911 restricted the size of the electorate by imposing a literacy qualification. The elections of May were an exercise in 'managed democracy', gerrymandered by the Democrats to the disadvantage of the Evolutionists, whom Bell preferred. The PRP, that had ruled since the Revolution, had divided over a bitterly disputed Presidential election in August, 1911. The more radical faction became the Democrats; the more conservative sub-divided into two groups – the more right-wing Unionists, and the more centrist Evolutionists.[15] An 'administrative dictatorship' was created in that the elections produced 'not a national parliament but a Party assembly' for the Democrats. They, Bell argues, reneged on their promise to establish a proper democratic link between parliament and the municipalities. The old, regional Lisbon appointees, were left in charge as the Government's patrons organising parliamentary elections.

For Bell, politics was conducted at two levels. Public politics officially sought consensus, but secret, illegal politics really underpinned Democrat hegemony.[16] Because the Republic had secured itself since the Revolution, Bell saw no excuse for keeping political prisoners. Although he has no gendered agenda, he emphasizes the arbitrary arrest of women like the charity worker Dona Constança Telles da Gama and the British journalist Miss Oram, both kept for months without trial.

Historians of dictatorships have uncovered the extent to which the Gestapo or the NKVD relied upon false denunciations as a form of social control.[17] Within the revolutionary Portuguese state, Bell finds the *Carbonária* pioneers of such abuse:

> the present War Minister issued an edict declaring that, in view of the large number of ungrounded arrests, false accusers would be severely dealt with. This was not done, however, till the prisons had been filled with alleged conspirators on the part of the Carbonários who may be called private persons in that they escape all responsibility, but who, receiving money from the authorities, are anxious to justify their salaries and at the same time to parade their zeal for the Republic by discovering conspiracies where no conspiracies were.[18]

The Catholic journalist, Francis McCullagh.

The disgruntled Royalist, Vicente de Bragança-Cunha.

Postcard print of Campolide College, 1910, where Father Torrend was a professor.

The Portuguese Pimpernel, Sir Philip Armand Hamilton Gibbs, who reported on Portuguese prisons in the *Daily Chronicle*.

Postcard print of Gaby Deslys (Marie-Elise Gabrielle Caire), King Manuel's companion in 1910.

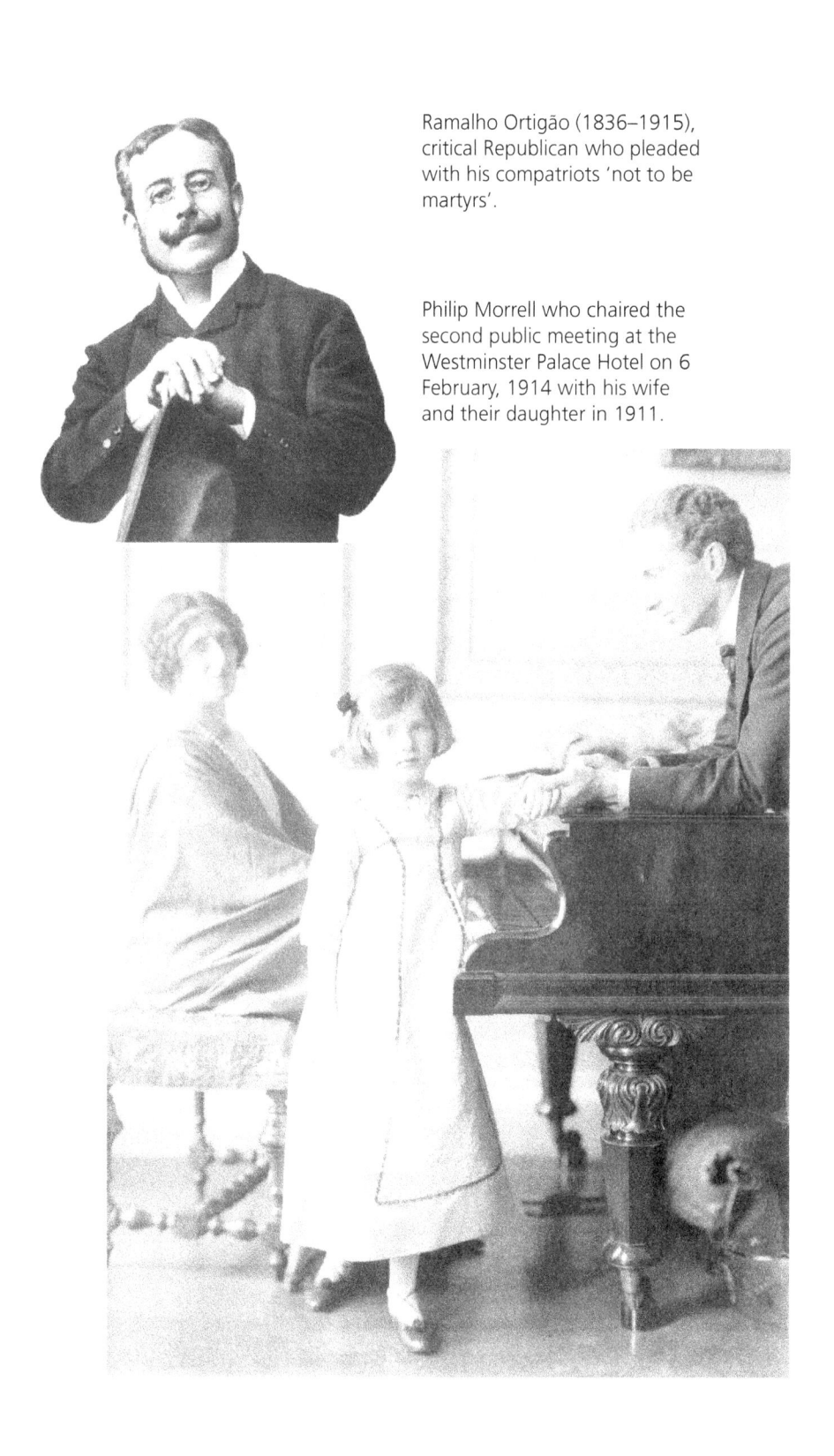

Ramalho Ortigão (1836–1915), critical Republican who pleaded with his compatriots 'not to be martyrs'.

Philip Morrell who chaired the second public meeting at the Westminster Palace Hotel on 6 February, 1914 with his wife and their daughter in 1911.

E.M. Tenison's close friend Musette Majendie (1903–1981) in her district scout commissioner's uniform.

Eva Mabel Tenison, Secretary of the BPC, on coming out, probably c. 1900–1901.

Adeline, Duchess of Bedford, vice-chair of the British Campaign, and prison reformer.

"Fearless but Intemperate." Reverend R. J. Campbell, minister of the City of Temple, speaker at the first public meeting on 22 April, 1913, as caricatured by 'Spy' in Vanity Fair, November 1904.

Alice Seeley Harris, missionary, photographer, lantern-slide campaigner and wife of John, with large group of Congolese children, early 1900s.

The 'black hole of Elvas' visited by Philip Gibbs in December, 1913.

1 View from inside a cell at Forte da Graça.

2 View of courtyard at Forte da Graça.

Carbonária acting as *agents provocateurs* is attested to by a number of different sources. The 'White Ants' were often drawn from the socially deprived of Lisbon, unemployed and anxious to denounce and be paid. But the denouncers covered a wide range of the disaffected. Historians of Nazi Germany and Stalinist Russia have shown that people with grievances denounced innocent neighbours. Bell shows intimidation seeping into the sinews of everyday life with the Press being silenced out of fear their offices will be ransacked by the mob. Philip Gibbs captures it, too, in his depiction of Lisbon in 1913 as 'a city of whisperers.' For Bell, the population was easily cowed into complicity by an historic indifference to urban politics. The only hope for Portugal, in the short term, was for the divided opposition to work together.

A precarious economy based on deficit financing did not assist this. Much of the problem was inherited, leaving the Republicans 'dancing on a rotten scaffold.' The new Government increased debt year on year to subsidise agriculture and industry. Tariffs raised from the protected colonial markets could not compensate. Capital flight was a frequent reaction to political uncertainty, causing dependency on the Bank of Portugal for loans. The consequence was lack of public investment.[19] Yet, still unaffordable promises were made. Too much was spent on the armed forces, too little on 'tramways and asphalt' – better communications infra-structure. Bell accused the Republic of worsening the public finances through waste: feeding a bloated state bureaucracy; fighting unnecessary wars on the Northern frontier; and financing the *Carbonária*. Economic failure caused flight as economic emigrants were joined by political refugees. So it must have surprised him when Costa balanced the budget by February 1914.[20]

Bell believed that if modernisation could not be financed by imperial revenues then colonies would have to be sold.[21] By early 1913, he was floating putting some of them up for auction, 'in order to exploit the others more profitably.'[22] Bell's Germanophilia alarmed Republicans who rejected his comparison with Spain's relinquishing of Cuba. For his part, he loathed the Francophilia of the Coimbra-educated, political class of the 'Generation of 1870'. Their way invited national decline:

> The educated speak, read and think in French; the Lisbon bookshops fill their windows with French publications, relegating Portuguese books to the more obscure corners. Lisbon, indeed, seeks to copy Paris in centralisation, politics, literature, in its virtues and its vices.[23]

Bell's Lusophilia accepted a subaltern cultural existence as the future for Portugal. It was derived from his reading of the Portuguese *longue durée*. Republicans had been more concerned to imitate past French republics 'than to develop a truly Portuguese civilisation.' He brushes aside the Revolution as a simulacrum, a blip on a linear contour: 'in the nature of things such revolutions as that of October, 1910, must ever resemble little limelight plays in the slow, small-grinding march of progress.'[24]

Mis-reading of history had led to bad government such as the anti-clerical reforms. It was 'one of the ready-made suits ordered from Paris,' that alienated the Northern peasants 'who care less for their King than for their religion.'[25] The marginalisation of the provinces was a parallel blunder that betrayed the heart of the Portuguese nation for the sake of Lisbon, a dangerous city of extremist bomb-throwers. He was surely wrong, however, to accuse Republicanism of lacking idealism. More to the point was his recommendation it focus on economic and social reform at home. Bell's formula to arrest national decline was: irrigate the land to grow more wheat, build more industry, improve communications, radically overhaul education, and think less about France.

3 Towards a plank couch: Bell's arrest

'Nobody is safe from sudden arrest and imprisonment.' (Aubrey Bell, Lisbon, October 23 1913)[26]

On Monday, October 27, 1913 *The Morning Post* relayed some difficult news for Anglo-Portuguese relations:

> Mr. A.F. Bell, Lisbon Correspondent of *The Morning Post*, has been arrested on a charge of being connected with recent alleged conspiracies against the Republic. Now, Mr. Bell is an English subject. He is an English scholar and a gentleman who has for some years acted as our Correspondent, and we can vouch for his entire disinterestedness. It has been the duty of a newspaper correspondent to give the truth, and the entire truth, of the situation as he finds it in Portugal. He has kept the British public informed of events as they happen, and of the conduct and policy of the Republican government. He has also written vivid accounts of the unfortunate Royalist prisoners who have languished in the dungeons and fortresses of Lisbon. It has been his duty to discover and report upon what happens on both sides without fear or favour, and in so doing if he has given the Portuguese

authorities chagrin it is because their treatment of these unfortunate prisoners has not been all that could be desired by civilised opinion. Here in England we do not yet regard it as a crime to have sympathies with the down-trodden and oppressed, even if they happen to be Royalists. Nor do we expect a civilised Government, founded upon Democracy, Liberty, and the other catchwords, that it should persecute a man for his sympathies and imprison him for his freedom of speech.[27]

Bell had been charged with conspiracy; different from corresponding with Royalists, the *Post* reminded readers. The Foreign Office was negotiating for Bell's release. In his absence, the *Post* relied on Reuters' Lisbon office for information. Documents had been seized from Bell's house because he was suspected of being involved in a recent plot against the Government. The newspaper reminded that, although a candid critic of arbitrary arrest and confinement who had inspired the Duchess of Bedford's recent 'crusade' over political prisoners, he had never been an opponent of the Republic, in itself. Indeed, 'he both admires and loves the Portuguese people'.[28]

Sir Lancelot Carnegie had just replaced Hardinge as British Ambassador. It fell to him to have released a man he thought had talked himself into prison:

I was not impressed by Bell and his views are erroneous and dangerous . . . much more was to be gained by giving fair play to this government than by conducting a campaign against it, which appeared to be his and his Editor's firm intention . . . he must be very ill informed or prejudiced.[29]

Carnegie expressed the official irritation of the Old Alliance diplomat. His agenda diverged from that of a Tory paper championing constitutional liberties in Portugal at a time of crisis in pre-war Britain. Liberal governments had imposed redistributive taxes consolidated by constitutional reform. Costa's Portugal was a warning of what unconstrained Liberalism could lead to.

The *Carbonária* raided Bell's house and took letters and a copy of the BPC's pamphlet, *Portuguese Political Prisoners*.[30] The Government had already confiscated two hundred copies in May. Still, he may have escaped arrest had it not been for the heightened security that followed the conspiracy of autumn, 1913. E. M. Tenison was very quick to come to his defence:

> The arrest of Mr. Aubrey F. G. Bell, the Lisbon correspondent of the *Morning Post*, is, like the Carbonários' threat to assassinate Lord Mayo, a convincing proof that while the Portuguese Government claims to be representative and popular it is in reality extremely vindictive towards anyone able and willing to expose its tyranny and injustice.[31]

Aubrey Bell is now a largely forgotten historical figure. But three years after his death in 1950, he was remembered by fellow scholars of Portuguese studies, who collaborated in a memorial volume for him and the historian, Edgar Prestage.[32] M. A. Buchanan, who knew Bell in Canada towards the end of his life, noted that 'His literary and scholarly production was vast, running to some thirty titles in books alone.'[33] The bibliographical appendix of over six pages lists publications from 1911 to 1950. Of course, it excludes Bell's journalism, of which there is no previous study, nor in particular, of the political reporting that saw him imprisoned. Buchanan's account of Bell's imprisonment by 'a sympathetic friend' is second-hand but the only one we have:

> Some time about 1912, possibly because of his association with *The Morning Post*, he was accused of aiding and abetting Monarchical reaction and summarily imprisoned as a political offender. Characteristically he baited his jailors by refusing to pay for his meals and hunger-struck for twenty-four hours, after which the police transferred him to a military barracks. There he was very well treated and had all the food he wanted. Indeed after the Commandant had allowed him to have some books sent in he settled down to a quiet period of study for – he told me – it was a great treat to have good and regular meals for nothing after his own sketchy housekeeping at Manique. Moreover, he found he could sleep perfectly well on a plank couch and made a mental note that as soon as he returned home he would install one and save himself the extra trouble of making his own bed. He was eventually persuaded to leave prison by the personal intervention of Mr. (now Sir) Charles Wingfield, then a Secretary at the Legation.[34]

Bell's wry sense of humour survived imprisonment. The importance of his journalism in providing evidence for the British campaign has been long acknowledged.[35] The case-study of his writing for the *Post* (1913–14) that follows provides the broad context of his arrest. Bell's journalism in 1913 is a partial, but invaluable window upon a First Republic struggling for survival. It draws extensively upon the

Portuguese newspapers through a period when censorship operated intermittently. Occasionally his own dispatches were delayed by the censor and *The Morning Post* never fails to capitalize on freedom of the press violations.

5 The costs of Costa: Reporting the economy

The reader of *The Morning Post* in 1913 had every reason to believe that the economy was a wreck. Bell challenged the Government's financial veracity, particularly the claim to have balanced the budget after only six months of government. He dismissed *O Mundo*'s boast that it was the most important event in Portugal since the Revolution. Money was being printed recklessly, causing a collapse of political confidence. Bell was not deterred by what the Democrats termed 'the crushing eloquence of figures.' He took his economics from the pro-Evolutionist, *A República*'s distrust of the so-called financial miracle.

Bell's attack upon Republican pride and joy nudged him towards the plank couch. Once freed, the *Post* called in an anonymous 'specialist correspondent.' This may have been a surrogate, but as he was hardly less critical, may well have been Bell, himself. He deplored the spiralling public debt and the many new hungry placemen feeding at the trough.[36] The Government's response was creative accountancy. At the same time, schoolteachers went unpaid and retired public servants had received no pensions for six months. The plummeting exchange rate made it more expensive to borrow abroad. Gold flowed out. Much revenue went uncollected. Emigration continued to increase, causing a labour shortage in the north where corn growing land lapsed into an uncultivated state. The over issue of paper currency caused increasing inflation, fuelling strikes and more urban unrest. At the same time, government attempted to limit the freedom to withdraw labour. Their only job creation scheme seemed to be the *Carbonária*.

6 The year 1913: Portugal, Britain and the European Crisis

A recent history of the world in 1913 managed to make only a single reference to Portugal in over four-hundred pages.[37] Bell's journalism is a corrective of historical negligence, providing an incomparable analytical narrative. Throughout the crucial year 1913, he was identified as the Republican Government's principal enemy in the British press. As War approached, Anglo-Portuguese politics became increasingly trapped within the nexus of the continental crisis surrounding them.

Bell's primary remit was to report on parliament. He chose to do this by being a vigilant critic of Republican government. But the role took him far beyond Chamber and Senate, reporting on political prisons, and the extra-parliamentary world of Royalist conspiracies and anarcho-syndicalist bombings. He treated the Church and state relationship as a political issue of governance. The future of the empire was recognized as a matter of international importance.

Portugal in 1913 was dealt with by a British Liberal Government in crisis. The *Post* reported the increasingly violent suffragette campaign. A letter in April from the Duchess of Bedford, argued that women's suffrage must be supported publicly despite the WSPU's militant tactics, not because of them. Faint-heartedness would only give the impression that there was less support for the cause than really existed.[38] In defiance of the Government's refusal of female suffrage, she refused to pay her taxes. HM Revenue confiscated in distraint a silver cup that brought 20 guineas at Hollingsworth's auction rooms; £6 7s 6d in excess of her tax liability.[39]

The three years to 1913 had seen the worst strikes since the 1890s, as prices outstripped wages and trades unions tried to keep up. Syndicalism became increasingly powerful amongst general unionists.[40] Rising prices and labour militancy paralleled the experience of Portugal in these early years of the Republic.[41]

Ireland was on the verge of rebellion in 1913 as the Ulster Volunteers mobilized to oppose the Home Rule Bill. The Balkans was actually at war for the second time in two years, as the Serbs confiscated and re-distributed the Bulgarians' gains of the first war against the Turks. This took place against the background of an arms race between Britain and Germany. Readers of the *Post* must have been tempted to conclude that almost any morning in 1913 brought bad news. Every few days, Portugal added to their gloom, a peripheral symptom of an old Europe falling apart.

In March, a scandal broke over the dismissal of the Governor of Mozambique, Alfredo de Magalhães. He refused to go quietly, exposing a web of corruption that, he argued, incited revolt. Colonial Governors were appointed by political patronage. Mozambique had become a hotbed of parasitic officials in corrupt relationships with foreign companies for mutual gain. Such venality had allowed the Germans to muscle in on much of Mozambique's export trade.

Bell, in the *Post*, argued that Portugal either reformed the colonies or lost them.[42] He was no anti-imperialist, he just favoured redistributing some of the Portuguese Empire to Germany. He thought the

Republic's unwillingness to address the problems had deprived them of any right to empire. However, he never overtly identified 'slavery' as a moral problem, as John Harris did. The scandal deepened with the intervention of President Braga. He gave newspaper interviews in which he supported Magalhães' accusations. Resignations were expected from within the administration, as Bell highlighted its growing division from parliament.

The *Post* got right behind Bell, utilising a long-standing Anglo-Portuguese dispute in Mozambique to launch a full-scale attack upon colonial maladministration. It argued the affair was an example of the double legal standards applied by the regime as a result of its revolutionary degeneration. The Rev. Arthur J. Douglas, head of a missionary college in Mozambique, was shot and killed by Corporal Annibal Alves Taveira in disputed circumstances. Taveira was suspected of preying upon the mission to kidnap some of its girls for forced labour, which raised the hackles of the Anti-Slavery Society. Tried by the Portuguese, he received only one year's imprisonment. The *Post* was highly critical of Grey, the Foreign Secretary, for not pressing for a more severe sentence and a considerable indemnity from the Portuguese. No-one should be surprised, it declared, at such behaviour from a regime that glorified in the assassination of its own monarch and imprisoned its own citizens without trial.[43]

Dona Constança Telles da Gama, descendant of Camões, was the most revered of these internees. The *Post* was appalled at tales of hooded aristocrats with shaven heads, dressed as convicts.[44] This was the *Carbonária's* work – 'the scum of its population' – worthy of France in the 1790s. And, it implored, 'tyranny, blackmail, terrorism, these surely are not the instruments with which Liberty builds her home.'[45]

This is good evidence of Carnegie's complaint about the *Post*'s prejudice. But its catastrophism amplified a genuine geopolitical concern for Iberia. Portugal was the front line. If liberty did not build a home there, then the rot might spread to Spain, where anarchists plotted a similar fate for their king. The *Post* put forth a catastrophic scenario for the European aristocracy, the like of which had not seen since the 1790s, unless Costa's 'Jacobinism' was stopped.

7 The years 1913–14: Insurrectionists, bombers, and political prisoners

Officially, the Government kept political prisoners for two reasons. The first was that they had plotted to overthrow the Government through armed insurrection. These were almost always Royalists. The second was that they had launched violent attacks upon civil society. A minority of these were anarchists who believed in the doctrine of the deed, that such attacks would inspire revolutionary upheaval. But more were anarcho-syndicalists, prepared to use violence to wage industrial disputes as part of the class struggle. The Government locked up both types for long periods without trial. Far more Royalists were imprisoned than anarchists, as they represented the more serious threat. Both were imprisoned on dubious or no evidence, pending trial. Bell sympathized with the Royalists, but he thought it equally unjust to imprison anarchists without trial. Not all bombs were planted by anarchists. Bell suspected the *Carbonária* planted them as a tactic of explosive disinformation.

The *Carbonária* exerted extra-judicial agency in numerous ways. They harassed the Church and its social organisations, and they interfered directly with the judicial process.[46] They whipped-up a hostile atmosphere in court during the trial of a retired policeman, who received four years' imprisonment followed by eight years' penal servitude. The evidence suggested he was guilty of little more than having Royalist views.[47] He settled into his cell just in time to receive the Duchess of Bedford, who visited Lisbon's prisons on 20–21 March 1913 after reading Bell's journalism. His reports, however, fell foul of the Censor just as she left.[48] Several Jesuit newspapers were closed in a last gasp of press suppression before the Amnesty Bill was introduced.[49] Bell predicted the Democrat dominated Chamber would block it,[50] but there were signs of a thaw with further early releases. Bell continued to press for the Bill to pass before the summer recess. He appealed to the Government's generosity, but Costa had none. Treating the issue as a matter of sovereignty, he dismissed the Duchess of Bedford's visit and British press coverage as being organized by enemies of the Republic.[51] *The Morning Post* met fire with fire. It dug up the still warm corpse of the Reverend Douglas to connect colonial decadence to the treatment of Royalist prisoners:

> the British Government can see to it that these barbarous customs of the revolutionaries are not extended to British subjects, and especially to the devoted missionaries who work among the natives of Equatorial Africa.[52]

Amidst this war of words, the BPC organized the public meeting at the Aeolian Hall on 22 April. The *Post*'s aristocratic conceit reports the Duchess of Bedford's tribute to Aubrey Bell and to the *Post*'s tutoring of Portuguese politics. His articles had propelled her visit to

Lisbon and the *Post* deserved great credit 'for having persistently brought the sufferings of the political prisoners before the notice of the English readers.' More controversially, she 'called upon the best elements in the Portuguese Republic to rise and overthrow this monster that was throttling their true life.'[53]

Five days later, there was an attempted coup in Lisbon, unlikely to have been inspired by the Duchess because it came from the far Left. Wheeler dismisses it as the work of radical syndicalists, prompted by Machado Santos.[54] Bell took it more seriously. 'Certain extreme radical elements, disgusted with bourgeois government' tried to take control of the Engineers' barracks in *Graça*, to defend the 'Radical Republic' against conspirators. Only the Fifth Infantry Regiment joined the Engineers, leading to mass arrests by the evening.

The Government accused Syndicalists and radical Republicans of joining in an unholy alliance with Monarchists. Bell even speculated that the *Carbonária* were acting as *agents provocateurs* to force the Government into sterner measures against Monarchists. Bragança-Cunha located the plot firmly within the Army. It was the work of recently promoted officers and sergeants who feared losing their control of the courts-martial.[55] There were more press closures, including the *Sindicalista* newspaper,[56] and increasing transportations of political prisoners to the Azores.[57]

In the spring of 1913, Bell became sufficiently concerned about political prisoners to go beyond his *Morning Post* brief and write a series of letters to *The Spectator*. For *The Spectator*, political prisoners ran a close second only to 'Portuguese slavery' as a campaigning concern. Tenison exaggerated shamelessly when she drew comparison with the French royalists of 1793, who at least knew they would be guillotined. Portuguese royalists just lived the agony of not knowing.[58] Bell disassociated himself from this, pointing out there was no capital punishment in Portugal of any sort. But he expressed sympathy with the campaign to release political prisoners, who were kept in worse conditions than under the Monarchy. These were just part of an overall decline in standards of justice, that included prolonged detention before trial, and farcical standards of evidence during trials, themselves. For Bell this was symptomatic of the moral decline of the anti-clerical state. The religious were imprisoned on the word of the state-financed *Carbonária*, while assassins were lauded as heroes. But he stressed the majority of Portuguese did not support persecution, so it was important to maintain their morale by defending the free press. With a glance towards Tenison, he commended the Evolutionist, *A República*, which approved of the British campaign for an amnesty.[59]

So, Bell was unsurprised when Afonso Costa reneged on his February promise of an amnesty. Costa's mouthpiece, O Mundo, announced it was not in the national interest while there was still a chance of conspiracy. Bell adopted a civil libertarian position. Policy should be based on evidence and there had been none of conspiracy for over a year. It was a ruse to justify draconian laws. But Bell allowed his frustrations with the Costa government to move him closer to Tenison's distorted historical comparisons. References to 'the bitter Jacobin wind now blowing'[60] smacked of her apocalyptic discourse. A fortnight later he had regained his composure, somewhat. Prompted by Costa's dismissal of British public opinion's support for an amnesty, he warned him not to under-estimate its strength. It should not be confused with the British Government's non-intervention policy.[61]

Once any hope of an amnesty bill in the spring parliamentary session had passed, Bell launched a broadside. Costa would lose even more support in Britain, not that he gave a fig for the Alliance. Otherwise, British protestors would not have been denounced as enemies and greedy chocolate makers with an eye on the Portuguese colonies![62] The latter was a deliciously sarcastic reference to Cadbury's, who had imported cheap cocoa from São Tomé. The anti-slavery campaign was dismissed by Republican propaganda as a tactic to bankrupt the colonies so that British capital could buy them up cheaply.

The Aeolian Hall meeting ratcheted-up the pressure to free political prisoners. The BPC's pamphlet *Portuguese Political Prisoners: a British National Protest*, united even the sceptical Portuguese press behind the Republic. O Mundo condemned it as 'a pack of lies', while O Seculo denounced the whole campaign as inspired by enemies of the Republic. Bell confronted the 'turncoats and apologists'[63] with previously unpublished material showing how bad conditions could be: freezing cells in which gas stoves were prohibited as dangerous; sane prisoners kept awake at night by the ravings of the mad.

The effect was counter productive. The political prisoners remained exactly where they were for another nine months. O Seculo published a photograph allegedly showing the flogging of a prisoner in an English jail and ridiculed the Duchess for hypocrisy. The Government seized a second batch of several hundred copies of *Portuguese Political Prisoners*. Lytton demanded their return from the Portuguese Foreign Minister on the grounds that they contained nothing illegal. He threatened to claim 'an indemnity for the confiscation of their property.'[64]

The reaction to the British Campaign was just part of a more general crack down. Arbitrary arrests continued, but some failed. Count Ervideira was freed when the principal prosecution witness could do no better than: 'having been a Count, he must be hostile to the Republic, which was hostile to Counts.'[65] Dona Julia de Brito e Cunha, provided bandages and other medical supplies to the Red Cross in case of riots. She was arrested for conspiracy to incite riots.[66] In Coimbra, there were reactionary riots as students supported the police against workers.

Parliament was prorogued on 30 May, with the Amnesty Bill still pending. In the second week of June Lisbon was *em festa* for the new secular holidays. Cheap rail fares encouraged peasants to travel in from villages to commemorate the death of the great Portuguese poet, Camões on 10 June. A band led a procession, composed largely of students and children, out of Rossio square, up the steep hill towards the Chiado. Suddenly the syndicalist flag was raised amidst the crowd and within seconds a bomb exploded. One member of the band lay dead, several more injured, the youngest of whom was a seven-year-old girl. Later that day a local syndicalist quiosque was burned down by an angry mob.[67] More than sixty arrests followed quickly, of syndicalists and anarchists, but also several newspaper editors. Detention prevented them reporting the shots fired at Monarchists leaving celebrations of the forthcoming wedding of the King of Spain.[68]

Two days after the Lisbon bombing, the Bishop of Porto was acquitted of baptising an infant whilst expelled from his diocese. Many other priests had already left, part of the 3,000 increase in emigrants in the first quarter of the year compared with the corresponding quarter of 1912.[69] Even Parliamentary life was becoming dangerous. On 25 June Senator João Freitas accused the Government of ignoring the corruption of colonial officials in São Tomé. The Prime Minister's brother, a Senator, repudiated his claims. After an abusive exchange, Freitas pulled out a loaded pistol, which was snatched from his hands by another brave Senator.[70]

On 30 June, Afonso Costa sailed through more safely on a wave of congratulation at the predicted budget surplus. *O Mundo* declared it the most important achievement since the Revolution. Bell, tried to spoil the party and pointed out that the surplus depended upon exceptional revenue from the maize and wheat tax, much of which had been imported in the poor harvest year of 1913.[71]

Novel strike action was taken by Coimbra's academics objecting to the establishment of a rival Faculty of Law in Lisbon. Shops were closed, newspapers suppressed, and the President even had to cancel a visit as troops were sent in. Observing this chaos at first-hand was a 24-year-old student of economics and public administration in the Faculty of Laws, António de Oliveira Salazar.[72]

The prospects of an amnesty in mid-1913 were lost amidst the reaction to the coup attempt of April. Bell responded with a tirade against the Democrat Party's record. The Amnesty Bill had been withdrawn despite the pledge six months before. The Democrat Party had conflated the interests of the Party with those of the state, so come to view all outside it as traitors. *O Mundo* seemed to strip Royalists of their civil liberties in asserting 'In Portugal there exists no right whatsoever to be a Royalist.'[73] Costa took a swipe at the English with the jibe that the Portuguese had no habit of hanging the innocent. That was a mistaken comparison, Bell's responded; the real one was with the Spanish Inquisition. The propaganda war had got completely out of hand.[74]

Through July 1913, Lisbon teetered on the brink of a left-wing insurgency. On 20th, another bomb, thrown from a car this time, killed a policeman. Over three hundred arrests followed the discovery of one hundred and sixty bombs. Children were injured as raided would-be-bombers tried to explode the evidence before the *Carbonária* got their hands on it.[75] It was so out of control it shot a photographer in the Rua Augusta who was, unsurprisingly, only carrying a camera.[76] On 26th, the police arrested an innocent, unarmed man on suspicion he was a Royalist agent from Brazil about to assassinate Costa.[77] Jittery Republicans were turning on themselves. On 28 July, one of the leaders of the 1910 Revolution, Américo Oliveira, was arrested.[78]

Bell was worried at Lisbon coming 'to rival Barcelona as the city of bombs' and noted that disturbances were becoming more anarchist inspired.[79] But he missed that anarchism came to Portugal from his detested France, in the 1880s, not Spain. A major influence was Elisée Reclus, a follower of Bakunin, but also a geographer of international renown. Reclus, however, did not advocate bombing. *The Times* attributed that tactic to Italian anarchists.[80] Reclus had published the first volume of *The Earth and its Inhabitants* on Europe in 1883, the last chapter of which covered Portugal.[81] More influential with revolutionary syndicalists, however, were his shorter polemics such as *Advice to My Anarchist Comrades* (1901), where he urged: 'If you throw yourself into the fray to sacrifice yourself defending the humiliated and downtrodden, that is a very good thing, my companions. Face death nobly.' But it was not until January, 1912, that a Setubal fish canner became the first Portuguese striker to die, closely followed by a rural labourer in the Alentejo.[82] From the 1890s, revolutionary publications had been suppressed, and anarchists deported to the colonies. But this failed to break links with radical Republicanism around anti-clericalism and anti-monarchism. The *Carbonária* were reported as infiltrating the armed forces, where 'Both Army and Navy are undoubtedly honeycombed with the principles of socialism.'[83] They were also spying in the prisons and police, where Bell suspected they planted evidence.[84]

Anarchism had implanted itself in the pre-Revolutionary labour movement. It developed largely amongst skilled workers in traditional industries, and from the co-operative, mutual traditions of local community crafts passed on through kinship networks. Trade unionism had expanded early across skill, class and gender, and the first organized unskilled workers included women. As the state was captured by new elites in 1910, labour militancy burst through the fractures of a stretched democracy, forcing Republicanism into concessions. Between then and 1915 numbers of unions grew by a further eighty-eight percent. Prominent were the big, single industry, public sector confederations: railway workers, government servants, and sailors (who had been in the vanguard on '5 October').[85] Rural labour unions, strong in regions such as Ribatejo and Alentejo, held their first federation in Évora in 1912.[86] Labour's co-operation with the Republican government quickly broke down after the Revolution. Strikes were legalized, but so too were lock-outs, indicating the limitations of liberal, Republican ideology, for the Left. They countered with demands for an eight-hour day and equalisation of wages. Industrial conflict flared-up from March 1911, when two striking fish canning workers were shot in Setubal.[87] In the same month, one thousand, five-hundred rail repair workers and lightermen on the river come out in a sympathetic general strike over sackings at the *União Fabril Co.*[88] Bell considered anarchist bombings a greater threat than syndicalist trade unionism, but had little sympathy for a regicidal state that invited them. By summer, 1913 he describes a society on the brink once more. The revolutionary movement of 1910 had split several ways between governing Democrats, an atomised old middle class sub-divided between smaller parties, and the Left. He blamed the Democrats' exclusive political practice for driving legitimate popular opposition into the arms of revolutionary politics.

The Evolutionist leader, Almeida, renewed demands for an amnesty, but his call for female franchise from a Government that had just disenfranchised illiterate males was unrealistic.[89] Almeida warned that Costa's continued extremism would provoke a new Royalist rising.[90] But Costa was not tainted with quite the 'fatal purity'[91] that opponents claimed. Both his premierships were ended through constitutional process. A closer comparator might be Combes' administration during the Third French Republic. The difference was that in France the Separation Laws of 1904 put the issue to bed; in

Portugal the Church remained hopeful of restoration. In fact, separation was permanent, even Salazar declining to reverse it.

By autumn, President Arriaga managed to pin Costa down over political prisoners. The Prime Minister acceded to a limited bill releasing those considered least dangerous. 'Mr' E. M. Tenison (the *Post*'s patriarchal error) uncompromisingly rejected this on behalf of the BPC. She contested the terms of release as many of the imprisoned had played absolutely no part in any rising or conspiracy. This was only possible because Portugal was effectively a *Carbonária* dictatorship. But she offered an olive branch: 'By granting a general amnesty to all political prisoners . . . the Lisbon Ministry might yet save the last remnants of its credit.'[92]

As usual, Bell retreated from Tenison's polemics. For him, the lunatics had not quite taken over the asylum. He hoped that they could get an amnesty in stages. His diplomacy was upset by five Syndicalists arrested in Sintra as they were about to assassinate Afonso Costa at his summer residence. The plot had been hatched from prison by Jayme Augusto, who claimed Monarchist involvement. A chemist, António Costa, had made eleven bombs, but he blew himself up at home in mid-September.[93] The evidence is unclear, but confessions of Syndicalist-Royalist collaboration appear to fit Government scaremongering so closely that they were probably scripted from the blood of a *Carbonária* beating.[94]

The Government made a virtue out of necessity and released almost five hundred prisoners to coincide with the third anniversary of the Revolution. Bell welcomed these as a first step towards the general amnesty promised. In London, the Howard Association added its voice to that of the BPC, demanding guarantees for those remaining.[95] There were still plenty. A hundred and thirty were transported from Lisbon to Elvas, probably to Forte da Graça. The highly volatile political mood hampered further releases. A large armaments dump of rifles and cartridges was found in Orense,[96] and rumours abounded of another Royalist rising in Chaves.[97] In fact, it occurred in Lisbon. On 21 October a small group of Royalists attacked the *Limoeiro* but surrendered after three of them had been killed by police. The arrested were taken to the police station, only for it to be attacked by fifty insurgent 'police' who turned out to be disguised Royalists. The latter planned to go on and liberate the prisons, but the cavalry of the Republican Guard restored order.[98]

The North was still insurgent, and the Church conspiring. The Vice-Rector of a Seminary, and the Canon of Porto Cathedral were detained. A former Minister of Marine, Azevedo Countinho was also linked but smuggled himself out of the country.[99] The 18th Infantry

Regiment had to be dispatched from Vila Real to Chaves where arms were seized and fifty arrests made. The opposition press was implicated there, so a press crackdown followed. Journalists were arrested and the offices of both O Dia and A Nacão were wrecked.[100] In Viana do Castelo, several soldiers of the Fifth Artillery Regiment were arrested. The sacking of two Spanish Governors in Orense and Pontevedra suggested they may have been assisting conspiring Portuguese Royalists.[101]

The Government insisted they were in control and that conspiracy was rooted outside of Portugal. Brazil was always a suspected home of Royalist intrigue. A round-up of the usual Royalist suspects began. On the other wing, another incompetent home chemist was arrested. Joaquim Oliveira survived, but he retained only part of his left hand. The other part, along with his right, was dispersed around his domestic bomb factory in Sete Moinhos, near Lisbon, which had exploded.[102] Bell expected Dona Constança Telles da Gama to be arrested again, so he paid a friendly call and found her still at liberty.[103] His choice of friends did not help him avoid becoming one of the hunted. His wires to London for the 23rd and 24th were 'delayed in transmission', a euphemism for being censored. His last wire of 24 October was insubstantial, reporting on the search for suspects and the pending reorganisation of the police.

On the morning of 27th, the *Post* reported Bell's arrest, it later transpired, 'on a charge of defaming the Portuguese Government and participating in the recent plot against the Costa Administration.'[104] There seems to have been no direct communication with the *Post* by the Portuguese Government. It was left to learn of the arrest from Reuters' correspondent in Lisbon, who had picked up the news in *O Mundo*. Assuming this was from the edition of 26 October, then it is likely Bell had been arrested the day before, the 25th. This is also suggested by the fact that he had been free to wire his report dated the 24th. He was not detained for long. The *Post* reported on the 29th that he had been released. If he was freed the day before, 28 October, then he had been in prison for a maximum of three days (25–28 October). It is likely that the hunger strike took up the first twenty-four hours, after which he was transferred to military barracks prior to the intervention of the British Legation.

The documents the police took from Bell's house seem to have been letters from Royalists. The *Post* conceded he had corresponded with them but 'only with the object of arriving at the truth on some point of interest to our readers, not . . . with any intention of conspiring against the Government.'[105] The offending article, 'Danger of Sudden Arrest', turned into a self-fulfilling prophecy, as Bell became a character in his own story. In it he argued the Government was bringing plots upon itself through relentless, unevidenced persecutions. He repeated his view that the Government were just storing up trouble in the shape of an unholy alliance between Monarchists and the Radical Left.[106]

The *Post* let fly with a piece of pompous, neo-colonial paternalism. It was one thing to deny Portuguese journalists their freedom of speech, 'it must not be true of a British subject in Portugal.'[107] On release, and possibly on the good advice of his employers, he opted for a period of silence. His next day-to-day report on Portuguese politics, was not wired until 13 November, and was published on the 15th. In between, the *Post* took him out of the front line by publishing a long reflective piece on the Portuguese character. This enhanced his scholarly reputation, whilst keeping him out of prison.[108]

The elections on 16 November were the first on the new reduced franchise. Costa won an increased majority despite contesting them amidst courts martial and mass arrests.[109] Bell returned to the frontline to condemn this 'Latin politics,' defined as elections designed to produce a foregone conclusion. Since his release, a balance of power between press and government had been restored. His piece was neither censored nor delayed, and he was still a free man.[110] He chanced his arm by denouncing Portugal as a one-party state.[111] Democrats' harassment of the opposition, he said, extended even to the shores of Britain. Dona Julia de Brito e Cunha had been arrested, again, for smuggling nursing materials into the *Aljube*. Neither had the elections quietened discontent. A labourer digging in Graça (Lisbon) had been blown up when his spade hit a concealed bomb;[112] and thirty bombs and a large supply of dynamite had been discovered in a house in Porto.[113]

The municipal elections of 30 November confirmed the parliamentary result of 16th. Far from producing moderation, his newly won majority saw Costa announce a tough programme. The police were to be reorganized and new prisons built. But this was assuaged by relaxation in the Lisbon *Penitenciária*, where the solitaries were being allowed limited fraternisation.[114] Bell sympathized with Machado Santos' attempt to unite the opposition parties against the Democrats, but passed over their lack of a majority in the Senate – an important constitutional restraint. In highlighting the Democrats' electoral rigging, he neglected the structural factors assisting them. The clientelist system advantaged whatever party was in power because it controlled patronage. The Democrats were historically well organized. Many voted for 'stability' after a period of almost permanent revolution.[115]

Almeida reintroduced his Amnesty Bill, from April, designed to free all but the leaders of conspiracies.[116] Bell reported an ambivalent

Government forced towards an amnesty, while still arresting and transporting opponents. Costa continued to warn all enemies that they would continue to be 'watched by friends of the Republic.' The watchers, presumably, included the two thousand 'White Ants' the Civil Governor of Lisbon admitted were employed as government spies.[117]

Bell knew pressure had to be maintained, so there were no good news days for Portugal in the *Post*. A negative discourse was maintained, particularly through vitriolic parliamentary exchanges. The political crisis was exacerbated by a railway strike. As a mass modern union of semi and unskilled workers, the railwaymen were untypical in Portugal. Imported syndicalist ideas circulated within, but never overcame the materialist focus on wages and working conditions. Bell avoids these, selectively citing the strike as evidence of political instability. His railway strike is symbolic of the train crash that Costa's government is heading for. The strike began, peacefully, becoming violent only after early arrests for sabotage. The railway system was militarized and the Cascais to Lisbon train had armed guards aboard when it was bombed amidst a shoot-out.[118] Bell was unable to collect his post or English newspapers. Sympathetic action by other workers followed as Lisbon taxi drivers, compositors and cork factory workers all came out. The tramcars kept running, though, along streets forcibly cleared by cavalry.[119] Bell dwells on the violence, neglecting the causes of the strike and its syndicalist character.

This is disappointing for the historian, as the railway strike was one of three reasons behind the fall of the Costa Government in January, 1914. The second was its failure to deliver the amnesty. But the immediate cause was party political strife. Costa was embroiled in conflict with the Senate where he did not have a majority. He called for the resignation of its leader, Goulart de Medeiros, who demanded the President dismiss the Government because it had violated the Constitution. Parliamentary deadlock persuaded President Arriaga to meet Medeiros' demand, with doubtful constitutional legitimacy.[120] The crisis saw Medeiros resign along with Costa.[121]

Bell could scarcely conceal his delight at the removal of the great amnesty blocker. He had been arguing vociferously that public opinion would accept nothing less than 'all the prisoners without a single exception.' Cleverly, he presented it as a deal everybody would benefit from, even the *Carbonária* who had nothing to lose but a bad reputation.[122] He sympathizes with President Arriaga's concern at the delay of the Budget.[123] Arriaga tried but failed to form a minority administration under the Evolutionists, so when Costa finally resigned Arriaga substituted 'a ministry of conciliation'. This first had to pass the

Budget, then to amend the law of public worship, and finally, introduce the amnesty.[124] Bernardino Machado was summoned from Brazil as a conciliatory replacement prime minister. He had been Minister in Rio de Janeiro since 1912, after Arriaga defeated him for the Presidency. From Rio, he advocated an amnesty and deporting exiles to Brazil. Arriaga needed all his diplomatic skills, for the day after Costa resigned his supporters exchanged gun shots with their opponents in Lisbon's Rua Carmo. Worse, a bomb exploded injuring ten people.[125]

Bell deeply distrusted the Democrats. He suspected they planned to provoke a constitutional crisis by the end of the parliamentary session in April. His lack of confidence in Machado proved misplaced, however, when an inexperienced administration of independents was cobbled together. With a pro-amnesty Prime Minister at its head, the release of political prisoners was at last assured. Machado introduced the bill into Parliament, himself, on 19 February, but it fell short of a total amnesty covering:

> all political offenders, tried and sentenced, who are in confinement or expatriated, except the leaders in question. Persons still awaiting trial will be released, but the Courts will decide as soon as possible whether they are to come under the amnesty or be exiled ... The amnesty includes crimes of rebellion, those against the Separation of Church and State Law, those of threats or disobedience against the authorities, of abuse of power, and of breaches of the Press Law, but does not apply to persons who used dynamite or committed offences against the person. Persons guilty of desertion and mutiny are covered by the amnesty, but officers and non-commissioned officers guilty of such offences will be expelled from the army.[126]

The Bill went through by one hundred and two votes to twenty-four. The Lisbon press estimated it amnestied about 3,000 prisoners.[127] Around one thousand, seven hundred were returning émigrés; another 572 were awaiting trial; the remaining seven hundred or so prisoners were released from 23 February. Bell entered into the spirit of conciliation, urging sceptics to accept the price of exile for the few who had admitted conspiracy. Resigned to its permanence, he hoped the amnesty 'will mark the beginning of a second and more peaceful phase of the Republic.'[128]

Not all 'Locusts' shared Bell's magnanimity. Lord Lytton, Chairman of the BPC, called the Amnesty 'a new engine of coercion.'[129] Although welcome, it was flawed compared with the complete amnesty Palmerston secured in 1847. Furthermore, Britain must exercise vigilance to ensure the released were not re-arrested and tried by courts martial. There was an entirely new and insidious power of banishment that could be used to keep out those exiles who had fled under suspicion of conspiracy, but had never been tried or imprisoned. Lytton's forensic eye settled on the Amnesty's exemption of the *Carbonária* and 'White Ants'. Excused were all those who might have been guilty of 'threats or public provocations of crime.' Lytton expressed the BPC's scepticism over the Amnesty, beneath which lay a subliminal discourse about untrustworthy Portuguese.

The Amnesty did not bring about the political reconciliation that Bell and Machado hoped for. Monarchists, and some conservative Republicans, agitated for the release of the remaining eleven deportees. 'White Ants' anticipated redundancy in a new political world without arbitrary arrest. Nevertheless, 23 February 1914 was a joyful day for many. Forty-eight prisoners walked out of the *Penitenciária* even before midnight chimed. A hundred more walked out of the *Limoeiro*, and five women accompanied Dona Julia de Brito e Cunha out of the *Aljube*. Another hundred – officers and rank and file soldiers – walked free from the *Trafaria* and *São Jorge* prisons.

The Syndicalists on the railways celebrated the Amnesty by derailing a goods train.[130] At 1 a.m. on the morning of the 25th two more bombs exploded at Rossio station in Lisbon. No-one was hurt, which was fortunate as many were awaiting the late arrival of trains from the North.[131] The next day passengers were advised that tickets were issued at their own risk, but there was no service to and from the North, anyway. Lisbon to Paris was taking four days. Sabotage had extended into Spain, causing passengers to have to change six times.[132] Bell went to Madrid, from where he had been tipped off about an expected swoop upon seventy-eight Portuguese nationals in Cadiz, suspected of Syndicalist conspiracy on the railways.[133]

After the Amnesty, the 'White Ants' finally began to be trodden on. The Senate had appointed a committee of inquiry into the conduct of the Lisbon Police, at the end of 1913. It reported in mid-March 1914. The 'White Ants' seemed to be crawling from under the door of the Civil Governor of Lisbon, Daniel Rodrigues, who had set them up illegally. The trail went back to Daniel's brother, the former Minister of the Interior. Neither was under arrest at the end of March, but João Borges, the chief 'Ant', was accused of organising the attack on the Ginásio Theatre the previous June. Other charges relating to illegal arrests were pending.[134] Without arbitrary arrest and political imprisonment to nourish them, Bell hoped the infestation would be extinguished as the shadow-state withered. This proved optimistic, even naïve. The nest was not in the Civil Governor's office, or even in the Ministry of the Interior. Nests were embedded throughout the social fabric of urban Portugal. They multiplied where there was underemployment, and a black market in arms kept from army service or the events of 1910.[135] For Aubrey Bell, they were criminals for hire; for revolutionaries, vigilantes defending the Republican state. Bell thought it time for them to disappear beneath the cracks. But they never really went away. Ants never do. They just slipped under the boots of the *Carbonária* as it retreated into the shadows of quasi-legality.[136]

After the Amnesty, Bell briefly recovered his optimism and made a plea for conciliation. Although the Republic had been a blunder, now it had a second chance of pursuing moderation. Censorship had ended. There were individual signs of hope. Dr Gama Pinto, dismissed for employing nuns as nurses, had been re-instated. In return, Royalists should put the welfare of the country above love for the Crown. Bell acknowledges Republicans' distrust of 'England' whose campaign they thought driven by religious opponents. Even some Royalists suspected the old ally 'wishes to foster anarchy in Portugal in order to seize the Portuguese colonies.'[137] Bell thought the best way to avoid the sale of colonies was to improve the national finances, and that could only come from moderate government.

By the summer, Bell's optimism had evaporated and he reported a return to politics as normal. He doubted whether there really was 'a new spirit in Portugal' because 'the Democrats and *Carbonário* had been attempting to fasten some new conspiracies on the Royalists, as a pretext for their arrest or rearrest.'[138] He had hoped that the amnesty might help unite the nation, but nothing had really changed.

8 Looking back from 1915

In June 1915, a year or so after the Amnesty, Bell published *Portugal of The Portuguese*, an attempt to place the Republic within the context of Portuguese cultural history. The Republic is presented as a distortion trying to rush a traditional culture of unchanging *mores* into an unwelcoming twentieth century. This was consistent with the arguments of *In Portugal* three years before. Bell was a traditionalist but his Lusophile scholarship discerning enough to reject national stereotyping. He respected rather than idealized the peasant. Conversely, he rose above characterisations of the urban Portuguese 'with a pistol in one pocket and a bomb in another.'[139]

Bell's Anglicanism colours his treatment of the religious question. But his core argument is that anti-clericalism was self-defeating. It had only produced counter-reaction, such as the early stages of the social Catholicism that attracted the young Salazar. Even more reactionary, *Integralismo Lusitano*, founded in 1913, was constructing an imitative fascism for the 1920s.[140] Bell praised the fresh new ideas of the young Integralists.[141] His establishmentarian instinct wanted to repeal the Laws of Separation, but that was to hope for too much.

In *Portugal of the Portuguese*, Bell is working towards a theory of the Republican state underpinned by a triad of forces. The first is traditional: a centralism, that went all the way back to Pombal.[142] Consolidation of the Republican state depended upon reproducing the narrow factional dominance that had characterized the Monarchy. He views the central control of elections given by the 1911 Constitution as constructed for the same ends. But he cannot explain how a constitution fashioned for one-party dictatorship, turned Costa out.

The *Carbonária* was the second, unconstitutional pillar of Bell's triad. He doubted such a structurally-embedded, quasi-legal state agent could be removed democratically. Originally founded in 1823, in imitation of the Italian *risorgimento*, its rise paralleled Republicanism's advance from the 1890s. Bell thought it had become endemic. Clad in antique black suits embellished with flowing black ties, he estimated there were some forty thousand members throughout the country. Some came from local *Carbonária* associations; others, from Radical clubs; still others, from the far left of anarchism. Bell was even more incensed by their affiliates, the 'White Ants.' As illegitimate state actors, some of whom were murderers, they should be stood down.

The third of the triad of forces was the press. *O Mundo* was the voice of the ruling party which, combined with repression of the opposition, provided Democrat control of the national discourse. Bell also identified the influence of the *Carbonária*'s own newspaper *Atta Venda*, ignored by most other British sources. It campaigned hard against both the Amnesty and the return of exiled bishops.

Portugal of the Portuguese is open to a double reading, as both survey of Portuguese cultural history and critique of the Republic's early years. It reflects Bell's literary, academic interests, while elucidating his journalism. It is a text written at a pivotal moment in Portuguese history, before the Republic seemed permanent. Like Bragança-Cunha, Bell struggles with change, measuring the present against the past and finding it wanting. Nostalgia is the covert discourse. At the same time he is resigned to loss – of Monarchy and Empire, if not quite the Church. But tradition is secured by culture: rich poetry and drama, written in a pure language without fear of its modern assassin, journalism. Bell is certainly no 'Whig.' His realism refuses any linear curve of historical progress. An amnesty was necessary because political imprisonment had got worse since the Monarchy in a degenerate state in which illegitimate agencies dispensed arbitrary justice. *Portugal of the Portuguese* can be read as a biting critique of the First Republic. But it is also a labour of love.

9 Bell the Locust

When Aubrey Bell coined 'The Locusts' metaphor he did so inclusively. He shared that group identity. As a journalist, he kept a certain professional distance from the British Campaign. But leaders like the Duchess of Bedford acknowledged their debt to him, illustrating how he acted as a bridgehead between metropole and semi-periphery. 'Locusts' like Bell flew just below the radar of formal diplomacy, enabling a critical discourse within informed public opinion. His journalism can be read as the bearer of the neo-colonial ideology of the metropole: patriarchal, entitled, condescending in his 'othering' of the subaltern. But, at the same time, ambiguity constantly breaks through. His representation of British neo-colonialist ideology was mediated by personal agency, particularly his Lusophilia.

This is more evident in his two early books than his journalism. Bell is already a published scholar on route to becoming the outstanding Lusophile intellectual of his age. *In Portugal* and *Portugal of the Portuguese* merely signpost the finest body of Lusophone scholarship by an Englishman before Charles Boxer.[143] Bell was twenty-nine when he arrived in Portugal in 1908. The decision to relinquish the career path that had led to the British Museum, for the lower status, dual identity of journalist and itinerant scholar must have been difficult. But, once made, he never looked back. He had merely cut his teeth on 'Costa's Law,' but all the amnestied political prisoners freed on that fateful morning of 23 February 1914 owed him a debt of gratitude.

CHAPTER

7

The Secretary

1 'Unexpected Activities'

When Eva Mabel Tenison moved, with her two aunts,[1] into Yokes Court, in the village of Frinsted, near Sittingbourne, Kent, in the early part of 1912, she anticipated a quiet life. Within weeks, however, the Tudor manor house was to become the joint centre of operations for the British Protest. The other was 51 Berkeley Square, London residence of Adeline, Duchess of Bedford. Mab, as she was always known to family and friends, was a 32-year-old spinster, bearer of a fragile beauty laced with an antiquated preference for Victorian costume, according to an old friend.[2] Her appearance spoke both of her love of history – she authored a multi-volume History of Elizabethan England – and of her profound conservatism. As a proud Tory she was uneasy with the radicalism of the pre-war Liberal Government. She clung, through her Anglican Royalism, to an imagined past, when all that was dear to her felt more secure.

She remained at Yokes Court for forty years. By 1952 she had a reputation as an old-fashioned, dilettante historian more typical of the nineteenth century to which Philip Gibbs thought she belonged. When Yokes Court burnt down in 1952, destroying many of her personal papers and the last two volumes of her history of Elizabethan England, she resolved to retrieve what she could by writing an autobiography. From her sanctuary at Hedingham Hall, Essex, where she was given rooms by a friend, she pieced her life-story back together. Much was completed by 1954, but it has remained unpublished since her death in 1961. An early section of nearly two hundred pages of typed manuscript deals with her period as secretary of the British Protest between 1912 and 1914.[3] For the historian, it presents the familiar problems of autobiographies. The greatest is the inclusion of much reported speech, which she admits elsewhere she no longer had the documentation for as her diaries were lost in the fire.[4] The memoir is partial and selective, like all such sources. At a distance of forty years, the septuagenarian Tenison was calling upon a memory she admitted was fading. These methodological concerns aside, her memoir remains an invaluable source for this history. It fills in gaps left by other sources, notably in respect of exiled Royalist involvement in the Campaign. In the absence of evidence of BPC meetings, it provides the best surviving account from inside that Campaign. It has proved a unique source. Reading *Unexpected Activities* is like entering a time-machine taking one back through the old wooden doors of the Yokes Court that perished in the fire of 1952. From Sittingbourne station, British, Portuguese and Austrian royalists come and go at a pace. It glows with commitment to a cause that Tenison was still able, in 1954, to bring alive with erudite prose.

Tenison was born in Liverpool in 1880 of a distinguished Anglo-Irish family. Her father, a barrister, had adopted the surname by royal charter as the descendant of Archbishop Tenison. Eva Mabel cherished her family history, although not her father from whom she was estranged before 1914. She remained in touch with her mother. Charles McCarthy Tenison seems to have disapproved of his daughter's political activities and cut off her allowance, although the problem may have begun before 1912. This was how she came to be living with, and apparently supported by, her maternal aunts at Yokes Court.

2 'Less than dust' kicks up a storm

On 17 September 1912, the three ladies had a distinguished visitor. Canon Harford was dropping in on his way from Wells to visit family at nearby Goodnestone Hall. Mab Tenison noticed a letter published in the *Daily Mail* he had left in the hall. It was from the novelist Dorothea Gerard,[5] whom she had known slightly before her marriage. Dorothea became Madame Longard de Longgarde, wife to an Austrian cavalry officer. The letter complained of the treatment of a Portuguese officer, Dom João d'Almeida, formerly of her husband's regiment. Almeida was imprisoned alongside murderers in Lisbon's *Penitenciária*, having been captured during the Couceiro rebellion of 1911.[6] Madame de Longgarde appealed to British readers to support prisoner of war status for such men.

Over dinner, Canon Harford expressed doubts that a Conservative newspaper like the *Mail* would obtain any joy from a radical government lacking compassion for Royalist prisoners. He urged Tenison to get on with her own work[7] and not get involved on their behalf. The Canon had made her feel 'less than dust.'[8] Despite this, she felt conscience-bound to respond to an Englishwoman's call. But there was also another pull towards Portugal. Tenison's uncle (on her mother's side), Vincent Ashlin, had married Maraiana Clementina de Moura, before becoming the Portuguese Minister to Argentina under the Monarchy. He later served in Brazil.[9] The family connection with Portugal promoted a lifetime interest in the country and the Monarchy her uncle had served.

Madame de Longgarde appears to have been alerted to Almeida's case from a letter that a friend had passed on to the Austrian newspaper *Zeit*. Almeida complained he had to wear convict clothes and was confined to a tiny cell with little light. But there was worse:

Upon my breast and upon my back the number 279 is branded . . . shall never forget the unfortunates and the souls in purgatory . . . name me in your prayers, whether I be among the living or the dead.[10]

Madame de Longgarde's shock that such things were done in a Christian country, betrayed an ignorance of the Republic's secularism. She does, though, acknowledge sympathy might be short for a rebel caught in the act. But she sought sympathy through relating the painful end to Almeida's career as an officer. His horse ran into a fence and performed a somersault during a steeplechase. He was unconscious for a week and left with long-term cerebral shock, impaired eyesight and double vision. As Madame de Longgarde said, it was a mystery how he was able to take part in an invasion.[11] The more discerning *Daily Mail* reader, reading against the grain, might have found a desperate Couceiro recruiting weak-headed, pensioned-off officers counting twice as many Republicans as there really were. Tenison was unconcerned about that, and responded eagerly to her friend's call for a press campaign.[12]

Tenison was a consummate networker. Through two contacts, she had Madame de Longgarde's letter reach the Duke of Norfolk. The nation's senior Catholic aristocrat shared Canon Harford's doubts about a radical government and the immovability of the Foreign Office. His stonewalling just made Tenison more determined not to be treated like dust. She was a high church Anglican, with very good Catholic connections. One was Bertha, Countess de Torre Diaz (1848–1925)[13], entitled through marriage to a Spanish nobleman. But Tenison met with an equally negative response from her. The realisation had dawned that Almeida's could not be an isolated case. Through a mutual acquaintance she was put in touch with a London friend of Madame de Longgardes's. Lady Goodenough, formerly the Austrian Countess Anna Kinsky, and the widow of a British General,

144 | *The Secretary*

invited Mab for tea. Her Ladyship confirmed that many innocents, like Almeida, languished at the Republic's pleasure. She encouraged Tenison to expose the facts about Portugal's reign of terror, because the British Government was turning a blind eye. Tenison had found an aristocratic supporter, albeit a foreigner confined to a role behind the scenes.

Tenison swallowed a little pride and took up a luncheon invitation to the Diaz residence. She opted for a high-risk strategy. In a Spanish household, she diplomatically persuaded the family that old national antagonisms with Portugal should be put aside. At stake was the defence of aristocracy itself. Conservatives needed to stand up to Grey's radicalism. She gambled again, and explicitly linked the matter to Anglo-German relations. Mab's brother Julian was a naval officer, anti-German, and a friend of the Diaz family.[14] She ruthlessly exploited this advantage, arguing the Germans had had a forty-year plan to capture Britain's place in the sun. If war occurred and the Kaiser treated British officers as convicts, what defence would there be if they had done nothing to assist the Portuguese? Her Germanophobia in the memoir smacks of the wisdom of hindsight. But the gamble paid off. The Countess was convinced and promised to help in any way she could, leaving Mab exultant.[15]

But she was at a loss as to how to proceed. Julian wasn't much use, except to urge her to get going before war broke out. The best she could think of was to go back to Canon Harford who had relatives in the Lords. Before having to resort to that, however, a stroke of luck befell her. The mother of the architect who had renovated Yokes Court, Mrs Ionides, knew the Second Earl of Lytton and mentioned Tenison's need of help. Lytton's father had been at the British Legation in Lisbon before becoming Viceroy of India. Here was someone, a reformist Tory, with both the pedigree and political clout she needed. She rashly allowed herself to think that the prisoners would soon be free. Then *realpolitik* broke in: 'this was to underrate the obstructive habits of His Majesty's Ministers.'[16]

3 The Networking of 'Senhor Tenison'

Tenison had great hopes of meeting Lytton, in January 1913, but he went down with influenza. She tried to exploit the Tenison family connection by visiting Lambeth Palace, but the Archbishop fobbed her off with his chaplain. He could not understand why she, an Anglican, would bother with persecuted Catholics abroad. She was equally frustrated by the Portuguese exiles around the Countess de Torre Diaz.

Tenison's Network

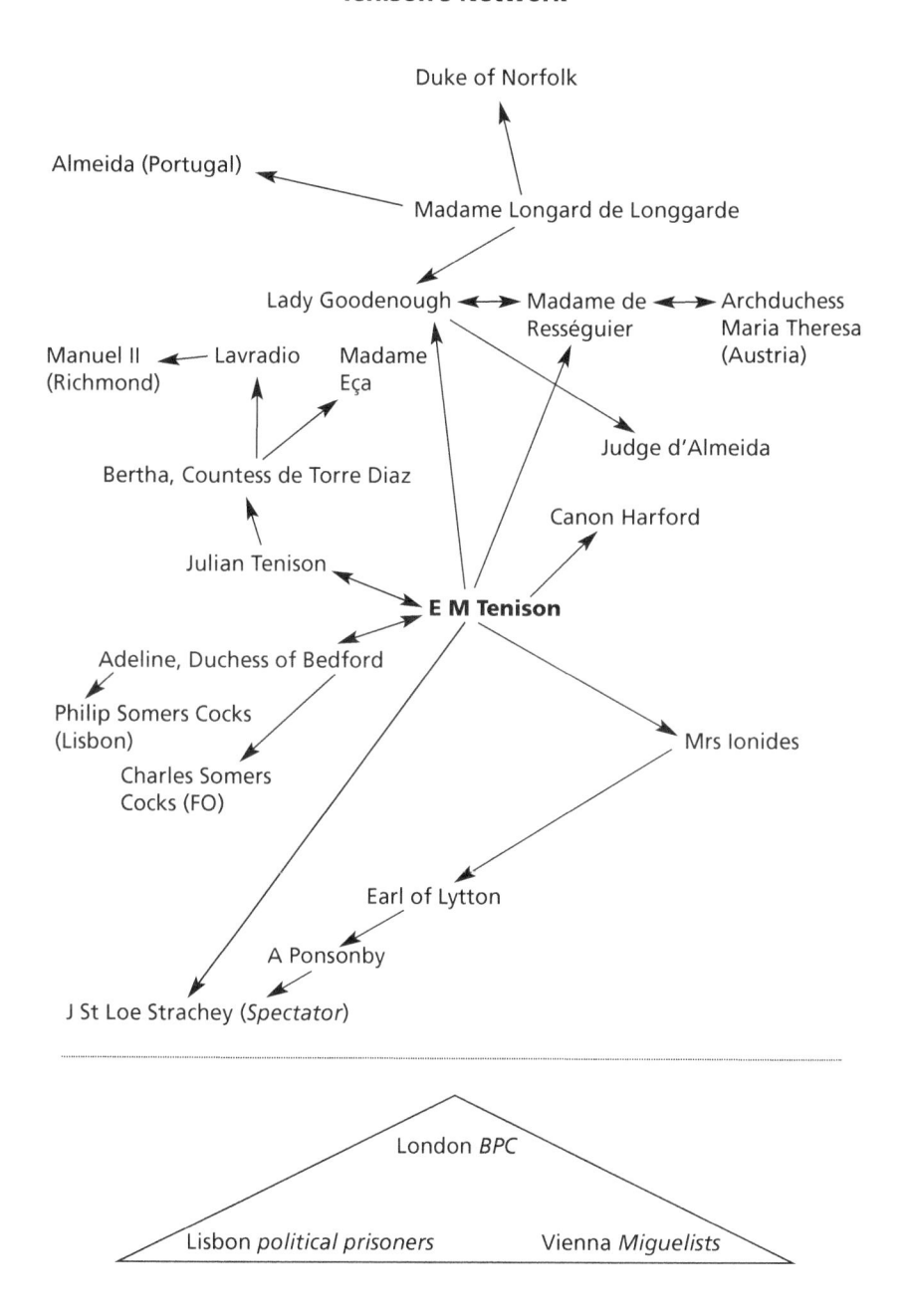

- Duke of Norfolk
- Almeida (Portugal)
- Madame Longard de Longgarde
- Lady Goodenough ↔ Madame de Rességuier ↔ Archduchess Maria Theresa (Austria)
- Manuel II (Richmond) ← Lavradio
- Madame Eça
- Judge d'Almeida
- Bertha, Countess de Torre Diaz
- Canon Harford
- Julian Tenison
- **E M Tenison**
- Adeline, Duchess of Bedford
- Philip Somers Cocks (Lisbon)
- Charles Somers Cocks (FO)
- Mrs Ionides
- Earl of Lytton
- A Ponsonby
- J St Loe Strachey (*Spectator*)

London *BPC*

Lisbon *political prisoners* — Vienna *Miguelists*

The Marquis of Lavradio was the nephew of the imprisoned Almeida. But she found Lavradio 'supercilious' and 'perplexing.'[17] He was unconcerned about his uncle, a Miguelist, because he served the Manueline court in exile at Richmond. Lavradio sought to avoid offending the Portuguese Government. Tenison was put out: 'Was Portugal offended when Wellington saved your country from Napoleon?'[18] Senhora de Queirós, Eça's widow,[19] virtually accused Tenison of being a press infiltrator.

Lytton had to recuperate abroad, but before he left he recommended using Arthur Ponsonby, the author of *The Decline of Aristocracy* as Parliamentary spokesman.[20] Ponsonby's pacifism and anti-aristocratic views earned him a left-wing reputation within the Liberal Party. He could hardly have been further from Tenison's high Toryism. Lytton suggested Tenison write a pamphlet about the Campaign, and convinced her that Ponsonby was necessary to balance it. Madame de Longgarde's letter appeared in the *Daily Mail*, a Conservative newspaper, so a Liberal ally was needed to establish its cross-party credentials. Tenison met Ponsonby at the Commons, but he behaved as if Lytton had handed him a poisoned chalice. He fobbed her off with a letter of introduction to John St Loe Strachey, the editor of *The Spectator*. Strachey would not see her, but suggested she write a letter. The correspondence in *The Spectator* proved a breakthrough because it amplified the issue beyond the small coterie of Portuguese exiles and sympathizers. *The Spectator* had long conducted a vigorous debate over 'Portuguese Slavery'; now political prisoners joined its agenda.

The British Committee of Residents in Portugal had first raised the treatment of the political prisoners in the February before Tenison read the letter in the *Daily Mail*. It had been specifically established to report on why 'Lisbon is once more in a state of siege.' The prisons were so full that the newly arrested were being detained on ships. Sir Arthur Hardinge came out of the report badly. He had stonewalled over claims of excessively filthy and punitive conditions until he was forced to make personal visits. Even then he 'whitewashed' them.[21] Amongst the imprisoned were Catholics suffering religious persecution, for example a law student punished for reading passages from a life of Christ.[22]

The matter was raised in the Commons in March when Joseph Devlin,[23] the Irish Parliamentary Party MP, questioned the Secretary of State for Foreign Affairs. In an impassioned intervention Devlin claimed that fifteen and sixteen year-olds were among the unjustly imprisoned. Older prisoners were subjected to physical humiliations. Men were condemned to 'filthy and verminous' conditions on the evidence of 'notorious perjurers.' Rigid press censorship prevented information on such injustices leaving Portugal. But, strangely, Devlin did not demand release, only 'relaxation of the treatment.'

Sir Francis Acland (Parliamentary Under-Secretary of State for Foreign Affairs) provided the standard diplomatic reply that Britain could not intervene in the affairs of a foreign country.[24] On 5 March 1912 Grey, himself, questioned by Joseph King[25] and James Hope,[26] replied similarly.[27] On 11 March, Acland was questioned again, by Mark Sykes,[28] who asked 'whether ... reports published in the British Press concerning the treatment of political prisoners in Portuguese gaols and fortresses are without foundation?' Acland stonewalled: 'the prison administration of Portugal is an internal affair of the Portuguese Government.' None of this encouraged Tenison, so she resorted to exaggeration. The Portuguese prisoners were worse off than the French in 1793. Death was preferable to indefinite detention in rat-infested dungeons. Hooded prisoners in tiny cells with little light went mad in 'living tombs.' The Monarchy had treated political prisoners better than the Republic, and Britain's failure to protest condoned 'the fanaticism of the *Carbonária.*'[29]

Adeline, Duchess of Bedford, sister in law of the Duke, read the letter. On 13 February, 'E.M. Tenison Esqre.' received a commendatory, handwritten missive from her, enveloped with the ducal coronet. (It was not the only time that Mab was to be mistaken for a man during the Campaign).[30] There is certainly a hint in her memoir that she took advantage of the gender confusion during its early stages. The Duchess assumed Tenison had a plan of campaign and invited 'him' to share it over lunch at 51 Berkeley Square. We do not know whether the lady in a frock who emerged out of the peasouper of a London fog disappointed. But the evidence she presented matched what the Duchess had heard from the wife of her cousin Philip Somers Cocks, Consul in Lisbon. The Duchess fulfilled all the hopes of leadership Tenison placed in her. She would go to Lisbon, stay with the Somers Cockses, and exploit her status as Home Office Visitor of Prisons to gain access to the *Penitenciária* and *Limoeiro*. Tenison sycophantically contrasted her response to the defeatism she had encountered:

> And here was the Duchess Adeline taking for granted that the evils must not be ignored. That she was the most regal looking mortal I had ever seen, increased my peculiar feeling that there was destiny behind all of this.[31]

Luncheon networking was enriched by the arrival of a further Somers Cocks; yet another cousin, this time from the Foreign Office.

Charles, however, adhered to the official line. Anxious to keep on good terms with Portugal he ruled out intervening. This brought out the neo-colonialist in Tenison, who asked him since when had the great British Empire taken to prostrating itself at the feet of a little Latin Republic. She invoked a favourite historical precedent of intervention during the Peninsular War. The Duchess indulged her new friend's history lesson to her cousin. The two women had discovered a shared youthful admiration for Marie Antoinette. Tenison now had a mature heroine; a pedigreed prison reformer prepared to go to Lisbon. Their first meeting ordained Tenison as Secretary-in-waiting, and she departed feeling she had known the Duchess all her life.

Tenison confesses she felt like a small woman in the man's world of 1912–14. Yet, she was overawed by the Duchess's leadership qualities that made Tenison feel in little need of a role for herself. This might have led her to reflect on Julian's opinions of the Suffragettes. He saw no need for women to descend into politics when they were already the superior sex by courtesy of the benefits conferred by 'Christian chivalry.' Mab Tenison was wrestling with a complex, gendered identity. She admired the Duchess as a woman, but agreed with Julian that the struggle for the vote could not be allowed to swamp their campaign. This ambivalence led her to go along with the mis-gendered identity. She contrasts the 'furious diatribes from the Lisbon press' against 'Senhor Tenison,'[32] with the courtesy she received from men in Britain who knew she was a woman.

3 Aristocrats

Strachey's insistence that she write to *The Spectator* thrust Tenison into the public spotlight, exposing both her gender and her history. Aubrey Bell was doubtful about the latter.[33] Thomas Glas Sandeman responded to her in defence of his cousin, Dona Julia Maria de Brito e Cunha, held for seven months awaiting trial and in delicate health.[34] Dona Julia was accused of funding ambulances, which Tenison had always thought politically neutral. Under interrogation, Dona Julia had refused to name any ambulance collaborators. 'Her only crime, apparently, is that she had the misfortune to be born an aristocrat,'[35] Tenison declared, making class prejudice, not ambulances, the issue. Aubrey Bell's championing of Dona Constança Telles da Gama showed this was no isolated case. She had experienced humiliation heaped upon injustice, imprisoned in a fetid cell alongside the lowest types of females who provoked the hoots of passing street boys – a clear example of anti-aristocratic prejudice, for the class warrior Tenison.

Once fully engaged in the Campaign, Tenison quickly connected to the Miguelist network active in England. She was close to Madame de Rességuier, sister of Lady Goodenough. Rességuier's grapevine ran through Archduchess Maria Theresa (of Bourbon-Bragança), and second wife of the Duke of Bragança, son of Miguel I and claimant to the Portuguese throne. She was born a German princess, the fifth child of Charles VI, Prince of Lowestein-Wertheim-Rosenberg in 1870. The Miguelist branch of the Braganças had been exiled since the 1830s and was long domiciled in Vienna. Miguel II had gone on to serve the Austrian monarchy as a Colonel in the 7th Austrian Regiment of Hussars. The Viennese connection Europeanized the British campaign. Money and contacts were supplied although, as Secretary, Tenison pleaded poverty.

Forty years later, she still veiled the exiles' involvement. This is explained by her continuing friendship into the 1950s with the Duke of Bragança, who subscribed to support the publication of her history of Elizabethan England.[36] The Duke was, by then, the recognized claimant to the Portuguese throne. After Manuel II died without heir in 1932, the claimancy passed to the Miguelist line. In 1950 the Salazar regime allowed a return from exile, but a serious car accident delayed the Duke's arrival in Portugal until 1952. His letters to Tenison through the 1950s are addressed from the house he inhabited once Salazar decided not to restore the monarchy after President Carmona's death in 1951: Casa São Marcos, near Coimbra.[37]

Madame de Rességuier was pulling Tenison's strings. She sent to Yokes Court a freelance journalist and former soldier with a Welsh name, whose identity Tenison withholds. He was convinced the Foreign Office would let Almeida die in prison, unless they bribed him out of jail (an easy practice in Latin countries!).[38] Tenison persuaded an American-Scottish friend, fortuitously in England at the time, to stump up the price in gold and notes. On the day of her first meeting with the Duchess of Bedford, Tenison was expecting a coded telegram from Gibraltar that Almeida had been sprung. She seems not to have considered the diplomatic implications of bringing him to London to promote the Campaign.

The jail-break was nipped in the bud by the Austrian Minister in Lisbon, Baron Kuhn. The Welshman managed to visit Almeida in the *Penitenciária*, but concluded he was unspringable. Kuhn tried to talk some sense into him. The only chance of releasing Almeida was to sweet talk Afonso Costa into it. Baroness Kuhn agreed to take personal responsibility for this more diplomatic strategy, as she indicated in a letter to Madame de Rességuier, who informed Tenison. However, diplomacy failed because Almeida refused to flatter 'the scoundrel

... the personal enemy of Christ. '[39] Baron Kuhn was unimpressed by Almeida's obstinacy and left him in the *Penitenciária*, to ponder his principles. Returning disappointed, the Welshman was keen to make a second attempt. Again financed by Tenison's rich associate, he became distracted by the charms of a Portuguese woman, instead. She offered to act in tandem with him, but Tenison smelt a rat and withdrew. *A Portuguesa* was later discovered to be a spy. Perhaps her new lover was too. Tenison seems unsure.

Francis McCullagh was more reliable. He was put in touch by Edgar Prestage, the English scholar of Portugal who lived in Lisbon. Julian had told her previously of McCullagh's fantastic adventures through the Russo-Japanese War of 1905, disguised as a Cossack. Knowing that McCullagh had been in Portugal in 1911, Tenison inquired about Almeida. McCullagh described him as a gallant fellow, like a Crusader from a nobler age. Although Tenison found McCullagh agreeably 'gentle, modest, shy,' she was warned off him as 'too sensational' by Lord Northcliffe.[40]

The Viennese Miguelist network made secret contact with the Campaign in London in spring, 1913. Duchess Adeline introduced Tenison to the Duke of Viseu. Tall, fair and elegant, she compared him to Prince Charlie. Perhaps his looks had won him the hand of Anita Murray, an American heiress of Scottish ancestry, in 1909. The marriage brought a high political price. He was the first son of the old claimant, Miguel II, but had effectively disqualified himself as Pretender by making a morganatic marriage. Because his half-brother Dom Duarte, was not even two years old then, the Duke of Viseu did not formally renounce his right to the succession until 1920.[41] Adeline had, however, declined to meet an anonymous 'Princess' who had also sought an interview with her. She may have been the Duke's stepmother, Archduchess Maria Theresa, herself.[42] Adeline, thought it too risky, because the imminence of the public meeting of 22 April required discretion. The 'Princess' proved perfectly understanding, and well-informed by the Duchess's letters to *The Times* and *Daily Mail*.

The Duke proved a more difficult customer. He slandered Grey for propping up uncivilized Lisbon tyrants who flouted all religion and morality. Tenison disapproved of Grey but assured the Duke that he could be brought round. The Duke was unappeasable, claiming most of the British press supported the Republicans, too. He clearly had not read much of it.

The Aeolian Hall public meeting proved a publicity triumph, although its chief agent, E. M. Tenison, took a back seat. We are not even sure if she was on the platform although, as a Committee member, it was to be expected. But she did not speak and is not mentioned in the press sources.

4 April in Paris: networking abroad

The Foreign Office disliked the Duchess's admiration for Aubrey Bell's journalism, and there were even rumours that 'the name covers a syndicate of five Portuguese at Richmond, in the pay of King Manuel.'[43] Tenison was detailed to prove Bell's existence. Fortunately, she knew his cousin, Mary Spring-Rice. *Bona fides* established, Bell was communicated with. In an incredible breach of protocol, the letter 'was to go in the Foreign Office bag under cover to Philip Somers Cocks at our Consulate.'[44] Bell was to read and destroy it on the spot. Tenison's memory is unclear from here. She says 'he read the letter' but took it home but 'before he had time to read it to the end' the *Carbonária* arrived. This is preposterous. Bell was not arrested until late October, 1913. The meeting was being planned for 22 April 1913. The author's memory fails her, confusing events six months apart. Other sources suggest Bell was arrested for possessing letters from Portuguese Royalists, not English ones. This throws into doubt Tenison's account of the whole episode.

Tenison interpreted the FO's policy of non-interference in Portuguese affairs as a lack of backbone. She solicited Francis McCullagh as a private envoy for the BPC to visit Lisbon prisons. 'No words at my command can adequately convey my indignation at what I have seen', he wrote in a published letter.[45] But he kept on trying. Unaware of his secret status, Philip Somers Cocks confided in him that he sympathized, but diplomacy came first. Lisbon in April was tense as all manner of rumours circulated. Tenison's favourite was that Afonso Costa had had a nervous breakdown requiring attendance by eight doctors.[46]

Tenison and Aunt Mabel went off to Paris to meet two exiled Monarchist ministers, Castello Branco and Aires de Ornellas. The two ladies stayed with family friends, Lys Forster and her sisters, long-standing residents in the Avenue de Longchamps. Lys was an artist who often wandered off to North Africa to paint Arabs. But painting Tenison defeated her because she had no permanent expression: 'one day of the 13th century and the next of the 18th, and never two days alike.'[47] The Tenisons met Portuguese exiles in the Forsters' house. Castello Branco was the first. No diplomat, he accused Lady Hardinge (wife of the British Ambassador in Lisbon) of accepting gifts of gold vases confiscated from churches, from Afonso Costa. Tenison reminded him Costa was an habitual liar. But Monarchist scepticism persisted. The British protest would fizzle out once the Duchess and friends had salved their consciences. Tenison's account has a gendered sub-text in which a pugnacious Portuguese male is forced to negotiate with two, single, English ladies on a political mission. The two Mabels were bullied, but the cause was greater than their indignation.

The two women received another male visitor, sent by Judge Azevedo. Tenison conceals his identity, but it was clearly Francisco Homem Cristo. Ex-officer, agnostic Republican, he had turned to editing O *Povo de Aveiro* out of exasperation.[48] Tenison asked him frankly if he could work with her, a Royalist and a Christian? They made a pact, in French. She got on better with him than with patrician aristocrats like Lavradio or Castello Branco. Politics was teaching her compromise and discrimination. There were agnostics, and agnostics. Give me the armchair scepticism of G. M. Trevelyan, 'neither militant nor dangerous', to Afonso Costa's 'active and venomous hatred of everything symbolised by Christianity', she wrote.[49] Homem Cristo was an agnostic with integrity, without the 'condescending superiority' she loathed. But Julian was unhappy about compromising with agnostics because 'they appeared to derive incongruous delight from a series of barren negations.'[50]

The Duchess of Bedford was in Paris, too. Privately, she met Tenison at the Hotel Meurice, on the site of the old Tuileries where the royal family had been imprisoned in 1789. The Duchess let slip she was resisting Tory Party pressure to drop the Portuguese agitation. Tenison reassured her that they were struggling for more than the freedom of one group of political prisoners. Paris affected Tenison as an historical site, deepening her sense of mission. The ghost of Marie Antoinette stalked the Hotel Meurice like an energising force.

5 Post-Paris

Paris was also the home of the exiled architect of the Portuguese Constitution, Cunha e Costa. But it was not there, but at Yokes Court that Tenison met him. She dissuaded him from publicly attaching himself to the BPC because he could be more useful as an independent critic. He might help dissolve some of the scepticism of the radical press. Many foreign sympathizers of the Campaign passed along the sleepy lanes of East Kent in 1913, to conspire against the Portuguese Government. One was a 'Princess' from Vienna.[51] Over luncheon, the two women compared grand theories of history. Tenison deferred to the 'Princess's' reading in several languages. But she was confident enough to argue they were part of a broader struggle against atheism, that would influence the world even more than the Kaiser's foreign policy. She placed this within the long-term crisis created by the French Revolution and its 'so-called democracy.'[52] This was compatible with the 'Princess's' moralistic view that history was made up of absolutes: truth against mendacity, justice against tyranny. But the short-term was practical. How to get the political prisoners released before a war broke out?

By summer 1913, Tenison's relationship with the Duchess of Bedford was so close that she was being invited to the latter's country house. Woodside, in Buckinghamshire, was built by John Russell, the first Earl of Bedford in 1530. There, Tenison admired the passing train of English aristocracy, but also made contacts more useful to the Campaign. One was Wilfred Ward of the *Dublin Review*, the Catholic publication that regularly aired the anti-Republican views of Portugal-watchers such as Francis McCullagh.

John Harris, the anti-slavery campaigner, was even more useful. He lent more support than most of the peers that had been approached. Yet, she still could not resist an implicitly racist jibe at the Liberal Nonconformist:

> Knowing as I did that he had toiled much in effort to bring about mitigation for "Portuguese slavery" of black men in the Portuguese colonial regions, it had occurred to me that he might extend his sympathies to white Portuguese at home whose predicament was actually far worse.[53]

Tenison met Harris at the rooms in South Eaton Place that she and Aunt Mabel used. Her concern was at the bad press the Campaign was receiving from the *Daily Chronicle*. Harris agreed to have a word with the leader writer, Harry Jones, but he warned that Jones hated Duchesses as much as grouse moors. Harris reassured her that Jones was still capable of sound judgement. But Harris's further suggestion proved vital to eventual success. She should urge Lytton to persuade the editor, Robert Donald,[54] to send a *Chronicle* correspondent to Portugal. The BPC should secretly pay the bill. So, it transpired that Philip Gibbs was employed to write the devastating critique of Portuguese prisons that also brought the *Daily Chronicle* to 'the front of the stage.'[55] Harris was confident that Gibbs' Catholicism would guarantee him to take on 'the agnostic terrorists' running Portugal. Invaluable publicity would be generated before the next public meeting. Lytton agreed to soft-soap the editor, while Tenison was to deal with Gibbs at Yokes.

The BPC raised the cash 'from different sympathisers at home and abroad.'[56] Some of these probably resided in Vienna, hidden behind Tenison's veil of discretion. Even the sceptical Duke of Norfolk sent the Duchess one hundred pounds. Lord and Lady Bute followed his example, alongside others 'amongst the most ancient and noble in England.'[57] Common folk like the children's writer Dorothea Moore, and her friend Daisy Lockwood were generous. Even Annie, the maid at Yokes, loaned her savings. That such contributions were gratefully accepted indicates how the Campaign was being run on a shoestring budget. Tenison shielded the Duchess from Campaign finances, sensitive to her always being badgered for charitable donations.[58]

It was a sceptical Philip Gibbs who arrived for lunch at Yokes Court to receive his instructions and expenses. The former were delivered with Tenison-like precision. He was to conceal the fact that he was a reporter. He was to visit the names on the list provided. He was also to go to the lunatic asylum where it was thought a number of prisoners, driven mad, were lodged.[59] He was not to confine himself to Lisbon but to visit provincial provisions, too. Perhaps Gibbs resented being spoken to like a servant. He retorted that he was quite prepared to disappoint 'the dear old Duchess' if he found she had exaggerated conditions. On the contrary, Tenison thought he would find she had understated the problem. Class tensions simmered between the aristocratic Anglican lady, recoiling at the rude manners of the middle class, Catholic journalist. She found Gibbs patronising, and admits she would rather have sent Francis McCullagh. So, she patronized Gibbs back by telling him not to 'eat official dinners and drink official wines' on expenses. Still, she sent him off with the fund collected for peasant prisoners, as well as his own expenses in notes and gold coinage. She dispatched a doubting Thomas, about to undergo a damascene conversion.

She welcomed back a convert but not a penitent, and one who spoke more to the triumph of experience over faith. Yet, she and Gibbs seem never to have been reconciled. It was a strictly working relationship. Her 1950s memoir is tainted with an opaque prejudice soured by a reading of Gibbs' autobiography of 1946. The relationship of 1913 is described in the full knowledge of his description of her as 'a strange little lady', of obsessively romantic temperament.[60] But worse was to follow when, 'Some while after 1917 I learnt that Philip Gibbs was describing me as denouncing Costa like a Russian aristocrat burning with indignation against Lenin.'[61] She had also read at least one of Gibbs' novels and been repelled by his depiction of county society as 'class war.'

Irritation with Gibbs' flamboyance made Tenison yearn for more of John Harris's pragmatism. It was he who urged a meeting with Grey, but the Foreign Secretary refused to discuss Portugal with the Duchess or Lord Lytton. Another foot in the Whitehall door was needed. As a last throw of the dice she turned to Henry Staveley-Hill[62] because she remembered he had confided during a cruise in 1900 that Grey sought his advice on Portuguese matters. She enticed him with a posted copy of *Portuguese Political Prisoners*, which he found irresistible. They lunched at the Commons. Staveley-Hill spoke to Grey, who agreed to formerly express concern to the Portuguese Government. But Tenison never trusted that the Liberal was not in the pocket of Costa's Government.

The sceptic Gibbs returned from Portugal a changed man. One would not glean this from his autobiography. Distressed, apologetic, and eager to make amends, he had not believed that 'a democratic Republic' could perpetrate the horrors he had seen. Tenison had no trouble believing. For her, atheism and horror were cause and effect. She forgave Gibbs his naivety and acknowledges the crucial role his articles in the *Chronicle* played. They were 'so excellent that our Committee decided to print them as a pamphlet,'[63] largely to get through to Conservatives who would not touch the *Chronicle* with a barge pole. The Campaign had quite as much trouble winning over Conservatives as Liberals. Arthur Balfour refused interest in Portuguese Royalists. So too, did Lord Robert Cecil, third son of the late Prime Minister Salisbury and Conservative MP for Marylebone North East. These Tories, remained perched on the same diplomatic fence as Edward Grey, Cecil's friend from Oxford. Tenison made several unsuccessful attempts, via Lytton, to recruit Cecil's star name. The Commons remained difficult terrain. Walter Guinness had been stonewalled by Grey on 10 April.[64] On 27 May, Grey remained unmoved when two Members compared Portuguese prisons to Russian.[65]

Undeterred, she turned her attention to an outright opponent, the editor of *The Westminster Gazette*, J. A. Spender, whose Catholicism she believed advantageous. The *Gazette* had a relatively small circulation before the War, but was particularly influential in London's political clubland, Tory as well as Liberal.[66] It entertained a fierce scepticism about the Campaign that resisted Tenison's entreaties. For example, it pointed out that in the week of the Aeolian Hall meeting four British policemen in India had been convicted of torturing prisoners in their care.[67] It later challenged Gibbs' reports, arguing prison conditions in Portugal were improving.[68] It was planned to seduce Spender through lunch with the Duchess at 51 Berkeley Square. But, fearing he was about to be presented with a libel suit, he sent his brother. Spender minor was delighted to find that, far from a writ, he received only an invitation – to the BPC's next meeting.

The charm offensive impacted upon Lambeth Palace, which had received copies of the BPC's pamphlets. The Archbishop of Canterbury offered to speak in the Lords on their behalf, but his chaplain was sent from Yokes with a flea in his ear. Tenison was offended by the Church's faint-heartedness, and had lined-up Lords Landsdowne and Mayo instead:

> I find it difficult to understand the morbid degree of caution embodied by the Archbishop in 1913, when bold initiative would have been more consistent with Christian chivalry than waiting till the eve of victory to offer assistance that was no longer necessary.[69]

But Tenison's refusal suited the Archbishop down to the ground. The Church could remain on the same fence as the British Government. By comparison, both Mayo and Tenison were living outside their comfort-zone. Each had received anonymous death threats from the same hand. Convinced it was the *Carbonária*, Mayo responded with a second speech in the Lords, wielding the threatening letter as primary evidence of Portuguese terror. Tenison published a second edition of *Portuguese Political Prisoners*, braving assassination with the confidence of another misgendered identity. Her letter had been sent in ignorance to 'Senhor Tenison.' The press was even more confused. Some conflated her with the 'five Portuguese Royalists at Richmond' who turned out not to be Aubrey Bell.[70]

John Harris put two useful networking suggestions to Tenison: his own Anti-Slavery Society, and the Howard Association, of which the Duchess was a long-standing member. On a cold winter's morning in London, Tenison went to see representatives of both and met with surprisingly frosty receptions. That resurrected her early doubts about Harris. A Liberal more concerned with black Portuguese than white, and Catholics, she gripes, discounting the many blacks who were also Catholics. She became equally cynical about that other Liberal, Philip Gibbs. His articles in the *Daily Chronicle* merely reiterated the exposures of the BPC's own pamphlets. This was unfair. It disregarded their much larger readership, and that Gibbs visited prisons beyond Lisbon. In addition, the Liberal *Chronicle*'s conversion left only the *Daily News* and *Manchester Guardian* clinging to Costa. Tenison preferred the journalism of the Frenchman Paul Vergnet, who wrote a series of pieces on 'The Terror in Portugal' in *La Libre Parole*, October to November, 1913.[71]

Tenison fell ill with acute neuritis[72] through early 1914. But, as the Campaign was building momentum, she ignored medical advice to rest in the warm. The second public meeting was arranged for the Westminster Palace Hotel and targeted directly at changing Foreign Office policy.[73] Unlike the crowded first, attendance was to be by invitation only. Places would be specially reserved for the growing numbers of Portuguese refugees flocking into London, including Homem Cristo who had assisted her in Paris. The Duchess implored Tenison to continue cultivating those sections of the Liberal press clinging to official non-intervention despite Gibbs' researches. As the Campaign's historian, Tenison was commissioned to write a declaimer, delivering a history lesson in the precedents for intervention. She rushed out a handwritten manuscript that Aunt Amy took to the printers in London at her own expense. The Portuguese Legation got wind of the impending *Will England Save Portugal?*, and tried unsuccessfully to intimidate the printers. But even before it could be published, its chief target, Costa, resigned.[74] Tenison praised the Duchess for not conceding to those who argued this pre-empted the need for a second meeting. The end of Costa was not the battle won.

Will England Save Portugal? was delivered first to 51 Berkeley Square. Next, it went to the clubs and foreign embassies, judged likely to be more sympathetic than the press. Tenison berated Portugal's sham democracy: soaring emigration, depopulation, starvation, muzzled press, prisons overflowing, disenfranchisement of seventy-five percent of the electorate. Ironically, Costa's determination to 'extirpate Christianity had only strengthened it.'[75] From Vergnet, she borrows the tired analogy of 'The Terror' and turns Portuguese politics into a *Thermidorian* bear garden devouring its own. Her own Elizabethanism sends out the good knight 'England' to fulfil its historic destiny by redeeming its ancient ally. This reads like an anachronistic, chivalrous discourse for the eve of the First World War. *Will England Save Portugal?* is a propagandist call to arms driven by fear of Republicanism.

It did add growing pressure upon Grey. Tenison's customary lack of diplomacy urged him to do what Palmerston would have done.[76] She remained annoyed that Grey had consistently refused to talk to the BPC, while the Liberal press had gradually come round. Freeloaders like the *Westminster Gazette*, which had originally refused to publish her letters, now wanted to share the glory. She bit her tongue in the knowledge that it was the price of a cross-party alliance. Henry Staveley-Hill took the pamphlet to the Foreign Office and claimed to have stood over Grey until he finished it. Fortunately for the Foreign Secretary, it was only twenty-four pages long.

Staveley-Hill expected Grey to use it to pressurize an insecure Lisbon as war loomed.[77]

The BPC had not been united over the pamphlet's timing. Eyebrows were raised at the Duchess's swift decision to commission it, but Tenison won them over by translating from Portuguese press cuttings insults to the Duchess.[78] Plans for a second public meeting were paused when Lytton was taken ill abroad. John Harris delivered again, suggesting the Liberal MP for Burnley, Philip Morrell as a substitute Chair. As the brother-in-law of the Duke of Portland, and a fine public speaker, he had impeccable connections. Tenison met Morrell at 51 Berkeley Square, but he took some winning over. He doubted the public gave a fig about Portuguese Royalists. She endured Morrell's interrogation of her motives in the interests of cross-party collaboration. She had never been to Portugal, had no Portuguese relatives (she must have discounted an aunt by marriage), and did not even drink port. Morrell succumbed. She had acquired a Chair for the meeting who would act as a bridgehead to stiffening his own government's policy on Portugal; one not lacking charisma.[79]

6 Trouble at the Westminster Palace Hotel

Mab Tenison was no Suffragette. Chistabel Pankhurst was, and prioritized campaigning on behalf of the unjustly imprisoned under the Cat and Mouse Act. Because women like Tenison had nothing to say on this, Christabel planned to bring militant Suffragettes to the Westminster Palace Hotel on 6 February. Leonard Corfe had picked this up, probably through the grapevine of clubland. Tenison was cognisant of Suffragette tactics; they had clashed with BPC supporters before.[80] She counter-attacked by bombarding Suffragettes with pamphlets, confident that 'truth' would prevail and Christabel's fighting talk melt away. Just in case, she prevailed upon Corfe to recruit bodyguards for the meeting. The Suffragettes were not the only worry. *Carbonária* had also threatened to disrupt the meeting. Tenison wondered whether mixing with the declared 'enemies of Christ'[81] would deter Suffragettes. It did not.

Whiteley's, the large Bayswater department store, boasted they would provide anything at all at the shortest notice. Tenison dispatched Corfe to recruit six tall, handsome, athletic stewards.[82] Little was left to chance in planning. Speakers were briefed not to repeat each other. The BPC's own reporters provided an account of the meeting independent from the press. John Harris lunched the editor of the *Manchester Guardian*, Charles Prestwich Scott,[83] but failed to overcome its Government loyalism. He urged Tenison to meet Scott, personally, but not to use 51 Berkeley Square's headed notepaper, because he disliked duchesses.[84] Aunt Mabel thought strategically. Scott might prefer Socialists, so Mab should emphasize the Portuguese Government was imprisoning them, too. Tenison arrived to find the editor had just read *Will England Save Portugal?* The light had dawned that the Campaign was no mere Manueline conspiracy. Tenison assured him, it was anxious to release *all* political prisoners, stressing that was its *only* objective; enough for Scott to guarantee the *Guardian's* objectivity.

Two days before the public meeting, Bernardino Machado transformed the entire context by replacing Costa as Prime Minister. Machado had already promised an amnesty, questioning the purpose of holding the meeting at all. Morrell's chairmanship assumed nothing. They would go ahead as planned. Support was broad, but the good wishes of the Catholic Archbishop of Westminster and the Chief Rabbi, contrasted with the absence of any from the Archbishop of Canterbury. Morrell praised the recent visits by the Duchess and Gibbs. But, as a Liberal, he was as attracted as the Tory, Tenison, by analogies with the 'French Terror'. Morrell moved:

> That this meeting protests against the violation of justice on the part of the Government of Portugal in arresting men and women on account of their religious and political opinions, and denying them the right of trial by due form of law; and calls upon the British Government to make representations to Portugal with a view to securing a General Amnesty for all political prisoners, so that the principles of ordinary justice and humanity may be established in that country.[85]

The resolution's subtext was that the Amnesty fell short of Palmerstonian totality. Refugees in the reserved spaces at the back of the hall let out a cheer. By contrast, a ticketless, German peace campaigner, had been excluded. The Duchess's speech placed the pending Amnesty within a Whiggish narrative. Aubrey Bell and Francis McCullagh were particularly praised, but Philip Gibbs received pride of place. His reporting had been 'an event of supreme importance.' Tenison was embarrassed that this concealed the murkier side of his recruitment: the stuffing of his pockets with Royalist gold.[86]

His secret safe, Gibbs strode to the rostrum. Unrecognisable from the sceptic she had first encountered at Yokes, Tenison gloated as the zealous convert played his audience. On arriving in Lisbon, he told them, he had refused to be fobbed off with a picture of a perfect

160 | *The Secretary*

Portugal ruled by Costa's 'spirit of most lofty benevolence.' He knew full well that three-quarters of the people were disenfranchised; and, that the *Carbonária* constantly violated individual liberties. He discovered prisoners kept in underground fortresses fit only for beasts; and that just working for the Red Cross could put a female humanitarian amongst them. Gibbs walked his attentive audience through the dark corridors of the *Penitenciária*, peeping at the loneliness of the solitarily confined. There were aristocrats clothed as convicts, driven to the edge of madness. But he also found scholars, doctors, and priests among humble peasants.

Cross-denominational co-operation came in the form of the Presbyterian, Reverend R. C. Gillie. He had abandoned his former sympathy for the Republic. Tenison notes that he stood tall and handsome amongst the speakers, glossing the eloquence of his oratory. Gillie reiterated Tenison's argument for the historical precedent of intervention in Portuguese affairs. By the time that Sir Arthur Conan Doyle rose, Tenison was glowing with pride that they had both read *Will England Save Portugal?* so attentively. Conan Doyle expressed confidence that the press now accepted their case. Grey, a notoriously slow mover, must follow. With such distinguished advocacy, it was perhaps elementary that the resolution passed. As Secretary, Tenison declined to take it to Grey. She thought Gibbs would be a more disinterested messenger. She omitted to add, he was also a Liberal.

The Campaign's role in freeing political prisoners was celebrated, but secondary. Its cross-party networking, press lobbying and even, ultimately, celebrity support had enhanced its profile and power. The public could recognize female political agency, if more in the Duchess than the reclusive Tenison. But in the end it was made redundant by events in Portugal. Neither 'England', nor an immobile Foreign Secretary, 'saved' Portugal's political prisoners. The fall of Costa was not caused by pressure from London or Vienna, nor by English visitors to Lisbon. It was made in Portugal, via Brazil; a consequence of the Cortes summoning Bernardino Machado to unpick the parliamentary deadlock. Tenison's narrative has an 'English' centre determining causation in the periphery. The real history lesson was that the semi-colonized retained an autonomous voice.

7 Planting a tree for liberty

Tenison's English narrative was more ethnocentric. By the time the Amnesty Bill was passed on 20 February, she was claiming acknowledgment of the BPC's work from Portuguese MPs. She was pleased to have company at Yokes Court on that special night. Edgar Prestage, the friend who had first put her in touch with Francis McCullagh, was visiting from Lisbon. The two had a great deal in common. Prestage was a supporter of the deposed Monarchy, and opponent of the Republic. A Catholic convert from Anglicanism, and a better historian than Tenison, he had married into the Portuguese aristocracy – a long way from the Manchester solicitors' office he left in 1907.

The Revolution had shocked Prestage because the Portuguese Foreign Minister had assured him 'that England would never allow a Republic to be proclaimed in Portugal.'[87] Naively, he had believed this neo-colonialist prediction, before a Liberal Government did precisely that. His account of the causes of the Revolution is conspiratorial in the extreme:

> So many of the Republican leaders seemed by their features to be of Jewish stock that the saying arose: 'King Manuel I expelled the Jews and King Manuel II was driven out by the Jews.' The assassination of King Carlos and the Revolution of 1910 was commonly believed in Lisbon to have been plotted between the French Grand Orient and the Portuguese Masonic Lodges.[88]

In Lisbon, he had lost a galaxy of celebrity friends – he was closely acquainted with both Kings Carlos and Manuel – but remained an enthusiastic name-dropper in his later years. Aubrey Bell was generously acknowledged as ' the most distinguished scholar to whom Portugal owes, among other things, the best survey of her literature.'[89] Prestage returned to England, as the Camões Professor of Portuguese at King's College, London from 1923. He maintained a scholarly friendship with the exiled Manuel II, until the latter's death in 1932. Prestage's history was unreliable in his later years. But stereotyping 1910 as a plot of Francophile, Jewish freemasons was, at least, consistent with praising its nemesis: dictatorship. Under Salazar, he maintained that Portugal was governed by a 'genius.'[90]

At Yokes Court, on the night of 20 February 1913, Prestage was tingling with triumph. His presence in England is rare evidence that Tenison's networking extended to English trojan horses in Portugal. Tenison asked him to plant a Scottish fir-tree to celebrate 'the victory.' She shared with Prestage her apprehensions that the *Carbonária* would make the released prisoners' lives a misery. Many had just been thrown into the streets with nowhere to go. Benevolent aristocrats, like Dom João d'Almeida and his cousin Dona Constança Telles da Gama, snatched a number from under *Carbonária* noses. Almeida celebrated his good work at a masked ball thrown by one of his cousins.

7 Endgame: After the Amnesty

Once the partying was over the text of the Amnesty left a hangover. Tenison suspected duplicity so the press was told that the Committee was not dissolved. In a letter published the day after the Amnesty, she criticized Machado for trimming over totality, again citing Palmerston.[91] A week later she warned against any illusion that Lisbon had been converted to 'European standards of justice and humanity.' The Special Watch Committee that the BPC had formed with the Howard Association would remain.[92] The latter wrote officially to Grey in November 1913.[93] Tenison further complained of Sir Eyre Crowe spreading disinformation from the Portuguese Legation via the FO.[94]

Lytton joined the counter-offensive. The Amnesty contained too many loopholes. Some 'chiefs, leaders or instigators' remained imprisoned or were banished. Banishment, itself, was a repressive tool that could nullify the Amnesty. The only group given a complete amnesty were the *Carbonária*, pardoned for all abuses. Military tribunals continued, with powers to re-convict the released. All this was followed by the customary reproach that Palmerston had done better in 1847.[95]

However, by his own assessment two months later, his worst fears had gone unrealized. Of the 572 untried, ninety-five had subsequently been tried, the rest released. Of the tried, eighty-seven were acquitted, the remaining eight banished. This did not prevent him seeking ideological validation for the Campaign: 'English Crusaders aided the Portuguese to capture Lisbon from the Moors' in the twelfth century . . . the link has remained unbroken.' 'English criticism,' he argued, is provoked only when the Portuguese government violates the interests of the nation.[96]

The tone of entitlement is palpable, accompanied by apprehension at Republicanism's challenge to the Anglocentric collective memory of shared values and co-operation. England must 'save' Portugal because it was the imaginary keeper of the Old Alliance. This narrative was pitted against Costa's revisionism, that refused the Anglicisation of Portugal. As surely as the Moors had once 'othered' the real Portugal, Costa challenged the ideological construct of a subaltern Portugal. Yet, 'Locusts' like Lytton invariably wrestled with an historic ambiguity. 'What beauties doth *Lisboa* first unfold, Her images floating on that noble tide,' extolled Byron in *Childe Harold*; only for Rose Macaulay to contrast its collision with 'the luckless Portuguese whom it was at the moment the English habit to despise.'[97]

Almeida took advantage of the Amnesty Bill to return to the Miguelist bosum of Vienna, from where he gave press interviews criticising it. He thanked Tenison by letter, but his wish to come to England was frustrated by the Duchess, who suspected he would use the trip to propagandize the Miguelist cause.[98] Tenison concurred and declined subsequent further Miguelist invitations to visit. The Campaign had also left her and her two aunts short of money, while the BPC was still functioning on amnesty-watch.

By contrast, the Duchess went on tour to recuperate. From the Holy Land, she dropped into Vienna as a reconciliatory gesture towards the Miguelists. She thought a frock-coat and top hat suited Almeida better than the convict's uniform he was wearing when last they met in the *Penitenciária*. Back in London, she dined with King Manuel at Apsley House, who was apologetic about distancing himself from the Campaign. Tenison acts as our fly on the wall:

> King Manuel had been greatly distressed by the plight of his country; but as he received an annual allowance from Portugal on the condition of neither returning nor countenancing any projects for his return, nor in any way acting against the existing regime, his hands had been tied. The Duquesa understood this; and emphasised to His Majesty how careful we had been to reassure all interrogators that no responsibility whatsoever attached to him for any of our actions.[99]

Tenison handled this delicate matter with kid gloves. If only she had known that Manuel had been playing a double game as a pensioned plotter. Instead, she thought Manuel consoled himself with book collecting, something Lady Bute thought he was more cut out for than kingship.[100]

Although the BPC intended to distribute *The Portuguese Amnesty* across Europe and the Empire, the Campaign dwindled away from the spring of 1914. Philip Gibbs was asked to encourage press vigilance over the Amnesty's implementation. But he could not get on with Tenison. She wrote him off as a pacifist over the prospect of war with Germany. He found her anti-Germanism provocative, but she did sympathize with the Austrians after Franz Ferdinand's assassination. The shadow of war was subjugating other politics by July 1914. The Liberal Gibbs, claimed to have been in the dark about her Conservatism during the Campaign.[101] If so, she had done a good job forging that cross-party alliance the BPC strategized. But, Gibbs and Tenison had rubbed each other up the wrong way from their first meeting at Yokes Court. This never improved, and her 1950s memoir is stung by the disparaging remarks in his autobiography.

8 Epilogue: Tenison and Portugal after 1914

The *Tenison Papers* trace a Portuguese thread beyond the chapters, *Unexpected Activities*. It enables us to glean what Tenison thought the long-term significance of the Campaign to be. She detects a disguised triumph in Republicanism's attempt to 'extirpate the Christian myth'[102] turning into Salazar's Portugal, one of the most Christian countries in Europe. That regime had retrieved much of what had been struggled for earlier: 'The condition of Portugal is a happy contrast to what it was in 1908–13.'[103] This echoes *Unexpected Activities*, itself:

> As Portugal today in 1954, is one of the best governed countries in Europe, there are probably few alive who remember when schoolchildren in 1913 were compelled to walk through the streets of Lisbon carrying banners inscribed "There is no God."[104]

Her interest in the Portuguese extreme Right stretched back to at least 1916 when she was reading *Integralismo Lusitano* literature. That makes it unlikely that she was only ever trying to free political prisoners. She continued to correspond with the Duke of Bragança through the 1950s.

It was a fitting coincidence that Tenison ended her days next to the twelfth-century Castle Hedingham where Elizabeth I had stayed, in August 1561, with the 17th Earl. Georgian Hedingham Hall had been turned into a home for 'very grand old ladies.'[105] Her friend Musette Majendie, whose family owned Castle Hedingham for 250 years, found space for her the year after Yokes Court burned down. There, she completed parallel histories: Elizabeth, her heroine's, and her own. The latter remains uncatalogued and unpublished, contrary to her intentions. But her 'Unexpected Activities' between 1912 and 1914, reconstructed from the ashes of Yokes Court, have now seen the light of day. In the small cemetery outside the village a headstone with a simple inscription looks out on a south-facing field. Around it, other tombstones speak of love and loss. E. M. Tenison lies in a lonely grave, genderless in death as she was in her early political life.

CHAPTER

8

The Duchess

When Adeline, Duchess of Bedford arrived in Lisbon in March 1913, on a mission to free political prisoners, it had, in more than one sense, been a long journey. Unlike the role she had played for some twenty years as a penal reformer in England, she had not sought this part. Still, she was pleased to add another, relevant cause to her considerable philanthropic portfolio. Adeline Mary Russell (*née* Somers Cocks) became the Duchess of Bedford in 1891, when her husband George William Francis Sackville Russell, the Liberal member for Bedfordshire, succeeded his father as the tenth Duke. Married in 1876 at twenty-four, the relationship remained childless, and at forty-one she found herself a widow. She retained the courtesy title of Adeline, Duchess of Bedford and took the advice her friend Benjamin Jowett, Master of Balliol College, Oxford, plunging her energies into philanthropy.[1]

1 Christian Philanthropist

For many Victorian, leisured women, philanthropy proved a choice enforced by a gendered career structure closed to the talents. But it was also extolled as the highest moral calling of the Christian life. Adeline took up the gospel of good works as a prison visitor. As Lucia Zedner has said, male officialdom 'believing that women were more malleable than men … permitted greater flexibility in female prisons in the hope that Lady Visitors and prison matrons could persuade criminal women to repent.'[2] Adeline visited poor women in prison, relentlessly. As a Lady Visitor, she followed in a distinguished train that stretched back to Elizabeth Fry's British Society of Ladies for Promoting the Reformation of Female Prisons (1821). Male chauvinism and institutional conservatism were thrust aside by a fortitude that disregarded the conditions that rugged masculinity would shield her from.

The prison world the Duchess entered in the 1890s was one in which, 'masculine officialism'[3] remained deeply resistant to the female reforming hand. Elizabeth Fry had been obstructed from the start. As late as 1894, Susanna Meredith regretted that she was unable to tell the Gladstone Committee more about life inside because the Prison Commissioners continued to conceal it.[4] But many of her sisters persisted. 'Masculine officialism' channelled them into work amongst the aid societies for the discharged, for example, where it was thought they could do less damage. This was the exclusive system Adeline Bedford confronted on taking charge of the Association of Lady Visitors in 1901; a system of neglect in which twenty percent of women prisoners had never talked to a female visitor. As she wrote in the very month the Portuguese Revolution was about to provide a new mission, before that Association had been set up, 'ladies were permitted to visit the female side of the prison; they did so in a tentative way, but without any recognised right of entry.'[5]

Amongst the visited, about half were admitted for 'immoral' reasons, meaning prostitution.[6] Separated or widowed alcoholics often struggled to escape the web of female philanthropists competing to save them. Aylesbury housed the worst cases. The 1902 Licensing Act had made habitual drunkenness by either partner a legal ground for separation. But drunken husbands were more adept at using it to dump their spouses and move on to a new partner. The discarded wife was then on the rocky slope to places like Aylesbury. If pregnant, she kept the child only until it could be placed with relatives, or in the workhouse.[7]

Earl Lytton, chair of the BPC, was a reformist Tory,[8] close to Adeline Bedford's Liberalism. He and his sister, Lady Constance Lytton, were founding members of the Penal Reform League in 1907. Imprisoned as a suffragette in 1909, for throwing bricks at ministerial cars, she left a vivid portrait of these hopelessly, disempowered women:

> Child-burdened women who were left without money, without the means or physical power to earn it, who had stolen in order to save their lives and that of their children – thieves! Women who had from their childhood been trained to physical shame, women who at their first adolescence had borne children by their own fathers under circumstances when resistance was inconceivable. Women who had been seduced by their employers. Women deceived and deserted by their friends and lovers. Women employed by their own parents for wage-earning prostitution. Women reduced to cruelty after being for years the unconsulted churning mills for producing in degradation

and want and physical suffering the incessant annual babies of an undesired family. Women who had been stolen in their bloom and imprisoned for purposes of immoral gain. If amongst such women there are many who are professionally thieves, prostitutes "by choice", immoral, "past redemption" . . . sodden with drink, undermined by drug taking, their maternity transformed by cruelty, their brains worn to madness, what cause is there for surprise or reproach, and what hope is there for cure by imprisonment?[9]

Constance Lytton was deeply affected by this cycle of depravity of poor women born to suffer. She resisted the privileged life she was born into, using a personal legacy to support penal reform and suffragism.[10] She self-harmed, went on hunger strike, and was force-fed despite having a heart condition.

By the end of the nineteenth century 'the new rationalism' was making some impression upon the masculine constructions that underpinned female imprisonment. Social environmentalism emphasized the moral degradations of urban working-class existence. The outworkers of the religious societies dived into the urban cesspools in a quest for moral cleansing. Later, like Constance Lytton, Adeline Bedford turned to the suffrage to raise woman in the eyes of man. But she never subjugated moral philanthropy to politics. She lived until 1920, an enfranchised woman inclined to see that status as earned through long public endeavour rather than equalizations borne of wartime service.

2 Penal Reformer

Adeline Bedford's evangelical Anglicanism preached that all members of society, even prisoners, were entitled to God's grace as children of a loving deity. It followed that she favoured special treatment for the 'feeble-minded', as a separate category of prisoner capable of being taught how to make moral choices. To advance this view, she worked with other pressure groups for increased female responsibility in prison management. The British Ladies' Society and the Howard Association were both convinced that the high motives of Lady Visitors brought female prisoners to an enhanced awareness of personal inadequacy. The Gladstone Committee of 1895 recommended the appointment of a female inspector of prisons. Sir Evelyn Ruggles-Brise became Chairman of the Prison Commission but stopped short of implementing this. Instead, he invited the Duchess of Bedford to act as occasional, voluntary adviser. She was to manage the planned increase in Lady Visitors. This interim arrangement persisted until the urgency of the suffragette issue led to Dr Mary Gordon, a Harley Street physician and suffragette supporter, being given a full-time appointment in 1908. But she was held in deep suspicion because of her feminism and was closely monitored. Even then, Ruggles-Brise struggled to abandon the gendered power model that had constrained Adeline Bedford:

> Ruggles-Brise held a traditional view of the charitable aristocratic or middle-class woman, in her good offices and with her good influences, mirroring to her fallen sisters and to young prisoners the class and gender relationships which should prevail in the good society . . . the middle class male owner/earner and the female, maintained, philanthropic nurturer.[11]

The new penal liberalism resurfaced in the 1908 Prevention of Crime Act that established the Borstal, a new institution for the most difficult sixteen to twenty-one-year olds.[12] Shorter sentences and revocable licenses allowed remission after three to six months. At Aylesbury, where the Duchess had been visiting since 1897, she hoped its new borstal would stem the flow of young women into adult prisons, despite its being no more than a converted wing of the prison.[13] Traditionally, it persisted with domestic instruction designed to prepare the female juvenile to cross the bridge to marriage and motherhood. That bridge was the refuge, to where you were released on license. But recidivism claimed the weak, as many rushed straight back into the arms of exploitative boyfriends who had showered them with love letters in borstal.[14]

The women's reformatory at Aylesbury received a damning report from the Inspectorate in 1904, despite a cascade of improvement launched by Lady Visitors. Lectures on abstinence taught moral virtue and good health; concerts refined the aural sensibilities; aftercare routed a path into the civilized world. But the 'inebriates' resisted improvement, persisting with their violent, passionate, alcohol-fuelled behaviour. A cacophony of shouting and swearing often went on for days on end.[15] The Duchess was more disappointed than Ruggles-Brise, not a man prone to tears. He reacted to the 1904 Report by toughening up the regime. This was greeted more favourably by the more extreme eugenicists who preferred the knife of sterilisation, while liberals like the Duchess glued themselves to the Bible as guide to reformatory behaviour. To 1914, liberals got the better of the argument. Parkhurst (Isle of Wight), from 1912, was the first prison based on the principle of preventive detention, rather than penal servitude.

Aylesbury, the Duchess's domain, imprisoned the most intractable. It developed a fearsome reputation, institutionalizing criminal poverty, and incarcerating women who, hungry or sick, had turned to minor theft and abuse of authority. Many saw prison as a preferable alternative to the workhouse. They came, went and returned with regularity. Aylesbury had been one of two state reformatories set up under the 1898 Inebriates' Act to receive the most intractable of habitual drunkards, from criminal prisons that struggled to deal with them. The Duchess put her head into the lionesses' den, a true believer clinging to the conviction that the 'blunted moral sense . . . of the enfeebled and degraded drunk' could be transformed into 'a model of healthy, domesticated femininity.'[16] Such optimism ran up against the scepticism of 'masculine officialism', causing reformers to argue for the feminisation of the staff.

Aylesbury boasted barrack-like cell accommodation. It was precious short of outdoor space to exhaust the 'energetic savage.' Social explosions were frequent. From its inception, it had had a detached reformatory block for 'humane control.' Even there, the Governor despaired, the inmates remained determined to make life unbearable for the authorities, as they continued to tear up their clothes and destroy the cells.

The grievance procedure at Aylesbury turned into a conflict arena. Inmates laid complaints before the monthly Visiting Committee. This led to an official inquiry into accusations of ill treatment by officers. In 1911, Caroline Teehan reported that she had written to the Pope about being attacked by warders in her bed. But officialdom accused the most unstable 'inebriates' of abusing the procedure, and even the Duchess proposed withdrawing some privileges from the most refractory.[17]

Yet, there had been so much more optimism when in 1895 the Gladstone Act had sent the first Lady Visitors into the prisons, tasked with arousing the 'dull intelligence' stagnating there. Women prisoners had never been visited by other women in a quasi-official educational role before. From 1900, when she was appointed first President of the Lady Visitors' Association, Adeline Bedford proceeded to establish a national network of Lady Visitors. To make this acceptable to a patriarchal regime, she worked hard to forge close relationships with governors and chaplains. Ruggles-Brise frequently called on her as his only female advisor to the Prison Commission. But he still shared the common gender stereotypes of his times. Women were not cut out for senior management because they were too emotional for the clear-headed, balanced decision-making necessary. Eventually, he was forced to concede the weight of the argument of women's organisations. First, female doctors were appointed to female prisons; then, ironically, his retirement was marked by the appointment of Lilian Barker as the first female governor of Aylesbury borstal.

Ruggles-Brise was no radical in opening doors to careers for women in the prison service. On the other hand, he was no reactionary either. The Duchess and other Lady Visitors found they were being treated in a more professional way. More generally, He turned around the previous reactionary regime of Sir Edmund Du Cane, influenced by Social Darwinist pessimism.[18] As a senior civil servant he applied, after 1905, the Liberal Government's more socially interventionist approach to prisons. It was an approach that Adeline Bedford found congenial as she cut her teeth as a prison reformer. Young offenders were major beneficiaries, spending more time in the classroom and in prison libraries. But morally hygienic Christianity remained paramount, as Constance Lytton observed inside Holloway

> At each end of the bed was a small iron shelf. At the head were kept a pint mug for water, toothbrush, soup, towel, brush and comb. On the shelf at the foot were a Bible, prayer book, hymn book, small devotional book called "The Narrow Way", and an instructive book on domestic hygiene, "A Perfect Home and How To Keep It."[19]

Lady Visitors provided a conduit for the ex-prisoner to the outside community, and acted as counsellors, even when rejected. The refuges had a high turnover, as most women fled the moral maternalism of the prison regime as soon as an alternative appeared. The many different charitable aid societies exhibited a competitive pluralism in working with Lady Visitors that continued the best traditions of philanthropic provision. Aylesbury was a prison that worked particularly closely with the aid societies.[20] The girls were shunted around between the societies and Duxhurst Farm Colony, from where the Duchess noticed too many returned. [21]

Historians have challenged the idea of a direct causal relationship between philanthropy and improvement in British prisons. Nonetheless, Adeline Bedford's evidence to the Royal Commission on the Feeble-Minded in 1908 is illustrative of liberal criminological thinking's influence by then. 'Feeble-mindedness' was an attempt to reconstruct the 'inebriate'. Until then, inebriety had been treated as a disease brought on by moral degeneracy. It implied a curable, not innate, condition. Feeble-mindedness, however, was a step back into a discourse of incurability. This raised more practical questions of funding. Was it worth spending more money on inebriate reformatories that practised curative therapy? Or should the feeble minded just be locked up cheaply for society's protection? The Duchess resisted the regressive turn. She argued that the feeble-minded should be treated separately from ordinary prisoners, implying that criminalising them was the worst solution. Indeed, she remained optimistic about their improvability: 'under the influence of a well-born and highly educated lady . . . they could be raised by their association.'[22] She referred to herself, of course, and spoke from the experience of Aylesbury, where segregation had already been effected the year before. The Duchess was well aware that the majority of habitual returnees were ageing drunks who might otherwise have been in the workhouse: 'The ravages of drink are beyond belief and beyond description, some middle aged women having spent thirty or forty years in and out of prison mainly for this cause.'[23] She recognizes the institutionalization of the habitual returnee, bed and breakfasting at the Aylesbury 'guest house' for inebriates. Not that the tea was an attraction, being regrettably weak and no alternative to stronger drink, she noted. Despite high rates of recidivism, she believed that criminalising these women achieved nothing. Although it took until 1921 before inebriate reformatories were closed, the Royal Commission was a step in that direction. Long before that, the Duchess had acquired the transferable skills that were to take her from Aylesbury to Lisbon.

Feminist historians have begun to fill the gap that once existed in respect of the role of women in the criminal justice system. Zedner has argued women's prison experiences do not fit a model of progressive improvement.[24] Forsythe questions the very idea that changes had any particular gender specificity.[25] But Anne Logan identifies, beyond the dominant feminism of suffragism, a plethora of associations concerned with criminal justice of feminist significance.[26] The Lady Visitors' Association was one, and played an important role in professionalising the female presence in prison management. Still, it ran up against a wall of 'masculine officialism' that shaped 'the context of a complex set of relations and processes which includes both men and women.'[27] Gender shaped relationships. Aspiring women like the Duchess were forced to negotiate hard over contested space in the prison system. Change only really arrived with the social consequences of the First World War.[28]

Yet, we should not under-estimate how advanced their challenge was by 1910–14. Adeline Bedford was a national figure as a public campaigner before the War who had challenged a resistant, gendered, prison system. Well used to dealing with difficult men with fixed ideas about women, Portuguese Republicans held no fears for her. Unlike her friend E. M. Tenison she did not seek to hide her gender. After Aylesbury's horrors – foul-mouthed rage, alcoholism, violence, even infanticide as surrogate abortion – what price a few hundred 'White Ants'? She carried the burden of the Christian reformer into the bowels of Lisbon's prisons wielding the trusty sword of truth and justice. This was God's struggle on behalf of the political prisoners, and against the anti-Christ Costa. But, hers was an idealism tempered by pragmatism. The focus was on conditions: space, constraints, access, and the dignity of the prisoner. Gender entered secondarily, in so far as female Christian philanthropists were not spared victimhood by the First Republic. She thought this unsurprising behaviour from an atheistical regime that denied its citizens human rights on the scale of revolutionary France. But she needed the empirical evidence to make an impact, which is where she drew upon her time-honoured experience of visiting. Her Portuguese visit reverberated across the Atlantic. 'The official contradiction of the Duchess's charges by the Portuguese authorities is not accepted here as adequate',[29] proclaimed one press voice in a city of immigrants that included many Portuguese.

3 Portugal and after

In late 1910, as the first Royalists passed through the gates of Portugal's prisons, the Duchess was unaware of the great cause that lay ahead. She was still reflecting on her Christian duty to imprisoned English women. This was to gather around her an educated, improving team of Lady Superintendents, to lift the inebriates and the feeble-minded to 'a higher plane':

> It is sometimes erroneously supposed that moral and spiritual forces make no appeal to the class under consideration, but I incline to the belief that close acquaintance with the subject would lead to a different conclusion. The human spirit, softened and rationalised by gratitude and affection, is, moreover, seldom incapable of response to a Higher Influence.[30]

The full weight of this Christian righteousness was transferred onto Portugal's Republican gaolers. Atheists who preferred incarceration to reason would be bettered by moral argument. The Presidency of the Lady Visitors' Association would eventually secure a visitor's pass into Lisbon's prisons, providing her with the public platform through which to beard Afonso Costa in his own den.

The previous chapter followed the Duchess's personal and political interactions with E. M. Tenison and other protagonists in the BPC. Here, the focus will be on her use of that key influence on public opinion: the press. Her reputation as a reformer of women's prisons played a part in obtaining access to Portuguese prisons. But there were key differences requiring adaptation, and the conciliatory skills she exercised in the British system were tested to the hilt. As frustrations mounted, she increasingly made the mistake of abandoning diplomacy as her humanitarianism became politicized.

She was now wrestling against two governments. She was quite familiar with burrowing from within on behalf of women prisoners. She now faced both the Portuguese and the foreign policy of Edward Grey. Undaunted, she convinced herself that the road to Lisbon went through Whitehall. She and the BPC gambled on a full-frontal publicity campaign to embarrass Grey into a change of course. But she miscalculated how strongly Grey would cling to a fragile ally in the perilous Europe of 1913–14. Within the intricate pre-war balance of power, Portugal's political prisoners were of little import. The Duchess also under-estimated the capacity of the Republic to reform itself. Instead, she took a leaf out of the book of her recalcitrant Aylesbury 'inebriates' and banged the drum outside Grey's window, loudly.

The Duchess's first press intervention on behalf of the political prisoners came in *The Times*, shortly after her visit to three Portuguese prisons. She implies that she had first been alerted to their plight by her cousin Philip Somers Cocks, Consul in Lisbon. But the catalyst for her had been E. M. Tenison's letter to *The Spectator* the February before. From 19 March, she had made several officially approved visits, to the *Limoeiro*, where she found some ninety political prisoners mixed with criminals. The prisoners crossed class boundaries: journalists, doctors, servants, tradesmen, nobles and priests, all sharing the criminals' minimal diet. Food parcels arrived from the families of the more fortunate. The Duchess argued that the *Carbonária* had been allowed to create a police state of trivial criminality. Detained for up to two years were a doctor, arrested for a remark made to his barber; a police sergeant, proud of serving under three kings; a Count, whose dinner guests sported miniature royalist flags as button-holes. Pity the poor priest who was given no reason at all:

> Herded together in cramped rooms and narrow passages, the men's faces wore an unspeakable look of anguish, which once seen could never be forgotten. Without exercise or employment of any kind, the endless hours drag wearily past . . . As I passed through the courtyard on leaving, dozens of dark, sad faces were pressed against the bars, and it was with a pang that I realised that my visit had aroused a passing gleam of hope.[31]

174 | *The Duchess*

The *Aljube* women's prison was little different: five peasants from the Azores, who had resisted a Republican attack on their local church; and the humanitarian charity workers, Dona Julia de Brita e Cunha, and Dona Constança Telles da Gama.

The *Penitenciária* contained the worst conditions. Politicals co-existed with long-term criminals; solitary confinement was common. Amongst them were, the Marques Belmont and Dom José Mascarenas, almost killed by the *Carbonária* on arrest. The Duchess made the amazing claim that it was intimated to their jury that both would be shot if acquitted. Safer to hand out life sentences. Through the *parlatorio*[32] she talked to Belmonte, and to Dom João d'Almeida, who she acknowledges was arrested for participating in the September 1912 rising. But she passes over his treasonable offence, in favour of a diatribe against a godless *Carbonária* state:

> the Republic has abolished every sign of the Christian state . . . The people of Portugal are undoubtedly opposed to these stringent measures . . . among them . . . a large proportion of moderate Republicans. A . . . handful of extremists surround the present Prime Minister and dictate the policy of terrorism which paralyses the entire country . . . the voice of England, speaking through its all-powerful press, will be raised on behalf of justice and mercy. Is our old and honourable alliance with Portugal to act as a shield to a secret society of men who treat with utter contempt the motives and principles which govern civilised nations?[33]

The visit proved pivotal in launching the campaign. Two days later, in a balanced leader, *The Times*, edited by Geoffrey Dawson from 1912, sought to contextualize the Duchess's invective against the Portuguese Government's authoritarian lurch within the need to conserve the Old Alliance. It concedes the instability caused by the Royalist invasion of 1912 provided an excuse for a 'war of extermination' against Royalists. But it credits Costa with a 'shrewdness and political insight . . . recognised even by his opponents.' He was thought to privately favour an amnesty but had been captured by extremists. Yet, *The Times* argued, anti-Royalist extremism was unnecessary because the Royalists were no longer a serious threat: 'a policy of conciliation and consolidation' is needed to rebuild the state, encouraged by the release of Dona Constança Telles da Gama.

> An amnesty at the present time could not be interpreted as a sign of weakness as it might have been a year ago. Far from exposing the new *regime* to danger, it could only strengthen it, by getting rid of a

source of unrest and disquiet in Portugal and by disarming criticism abroad.[34]

The Times had differentiated itself tactically from the Duchess. It preferred olive branch diplomacy to the sceptre of angered Christianity in dealing with Costa. This was closer to Grey's position than the Duchess's. Costa had displayed cynicism about British motives and could be headstrong. But *The Times* believed that persuasion, not moral indignation, was more likely to squeeze an amnesty out of him. The Duchess's more offensive tactics expose the contradictions immanent within the Campaign's covert politics. Publicly, it could only declare for the freedom of political prisoners. But, simmering below, were volcanic seams of Royalism and Christianity that loathed the Republican state's secularism.

The Duchess seemed to think the readers of the *Daily Mail* required a more bathetic approach. A burst of purple prose extolling the joys of a Lisbon spring greeted them:

> The Judas trees in the Avenida da Liberdade are showing their purple pink blossoms against the grey skies of an early spring morning, and a feint tint of green gives brightness to the fine broad space surrounding the monument which commemorates the freedom of Portugal from the Spanish domination . . . a certain sense of prosperity seems to pervade the streets of Lisbon. But beneath the brave show of well-being presented to the stranger by the capital there flows a secret poison the effects of which recall the conditions of Naples or Sicily in the worst days of King "Bomba."[35]

The historical analogy with Neapolitan dungeons in the age of Palmerston preface the familiar clichés about tyranny: 'spies in every household', and 'walls that have ears.' She regrets that provincial prisons and the Castle of St George went unvisited, as did many prisoners in the *Limoeiro* and *Penitenciária*. But she did encounter willing denouncers hanging around court-rooms looking for payment to swear false accusations. This was nothing new, but another nefarious practice derived from British Liberalism's *bête noire*: Bomba's Naples.[36] Amongst the victims was an old priest in the *Limoeiro*, dragged through the streets by the *Carbonária* who reminded her of similar abuses during the French Revolution. Worse, 'the graves of some nuns were violated and their remains cast into a pit.' Through all this, the released Dona Constança da Gama continued to raise funds to clothe the poorest prisoners at Christmas.

But, what to do about it? Trust in the God-fearing English was her rhetorical reply, and cognisant of her reading audience she aimed a swipe at the Old Alliance in her plea for an amnesty:

> The word "Inglês" has not lost its meaning. In Portugal it has the force of centuries of tried friendship behind it . . . The English Press above all is a supreme power; its criticism is feared, its applause desired . . . Has England in all her history ever before been the friend and ally of a nation ruled by a vile Secret Society?

The Duchess's *Daily Mail* article was a clever piece of ironic propaganda, amplified in its paradoxical leader 'Crimes in the Name of Liberty.' Urging support for her 'humane campaign' it recommended *Portuguese Political Prisoners*, as an essential pamphlet analysing the contradictions of the Republican state. Condemning its 'mediaeval inquisition' and 'arbitrary justice' it warned Costa to honour his pledge of an amnesty or face 'a storm of popular indignation which European governments will be forced to obey or be put on notice by civilised Europe.'[37]

The Spectator also endorsed the Duchess's campaign, despite its partiality towards republicanism. Praising her Gladstonian selflessness, it also singled-out her practical experience:

> The Duchess of Bedford is, moreover, a witness not merely free from political motive, but one devoid of the sentimentality of inexperience in penal affairs. Her connexion with the British Home Office – she holds an official post – in the matter of the treatment of female convicts has given her a firm standard of judgment. She has visited prisons all over Europe. She is not just a kind-hearted traveller who has given way to a panic of pity.[38]

But the Duchess was less adored outside of Fleet Street. *The Manchester Guardian* was one of the few newspapers to defend the Republic against her. Commenting on her letter to *The Times* it pointed out that a court martial had just acquitted six prisoners of charges of monarchist conspiracy. The effect was to undermine her charges of grand-scale, illegal imprisonment.[39] However, she was also the victim of mis-identification. *The Observer* was provoked by an unsolicited copy of *Portuguese Political Prisoners*. Wrongly attributing its authorship to the Duchess, it implied that it was missing the big picture: 'the pamphlet as a whole leaves the impression of a strong animus in its author's mind against those who have released Portugal from the weakly vicious rule it suffered under the late monarchy.'[40] Indeed, the Republic merely inherited its prison conditions. Furthermore, the pamphlet made outrageous claims, conflating the British public's opinions with those of a single letter writer to *The Spectator* (Tenison's). Finally, it sensed double standards within the Campaign, which needed to be more open and honest.

The Observer drew much of its evidence from *O Seculo* whose Republicanism defended the *Carbonária* and the impartiality of the justice system. And, it reminded, the Republic had abolished capital punishment. Furthermore, the prisons were the same ones used under the Monarchy. But, *The Observer* erred in repeating *O Seculo's* claim that no prisoners were kept in fortresses,[41] the falsity of which was shortly to be revealed by Philip Gibbs from Elvas. Tenison went into battle with *The Observer* to defend the Duchess's evidence. She complained that the regime was indulging in counter-propaganda on a grand scale. Fifty thousand copies of *O Seculo's* apologia had been sent to Britain by *Carbonária* agents. Unlike the Monarchy, the Republic filled its prisons with untried suspects: 'The Portuguese are free to think as Senhor Costa thinks, otherwise they go to prison.'[42] The Duchess was accused of not visiting many prisons, but she was prevented from seeing more. The 22 April protest meeting had not been trying to dislodge Republicanism, but to reinstate justice. There should be no long periods of detention without trial at the whim of court martials packed with government placemen.

Tenison's defence spurred the Duchess to return to the pages of *The Observer*. The Campaign was not a Royalist front, she complained. That insulted the reputations of prominent supporters like Trevelyan, who defended liberal values not monarchs. *Portuguese Political Prisoners* was a much more accurate guide to what was happening than *O Seculo's*. The pamphlet's account, she insisted, was corroborated by the *Morning Post*'s which evidenced the use of fortresses at Alto du Duque and Caxias. She appealed to the liberalism of *The Observer*'s readers to condemn solitary confinement of political prisoners.[43]

The chastisement of *The Observer* far from concluded the press battle. The *Manchester Guardian* pushed an English resident in Portugal, W. A. Bentley, into the front line of defending the Republic. Bentley had accused both the Duchess and Aubrey Bell of exaggeration. He also lambasted the Reverend R. J. Campbell, minister of the City of Temple, for being too influenced by the Duchess in denouncing the Republic. Bentley had an axe to grind. He had written to Campbell personally two weeks before, asking for a meeting with him, the Duchess and Lord Lytton, but had been ignored. He despairs at the attitude of the Free Churches. Bentley confronts the Campaign's arguments with the evidence of the Positivist, S. H. Swinny, who visited the

Limoeiro on 11 April.⁴⁴ Swinny reported political prisoners separate from common criminals, free to mix amongst themselves, to receive visits from relatives, their rooms adorned with pictures and photographs. Bentley confirmed this impression from his own visit to the *Penitenciária*, where he found conditions comparable with English prisons. Gifts of tobacco, fruit and flowers flowed in, and there were definitely no plank beds, nor corporal punishment. 'These are the prisons that the Duchess of Bedford compares with Naples and Bomba!'⁴⁵

Bentley thought Campbell confused over Grey's foreign policy. Portugal was not comparable to the small Christian states that Grey had given little support to against the Turks. Campbell saw in Portugal another threatened minnow, this time by a 'Teutonic alliance.' Just a week before the Aeolian Hall meeting, he wrote:

> It may be questioned if Turkish misrule was ever worse than that of the new Portuguese Republican Government in respect of persons suspected of Royalist sympathies . . . Here is a case in which pressure could be effectively exerted immediately by France and England or either of them without the slightest danger of European complications. We are morally bound to do it, and I trust that public opinion will speedily make itself felt on the point.⁴⁶

Bentley was not Campbell's only critic. G. M. Trevelyan brought the historian's perspective to criticize Campbell's grasp of Grey's foreign policy. Trevelyan was annoyed by Campbell's reckless discourse comparing Portugal's 'terrorists' to King Bomba's treatment of political prisoners in darkest Naples. 'It is greatly to be hoped that the better elements in Portugal can make the Republic once more as civilized as it was when it began its career.'⁴⁷ Trevelyan's Liberalism differentiated between the radicalism of Costa and more moderate Republicanism. It is a useful corrective to the increasingly strident tone of the Campaign, itself. Trevelyan acted as something of a bridgehead between it and Grey's delicately poised diplomacy in a Europe perched on a knife-edge.

E. G. Browne added to Trevelyan's academic disdain of Campbell. He considered Campbell's understanding of Portugal as 'questionable' as that of Albania or Austria.⁴⁸ Edward Granville Browne was the Sir Thomas Adams' Professor of Arabic at Cambridge University, although he was equally renowned as a scholar of Persia. He had been a key figure in bringing radical Liberals and Socialists together on the Persia Committee through which they campaigned against Grey's support for pro-Russian meddling in Persia in furtherance of the 1907

Anglo-Russian agreement. Browne regarded Grey's policy as undermining Persian constitutionalism.[49] By contrast, he implicitly defended Grey's policy over Portugal against the criticisms of people like Campbell.

These examples allude to the Campaign's status as a cross-party coalition, but more importantly the divergence within Liberalism caused by Portugal. While the high Tory, Tenison was intervening in the Liberal *Observer*, no less a Liberal than Sir Arthur Conan Doyle lent celebrity endorsement to the Campaign in the Tory *Times*. Conan Doyle's reputation as a campaigner against injustice was well established by 1913. Although he had defended British participation in the Boer War he worked with those like E. D. Morel to expose the evils of the Congo. He published a pamphlet, *The Crime of the Congo* in 1909. He also worked to overturn miscarriages of justice within the British legal system. As a Liberal Unionist he was well practised in the arts of cross-party co-operation, which he applied to the Campaign. He was also a Catholic, having been educated at Stonyhurst College, alongside the future Attorney-General for Ireland (1913–14), J.F. Moriarty.

In contrast to Trevelyan, Conan Doyle adopted the Duchess's historical imagery. He thought the present Portuguese Government as unrepresentative of their people's interests as the Jacobins had been of the French. He echoed her Palmerstonian comparison of the condition of Portuguese prisons with those of the Naples of King Bomba. In an historical comparison with Serbia, that showed how fast national narratives could change, he wrote of the abused ally of summer 1914:

> There is a precedent in the case of Servia. That nation murdered its King and Queen under atrocious circumstances. We showed our sense of the crime by withdrawing our representative. The Portuguese – or a section of them – have also murdered their late King and his son. The present Government have made the deed their own, since public demonstrations have been permitted this very year in Lisbon in honour of the murderers. Why should we not do what we did in the case of Servia? It would make the powers that be in Portugal realize as nothing else would do how utterly unworthy they are to belong to the comity of nations. The mere threat of such an action might bring about an amnesty. If not, we can only show our displeasure by refusing to have any dealings with people so devoid of justice and humanity.[50]

The comparison of the assassination of King Alexander I and Queen Draga by a group of Army officers in 1903 was stretched. King

Carlos was not murdered in a palace coup. But, to be fair, Conan Doyle uses the example instrumentally to argue for an equivalent diplomatic response. He does not claim there was a similarity of motives. However, the Serbian events had taken place ten years before 1913, when it was, unlike Portugal, no ally of Britain. Conan Doyle was not a front-ranking activist on the political prisoners' issue, but he was marginally engaged. While there is no record of him attending the 22 April 1913 meeting at the Aeolian Hall, he was at the one in February 1914.

Unsurprisingly, *The Observer* dismissed the Aeolian Hall meeting with brevity. The Duchess's speech was afforded roughly the same space as a suffragette's challenge to Lord Lytton's opening address: 'why not put your own house in order?'[51] This was too much for George Birdwood who leapt to the Duchess's defence in the letters column of *The Times*. Why had no reader so far written in support of her original letter of 7 April? He cited in her defence the cases of two political prisoners, Francisco and Carlos de Melo e Costa, both innocent young men under thirty. Francisco had already been sentenced, but Carlos was held without trial. Their only offence was 'to be obnoxious to the scoundrelly "Carbonários" who for the present overawe all of Portugal from the Government downwards to the porters in the streets of Lisbon.' Neither should the gullible reader be fooled by the odd act of apparent clemency. Dona Constança Telles da Gama may have been released, but her maid-servant had been further detained.[52]

After setting the letters' columns alight following her Lisbon visit in April, the Duchess stood back and admired her arson, for a bit. From 51 Berkeley Square she watched as her friends fanned the flames of discontent with the Alliance, her critics pouring water on their incendiarism. We know from Tenison that the two friends were working together behind the scenes, not least to arrange Gibbs' visit. The Duchess did not return directly to the press until the end of the year, when a letter to *The Times* about the forthcoming second public meeting, turned out to be her swan song. In addition to drumming up support for the meeting, she renews the reckless threat against the Portuguese Alliance. Trotting out the usual catalogue of Republican violations of natural justice, she continues:

> a general amnesty to political offenders (on the lines of the bill which before long will again be presented to the Portuguese Chamber by Dom José d'Almeida), accompanied by a complete reversal of the prevailing system of tyranny, will alone serve to reconcile the British people to the continuance of the alliance with Portugal.[53]

Absence from the British press had not made the heart grow fonder of the Portuguese Government. Despite being a lady of breeding, she was not averse to aiming the kitchen sink of 51 Berkeley Square at Afonso Costa and his cronies in the *Carbonária*. Her old ally, *The Times*, used its leader to send an accompanying volley up the Tagus. Rejoicing in its own objectivity, *The Times* extolled the aims of the forthcoming meeting, insisting that all Portugal's critics approached the issues as Lusophiles. But it warned against taking the goodwill that underpinned the old alliance for granted. It reminded that both Bomba's Naples and the Turkey that massacred the Bulgarians were also allies who had to be denounced. *The Times* conceded the difficulties of succeeding a decadent monarchist regime and operating the rule of law amidst two major uprisings in three years. But that was no excuse for the perpetuation of the conditions reported by the Duchess and Philip Gibbs (unnamed, as he was a *Chronicle* journalist). Yet, *The Times* stops short of endorsing the Duchess's demand for an end to the alliance without a complete amnesty. It came down somewhere between her and Grey:

> it is our earnest hope that the Portuguese Government may soon see their way to mitigate the lot of the political prisoners, even if they do not take the bolder course proposed by the PRESIDENT of the REPUBLIC a year ago, and grant a general and comprehensive amnesty.[54]

The Duchess was rudely shaken four days later by the clatter made by the Managing Director of the Anglo-Portuguese Tin Company. H. W. Hewitt took industrial aim at the critical alliance of Berkeley Square with Fleet Street. In a rare defence of the Costa Government in a British newspaper, he developed an impassioned case on behalf of the Republic. Firstly, the conditions in Portuguese prisons had much improved over the past year. Secondly, many political prisoners had been released during the course of that year. Thirdly, the Royalists had, themselves, retarded the chances of clemency by their own behaviour. Continuing to plot throughout 1913 encouraged *Carbonária* extremism and damaged the chances of release of the remaining political prisoners. Fourthly, he offers an important explanation of the slowness of the Portuguese criminal law. For a warrant to be issued for arrest, a judge had to affirm signed statements by witnesses of the alleged offence. This slowed the process of arrest, encouraging arbitrary action by quasi-legal groups such as the *Carbonária*. If the criminal law was amended, to allow swifter apprehension by the regular police, then much of the rationale for using the *Carbonária* would be erased. Finally, Hewitt argued, Costa had received an unfairly bad press in Britain. He had shown outstanding statesmanship and leadership of his country, particularly in the areas of educational and civil service reforms, much neglected under the Monarchy. He concluded by suggesting that both Her Grace and *The Times* were employing the wrong tactics:

> The best course for the Duchess of Bedford and her supporters to pursue would be to use their influence with the Monarchists in order to persuade them to cease their efforts to upset the Republic by armed conspiracy, and to rely upon constitutional methods. If that were done, Dr Affonso Costa is too prudent and enlightened a minister to neglect the opportunity for a general amnesty, which a settled government could well afford to proclaim.[55]

Hewitt illustrates how different the view of Portugal could be from the house of industry. Beneath the argument that a flawed legal system, inherited from the Monarchy, impaired the prospects of improved justice under the Republic, lay a concern for business continuity. His company had been mining wolfram in the Beira Baixa region of eastern Portugal since 1910.[56]

As the Duchess was resting, Tenison, leapt in with a selective defence of the BPC's vice-chairman. She by-passed completely Hewitt's substantive point about the inherited deficiencies of the legal system. She also missed the opportunity to expose his underlying business agenda. Rather, Tenison prefers to take aim at the alleged slur by Hewitt, that the British Campaigners were a mouthpiece for the Monarchists. 'The National Protest Committee . . . has no influence or connexion with any Portuguese Monarchists,'[57] she claimed. In respect of the collective body, the Committee, this may have been true. In respect of individual members like herself and the Duchess, it was not. As we have seen, both of them were in contact with Miguelists in Vienna and Paris, and only a discrete distance was kept from Dom Manuel's circle in England. Tenison was being disingenuous. There were other distortions. Secondly, she falsely accuses Hewitt of suggesting that the risings of 1913 were all Monarchist ones, when Syndicalists and other leftists had also been insurgent. He had not actually said this. His argument had been that Monarchist risings gave license to other extremist political behaviour on the part of groups such as the *Carbonária*. His tone clearly disapproves of the behaviour of both extremes. Finally, Tenison turns Hewitt on his head. The latter had argued that cessation of insurgency would allow for speedier release of political prisoners. Tenison replied that an amnesty was a pre-requisite for such a cessation. In the long run an amnesty did not end plotting, but it was the military not monarchists who overthrew the Republic in 1926.

The Duchess reappeared in the public life of the Campaign at the 6 February meeting at the Westminster Palace Hotel. It proved the Campaign's swan-song, but her role was eulogized despite its episodic pattern:

> Nearly a year has passed since the Duchess of Bedford, fresh from a visit to the prisons of Lisbon, addressed to *The Times* the letter which first called attention to the unhappy lot of the Portuguese political prisoners . . . Since that date the Duchess has never relaxed her efforts to secure justice and mercy for the victims of oppression . . . what Senhor Costa refused to do has now been done by others, and we may heartily congratulate her GRACE upon the conclusion of her delicate and honourable task.[58]

The Times basked in the glory shone by a heroine of its own creation. Its narrative was that an Englishwoman had indeed saved Portugal. But if that was true at all (which it wasn't) that woman had since retreated to East Kent, far from the spotlight which she was always happy to cede to her adored Duchess. Since it wasn't true, it feeds the historian with further evidence that there is nothing new in a campaigning press creating false heroes.

The press, of course, runs competing narratives, and the *Manchester Guardian* had different heroes. In its account of the 6 February meeting, Conan Doyle, Morell and Gibbs' contributions were fully reported, while the Duchess's was afforded just three lines.[59] Its analysis required no heroes, though: a reshaped Portuguese Government was in a position to grant a general amnesty from a position of strength. But the terrier Tenison was not about to let them get away with transferring the credit to Lisbon. She pointed out that the amnesty was not general. It excluded a few exiles still regarded as dangerous. Returning to Palmerstonian lessons, she reminded that he had stood out for a general amnesty in 1847, when the Portuguese Government had wanted to banish a dozen or so of the rebel leaders: 'May we not hope that in 1914 as in 1847 the voice of British public opinion may successfully influence the Portuguese Government to show its strength by justice and mercy.'[60] Or, let England save Portugal another time.

184 | *The Duchess*

4 Conclusion: Adeline, Duchess of Bedford and prison reform

When Adeline Bedford died of influenza, in 1920, eulogies flowed from both wings of the British press. *The Times* obituary commented that she was 'known for her excellent social work, especially for women.'[61] The list of charitable endeavours was formidable. It cited her rescue work with young women at Victoria Station, her membership of the Associated Workers' League through which the problems of young working women were addressed, her championing of women's education, but most of all her chairing of the Association of Lady Visitors of Prisons. During the war, she worked hard as a committee member of the British Red Cross Society, and the Order of St John of Jerusalem (a history of which E. M. Tenison published). After the war, she worked on schemes for adoption and, in particular, on behalf of blind babies. Portugal was not forgotten:

> Her interest in prisons was not confined to prisons in this country. Her disclosure of the condition of those of Portugal, largely based on her own personal observation, provoked a storm of controversy. Whatever may be the merits of the dispute, her intervention did much to secure the eventual release of the Royalist prisoners.

From the other political wing, *The Spectator* focused much more heavily upon Portugal. It argued that her great contribution was to bring unity to a previously divided press. She took on fellow Liberals by launching the Campaign in two Conservative newspapers, enabling interest to be generated that spread beyond British shores. This was key to its success in forcing the Republican Government to change policy. Finally, her timing was immaculate, as the Amnesty was won just months before 'the German challenge broke upon a bewildered world.'[62]

But historians have hardly mentioned her contribution since. This is one reason for putting the record straight. Another is that her attitudes towards the government of Portugal in the years before the war reveal another Duchess. *The Times* obituary hints at her unpopularity with suffragettes, whose militancy she distanced herself from. It also highlights the controversial nature of her interventions over Portuguese political prisoners, which have been much evidenced. Significantly, *The Times* slipped an ambiguity into its obituary, suggesting it was Royalist prisoners that she sought to release. The Campaign was always careful to avoid accusations of partisanship by claiming that it worked for *all* political prisoners. The newspaper had, in fact, revealed a deeper truth: that members of the Campaign held ambivalent public and private positions. The Duchess was more prepared than most to argue the religious case against the First Republic in public because she felt she occupied the high moral ground. But her aristocratic, class background was an embarrassment. She was anxious to avoid looking like an English aristocrat campaigning on behalf of equally privileged Portuguese. The British political landscape is vital in understanding her problem. Defending aristocracy in these years went against the policies of a government of her own persuasion. In his budget of 1909, Lloyd George had taxed the landed classes to finance social insurance so radically that they provoked a constitutional crisis in retaliation. The period between the general elections of 1910 and 1914 experienced political strife that extended to labour, women and votes, and Ireland. It was no time for a Liberal duchess to be defending aristocrats. The only way out was to arm oneself with a narrative of liberty, constitutionalism, and religion, that was inclusive of all classes.

It is easy to discern a linear continuity in her penal reform work that leads from Aylesbury to Lisbon. But there was a key difference. At home she worked across the spectrum on behalf of under-privileged women. In Portugal, she was not particularly concerned to reform the penal system institutionally, just to release the political prisoners. She had not been concerned with the condition of Portuguese prisons under the Monarchy before 1910, and she retreated from the Republic after 1914 until her death in 1920. In each case she was a narrow reformer: for women in England; for political prisoners in Portugal. Whereas *The Times* commented on the *social* nature of her reform work in Britain; in Portugal, it was *political*. If she had few illusions about overthrowing the Republic and its perceived atheism, the Campaign she figure-headed did play a small part in getting rid of Costa. This was informed by a condescending neo-colonialism that paralleled some of the class attitudes she exhibited towards women prisoners. The Republic might have been behaving like one of her refractory young girls in Aylesbury: noisy, rebellious, and unwilling to take the wise counselling of their betters. Lisbon needed a Lady Visitor in 1913 but it was not the gentle matriarch, familiar in Aylesbury and Holloway, that arrived. This 'other' Duchess was a pedagogue, come to sort out not only the prisons of the Portuguese but their value system, too. Their lapse into secularism required the re-moralization of government. This was a gargantuan task. She settled for releasing the political prisoners.

CHAPTER

9

Captives, Campaigners and Citizens

1 Captives

Competing narratives

From its inception in October 1910 until the Amnesty Bill of February 1914 up to two thousand political prisoners were incarcerated by the first Portuguese Republic.[1] The prisoners were drawn from a wide range of political opponents, from royalists to syndicalists and anarchists. The vast majority were royalists, although debate persisted about proportions. British critics directed two principal lines of attack. Firstly, for a parliamentary regime to keep political prisoners was a violation of the rule of law. The Republic replied that such idealism ignored the constant insurrectionary threat from royalist conspiracies. Royalists retorted that the Republic had itself come to power by insurrection, and so the argument came full circle. Secondly, the conditions of political prisoners ill-befitted a regime professing liberal values. The first line of attack was easier for the Republic to defend than the second because of the frequent insurrections. But, even a government under threat had no need to treat its political prisoners cruelly. Thus, political prisoners became the Achilles heel of the regime. The issue also became emblematic of the hypocrisy that critics insisted lay at its heart. A government standing for freedom, democracy and justice imprisoned its opponents, gerrymandered elections, and violated the rule of law. The Republic was a charade behind which lay the self-interest of little dictators who would replace the gently decaying royalist state with something worse: a kleptocracy guarded by low-bred gangsters, freemasons and *Carbonária*.

Captives' narratives were used by the British Protest Committee as an important element in the campaign to free political prisoners. Linda Colley has reminded us that such personal evidence is open to a plural reading.[2] At the micro-level, the Portuguese narratives provide valuable, often verbatim reportage of the testimonies of prisoners about their conditions. At the macro-level, they evidence the arbitrary exercise of the rule of law and the severity of punishment in the new Republic. They can also be read against the grain, for example for the unwitting testimony of a dethroned royalist class.

A critical methodology also needs to mediate this evidence as selective accounts with a strong propagandist function. Conditions of imprisonment are compared unfavourably with those pertaining under the Monarchy. As Colley points out, using captives' narratives requires the historian to ask questions about how the tales were constructed.[3] Most of the narratives of Portuguese captives are contained in the first section of a pamphlet published by the British Protest Committee,[4] although some also appeared in *The Spectator*. They appear in two, lengthy polemical pieces that preface the pamphlet. They are 'constructed' by the Honorary Secretary of the British Protest Committee (and historian), E.M. Tenison. Tenison's editing of the narratives is disingenuous. Her opinions, prejudices even, intervene into narratives that are not always reported verbatim or clearly sourced. They reveal as much about the propagandist practices of the British Campaign as they do about the evidence of the informants. But this is valuable because it illustrates the Campaign's tactics. Tenison's partisanship reflects that Campaign's anxiety over the British government's evasiveness. It needed pushing. But, Tenison's mediation also divulges her own ideological predilections, broadly shared by the BPC.

The pamphlet went through five editions in seven months between January and July, 1913. Copies were sent to Lisbon in May, and two hundred bound for the English Library, there, were confiscated by the Portuguese Government. It did not go unchallenged as evidence. The pro-government newspaper *O Mundo* condemned it as the fraudulent work of a Portuguese Royalist conspirator. Prime Minister Afonso Costa countered its claims with his own about the lenient treatment of prisoners. The British protest smeared him by declining to trust the word of any politician in league with the *Carbonária*, which 'kills with poisoned weapons'.[5] The Government stood accused of trying to eradicate Royalism from Portugal through imprisonment. But in April, 1913 it changed tack as outright repression gave way to counter-propaganda. The excellence of prison conditions was 'constructed' by circulating in Britain translated articles from sympathetic newspapers and pamphlets. If the prisons were not exactly opened, they were opened for inspection, and a flood of competing narratives unleashed.

The humiliation of Dom José

Dom José Mascarenhas, sentenced to sixteen years, smuggled out his captive's narrative in the stockings of a sympathetic warder. It appeared in *O Dia* of 26 April. The warder subsequently joined the prisoners' ranks. Mascarenhas retained a creditable sense of humour towards his conditions, tinged with class prejudice. He mused that the rough and ready types from the mountains were more attuned to the cold and appalling food than aristocrats like himself. Tenison intervened to compare these prison rations with Costa's when he was imprisoned under the Monarchy. She recalls his diary, in which even breakfast read like a full meal: 'A nice fried sole, an excellent beefsteak, potato straws, cheese, wine, an apple, a tangerine orange, and a banana.'[6]

Mascarenhas was emotionally traumatized by his moral degradation. His class prejudices rebelled against Royalists being forced to share conditions with common criminals. Regulation prison clothing, shaven heads, and straw pallets were all great levellers. Family visits could only take place from behind the *parlatorio*, and not at all if one complained. He experienced emotional deprivation at not being able to embrace or kiss his children or wife. When he applied for special permission to have his family admitted to his cell in the *Penitenciária*, the Minister of the Interior refused him. He urges readers not to believe the evidence of the Governor to the press.

The reneging of Francisco Homem Cristo

Homem Cristo's narrative, originally published in *The Spectator* (28 June 1913) was republished in the BPC's pamphlet. He contrasted political imprisonment under the Republic unfavourably with that under the Monarchy, under which, as a Republican, he had served five sentences. The first of these resulted from a false conviction for being one of the leaders of the 1891 Oporto insurrection. At the other extreme, the indolent Monarchy failed to prosecute several members of the present Republican government in 1891. He contrasts this with the Republican government's vengeance in convicting on *Carbonária* evidence, alone. Secondly, Cristo contrasts his humane treatment under the Monarchy with the Republic's attempt to assassinate him in custody. He had been sceptical about the 1910 Revolution. Sentenced for 'libelling' several Republican leaders, he claimed there was an attempt to poison him in the *Limoeiro*. He had been saved by Costa Cabedo, a political colleague of Machado Santos,[7] who burst into the police station to warn him not to eat any food once inside the

Limoeiro. A sympathetic a police lieutenant gave Homem Cristo his own dinner lest he went hungry. Homem Cristo managed to escape to France, evading six years' solitary confinement and ten years' penal deportation. He regretted leaving behind some three hundred and fifty others, mainly Royalist, political prisoners.[8]

For Tenison, cases like Homem Cristo's illustrated the artifices of the Costa government, and the naivety of those Liberals who supported it. Homem Cristo complained that the regime represented only a Lisbon clique, not the whole nation. He called for a traditional English intervention in Portugal's affairs. Consistent with Tenison's mantra, such pleas were treachery to Costa's government and justified his prosecution.[9]

The martyring of Father Avelino

Father Avelino de Figueiredo was arrested in March, 1911 and kept for some two years under the emergency laws relating to 'preventive imprisonment'. The harsher regime imposed after the Couceiro Rising of 1912 allowed for him to be brought before the new military tribunal retrospectively. He was sentenced to six years' solitary confinement and ten years' penal deportation. Tenison intervened: 'the martyrdom of Father Avelino de Figueiredo has been the cause of widespread and repeated protests.'[10] By the time he had reached his solitary confinement, his health was already broken by two years in the *Trafaria* and *Limoeiro*. The bread and water diet and rat-infested cells had induced suspected tuberculosis, loss of sight and mental instability.

Yet, he provided cogent testimony for *A Nação*, (3 November 1912), where he explained that he had originally been arrested on 20 March 1911 for instigating a general strike. This charge had been changed to conspiracy, implying the strike was designed to recruit support for a Monarchist rising. At the trial, the crucial evidence had been the word of an informer, and Avelino had been prevented from calling witnesses in his defence. In March 1913 he smuggled out a letter to the *Catholic Review* (of Viseu) in which he laid down the preconditions for his own martyrdom. He had been persecuted by 'atheistical clubs', his health would not withstand years of imprisonment, and his old father would probably die of hunger without his support:

> I pray I may know how to die . . . My mind is calm and tranquil . . . Someone must suffer for the sake of our country and our faith, and I happen to be one of those chosen – blessed be God. Disciple and minister of Christ, in Him, I will seek strength for the great struggle;

from Him I may learn resignation and courage such as supported the martyrs of old ... None of the prisoners have suffered so atrociously as I; but do not weep for me.[11]

Father Avelino was transferred to the *Penitenciária* on 7 April 1913. Several of his fellow prisoners cheered as, on departure, he uttered a forlorn farewell in favour of the Monarchy and King Manuel. Tenison added her eulogy. Father Avelino entered the history of Republican injustice, for 'the crime of fidelity to a fallen cause.'[12]

The silencing of the lawyers

Portuguese Political Prisoners further argued its case from examples of attacks upon the legal profession. José Arruella was a Republican lawyer who had defended rebels against the Monarchy in 1908. By 1913, however, he had spoken out against the new Republic. Visiting prisoners in the *Penitenciária*, he was arrested 'for carrying a revolver.' Tenison wove in the ironic lesson: those who visited prisoners ran a high risk of becoming prisoners, themselves.

Lomelino de Freitas, another dissident Republican lawyer, was among a batch of one hundred and eighteen political prisoners deported to the Azores. They had been put under preventive detention, accused of participating in the uprising of 27 April 1913. His testimony was sent by letter from the Castle of St John the Baptist on 22 May. He complains of being ill before being transported. Neglected, he was then thrown into the insanitary hold of an old cargo boat, the Cabo Verde, where his condition worsened until the ship's doctor intervened. Imprisoned, nevertheless, in a small, dark, airless cell he dreaded his heart condition would worsen. He survived and, back in Portugal, feared for Royalists who had suffered such preventive custody for far longer than he. He reflected on the irony of his situation that, as a lifelong Republican, he was watching democracy metamorphose into tyranny. Liberty and freedom of thought were no more. Tenison was in no doubt who was responsible: 'Under the "free-thought Republic" Portuguese subjects must think as Costa thinks; otherwise they go to prison.'[13] De Freitas's fellow prisoners in the Azores wrote to the moderate Republican newspaper *Intransigente*, comparing their conditions unfavourably with the Monarchy, but it was silenced.

'Contradicting slander': Counter-narratives

The captives' narratives presented by the BPC did not go unchallenged. At 69 Brookfield Road, Chiswick, a Republican agent, put together a pamphlet, designed to present a counter-narrative. He targeted the Duchess of Bedford, rather than the reclusive Tenison, for circulating misleading rumours to the London press culled from her visit to Lisbon in April 1913. It contained nothing new, being sourced from Lisbon's *A Capita* and the London *Times*. Its significance lies more in demonstrating the Republic's active counter-propaganda within London, itself.

On 19 April, *A Capita*, had interviewed the political prisoner, Francisco de Melo Costa (son of Countess Ficalho). He is reported as working in the Secretary's office in such amenable circumstances that the authorities even allow him to make a little money. He blamed the Duchess for deliberately bypassing well-treated prisoners like himself, accusing her of bad faith in selecting only evidence that suited her case:

> he said that her conduct was most incorrect. As a foreigner she goes about reporting things she did not see. When that lady saw him, she only asked after his brother and his mother's address. Nothing else. When he was leaving the prison he was in the corridor and she said 'be confident' Ficalho assured me that between the Duchess of Bedford and himself no other conversations took place.[14]

A Capita's correspondent returned to the *Penitenciária* on 24 April to continue interviewing contented prisoners. Ficalho made for an even happier sight than before, dressed like a gentleman in well-pressed trousers and black silk socks, working in an office full of flowers and smelling of spring. Whole families had been allowed to visit prisoners, bringing gifts ranging from sweets, fruit flowers, and tobacco, to books and bedclothes. Ostensibly well-fed, well read and warm, one prisoner felt moved to tell the correspondent that 'if allowed to do so they would all doubtless sign a message expressing themselves captivated by the good treatment afforded them.'[15] The rotund Father Barroso, a man of large appetite, agreed that the meals were so good that even he could rarely finish them. He illustrated the civic spirit presiding at the *Penitenciária* by relating the tale of the enormous nineteen year-old field labourer, António Feliciano, who had apprehended a mad prisoner who had gone on the rampage. He was rewarded with extra food.

The *Penitenciária* was apparently full of satisfied clerics. Father Avelino de Figueiredo ('martyred' by Tenison) had a cushy job typewriting for the locksmith workshop. Small, refined and delicate, he contrasted with Barroso, but was also a picture of health, as exemplified by his white, well-kept teeth. He claimed he could not have been better treated. Our correspondent invited him to comment on 'the malevolent campaign raised in London by Bedford', to which he responded with energised patriotism:

> Portuguese life is only for the Portuguese; foreigners have nothing to do with it. Much less when they go abroad to spread falsehoods and slander. On this point, although a Royalist, he agrees with the Republicans. Slander must be contradicted.[16]

The correspondent concludes his visit with the 'truly moving scene' of political prisoners 352 and 362. Father and son, they had been incarcerated separately in different parts of the prison for a full nine months. Without explanation, the son suddenly decides he wants to see his father. The Governor naturally invites both to his office, where they fall into each other's arms 'after cruel hours of uncertainty, sorrow and despair.'[17]

The Times published an edited version of a letter from the Director of the *Penitenciária*, Henrique Caldeira Queirós. Gomes' pamphlet published the full version to complete the rehabilitation of the *Penitenciária*. Queirós complains of much previous correspondence designed to stain the reputation of Portugal as a civilized country. He reminds of conditions under the Monarchy when his prison was built in 1885. Modelled on the Penitentiary at Louvain, it was especially designed for cellular isolation of serious criminals. Prisoners were hooded. When taught in a class group, they had to stand in wooden boxes to prevent them from seeing each other. Teaching was by instruction; no questions were allowed. After class, they would return to cells to perform the instructed tasks.

The Republic had reformed these conditions. Both hooding and corporal punishment had been ended. Wooden boxes were being phased out with the intention that all prisoners should be instructed on benches. For the moment they still stood in the boxes, although, unlike under the Monarchy, they were open. Selection for class was by aptitude and experience, taking account of health and physical condition of the prisoner. Teaching proceeded by modern question and answer technique. Special workhouses were set up for tailoring, shoemaking, carpentry, bookbinding and other crafts. In some of these the men worked together, no longer in isolation. They were paid a wage.

When not working, prisoners could avail themselves of literary instruction at any one of three different levels, all supported by a library service. As full religious freedom operated under the Republic, nobody was obliged to attend mass. Indeed, Queirós is anxious to point out that only one political prisoner chose to have mass in his cell on a Sunday. Others declining the spiritual light all inhabited clean, airy, well-ventilated cells with a window to the outside. Each had a bed, small table, bench, lavatory and electric light until 9 p.m. Under the Monarchy, communal exercise was not allowed; the Republic had introduced it for one hour per day, during which prisoners might walk, talk and even smoke in groups of three. At pains to emphasise the phasing out of an isolatory regime, Queirós stressed the contact permitted with families. The public meeting area, was being made more user friendly by replacing the iron bars and brass wires with glass frames. Not only were gifts such as reading matter, fruits and sweets permitted, but meals could be brought in from the outside up to twice a day. Such nutritional benefits were designed to sustain hygienic prisoners free to wash and bathe often.[18]

Given such pristine conditions, it is perhaps no surprise that Queirós reported there had been no need to exact special punishment upon any of the political prisoners. Indeed, he claimed their good behaviour as tacit acknowledgement of their treatment. He stood ready to hear any complaints they might have, and the prison was open to visit by any foreigner. One did visit on 14 April, S.H. Swinney, President of the London Positive Society. Queirós signed off with a final rub of salt into English wounds by citing his entry in the visitors' book: 'I think the arrangement and management of the prison excellent – In many ways the prisoners are better treated than in similar institutions in England.'[19]

How should we evaluate this war of words? Both sets of captives' narratives were mediated by the subjective agendas and interventions of their collectors. The competing 'constructions' were so driven by propaganda that a prison like the *Penitenciária* was narrated as both hell on earth and the Hotel Lisboa. But there is more certainty over which narrative most influenced British public opinion. The Portuguese counter-narrative emanated from a sense of the righteousness of a wronged Republic. But it was crude in the extreme. It was permitted limited discursive space by an unsympathetic British press. The Campaign's 'construction of reality' prevailed in this respect, but also because it claimed to afford to Republicans the freedom of debate they denied their captives. At the macro-level of ideology, the dominant out-competed the subordinate narrative. The Portuguese case had been heard, but marginalized, despite Gomes and Queirós being agents of their own destruction. The British knew best what Portugal's prisons were like.

2 Campaigners and Citizens

Planning the first public meeting of the Protest began while the Duchess of Bedford was away in Portugal. E. M. Tenison, as Secretary, constructed the pamphlet that became *Portuguese Political Prisoners: A British National Protest*, in preparation. On her return, the Duchess wrote her open letters to *The Times* and the *Daily Mail*. It was felt that the platform ought to include a broad cross-section of views. As a well-known agnostic, G. M. Trevelyan's name was floated as a main speaker, but it proved difficult to commit other such public figures.

Obtaining a venue proved as problematic. The Duke of Wellington made his excuses for Apsley House. He was afraid the 'militant and fanatical suffragettes' would take advantage and invade. Surrey House, offered by Lady Battersea, was too small at 300. The Aeolian Hall provided 800 seats, which signalled to detractors that the meeting would pull in a big audience. Much letter writing by Tenison and her two aunts met with an improved response. Trevelyan, Republican as well as agnostic, finally signed up. Portuguese Royalists in exile had been forbidden to attend, however, by the Marquis de Soveral, Dom Manuel's confidante at Richmond. Tenison made no connection between this and the ex-King's pension arrangement with the Portuguese Government. It is, however, evidence of the falsity of rumours that the Protest was manipulated by the exiled King. Tenison is adamant:

> None of our Committee knew King Manuel personally; not even Lord Lytton or the Duchess. In all our words and actions we were careful never to rebuke the Republic for being a Republic, only for the atrocious conduct of its myrmidons.[20]

Disinformation emanated from the sceptical press. A few days before the meeting, a journalist seeking an interview called upon Tenison at her lodgings in South Eaton Place. She had no permission from the Committee to grant one. Nevertheless, the unnamed newspaper published a full 'interview'. Alarmed, she rushed round to 51 Berkeley Square, where the Duchess reassured her that she, herself, had been similarly door-stepped.[21]

The Aeolian Hall in New Bond Street was full to the brim on the 22 April. Inside were a few disruptors, including some '*Carbonários*' (probably just Republicans resident in London). In addition, a handful of noisy Suffragettes expressed displeasure that the Duchess was putting the freedom of Portuguese political prisoners before that of unjustly imprisoned women. They were escorted out by a steward.

Tenison's personal reflections on the meeting are sketchily written down and are not as reliable as the verbatim report in *Portuguese Political Prisoners*. But she adds two particularly useful pieces of information. The first illustrates tension on the Committee caused by Evelyn Cecil toning down the final resolution. Cecil was no radical. Liberal MP for Aston Manor in 1913, he had supported the Boer War, and opposed both social reform and female suffrage. Tenison had wanted to demand the British Government withdraw naval support from Portugal. The Committee, however, preferred Cecil's more moderate appeal to the Portuguese Government's humanity and justice. Tenison's anger incited her to ugly metaphor: 'I felt we might as well have played a violin solo to a traction engine as expect compassion or justice from Costa by appealing to his non-existent humanity.'[22] The second, comes from Leonard Corfe, who had first suggested holding a public meeting. At his club there were whispers that the Protest was no more than a Stock Market conspiracy by international financiers. Tenison omits to explain why, but it is possible that international finance was anxious to destabilize the Republic in favour of a return to the Monarchy. More probably, Liberal defenders of Grey's foreign policy were peddling gossip to discredit the Protest.

After much networking, the platform comprised an impressive coalition. Most were not anti-Republican *per se*. However, a minority did have an anti-republican axe to grind. Royalists opposed a Republic that was only the third in modern Europe (after France and Switzerland). They were the tip of an iceberg. Subsidiary agendas ran deeper into questions of anti-clericalism, divorce, freemasonry, the franchise, and vigilante political activity. These were issues that traversed party lines.

These protesting British citizens claimed to have been brought together by a single issue. But the road to the Aeolian Hall stretched back to the Third French Republic, of September 1870. Then, another British protest had defended the Commune.

Ultimately, the Portuguese Republic of October 1910 modelled the new constitution of 1911 upon the more pragmatic republicanism that emerged after 1870. A Law of Separation followed, after the French example of 1905. As in France, the Separation Laws settled the religious issue, although it was difficult to predict that in 1911. Royalists lashed out at Freemasons and *Carbonária*, who had usurped the Church's power and brought Jacobinism to the streets. This volatile context met an equally disturbed British politics. Liberalism was locked with Conservatism in a bitter struggle. Two elections in the very year of the Portuguese Revolution had failed to return the Conservative Party to power. Its poodle, the House of Lords, had been neutered. Taxes on property punished the 'natural rulers'. As in Portugal, Syndicalist inspired strikes reflected a new labour militancy. Suffragettes were subjected to the tortures of the Cat and Mouse Act,[23] and Ireland threatened civil war over Home Rule. With their own Constitution in crisis and the Foreign Office juggling Lisbon against Berlin, the British National Protest gathered in New Bond Street to instruct the Portuguese on how to govern.

From its height of arrogance, it failed to delineate nineteenth-century Portugal's crooked line to citizenship. The new Constitution of 1911 was the first serious revision of the long-standing Constitutional Charter of 1834. The latter had laid the foundations for a liberal, constitutional monarchy after the tumult of the civil wars. 1911 preserved both the bicameral legislature (eventually) and the separation of powers of 1834. But it went further. A President, elected by the legislature, replaced the monarch as head of state. The state was secularized.[24] However, the key test for Portuguese democrats was to attend to the franchise. The Republic's reforms proved perverse. Between 1895 and 1910 Portugal operated an income-based franchise that increased the size of the electorate. Replacing income with household franchise in 1911 raised the percentage of the population voting from 11.8 to 14.2 but introducing a literacy test in 1913 reduced it to 7.7 by 1915.[25] The right to vote was not even enshrined in the Constitution of 1911 and had to be affirmed by separate legislation. This ambivalence towards electoral democratisation undermined the legitimacy of the regime at home and abroad. The turnout for the elections of 1911 of 61 percent was only a little above that at the end of the Monarchy. Worse, slightly more than half the members in 1911 had been returned uncontested. Even amongst the elected, the 'filled hats' of bought votes (*chapeladas*) often made the difference. The 'new men' empowered were doctors, lawyers and teachers – machine-Republicans who had matured on the corruptions of the old regime.[26] A more charitable view is that Republicans had insufficiently thought through the idea of representation, resulting in a constitution caught between parliamentarianism and authoritarianism.[27]

The Revolution's ambivalence was epitomized by the men on horseback. 'Please show me a revolution in which troops did not intervene as an instrumental and the most powerful cause' was the challenge trotted out by José Agostinho de Macedo in the 1820s.[28] Ninety years later it had still not been met. The Navy and the Army delivered the 1910 Revolution, a set of armed forces deeply influenced by Positivism and Freemasonry. The officer class had come through the polytechnic schools founded through the nineteenth century, later the Science faculties of the universities. It had emerged from the civil wars committed to liberal, not authoritarian, monarchy. In Saldanha, mid nineteenth-century Portugal produced that rare political animal, a liberal, military dictator. Francophile, populist, and interventionist, the Army was always a potential instrument of political change. This left it far from thoroughly democratic. It was neither uniform in opinion, nor in civic rights. Before the Revolution, non-commissioned ranks could not vote. In 1911, the common soldier, who had been instrumental in making that Revolution, had to fight very hard to be included. Then, in 1913, all members of the armed forces were disqualified from voting in uniform, a slight not well received. Afonso Costa seemed to hold soldiers in only marginally less contempt than priests.

Republicanism's new elite had mostly ascended on the same Positivist, educational escalator. Doctors and lawyers emerged from institutions like the *Escola Polytécnica* alongside officers in the making. Under the liberal monarchy, medical science had reached a pinnacle of social prestige. This was one reason why the assassination of Dr Bombarda had been so shocking. Medics were entrusted with national regeneration. Their perceived task was to rescue the Portuguese from racial decline brought on by a degenerate physiology. Their solutions were not restricted to medicine. Bombarda himself had been a Republican political activist, just one medic who advocated the health benefits of social reform. Housing and sanitary improvements were essential. That is why so many – thirty-seven doctors and two medical students – were elected to the 1911 Cortes. But they ran up against the vested interests. Winemakers proved stronger in countering medical discourse on the dangers of alcohol. Financial austerity won out in substituting public assistance for new house building. But once drawn into the comforting cosiness of Cortes politics, the medics did not fight hard enough.[29] Lawyers proved even less astounding in their social impact. They were hardly new members of the political class in 1910. The Republic decided not to purge the judiciary, but to force the old one to conform. The judiciary did conform, condoning some quite draconian restrictions of civil liberties, like political imprisonment.[30]

This throws into question the 'revolutionary' nature of the Republic. Its continuities with the last years of the Monarchy have been emphasized in that Progressives, as well as Republicans, favoured democratisation and social reform. But their leader, José Maria Alpoim, shot himself in the foot with admissions like: 'I want and desire power for the sake of power: nothing else.'[31] In practice, it led to rotation with the Regenerators, and an abuse of the 'spoils system' that tipped both parties into disrepute. Alpoim had not read the runes. The Republicans had, and presented themselves as above all that. They were modern men, in thrall to the Comtean paradigm of progress, justice and science. But did this amount to more than a 'cultural revolution'; an alternative faith that countering religion could transform traditional customs and beliefs. The state was treated as a transferable asset, not a candidate for social transformation. By the time that Marxists and Weberians arrived in the salons of Lisbon's intelligentsia they had found all the best armchairs occupied by Comteans. So, If '5 October' was a political revolution at all, they saw it as a necessary 'recourse to violence to unblock the system.'[32] Embolic metaphors appealed to medics educated in organicist theories of the state, but soldiers and workers saw themselves as the plumbers who had done the dirty work. Even when Republicans split, in 1912, into Democrats and Evolutionists, the voter had to look hard to spot the difference. The latter leaned slightly to the Right in favouring a tax system more sympathetic to property, a stronger Presidency, and review of the Law of Separation. Behind the split lay factionalism rather than policy. By 1913, personality politics festered, while political prisoners rotted in jail.

The fact that the platform at the Aeolian Hall consisted of three Conservatives and a Liberal cast doubt on the Campaign's claim that it was 'A British National Protest.' Tenison was Secretary of the Committee, Earl Lytton, Chair, and Adeline, Duchess of Bedford, Vice-Chair. They were joined by Aubrey Herbert, MP, arguably the most extraordinary of them all. Conservative MP for Somerset South, he was otherwise engaged in spring 1913, almost becoming King of Albania after securing its independence by the Treaty of London. Albanian was one of his seven foreign languages. He was a close confidante of both Edith Durham (author of *High Albania*, 1909) and the Orientalist, Mark Sykes. Herbert was to work in military intelligence during the First World War and was probably the model for John Buchan's 'Sandy Arbuthnot' in *Greenmantle*. Of the Committee, only Lytton and the Duchess spoke. Thus, diversity was a pre-requisite for the other speakers: non-conformist clergyman, Reverend R.J. Campbell,[33] three members of Parliament – Sir Mark Sykes, W.G. Gladstone,[34] and Mark Lockwood – African expert, Sir Harry Johnston, and historian, G.M. Trevelyan. The verbatim report of the meeting reveals that, despite Lytton's claim that political prisoners was the sole issue, speakers expressed widespread opposition to the Republic.

Born in India in 1876, Lytton was the son of the Viceroy. He inherited the Earldom while still at Eton, from where he went to Trinity College, Cambridge, emerging with a second-class degree in History. From there he failed the Foreign Office exams. He recovered by marrying Winston Churchill's former girlfriend, Pamela Frances

Audrey Chichele-Plowden. Churchill wished them well as a combination of wit and beauty. A Tory peer from 1902, Lytton was so liberal sceptics believed he was in the wrong party. He supported free trade against the tariff reformers in his own party in 1903; refused to vote against Lloyd George's 1909 budget; then voted in favour of the Parliament Act in 1911. He supported his sister Constance's advocacy of female suffrage and chaired the all-party committee that drafted the Parliamentary Franchise (Women) Bill in 1910. Later, he committed to 'creative love', a personal philosophy based on the ideas of the American, Homer Lane. Lytton interpreted it as an amoral synthesis of the ideas of Christ and Freud to restore belief in the original virtue of all human desires.[35]

Lytton was anxious to establish his non-partisan credentials as a friend, not an enemy of Portugal. It was not the Republican nature of the regime that concerned him, but its violations of basic principles of justice and civilized government. He made three specific charges. Firstly, the prisons were full of people for having incorrect political opinions. Secondly, new special tribunals were purposely set up to convict them arbitrarily. Thirdly, some prisoners were subjected to 'barbarous and inhumane treatment.'[36] Lytton was interrupted by Monteiro Gomes, authorized by Costa to write the official reply to the Duchess of Bedford's description of prison conditions, previously discussed. Gomes was given short shrift. Lytton denied him any right of reply. It was implied that the platform was open only to critics of the Portuguese Government's policies. He was advised to organize his own meetings elsewhere and publish his views in the press. The irony of denying freedom of speech at a meeting against political imprisonment seemed to escape the Chair.

Lytton was stung into a clear warning for the disgraceful Portuguese administration: end their tyranny, oppression and injustice or forfeit the friendship of other 'civilised nations.'[37] This was strong language to use about an ally but utterly consistent with the Campaign's policy, echoed by *The Spectator*. The Liberal Government was more cautious. Having survived the 'slavery' issue to 1913, it valued the Alliance as insurance against possible hostilities with Germany. However, the Republicans continued to neglect the armed forces. In the event of the Atlantic becoming a conflict zone, the Portuguese Navy could not be relied on. If conflict occurred in the Empire, the Army in Angola or Mozambique would be unable to resist German incursions from their colonies in South West and East Africa.[38] It was little compensation that Republicans were more   suspicious of Germany than Monarchists. Portugal was a lame duck because the armed forces were weak. Better to keep her neutral and the empire uninvaded. Populist rhetoric over reinstating the rule of law glossed over the problems of Portugal's Government in 1913. Whilst it was in violation of its own Constitution in its treatment of political prisoners, release was opposed by the majority Democrats. They believed to free Royalists was to invite conspiracy. In fact, the two failed uprisings of July and October 1913 were already in the bud in April.[39]

It was left to the recent press controversialist, R.J. Campbell, to move the resolution.

> That this meeting desires to express a strong and indignant protest against the unjust and arbitrary detention of political prisoners in Portugal, and in consideration of the traditions of friendship and goodwill which have long existed between the British and Portuguese peoples, earnestly appeals to the Portuguese Government to pass the Amnesty Bill now before the Portuguese Chamber.

Campbell personified the great Free Church preachers of the Edwardian 'age of mild dissent.'[40] He was born in Bermondsey in 1867, the son of an Ulster Presbyterian, and Unionist, who had migrated and become a Methodist minister. He taught elementary school while studying at University College, Nottingham, before going up to Oxford as a married, mature student. Prominent in Oxford Nonconformist circles, he became attracted to social reform. Graduating with a second in History and Political Science in 1902, he joined the Congregational Church. A move towards Liberal Imperialism was empowered by the belief that God had endowed Britons with unique racial powers. 'Millions of swarthy subjects receive, or ought to receive, at her hands peace and good government,'[41] expressed his imperialist mission. His jingoism is typical of the attitudes that divided 'Limps' like him from the pro-Boer Liberals in these years.[42] He seems little changed by the time he addressed the Aeolian Hall on the Portuguese. Campbell's first ministry was in Brighton, but in 1903 he moved to the City Temple. By that time, he was incubating the ideas that led to 'The New Theology', published in 1907. His sermons became so popular that he was elevated to celebrity status, not only in Britain but also in America. Still, he had to survive an attempt within his own church to expel him.[43]

'The New Theology' was an appeal for more liberal doctrinal thought. Biblical literalism was rejected in favour of a contemporary interpretation of Christianity that emphasized social action; 'the religion of Jesus is primarily a gospel for this life and only secondarily for the life to come'[44] captures its core message. But, its earthly agency, the Progressive League, never took off as a force for social change due to Campbell's recurring bad health. 'The New Theology' marked Campbell's conversion from Liberal Imperialism to Socialism, which he now saw as the practical demonstration of Christianity. Christian Socialists were hardly new in 1906, but his less well remembered *Christianity and the Social Order* (1907) is a better guide to his revisionist political thinking, by then.[45] 'Socialism needs to be hitched to the star of religious faith' he preached. Even more controversially he argued that John the Baptist would have led the storming of the Bastille in 1789. At a labour meeting in Hyde Park in 1907, he stopped short of claiming Jesus for Socialism, but only because he lacked economic theory. Anachronism never detained Campbell. He joined the Finsbury branch of the ILP and the Fabian Society, from where he advocated female suffrage.[46] Such progressiveness was greeted with scepticism when the labour movement remembered Campbell's support for the Boer War.[47] His credibility was further tested when he criticized the alcoholic lifestyle of the working man. He claimed to have been misrepresented. He survived as a Socialist to share platforms with Keir Hardie and spoke for him at Merthyr Tydfil in 1910. By then he was becoming estranged from the congregation at the City Temple, over his drift towards Anglo-Catholicism. He eventually joined the Church of England in 1915, where he remained, much less controversially, until his death in 1956.

Campbell was a valuable acquisition. As a charismatic, Nonconformist preacher, and the only Socialist, he balanced the dominant Tory-Liberal consensus. He claimed the meeting was supported by a broad cross-section of British society. He had confused society with the press. True to form, he controversially used the political prisoners to launch a broader attack upon the Republic. He was unsurprised that a Government that had abandoned Christianity to Freemasons and *Carbonária*, would abuse its opponents. Seeking validation, he reminded he had initially welcomed the Republic's ideals of liberty, enlightenment and progress. But the Government had betrayed these in favour of a 'systematic terrorism' that made it worse than the government it had overthrown. Worst of all, the Government's payments to *Carbonária* to spy and arrest caused excessively zealous behaviour on their part. Inside prisons, general deprivation was exacerbated by flogging,[48] causing moderate Republicans to dissent. Campbell implied that the Government had become a rump, a police state that could only survive through terror.

He had no confidence the Government would improve because it had no strategy for reform. Far from it, it was institutionalizing terror. The special tribunals were packed with Government appointees to eradicate not only Monarchism, but Christianity itself. Schools dismissed religion as foolish. The British Government must put aside concerns about interference in Portugal and invoke higher ideals: 'laws of God . . . and . . . the moral standards of the civilised world.'[49] Campbell concluded by presenting the struggle as one above nationality. It was the family of mankind against the barbarism of the Portuguese Government. He sat down having attacked the Portuguese state from policing to religion.

Adeline, Duchess of Bedford accredited Aubrey Bell with arousing her interest in Portugal, in the *Morning Post*. Tenison had then confirmed for her disturbing reports received from Lisbon contacts. Sir Arthur Hardinge, the British Ambassador, helped arrange the visit to Lisbon in mid-March. Henry Gurney, her Howard League colleague, had urged her, from his Moroccan experience, to be prepared for many visits. But, she told Hardinge that the success of the Campaign in the British press meant once would be enough. The Portuguese authorities raised no objections to her inspecting the *Limoeiro*. For the meeting she reiterated much of the content of her press articles: over-crowded, light deprived cells housing too many abused professionals. Unable to visit every prisoner personally, she took, to group meetings of twenty-five to boost morale. Fatigued, she retreated to the Cathedral opposite the prison to reflect on the irony of it being the Wednesday of Holy Week, when Judas bore false witness to Christ. She left pondering an overheard conversation in the surrounding streets; that it was for women to right the wrongs of Portugal. Women without such freedom were inside the *Aljube* prison where Azorean peasants rubbed shoulders with aristocrats like Constança Telles da Gama. In the *Penitenciária* she found ninety political prisoners alongside criminals awaiting deportation to Portuguese West Africa. The *parlatorio* forced her to converse with them on her knees.

Like Campbell, the Duchess dramatized a monstrous *Carbonária*. Moderate Republicanism had been throttled by a leviathan numbering 32,000 spies who broke into private homes, robbed banks and even committed murder. It was only its insidiously, secretive nature that enabled the Portuguese Ambassador to deny the *Carbonária*'s existence:

> He may be the gentleman who sits next to you at dinner, or the waiter who hands you the dish, or both. He may be the colonel of a regiment, or the private soldier in the ranks, or both. He may be the editor of a democratic newspaper, or the ragamuffin hawking the paper in the streets, or both. He may be the Minister of Foreign Affairs, or his cook, or both. He is anything and everything in all

classes of life, and in all ranks of society. He stabs you in the back, either by word or act; he throttles the young republic like a boa-constrictor, till nothing is left of it but a jelly.[50]

The Duchess too had gone off script. Her theory of a secret state amplified the political prisoners' problem into an existential struggle for the 'inner soul of the nation.' The *Carbonária* were out to exterminate Christianity. Schoolchildren were forced to wear badges that proclaimed no need of God or religion. Cemeteries were desecrated by having the bodies of nuns and all signs of the Cross removed. A bomb attack on a Lisbon church had been foiled, but atheistical mobs still dragged priests through the streets. She shocked moderate Republicans into confronting the anarchy of Lisbon 1913 with the imagery of Paris 1794. 'England' could not stand by as Portuguese Jacobinism devoured its own enemies. The Duchess called for a moral crusade, like Britannia straddling the globe calling the semi-colony of Portugal to order.

Sir Mark Sykes[51] was the Unionist member for Kingston upon Hull from 1911. Son of a Yorkshire squire, and a Catholic convert mother, he was educated by Jesuits in Britain and France, before leaving Cambridge without graduating. This gained him a reputation as an amusing lightweight, although he had authored several books by 1913. Sykes was much travelled across the Middle East and, as a Conservative, was known for his open-mindedness towards other cultures and religions. Commissioned in 1897, he served in the Boer War; then as political secretary and diplomat before being elected. His politics looked back to the romantic Disraelian era of Tory democracy. Sympathies with 'one nation Conservatism,' his cosmopolitanism alongside his Catholicism, gave political breadth to the platform. This was no rash Tory reactionary lashing out at the Portuguese Republic. After the First World War his special knowledge of the Middle East led him to be delegated to negotiate the Sykes–Picot agreement. With the French, he played a key role from 1916 in picking up the pieces of the Ottoman Empire. But, he became disillusioned with what he had done. Like the Duchess, he fell victim to the influenza pandemic, dying in February 1919.[52]

As a diplomat, Sykes discoursed on the values of the Old Alliance. The narrative of Wellington's joint command of both British and Portuguese troops during the Peninsular Campaign was recycled. He conceded the Portuguese 'right' to Republican government and a secular state, but not to imprisonment or torture, nor abuse of Royalists and Christians. In a clever inversion of the Republic's liberalism, he accused the Portuguese Government of practising medieval barbarities as if the Enlightenment had never happened. It set a bad example of intolerance in violating 'the ethical teaching of all time.'[53] In asserting what sounded like a moral universalism, Sykes was actually accusing the Portuguese of breaching *European* ethical standards. But his neo-colonialist construct presented these as universal benchmarks of civilized progress. In inferring that the Portuguese were culturally inferior, he had come perilously close to racializing them. They had produced a regime that was a defeat for European ideas. The political violence of 1910 should have been consigned to the past, unless Republicanism intended to institutionalize state criminality as a permanent system of government. Supporting an amnesty was the responsibility of all God-fearing and humane people.

The diplomat, Sir Harry Johnston, had served in some of the Portuguese colonies. He legitimated his criticisms through a long association with, and love of Portugal, dating back to 1876. The son of an insurance broker, Johnston had learned Portuguese at evening classes at King's College, London in the 1870s, as one of his several languages. He put it to practical use on an expedition to Angola in 1882–83. In the Congo he met H. M. Stanley. A committed imperialist, it was Johnston rather than Rhodes who devised the 'Cape to Cairo' concept to encapsulate British ambitions. His work, financed by the British South Africa Company, enabled the Salisbury Government to strengthen its interests there. Johnston was a key figure in the Anglo-Portuguese crisis of 1890 that led to the Ultimatum. As British Consul in Mozambique, he had visited Lisbon in 1889 to try to negotiate an agreement on spheres of influence. Back in Central Africa, he set about securing British interests against the Portuguese by making treaties with local chiefs. His great adversary was Alexandre Serpa Pinto, just as distinguished an explorer and honoured by the Royal Geographical Society. Crisis ensued over the Shire Highlands. Two forces met in August 1889. Johnston warned Serpa Pinto not to proceed and was ignored. Shots were fired. The British dug in and declared the British Central Africa Protectorate, of which Johnston became the first commissioner in 1891. The 1890 Ultimatum put the Portuguese in their place, although Serpa Pinto was promoted to colonel and national hero.

Johnston was for most of his life a social Darwinist, and a racist who talked about savages and wrote comic verses about cannibals.[54] The title of his later book, *The Backward Peoples and Our Relations with Them* (1920) captures his paternalism. But Johnston was a conciliator and negotiator at heart, not an enforcer. His lightweight colonialism was regarded as radical by conservatives. In 1913,

Johnston published *Common Sense in Foreign Policy*. Aimed at the man in the street, it summarized his views on how Britain should arrange its foreign relations to maximum imperial advantage. A contemporary reviewed its Liberal Imperialist sentiments succinctly:

> If he takes considerable liberty in assigning to the great powers their future position in the world at the expense of the independence of the native races and smaller nations of Africa and Asia, it is but fair to say that he has in view not the exploitation of those countries, but their gradual development into self-governing colonies.[55]

Such was the half-way house of Liberal Imperialism, at the turn of the century. Knighted in 1896, at only 37, Johnston was the youngest member of KCB. He returned from Africa by 1903 and stood unsuccessfully for parliament as a Liberal, an experience repeated in 1906. From home in West Sussex, from 1906, he continued the writing begun in Africa. His considerable reputation as a scholar earned him an Honorary Doctorate of Science, from Cambridge University in 1902. Johnston's academic work drew praise for its fairness towards Portuguese imperialism, even from Portuguese academics:

> The work now under consideration contains an introduction to the whole subject, vindicating the claims of the Portuguese as pioneers in exploration and colonization, claims which have already been fully recognised in this country by Sir Harry Johnston and others who have written on the dealings of European nations with Africa.[56]

Two months after the Aeolian Hall meeting, Johnston published a learned article on David Livingstone that exposes his taste for racial categorisation:

> David Livingstone, it is scarcely necessary to remind you, was of Highland descent, his grandfather having been a crofter on the island of Ulva, off the west coast of the larger island, Mull. In appearance he showed clearly the predominant strain in his ancestry was what we call Iberian for want of a more definite word. That is to say, that he was of that very old racial strain still existing in western Scotland, western Ireland, Wales and Cornwall, which has apparently some kinship in origin with the peoples of the Mediterranean, and especially of Spain and Portugal.[57]

Johnston brought the erudite voice of academia and diplomacy. Liberal Imperialist but Lusophile, he would only criticize fellow imperialists like the Portuguese *in extremis*. In a Britain preoccupied with such worries, he put a national resources argument. Political persecution threatened catastrophe for Portugal's national existence. He appealed to its leaders to clear the prisons of people who should be playing an important intellectual role in the national life, even at the expense of suppressing violent protests. Johnston's Liberalism held no brief for the deposed monarch, whom he thought lacked the wisdom to deal with his circumstances, despite his constitutionalism. The Church, he thought, had made circumstances worse through neglecting much needed popular education. But none of that excused political imprisonment, a characteristic of a *Carbonária*-driven dictatorship. Johnston called for a coalition of patriots of Monarchists and Republicans against political coercion, to salvage Portugal's reputation. His call for regime change to free political prisoners revealed the misrepresentation behind the single-issue strategy.

William Glynne Charles Gladstone was the grandson of the great Liberal Prime Minister. Born in 1885 at the family's London home, 41 Berkeley Square, he was a neighbour of the Duchess of Bedford. In his maiden speech in the Commons Gladstone confessed to feeling burdened by the family name, but it did the Campaign no harm. He had not done badly in his grandfather's shadow. After Eton, he was President of the Union at Oxford (1907), then Assistant Private Secretary to the Lord Lieutenant of Ireland (1909) and an Honorary Attaché to the British Embassy in Washington (1911). In that year he was elected to Parliament as Liberal Member for Kilmarnock Burghs. A fresh-faced twenty-eight year-old, he contrasted with the distinctly world-weary, fifty-five year-old Johnston. Sadly, Gladstone was to be killed in action in France in April 1915, shot dead in the trenches endeavouring to locate an enemy sniper, aged forty-three.

On 22 April 1913, he did what his grandfather had done to the Turks in 1876: he instructed the Portuguese on how to live up to British standards. Portugal had to be saved from itself because it was in danger of dishonouring the Alliance. Portugal was letting Britain down. Imprisoning in inhumane conditions was bad enough; inflicting it without trial was beyond the pale. It offended the constitutional principles of the British people, but more immediately would provoke instability within Portugal itself. A prosperous Portugal, honoured abroad, depended upon the restoration of justice. Good social relations arose, he universalized, only from sound constitutional principles. W. G. Gladstone kept faith with his grandfather's Europeanism. Like Sykes before him, he called Portugal back to the European family of values.

As a prominent freemason, Mark Lockwood, Conservative MP for Epping (1892–1917), might have been expected to sympathize with Republicanism. But English freemasonry was cut from a more conservative cloth. Lockwood was from an old Essex family who owned the Lambourne estate near Abridge, about fifteen miles from London. An old Etonian, he had retired from the Army in 1883, with the rank of Lieutenant Colonel, at the tender age of thirty-six. In 1894 he assumed the Lord Lieutenancy of the county. Lockwood seamlessly combined politics with freemasonry. In 1902 he became Provincial Grand Master of the Essex Freemasons. He took his duties very seriously, travelling from one end of the county to the other despite his parliamentary duties. In 1909 he refused to consecrate the new lodge at Loughton, named after local mason Edward Catesby, on the grounds that it bore the same name as Robert, co-conspirator of Guy Fawkes, and a Catholic.[58]

Lockwood's contribution was a patriarchal narrative. He urged intervention in the British spirit of helping those who cannot help themselves. Britons confident in living under a just system had a duty to persuade the British Government to place pressure upon the Portuguese one. Returning Portugal to constitutional rule meant invoking the first law of liberty: the right to trial. This required an end to the *Carbonária*'s 'suborned and perjured evidence.' As a Tory, he was flexible enough to cite Garibaldi's history as assister of the oppressed.

Lockwood had an eye on the star-turn and final speaker. G.M. Trevelyan had published his biographical trilogy on Garibaldi between 1907 and 1911.[59] He was that rarity in early twentieth-century Britain: the historian as public intellectual. As he said, 'If historians neglect to educate the public . . . then all their historical learning is useless except insofar as it educates themselves.'[60] His books were accessible, and their sales granted him a special cultural authority. From a distinguished Whig family of historians and politicians, his great uncle was Thomas Babington Macaulay, and his father George Otto Trevelyan, Chief Secretary for Ireland and Secretary of State for Scotland under Gladstone. He emerged from the Cambridge of J. M. Keynes, Bertrand Russell, Vaughan Williams and E. M. Forster with a First and the intellectual confidence to chart a secular path through Christianity. Kept on as a Fellow at Trinity in 1898, he resigned in disgust in 1903 at the new Regius Professor, J. B. Bury's, condemnation of his style of literary history. His early work on the Age of Wycliffe and the Stuarts emulated the style of his great uncle. From Cambridge he moved to live in Chelsea to hone the Whig interpretation of history begun at Trinity. In 1913, itself, he produced a biography of John Bright, that transformed the free trader into a campaigner for international peace.

Trevelyan echoed the non-partisan spirit of the meeting. He contrasted Lytton's 'sane and single minded' chairmanship with some of the hysteria and exaggerated reporting in the press. He welcomed an audience that represented people from both the political parties and different religious persuasions. Still, 'I would especially appeal to Liberals, and especially appeal to Free-thinkers, not to wink the eye at crime and injustice because it happens to be committed in the name of an anti-clerical Republic.'[61]

Predictably, Trevelyan's Liberalism validated the BPC's protests through the analogy with Gladstone's campaign against the Neapolitan prisons in 1850–1. In late 1850, a family holiday to Naples, to restore his daughter's health, had led Gladstone into a nest of vipers. Climbing Vesuvius, James Lacaita, a legal adviser to the British Legation drew his attention to King Ferdinand II's extreme repression of his liberal opponents, in violation of the 1848 Constitution. Gladstone then attended court as Carlo Poeiro was sentenced to twenty-four years in chains. Gladstone visited Poerio in his filthy dungeon, concluding his case was the tip of an iceberg. The Austrians refused to intervene in Naples, so in July 1851 Gladstone published a letter he had written to Lord Aberdeen some months earlier. He described Ferdinand's prisons as 'the wholesale persecution of virtue . . . the awful profanation of public religion . . . the perfect prostitution of judicial office . . . the savage and cowardly system of moral as well as physical torture . . . the negation of God erected into a system of Government.'[62]

No prisoner was kept in chains in Portugal, let alone for half a lifetime. Still, many condemned it as a negation of God. Trevelyan cared little for gods, but he was capable of equally exaggerated comparisons. Gladstone had disassociated his party from conditions in Naples, he reminded. Supporters of all political parties should do the same in respect of Portugal. This abuse of history continued by application to the French Revolution. A little humour intervened. Portugal's problem was not merely the condition of the prisons, but that the wrong people were in them. He labelled a political system that imprisoned people for their opinions 'Jacobinism.' Warning of parallels with Spain, 'the Liberal Internationalist'[63] announced that he had signed a petition protesting at the execution of Ferrer.[64] Drawing further parallels with Russia, he criticized newspapers that castigated Portugal, but not Britain's other ally, where untried political prisoners languished in Siberia. Nor did he accept that the British public had succumbed to a kind of compassion exhaustion, caused by saturation press coverage.

Recent protests about the Belgian Congo and Brazil gave the lie to that. Trevelyan ended with a plea for diplomatic moderation: 'we are not calling for Palmerstonian gunboats to go to the Bay of Lisbon.'[65] The pressure of public opinion should see through an Amnesty Bill already before Parliament.

Trevelyan used his 22 April speech to demonstrate his internationalism. The Spanish, Russians, Belgians and Brazilians had all been lectured on human rights. When Edward Grey read the newspapers next day, he might have ruminated on the inconsistencies of historians. The Germans had escaped Trevelyan's aim but he had still abandoned measured historical criticism to rhetoric. He contradicted his own reprimand of Campbell, a few days before, for his 'Portugal as Naples 1850' depiction.[66] Trevelyan in full public voice had succumbed to the Duchess's disease. As Disraeli had once said of Gladstone, he had become exuberated by his own verbosity. By contrast, Edward Grey was famously unexcitable.

Lytton in the Chair terminated the meeting in the way he had begun, by excluding debate. He insisted on questions only, no opinions. An atheist in the audience refused censorship and shouted that the Republic had improved educational opportunities by some 75 percent since the end of the Monarchy. Furthermore, despite the presence of Freethinkers like Trevelyan, the Church of England was strongly behind the Campaign in Britain. Lytton dismissed the interjector – even if his assertions about education were true, that was no excuse for keeping political prisoners. The Portuguese went the way of the interruptive Suffragette; led from the Hall by stewards, after being attacked by a compatriot.[67]

A fuller history from below would attend to the social composition of the audience at the Aeolian Hall. About this we can only make inferences. The evidence we have reveals the self-proclaimed 'British National Protest' was little more than an upper to middle class, cross-party alliance. The only Socialist in sight was a former Liberal Imperialist, non-conformist minister with tenuous links to a labour movement, largely silent on the sins of Republicanism. The sympathetic press reported that only three voters opposed the motion for an amnesty. Impressive was the cross-party consensus achieved at a time when Liberals and Conservatives were tearing each other apart in Parliament. It seemed like a triumph for carefully managed citizens' protest. If so, then such modernity was built on an abiding discourse of entitlement: that England had every right to save Portugal – from itself.

CHAPTER

10

The Portuguese Pimpernel

1 The lady expects

News came that they were being treated with great cruelty in horrible conditions – these aristocrats who had been loyal to the young King and had put up a bit of a fight for him. A strange little lady in England who was in touch with their families and agonised over their sufferings received this news constantly and resolved to attempt their rescue. For some reason, which I have completely forgotten, I was chosen by her and a group of friends, among whom were the Duchess of Bedford and Lord Lytton, to play the part of the *Scarlet Pimpernel* in Portugal, or at least to get into the prisons, if possible, and unlock their doors by revealing their misery to the world.[1]

So began the journalist Philip Gibbs' 'adventure in Lisbon' on behalf of the BPC. Gibbs had been recruited by Lord Lytton, via his editor Robert Donald at the *Daily Chronicle*, at the suggestion of John Harris. Lytton asked him to go to see E. M. Tenison 'on behalf of a committee'[2] and warned him to be prepared for a long journey. Yokes Court, Frinstead, was really not that far, even in the winter of 1913. Gibbs was probably collected from Sittingbourne station, in common with other guests. On meeting Tenison for the first time, in late 1913, Gibbs

> found her obsessed by romance and pity for these Portuguese gentlemen, and especially for one noble and gallant fellow who, according to her, was a kind of Portuguese D'Artagnan . . . She did not seem to belong to modern England. She was pre-Elizabethan, I thought, and looked like the pale ghost of a Plantagenet lady looking out upon the world from a castle turret, and waiting for a "very parfit gentil knyghte", who was long in coming.[3]

Tenison was thirty-three, enough for Gibbs, thirty-six, to detect a fear of being left on the shelf. She never married, and Gibbs missed the reason why. The search for a 'gentil knyghte' lay in his imagination. The references to her pre-Elizabethanism, in an autobiography published in 1946, were almost certainly a reference to her multi-volume *History of Elizabethan England*, begun in the 1930s. Gibbs' pen portraits of the woman at the centre of the Campaign (written more than twenty years apart) are brief, but rare sources of their type. In 1923, she is fiercely political, combining the Duchess's agonies for the political prisoners with a hatred for Afonso Costa. She gave him letters of introduction to abused nobles in Lisbon, probably from the Duchess and possibly from Vienna. By 1946, Tenison has lost her soft edge, and the Duchess is 'a very dominating old lady with all the tradition of the 18th century.'[4] The Gibbs of 1946 was a famous journalist of international repute reflecting on being hired as a young man by two women. His chauvinism baulks at this, and he is inclined to distance himself from the neo-colonialism expressed by Tenison in the introduction to the original pamphlet collection of his own articles.[5]

Even in 1946, Gibbs pretends to be at a loss as to why he was recruited. It is not difficult to fathom. His ancestry could not compete with the aristocratic Duchess, nor even with the lesser but well connected Tenison. Nevertheless, he was minor gentleman. His father, Henry James Gibbs, had actually been born beneath the royal roof of Windsor Castle because grandfather Gibbs was serving there as Queen's Messenger. Philip's father went on to become a civil servant at the Board of Education. The family resided in the modest middle-class surroundings of Clapham Park. His salary, rising to £800 a year, was sufficient to stave off genteel poverty, although Mr Gibbs educated all seven children at home, Philip says, to save school fees. The elementary school option is unmentionable by omission.[6]

Such familial frugality destined the young Philip for the university of life, more specifically for the faculty of journalism he later portrayed in his first novel as *The Street of Adventure* (1909). At sixteen, he had his first article published in the *Daily Chronicle*; by twenty-two, his first book, an early venture into children's history writing, *Founders of the Empire* (1899). By his own admission, Gibbs was no historian, and through the remainder of his twenties he worked for three of the leading newspapers of the day, the *Daily Mail*, the *Daily Express* and the *Daily Chronicle*. By then he had shed his former anti-Boer attitudes in favour of a lightly-held Liberalism, mulled over at the Reform Club. He had married the Catholic convert, Agnes Rowland, the daughter of a West Country vicar, in 1898. This was probably the reason for Gibbs' own conversion to Catholicism. The young Anthony had arrived quickly after marriage. Gibbs admits to the strain of Fleet Street upon family life, but the ill-judged switch to the new Liberal daily *The Tribune* solved no problems. Despite boasting G. K. Chesterton, J. L. Hammond, Henry Brailsford and Leonard Hobhouse as fellow contributors, Gibbs found himself out of a job again when it closed after a short period. He sat down to write *The Street of Adventure* as therapy. Sadly, the *Tribune's* naval correspondent lacked Gibbs' personal resources, and shot himself.[7]

After his brief literary sojourn, pressing financial worries forced him back to a job with the *Daily Chronicle*, in 1909. There, he was to excel as Special Correspondent, a job that took him all over Europe. By 1912 he had moved to the *Daily Graphic* for whom he was covering the first Balkan War, first from Serbia, then from Bulgaria, from where he was expelled alongside the Futurist, Marinetti. By 1913 he was reporting mainly for the *Chronicle* again. Thus, when the Campaign needed an agent to expose the iniquities of Portuguese political imprisonment Gibbs fitted the bill. Liberal, Royalist through his Catholic sympathies, he was a widely experienced freelance hack. What Gibbs never tells us is that he left Yokes Court with Viennese gold in his pockets.

Letters in hand, Gibbs arrived in Lisbon feeling, initially, that he had been sent on a fool's errand.[8] Several of the noble houses on his list were closed up. The men of the house were in prison, and the women gone away. Eventually, he found one who had not. The aged aunt of one of Lisbon's great families welcomed him but insisted on speaking in French. He recounts only one other such case – a much younger, and beautiful, aristocratic woman, who told him she was alone because her relatives were imprisoned.[9] But before any of this disappointing house-calling, Gibbs had an even more unpredictable introduction to Lisbon.

2 Strange meeting off Black Horse Square

Gibbs wrote autobiography like the novelist he was. He even compared himself to that figment of Baroness Orczy's imagination, Sir Percy Blakeney, whose adventures had been published in 1905. He arrived in Lisbon with a bag of gold sovereigns and a list of Portuguese ladies of high society to call upon. But such pleasantries were delayed. Gibbs' account of his first night in Lisbon reads, at first, rather like a pick-up. Dining alone at his hotel table, a handsome stranger, whom he takes for a Spaniard, comes over and asks if he is Philip Gibbs of the *Daily Mail*.[10] Gibbs corrects him: he was working for the *Daily*

Chronicle (he had left his post as literary editor of the *Mail* several years before). The man, undeterred, asks him if they can have a chat because he is a lonely, wandering Englishman. Surprisingly incautious, Gibbs allows himself to be regaled with the stranger's life story. There were tales of ranching in South America, mining in South Africa, as they flowed out into a café in Black Horse Square.

Here, the scene changes. They are being spied upon by several lynx-eyed fellows. Gibbs wants to know if they are watching him or the stranger, who only replies that they must give them the slip. At that moment, he makes a bolt for it down a side alley. Gibbs follows, only to spot that a couple of *Carbonária* had already closed off the exit to the alley. By now he remembers to inquire what's going on. The stranger just replies 'a dangerous game' and drags him into a wine bar half way down, where it is suddenly safe to order drinks. But, the two *Carbonária* come in and sit opposite. All other exits seeming closed, the stranger sprints out through the kitchen and leads Gibbs into the alleys beyond, whereupon they make their escape, back to the hotel from whence they had started! Gibbs declared himself unamused. The stranger was quite open about using Gibbs as a cover, believing that he would not be arrested whilst in the company of a visiting Englishman. Gibbs is beyond asking what for, but insists he will not be used for such purposes again.[11]

As a personal narrative, it is an unlikely tale because so much is left unexplained. Less important is Gibbs' propensity to be led into falsely-concocted danger. But it provides a flavour, however exaggerated, of the *Carbonária*'s Lisbon. If we believe it, people were going on the run to avoid arbitrary arrest. This is the pre-war espionage world of Buchan, in which reality is never quite what it seems. Aubrey Herbert would have recognized it intimately. Gibbs had been briefly caught up in a moment of madness yet retained sufficient alertness to disengage quickly. But it must have influenced the article he wrote on the *Carbonária* for the *Chronicle* on 13 December 1913 in which fear of the spy stalks Lisbon.

And Gibbs continued to be stalked. The next morning, the stranger made another extraordinary request. Would Gibbs go to Cascais (a few miles from Lisbon) and bring him back a handful of pebbles? In return, Gibbs could choose any gift from any shop in Lisbon. He would offer no further explanation, so Gibbs refused. His suspicion that he was a police spy was confirmed when the stranger kept turning up in cafes he was using. He appeared on the platform at Rossio station the morning Gibbs left for Porto, having said the previous day he was going to Vigo. He stayed with Gibbs in Porto, shadowing him with ridiculous excuses. And it got worse. Would Gibbs go to a beach near Porto and bring him that handful of pebbles? No! So, the 'shadow' nipped into a jewellers to buy a box for the pebbles that Gibbs refused to fetch. He also nipped into an umbrella shop, emerging not with an umbrella but a sword-stick. This is fortunate because it enables him to gift his walking cudgel to Gibbs. When he finally left Porto two days later, he asked Gibbs to send a telegram for him to an address in South Kensington: 'Arriving London Saturday. Cannot get the pebbles.'[12]

Only the reader of *Adventures* (1923) gets the Porto appendage of the story. Perhaps by the time of *Pageant* (1946) Gibbs decided to omit it because he thought nobody would believe it. In 1923, he had been unable to figure out what had happened himself: 'I cannot give a guess, and have sometimes thought of offering the problem to Conan Doyle',[13] he moans. But he did make a guess. The most obvious explanation was that the man had been a police spy, albeit an incompetently eccentric one. However, there was an alternative, and even more preposterous theory. Shortly after King Manuel had fled, three men had been shot at in the grounds of the abandoned Necessidades Palace. It was thought they were searching for royal treasure reputed to have been buried there. Gibbs speculates that his 'shadow' might have been one of them, on the run, and engaged in some kind of unlikely subterfuge. He couldn't do better than that, so it may have been a wise decision to edit out the final Porto leg of the tale in 1946.

Gibbs turned his attention to strangers in prison. His Portuguese trip took place just before Christmas 1913. He published six articles in the *Daily Chronicle*, which were, themselves combined, along with another piece from the *Contemporary Review*, and published as a pamphlet by the BPC in January 1914. The Duchess and Miss Tenison, who wrote an introduction to the pamphlet, wasted no time. Gibbs reported on prisons throughout Portugal, not just in Lisbon. Conditions in Porto (the second city), Coimbra (the oldest university town and site of conservative dissent) and Elvas, were scrutinized. In Lisbon, itself, he went not only to the *Penitenciária* and the *Limoeiro* but also to the *Aljube*. A further article on the *Carbonária*, exposed the work of a notorious spy, Homero de Lencastre. He interviewed a number of disaffected prominent Republicans, and a leading lawyer.

3 'City of whisperers': Lisbon, 1913

'Nothing Gibbs ever wrote was uninteresting', a reviewer for the *Manchester Guardian* observed. 'He could not be unreadable if he tried.'[14] His account of Lisbon, on arrival in mid-December 1913, as 'a city of whisperers', examples a reputation in the making. Immediately revealing his monarchist sympathies, he attributes the Revolution of 1910 to the betrayal of the young king by his ministers. The rebels are treated as secondary actors. The opportunist Afonso Costa is cast as treachery's heir, a prime minister adroit only at alienating his own revolutionary colleagues. Costa had humiliated Machado Santos, the naval officer who led the '5 October', by comparing him to a shoemaker who had delivered the Republic like a good pair of shoes. Costa's offer of a pension for Machado, Gibbs sees as a stratagem to get him out of the way. Machado was not a full member of the Costa club; an artisan among bourgeois intellectuals. Costa misjudged his man, and one wonders whether Gibbs gave Machado another thought after 1914. Perhaps he did in October 1921, if he heard that the hero of '5 October', had been murdered like a thief in the night by a small group of leftist sailors. If so, he might have reflected on his shameful end, arguably the nadir of a Republic of which Machado Santos' fortunes had always been a barometer.

Famously independent and unvenal, Machado Santos was in thrall to neither Left nor Right in the years after 1910. In his published 1911 account of the Revolution he claimed little for his own officer class, most of whom he saw as apolitical. Inaccurately, he sketched a narrative of a people's revolution. In his *Order of the Day No. 1* (anticipatorily Leninist in its title), he pronounced the end of national enmity in favour of an age of fraternal regeneration. The agents of national rebirth were the ordinary people aided by the sailors. The Army, decayed under the Monarchy, would be similarly radicalised. Having broken from Costa's Democrats to form a more conservative Republican bloc, he turned *O Intransigente* (1911–14) into a belligerently critical voice. A few months before Gibbs' arrival, Machado Santos only just stayed out of prison, accused of supporting a coup of Syndicalists incensed by Costa setting the *Carbonária* upon the trades unions. Yet, not only did he remain free, but in the month before Gibbs arrived he founded the 'Oppositions' League', to dispute the election results that had confirmed the Democrats in power. It brought conservatives together with socialists against the centre.

Gibbs might well have written it off as chaotically Portuguese. But, as he disembarked the train at Rossio station, his journalistic antennae were attuned to what authoritarian Republicanism had done to the national character. Descending the steps of Rossio, to his left, Gibbs would have seen Praça dos Restaurodores, with its huge central obelisk commemorating Portugal's regaining of its independence in 1640. Aubrey Bell would have explained that aphorisms such as, 'Respect the silence of the Portuguese – or go to Spain' express an historic anti-colonialism that goes back to the Restoration. But Gibbs detected an enforced silence broken only by a fearful whispering. Entering the Republic from Spain had been no stroll along the Avenida da Liberdade. Customs went through Gibbs' baggage with a fine-toothed comb, at one stage accusing him of being a disguised monk. They had mistaken his dressing-gown for a habit. The entire train was searched by the police for armed conspirators, and no particular distinction was made between them and journalists. Eventually Gibbs was allowed in on the understanding that he would report impartially. The Republic was, perhaps, as naïve as it was insecure.

Gibbs possessed the journalistic ear for turning the street whisper into sensational newsprint. All the portraits of ecclesiastical scholars had been put into the cellars of the National Library as an act of cultural censorship. And the whispers got louder as they became more visible. Celebratory lists of new political prisoners were appearing in the windows of loyal government newspapers. Two Englishmen were even taken off a ship in the harbour for speaking ill of Prime Minister Costa. No citizen was safe from the *Carbonária* appearing at the door with a search warrant. 'Queer-looking fellows,' they were, 'with big black ties and supple sticks.'[15], strolling the streets of Lisbon with swaggering insolence. They were everywhere, staring at you as you crossed Rossio square, eavesdropping as you sat in a café. Gibbs evaded them to visit an editor whose offices had been smashed up. Things had got so bad, he was told, that they might as well be in Mexico, or even Russia. Take good advice and don't write letters, for they will be opened. If you use the telephone, have a prearranged code; if you visit, have a secret knock that your contact recognizes. When Gibbs visited an old aristocratic lady he had to identify himself by announcing, 'I am the Englishman' because the *Carbonária* sought a pretext to arrest her. In terror, because all her relatives had been imprisoned or exiled, she 'stood there alone like one of those *grandes dames* who, in the time of the French Revolution, would not abandon the old chateaux until the mob forced their gates.'[16] When the grand ladies back in England opened the *Daily Chronicle* of 13 December 1913, they might have felt they were re-reading Baroness Orczy. Gibbs' portrayal of Lisbon 1913 claimed a false, but seductive, acquaintance with the Paris of 1793–4. He had infiltrated deeply into Portuguese Jacobinism's dark secrets.

4 'A horde of state paid spies': *Carbonária*'s Lisbon

Strolling through the centre of Lisbon at the end of 1913, the ordinary tourist might perceive, according to Gibbs, a city and a country at peace with itself. This was a superficial impression. True, elections had recently returned Afonso Costa to power, but only after new literacy regulations had disqualified two-thirds of the old electorate. Even in the Republican stronghold of Lisbon the turnout had been unusually low. Amongst the newly disenfranchised were political prisoners, so numerous that the overflow was incarcerated in confiscated convents and bishops' palaces. One cause of the backlog was the Government's violation of its own law: a maximum eight days' imprisonment without trial. Another was the return of prisoners from places as far afield as the Azores, to await final trial in the capital. Neither were they all Monarchists. Gibbs notes the irony of many Republicans 'being persecuted by the Republic they helped to establish.'[17] The unsuspecting tourist had been told the *Carbonária* had been disbanded because they were no longer needed. But Gibbs knew better because he talked to some who continued to boast 'we are the Republic.'[18]

Gibbs' piece for the *Chronicle* of 16 December explains the *Carbonária*'s inconspicuousness through the secrecy of the police state. The 'horde of paid spies' nicknamed the 'White Ants' were drawn from the irregularly and unemployed, then paid three times the average workman's pay. Little wonder they were not just loyal but enthusiastic state servants. They broke up Bible meetings, even when run by Englishmen. They frequented cafes, eavesdropping the conversations of fellow citizens. Every day they ransacked peoples' houses on suspicion alone. Being a middle-class professional provided no immunity from such enthusiasm, as two leading lawyers found out. Sometimes enthusiasm overstretched the boundaries of decency, as when a young woman was forced to strip on the pretext she was concealing incriminating papers. Still, that was a less terrible outcome than that of the naval officer shot on leaving his hotel in July 1912. His 'offence' was to have been recently acquitted on charges of anti-governmental activity. His fiancée then committed suicide. No-one was arrested for the crime. Street beatings were on the increase. One victim received one after refusing to take his hat off to a *Carbonário*, then received a fifteen-month sentence for attempted manslaughter. He was working class, but class did not save 'Horatio of the Millions', a well-known rich *Lisboan*, beaten prior to arrest on charges of sheltering a Royalist conspirator.

The *Carbonária*'s power was so extensive that they ordered the regular police around. Newspaper offices were ransacked while the police station a few doors away cocked a deaf ear. The editor, Moreira d'Almeida's offence had been to publish in O *Dia* a story criticising the prime minister's private financial dealings in the Portuguese West African island of São Tomé. Fearing arrest, Almeida tried to flee the country but rough weather forced his ship back to port in Porto, where he was imprisoned awaiting trial. Intimidation of newspapers was common practice. Machado Santos's O *Intransigente* was a regular victim once in opposition. As an MP, he protested in Parliament but was howled down from the gallery by *Carbonária* specially appointed for the task.

When Gibbs used the phrase 'the rule of the *Carbonária*' to headline his 16 December article, he meant to draw attention to what was not ruling, namely law. The *Carbonária* exercised power on the streets only by virtue of state endorsement. In the rural areas, especially the North where there was a constant threat of invasion from Spain by Royalist exiles, they were little more than an auxiliary force to the Army. It was in urban areas, notably Lisbon, that their powers had become excessive. Gibbs had no doubt they took their orders and pay from government, who covered this up. When pressed, ministers defended them as spontaneous vigilantes, drawn from the revolutionary enthusiasts of the people. Gibbs thought that might once have been true, but it now raised the question of what had become of that revolution? As the state degenerated, it turned in upon its critics. Gibbs was no Conservative; he remained a Liberal all his life. But he began to draw the same analogy as those of his sponsors who were – the Terror of the 1790s.

5 'A Judas sign': The *agent provocateur* of Porto

Gibbs left Lisbon for Porto, where he seems to have been given unrestricted access to prisoners who provided the raw material for his report from the second city, published on 17 December 1913. There, he discovered a plot that exceeded even his vivid imagination, 'like a story written by a sensational novelist.'[19] It was in good hands for he relayed the incredible story 'of students and scholars, of soldiers and lawyers, of noblemen and peasants, united in a brotherhood of misery.'[20]

That misery had been created by Homero de Lencastre, born into privilege not deprivation. The son of a lady-in-waiting, he was well educated by the charitable noblewoman to whom his mother was in service. Tasked with the sale of a valuable necklace on behalf of the family, at an early age, he disgraced himself by embezzling some of the funds. The scandal seems to have been hushed-up, but it proved to be the start of a promising career in deception. Surviving this earlier scandal may have enabled Lencastre to retain many of his Royalist connections. Certainly, it was these that got him into government service.

The context surrounding his new job offer was the aftermath of Afonso Costa's São Tomé difficulties and the November 1913 elections. Wheeler's view is that these elections were not rigged; the Republican party merely benefited from the prevailing political circumstances.[21] Gibbs, however, implied that Costa plotted with Lencastre to cook up a Royalist conspiracy designed to help the Republican electoral position. This is taken from Lencastre's personal confession. Lencastre seems to have been arrested in Galicia, in Spain, after fleeing Porto. The confession was given to a public notary in Vigo. In it he stated that the whole plot had been cooked up by the Government, with whom he had dealt directly, although he does not mention Costa's name. It had been mediated through the Superintendent of the Porto police, Caldeira Scovola. The latter had provided him with a list of names of Royalists in Galicia whom the Government wished to compromise. To this end he had concocted a report of false evidence of conspiratorial activities and had it signed by false witnesses who were other police agents, before making contact with the exiles in Galicia. All but one who suspected betrayal, were arrested as they re-entered Portugal. Beforehand, the police planted arms in selected houses. The confession ends with Lencastre's pathetic expression of remorse for his actions. The report notes that arrests of the innocent extended far beyond the few duped Galician exiles:

> the professors, doctors, newspaper editors and other distinguished men interviewed in their cells by Mr Gibbs after their false accusation by this spy still remain in prison without trial.[22]

Gibbs collected further evidence from the prisoners in the *Aljube* prison, Porto, that adds flesh to the bones of the confession. It implicates Lencastre in a malicious plot to fit-up the innocent for his own personal gain. His list of false conspirators contained as many as 3,000 names. Lencastre would visit the homes of the gullible, ostensibly to discuss financial backing for the supposed conspiracy. He then coaxed loans from those who were persuadable. The refusers were added to the list, anyway. The next day, a visit from the *Carbonária* would uncover pistols planted under their floorboards – Lencastre's rough justice for Royalists who had kept their distance from his web of intrigue.

In Lisbon's *Penitenciária*, Gibbs met Pedro Velladas, a political refugee whom Lencastre had persuaded back from exile. Velladas bore facial injuries, the result of a pistol-whipping by the *Carbonária*. He had been tempted back expecting to take part in a rising led by Azevedo Countinho, one of Lencastre's other duped Royalists. In a side street in Porto they were to make first contact with the man they thought to be their leader. Lencastre kept his distance, then raised his hat in 'a Judas sign'[23] to set loose the *Carbonária*. Velladas' companion got twenty years because he was already wanted for participating in a previous conspiracy. This was likely to have been the aborted Monarchist plot of July 1913.[24] Velladas, himself, was awaiting sentence. Gibbs never contextualizes the Lencastre conspiracy within the genuine plotting that had been ongoing since mid-summer. The British foreign secretary, Sir Edward Grey, was certainly aware of a real Royalist conspiracy,[25] but was suspicious of journalistic accounts, upon which the BPC based much of its evidence. Gibbs' prime concern was to file a good story and he had found an ideal villain.

Heroes he found in abundance in the prisons of Porto; one or two very distinguished indeed. In the *Aljube*, was lodged Dr Constâncio Roque da Costa, once Minister to the Argentine. He had refused Lencastre money on three occasions. Neither would he agree to purchase arms. The rough justice of Lencastre's denunciation saw him initially thrown into the military prison in Lisbon 'where he was confined for eight days in a cell only large enough for his bed, and through the bars of which came a pestilential stench from an undesirable place.'[26] From there, he was transferred to Porto, where he had been held for forty days, before meeting Gibbs.

Lencastre was no respecter of reputations. He denounced many other notables detained in the *Aljube*. They included the academics Dr Barbedo Pinto, director of the Pasteur Institute, denounced for refusing to give money; Dr Oliveira Lima of the University of Porto; Dr Lubo d'Avila a professor at the University of Coimbra; and, Dr Santos Motta, a professor at the Lyceum in Braga. Their fellow prisoners included medics, lawyers and journalists. The detention of Senor Lopes Coelho might have provided Kafka food for thought. He was being held until he revealed the names of collaborators in a conspiracy of which he denied all knowledge. His wife was also being held until her memory improved. Elsewhere, in Porto, there seems to have been some class segregation of political prisoners. Compared to the Bishop's Palace, the *Aljube* was more like a university behind bars. The Bishop had been evicted in 1911, victim of the secularisation policy, and the place had been inhabited by armed guards until it was turned into an emergency prison for the humble. Gibbs found over a hundred shopkeepers, artisans and peasants, crowded up to eighteen per room. Their families were at least allowed to bring them in food parcels and a lot of this charity was organized by the veritable Dona Constança da Gama, a *Carbonária* target. Even grimmer was the prison known as the *Relacão*, intended for more serious convicted criminals but extended to politicals. Gibbs found one poor wretch who had fled to Brazil after an earlier rising but had returned to Porto on the misinformation that there had been a general amnesty. Lencastre put the *Carbonária* onto him. They broke his ribs first, then left him to heal in the *Relacão*, where Gibbs found him still in pain two months later.

Gibbs' grand tour of unfree Porto concluded at the military prison, where he learned that republican justice reached all institutions, however powerful. Inmates told him that officers were imprisoned without trial, and that once detained their salaries were stopped, illegally. With a proper sense of class indignation, one imprisoned officer told him that they were being forced to eat less than soldiers' rations. The *Carbonária* had no time for class discrimination. They burned down the Catholic Working Men's Club. But, in an act of social levelling, they beat up General Jaime de Castro in the street on no more evidence than Lencastre's denunciation. From his prison cell, the General counter-denounced a government that sanctioned this but promoted to Senator an army captain who had been convicted as a bond forger under the Monarchy.[27]

6 Rooms with a view: The *Limoeiro*

Gibbs had no official permission to visit Portuguese prisons, so he was grateful for the letters of introduction given him by the Ministry of Foreign Affairs. These obtained access for the reports on Porto. They worked for Lisbon, too, and there is more objectivity when writing about the *Limoeiro*,[28] the Governor of which he found 'courteous and humane.'[29] Description of conditions is taken more from personal observation with less dependence upon prisoners' testimonies, many of which were unverifiable from other sources. So, the *Limoeiro* is overcrowded, but clean and contained no special horrors. The upper level, that housed about ninety political prisoners, was a rabbit warren but there was plenty of fresh air, light and there was a nice view of the Tagus through the iron bars! Prisoners were not confined to their cells; they wandered about like the debtors in the Fleet in London of old. They were regularly visited by their families. Indeed, gender and class discriminations were notable for their absence. Peasant women with babies in arms passed 'ladies of quality' in the corridors. Prisoners' complaints were directed at being held for so long without trial, rather than conditions. Gibbs found Royalists and Republicans, alike, equally vociferous.

7 'An institution for killing the minds of men': The *Penitenciária*

Lisbon's penitentiary gets a more mixed report. Architecturally and technologically modern, and clean, it had decent in-house educational facilities. But wood-carving and bookmaking were not enough for cultivated minds, Gibbs laments, and laying it on with a trowel he bemoans it as 'an institution for killing the minds of men while preserving their bodies . . . I am told that gibbering idiots are taken away in cartloads.'[30]

Gibbs suspected that recent improvements had been brought about by the British protest. Prisoners were able to visit each other in their cells, converse and smoke in corridors, and take regular exercise. But he also found the Austrian Imperial Guards captain, Dom João d'Almeida,[31] with his head still shaven. This could be counted improvement of a sort, for previously he had been hooded. His stern treatment is explained by his participation in the Couceiro conspiracy of 1912. But hooding continued into 1913. Gibbs encountered the young aristocrat Ficalho (visited by the Duchess in March) who claimed to have been hooded for a whole month after attacking a warder who called him a dog. Then, there was one of Lencastre's victims, Mangualde, of whom Gibbs had heard in Porto. He was serving twenty years, 'a living death' alongside common criminals.

8 The black hole of Elvas

The ancient town of Elvas, situated just a few miles from the Spanish border in the Eastern Alentejo, has been fated by geography to a contested history. First fortified by the Moors after the occupation of 714, the defences proved strong enough to resist even the onslaught of Gerald the Fearless in 1166. Unafraid, the Moors held out until Sancho II finally expelled them in 1229. For more than three centuries until the Spanish conquest of 1580–81, Elvas was the frontline of the historic Portuguese-Spanish conflict. When Philip II of Spain laid claim to the Portuguese kingdom in 1580 the walls of Elvas were only penetrated through bribery. The next year he was crowned King Felipe I of Portugal. Elvas had disgraced itself, the Spaniards ruling the Portuguese for another sixty years until João IV of Bragança overthrew the Habsburgs' Lisbon court on 1 December 1640. Spain did not take the *Reconquista* lying down. But the Wars of Succession, which lasted until the Treaty of Lisbon in 1668, gave Elvas a chance to redeem itself. Twice in this period it endured dreadful siege. For nine days in 1644 it resisted Spanish attack, and again in 1658, when an epidemic reduced the population to a mere thousand inhabitants, it defied a 15,000-strong Spanish army. After that, the Portuguese rebuilt the walls of Elvas even stronger. Through the seventeenth century the outer walls were added to the inner ones that dated from the thirteenth. They were supported by extensive moats and ramparts, designed by the French military engineer Vauban, making Elvas the best-defended town in Portugal. Similar fortifications were put in place all along that part of the Spanish border.

They were not strong enough to resist Godoy who arrived on behalf of the Bonapartes in 1801. The Portuguese had refused to sever their vital trading connections with the British, as Napoleon's Continental System required. The Marshall celebrated the surrender of the town without resistance by cutting down two orange branches from the foot of the ramparts and sending them back to Queen Maria-Luisa in Madrid. Sharing the good news with *Madrilenos*, their epithet 'the war of the oranges' rather neatly described its soft outcome. It left Elvas another humiliation to be avenged. Wellesley's Peninsular campaign is best remembered for the operations along the lines of Torres Vedras in the west of Portugal.[32] But the retaking of Elvas in the east provided the base for the sieges of the Spanish garrison in Badajoz of 1811 and 1812.

Elvas remained peacefully uninvaded from the end of the Napoleonic Wars. Over two years before Gibbs, within months of the Revolution, Aubrey Bell paid his visit, his impressions published in, *In Portugal*. As we have seen, Bell's Elvas is a construct of the 'real Portugal' of the *longue durée*, prior to the conversion of Forte da Graça into a political prison. The towers and houses of the town gleam from its hill above dark ramparts, with the Fort to one side of the view and the immense aqueduct to the other. The entry to the town is across a moat and an archway in the fortifications. Enraptured by tradition, Bell's Alentejan rhapsody removed the Republic without trace. Donkeys rattle along the cobbled streets. Men in long dark brown fleeces and tanned leather boots stand on street corners, carrying huge umbrellas. Their trousers are in the traditional style, tied tightly at the knee, then flared from the ankle. They boast bushy whiskers beneath

224 | *The Portuguese Pimpernel*

gigantic black hats, as they stare at passers-by with the gloomy look of ruffians.

When Gibbs arrived after the long cross-country journey from Lisbon, he was interested in none of this. No Lusophile, he may have been too tired to take note of the prehistoric dolmens and large black Alentejan bulls that represent the regions greatest attractions, before the magnificence of the town itself. Even if his mood had been lifted, it swiftly changed as he visited the cells of Forte da Graça.[33] His report is scathing. Dumped in the dungeons were no Royalists, but 133 Syndicalists. The underground cells had no natural ventilation, causing dampness that brought on bronchitis and rheumatism. In the worst black hole of a dungeon he found 'seven poor beasts' whose conditions would not have been out of place in the Middle Ages. 'But in the twentieth century one does not expect to find such cruelty.'[34] It would seem that prison conditions deteriorated beyond the capital. Porto had been worse than Lisbon, but in a backwater like Elvas, an isolated military relic on the Spanish border, they reached their nadir. Like Monsanto, Elvas was a fort badly adapted for prison conditions.

The difference between capital and provinces was confirmed when Gibbs moved on to Coimbra. As the country's leading university town, it was more significant than Elvas, but still seemed unprepared for substantial numbers of political prisoners, despite having a proper penitentiary. Gibbs' *Daily Chronicle* report of 19 December, is dominated, however, by a sensational interview with the thirty-seven year-old Padre Avelino de Figueiredo. The priest was charged with having instigated the general strike of 20 March 1911 and had been one of the featured captives of *Portuguese Political Prisoners*. Gibbs caught up with him a few months later, at the end of 1913, in Coimbra. Figueiredo repeated much of what had appeared in the pamphlet but added a disturbing twist to his tale. While in the *Limoeiro*, he claimed there had been a plot to murder him. Neither was this unique. A prisoner named Silva Feijas had already been killed with a butcher's knife, and his murderer acquitted. The Padre claimed that the common criminals were being put up to it, although he does not suggest they were rewarded. When he got wind that he might meet a similar fate, he had some friends outside smuggle him in a gun. Unfortunately, he was caught in possession, and put in solitary confinement (*segredo*) in a damp, filthy cell where he was given only sour bread to eat. On falling ill, the doctor ordered he be removed from *segredo* within twelve hours, for fear of death. He was kept there for another five days but stayed alive. After that he was removed to the *Penitenciária*.

At the end of Gibbs' report, published on 19 December, there is acknowledgement that he has selected the most damning evidence. He concedes that although prison conditions were uneven, much of what he had seen was good. A close reading of his pieces reveals that much of the most damning evidence was hearsay from interviews – Figueiredo's seems an unlikely tale – rather than reported observation. Since the British Protest had begun he thought that *segredo* had almost ended. But, that aside, the Republic was still arresting on the barest of suspicions and violating its own laws by keeping prisoners months without trial, before military tribunals. Behind this lay a network of terror – spies, *Carbonária*, 'White Ants' – 'who with their methods of espionage, blackmail and violence had wrecked the moral credit of the Republic.'[35] His conclusion, that the full force of international opinion needed to be brought against such government, reflects disillusionment but also an internationalism Trevelyan would have approved of. Reading Gibbs' reports against the grain, the Republic compares unfavourably with the Monarchy, something that must have pleased his paymasters. But more conspicuous is the conviction that the Republican government had fallen below its own professed standards. Worse, it was saying one thing in public and doing another in private. It spun a tale of liberty, but Gibbs proffered the competing narrative of a clandestine police state.

9 Lessons from a lawyer

Dr José Soares da Cunha e Costa met Philip Gibbs as they were both heading for London. The former was a well-known Lisbon Republican lawyer who had helped draft the Constitution of 1911, but defected to Monarchism. In October 1913, with the city alive with rumour of a Royalist plot,[36] he was visited by a stranger who proved to be that rare thing, a *Carbonário* with a conscience. The news was bad: he was about to be murdered, although not by his visitor. On this occasion, at least, it seemed prudent to believe the *Carbonário*. Cunha e Costa fled to London.

Wheeler distrusts Cunha e Costa's evidence as exaggerated and criticizes Gibbs for accepting it uncritically.[37] But he does not interrogate it, nor indeed any of the other evidence from Gibbs' visit of late 1913. Cunha e Costa's evidence to Gibbs links the spy Lencastre to Afonso Costa through the Porto Commissioner of Police. Lencastre's subsequent confession admitted as much without naming Costa. Cunha e Costa claimed to have photographic evidence to this effect. That he did not produce it suggests Wheeler was right to be distrustful.

That does not invalidate all of his evidence. He raised pertinent criticisms of the partiality of military tribunals. The judges were army colonels appointed by the Minister of War; the lesser members of the tribunal were young men in their twenties, compliant because they had a career to make. The adviser on points of law to the tribunals had been condemned by the High Court for gross professional misconduct. Political prisoners were denied the right possessed by common criminals of appeal to the High Court. They had to appeal to the General Commandant, the very person who had decided there was enough evidence to prosecute them in the first place.

Cunha e Costa was gunning for Afonso Costa, his old colleague turned bitter enemy, who had signed the warrant for his arrest that forced him into exile. But again, this does not disqualify all his criticisms. He told Gibbs that Costa was a bluffer who claimed too much financial stability, had not met his schools-building promises, and had taxed the rich highly without re-distributing the benefits to the poor. The North continued to be de-populated, and the peasantry were turning against the government. But then, critical observation spills over into wishful thinking. There will be a coup to re-establish the Monarchy – the only way to end the terror. In Cunha e Costa, Gibbs travelled home with a new Monarchist who would reside very comfortably with his associates in the BPC.

Wheeler's charge against Gibbs' uncritical journalism misses the point. This was not mere campaigning journalism for the *Daily Chronicle*. The 'paper had sent him to Portugal with BPC money in his pocket. To be able to conclude his Portuguese reports with a dissident lawyer, and one of the founding fathers of the Republic, was gift enough. That Cunha e Costa was predicting counter-revolution was manna from Heaven, and quite enough to satisfy the mission of a liberal journalist seeking a general amnesty. But Gibbs was more than that. He was a paid agent of the BPC, and only Tenison's memoir gifts us that.

10 'War against God'

Gibbs returned from Portugal just in time for the publication of his final article for the *Daily Chronicle* on 18 December. He reported back to Lytton the same day.[38] Before the ink had quite dried on his newspaper articles, he wrote a long retrospective piece that was published in January. Perhaps the time of year accounted for its particularly religious tone compared with the *Chronicle* pieces. But it does not begin in this vein. It combines the descriptive reporting of prison conditions with the more sombre reflections on the state of Portuguese justice, typical of the newspaper articles. For periodical readers who did not take the *Chronicle,* here was a chance to catch up with what they had missed. Gibbs' ears are still ringing with Cunha e Costa's rant over broken promises:

> There was to be liberty of conscience throughout the land. There was to be freedom of speech for all schools of thought. Large sums of money were to be spent on public elementary education. The wages of working people were to be increased, and the cost of living was to be reduced by relieving the country of its high tariffs. Justice, above all, was to be administered without fear or favour, and the Republic of Portugal was to be like a happy family, animated by the same high moral purpose, and marching on to new triumphs of civilisation.[39]

If prisons had improved at all, a senior prison official told him, this was largely due to pressure brought by the British Campaign. In any case, he suggests, such improvement was largely confined to the capital. He had a ream of letters from rheumatic and bronchitic prisoners in Forte da Graça, complaining about the destruction of their health. And, even in the conspicuously decent prisons of the capital, there were many ways to skin a cat. Mental health was being eroded by the insidious torture of being falsely accused without trial.

For Gibbs, Costa had failed both as a liberal and a social reformer. Resisting the temptation to compare Costa's record to the impressive one of contemporary British Liberalism, he hoists him on his own petard. No indent had been made upon poverty. Urban workingmen had seen no increase in earnings while the cost of living had doubled in a decade, aggravated by high tariffs. High taxes on landlords only forced up peasant rents. The result was flight. Emigration had reached 90,000 in 1912. Everywhere schools and churches were closed as farms were abandoned. But not all left for economic reasons. Royalists feared imprisonment. Portugal was becoming a spiritual and economic wasteland. It was literally and metaphorically rotting.

Writing at Christmastime 1913, Gibbs composes a dirge for the Republic's destruction of 'the Christian Myth' and the spiritual bereavement it wreaked. The suffering poor were denied even religious consolation. Church closures punished their children. About half the schools in Portugal had been closed, not all for the poor. Two hundred boys lost their places at the College of Boa Vista in Porto because their education was deemed to be too Royalist and too Jesuitical. Monks and nuns had become as rare as trial by jury. More than secularisation, far more than a war against the religious orders, the Church or even religion itself, this was a war against God. God had been expelled from the classroom and teachers suspended for using the three-letter word, which was disappearing from textbooks. In Porto, Miss Powers, an Irish teacher, had her school closed for 'practising cult in the community,' which amounted to saying morning and evening prayers.

Priests had withdrawn from them the 'full liberty of conscience' promised by the Law of Separation. They could not preach against divorce. They could not even follow their conscience by refusing government stipends, without being expelled their parishes. Around four thousand had sought refuge in private teaching. It was illegal for more than six of them to meet together. As they wandered forlorn from their churchyards into public places, they found all religious figures and symbols removed.

The 'war against God' threw deprived youth into the depraved city opened to the floodgates of licentiousness. A young man would pass shop windows that flaunted 'filthy pictures and obscene books.' If he dropped into one of Lisbon's cafes, he was not safe from openly displayed cures for 'vile diseases' placed on its tables. Gibbs' Catholicism fulminates against the moral decay evident in the state's official policies. He then fuses his spiritual concerns into a neo-colonialist discourse of salvation:

> To England, which once rescued it from foreign domination, there comes a cry for help and intervention from those who are falsely accused, and falsely imprisoned, as victims of the reign of terror. I was asked to carry that appeal home to my countrymen from the prisons in which I heard so many tales of tragedy.
>
> Will England turn a deaf ear to that tragic cry?
>
> If so, we have lost all spirit of chivalry, and that love of justice that made us great among the nations of the world.[40]

'The war against God' tirade echoes *Will England Save Portugal?* but embraces also McCullagh's Catholic anti-Republicanism. It therefore contrasts with his more secular pieces for the Campaign, by proxy, in the *Chronicle*. Yet it is still voiced from the British Campaign's shared neo-colonialist ideology. In particular, Gibbs' language sites Portugal's subaltern status in a paternalist discourse that constructs a Portugal that must be rescued from its own, infantile errors. Portugal needed to feel the directing hand of 'English' moral superiority. Liberal humanitarian interventionism in 1913 was premised on 'England' performing its moral duty in the world. The trusty sword of justice, however, had to be invisible, sheathed only in moral authority. A Republican government that had refused the lesson of its semi-colonized status could only be pressurized or isolated. Unlike many of his fellow campaigners, Gibbs did not call for an end to the Alliance.

As a Liberal, he was in no rush to upset Edward Grey's apple cart. He performed as a functionary, positioned to provide the evidence on Portuguese discontents. Overall, he succeeded well as propagandist, but at Christmas the Catholic was inspired to proselytize.

Seven months after returning from Lisbon in December 1913, Gibbs bade farewell to the white cliffs of Dover once again, to embark on a distinguished spell as a war correspondent. His next encounter with a Portuguese may well have been on the Western Front in April, 1918. It was 'Old Bumface', The Portuguese Chief of Staff, who spoke no English, so responded to ridicule with a warm handshake. The Portuguese had arrived near Neuve Chapelle dressed more for the Algarve in spring than Flanders. Their naivety brought them laden with essential straw plunder baskets to carry home anticipated German loot. But they had got ahead of themselves. Ill prepared for the still explosive intensity of trench warfare, their lines broke. The Germans recklessly poured too many troops away from the Amiens front towards the Portuguese hole, allowing the good men of the 55th Lancashire division to break through. Inadvertently, the Portuguese had provided a strategic advantage. Gibbs could not resist condescension: 'I have always said, with some seriousness, that the Portuguese won the war.'[41]

Gibbs' casual irony was derived from an ideological trope with deep historical roots. This had led him to construct a narrative of Lisbon, 1913 in which the Portuguese could not run a prison, let alone a republic. As for war, best not to mention it. However, in hindsight, he did not exaggerate his personal role in freeing the political prisoners. Reflecting from 1946, he was optimistic about the effects his visit had on influencing the Portuguese Government. But he claimed less than the BPC had done in their other propaganda. This does not make Gibbs devoid of ego. 'A cat may look at a King', he proudly declared, then proceeded to list all the monarchs he had met.[42] One of these was Amélie, the Portuguese Queen Mother who invited him to her country house (probably Wood Norton) to thank him for his efforts in releasing the aristocratic prisoners. Several of them had already turned up at his house in Holland Street, Kensington to thank him personally. Gibbs was singularly unimpressed at what he felt was a token gesture. He was equally unimpressed by the minor honour Amélia bestowed, and least impressed of all by Manuel, who was also present.

> He was not overwhelmed with grief for the loss of his crown. He was, indeed, in a larking mood, and when he went upstairs he leaned over

the bannisters and one by one knocked off the tophats of his gentlemen in attendance. Their laughter did not ring quite true.[43]

Gibbs' sense of disappointment is palpable. Was it on behalf of fools like this that he had gone to Lisbon, Porto and even 'the black hole of Elvas', and braved the depravities of the political prisons? Was it for them that he had endured the insults of the Portuguese press? 'An apache who lies for money as others murder for many',[44] they had called him. He left; moved on. Very soon there would be a Great War to report.

CHAPTER 11

The Missionary

1 Brief Encounter

When John Harris met E. M. Tenison in South Eaton Place in 1913 two English, but different, religious worlds collided. Tenison, the traditional Anglican bearing the name of a famous Archbishop, looked down upon the Baptist from humble stock. The dilettante, historian from remote East Kent reached out to the missionary from metropolitan Dulwich who had traversed two African empires. Tenison needed the campaigning experience of the man who had transformed the Anti-Slavery Society into a well-oiled pressure group. Their common ground was distrust of the Portuguese. Harris thought they practised slavery in the African empire. Tenison cared little about Africans, much more about the 'white slaves' in Portuguese prisons. To his credit, Harris agreed to assist, and provided her with some invaluable contacts. They were 'Locusts' of different hues. Tenison loathed the Republic; Harris slavery. Harris facilitated the BPC network in two ways. We have seen, already, how he shared his public contacts. The second was more circumstantial. The anti-slavery campaign voiced an extant public discourse within which the political prisoners' narrative could be sited. Few did more than John Harris to make that possible.

2 The Portuguese West African Empire

From around 1900, the Portuguese Empire resembled a corpse awaiting dismemberment. The prime predator was Germany, assisted by duplicitous friends in Britain. Through the late nineteenth century, Portugal nurtured an ambiguous relationship with the slave trade. Abolitionists tended to remain silent. Tolerationists – the majority – implemented abolition as gradually as possible, concerned that it endangered the empire. Slaving capital was embedded in Portuguese finance and oiled the factional wheels of Portuguese politics.[1] From the reluctant abolition of 1836 onwards, cries of 'national honour' were raised in defence of Portuguese autonomy against Palmerstonian, abolitionist, neo-colonialism. The Cortes submitted in 1842 amidst objections that the slave trade was divinely inspired to prevent 'negroes' eating each other.[2]

But the British lacked the capacity to police all slave routes. Off West Africa, São Tomé and Principé planters continued to supply labour from mainland colonies like Angola. From the 1850s, land grants were designed to attract settlers towards an 'uneconomic imperialism.'[3] From the 1870s 'public tutelage' legislation seemed to point towards complete abolition but was contradicted by forced labour contracts analogous to slavery. Draconian vagrancy laws undermined any notional free market in labour by restricting mobility.[4] Vagrancy was left deliberately vague as an offence to perpetuate forced labour. Vagrants could not be full citizens, merely 'natives'. 'Natives' were denied the vote due to their 'civilizational backwardness,' a view that changed little under the Republic.[5] 'It has long been established that laziness is a quality of the individual in Whites, and an attribute of the race in Blacks', wrote the Republican Deputy Manuel de Brito Camacho,[6] in a publishing skirmish with John Harris's book *Portuguese Slavery* (1913). Freire de Andrade argued, 'The black of Angola is effectively a savage and one of the lowest on the scales of civilisation and intelligence.' All humane means were justified to open the doors of the 'guild of civilisation' to the blacks.[7] The Portuguese 'civilising mission' was turned into a legitimating ideology of 'redemptive labour' for the 'empire-state.'[8] Moral education could be left to the missionaries. In 1907, the Portuguese 'empire-state' imposed its sovereignty upon Angola.[9]

A discourse of servitude enjoyed British confirmation. Acting Consul Brock reminded, in 1894, that 'they ... [forced labourers] ... are drawn from the lowest types of humanity, and have none of the instincts of civilization; and that morally they are improved rather than deteriorated by the more regular life and work.'[10] Ten years' earlier the Liberal imperialist, Sir Harry Johnston, discovered, 'the ideal of a black man's paradise, and the negroes of San Thomé the happiest in the world.'[11] This was imagery unrecognisable to humanitarian reformers like Harris, later. But even he conflated Christianity with civilisation in Africa, excepting Portuguese Catholicism. Johnston, on the other hand, confessed to liking the Portuguese and 'their wonderful achievements in Africa.'[12] These were not evident to Consul Mackie three years earlier. In mainland Angola he thought labour recruitment still brutal, and 'closely akin to slavery.'[13] The 1903 law regulating labour supply to the islands made only a few cosmetic changes because vested interests retained power. A claimant for repatriation at the end of a contract had to negotiate the built-in deterrence that a single claim for repatriation could require thirty-six separate accounting operations.[14]

On such evidence, modern Portuguese historiography has dismissed the uniqueness of the 'civilising mission.' For Jerónimo its only exceptionality is as a construct.[15] Ferraz de Matos similarly explains colonial exhibitions, not as representations of cultural realities, but as celebrations of 'civilising mission.'[16] The production of imperial knowledge by the Portuguese state was extremely narrow. The public lacked any film evidence as to what the inhabitants of São Tomé and Príncipe looked like until 1909.[17] Literature was also neglectful, for example Eça de Queirós wrote no novel set in the empire. However, as a mystification underpinning national confidence, 'the civilising mission' became increasingly necessary as Africa failed to materialise as a new Brazil.[18]

3 The British campaign against 'Portuguese Slavery'

In the years before 1914 Britain and Germany increasingly regarded Portugal's empire as negotiable. This placed Britain on the horns of a dilemma. The Alliance provided Atlantic and imperial security. But as the Cadbury Case proved later, British business was sometimes complicit in 'slavery.' Non-state actors such as journalists and missionaries had no hesitation in exposing this contradiction. Harris encountered 'slavery' as a missionary, then campaigned about it through the Anti-Slavery and Aborigines' Protection Society (ASAPS). But it was a journalist, Henry Nevinson, whose articles in *Harper's Magazine*, from August 1905 to February 1906, first stirred the FO out of its masterly inactivity. By the time the Liberals entered government, from January 1906, a tide of humanitarian fury was mounting. ASAPS trusted the new government no more than the old. William Cadbury knew that his firm were using cocoa produced by 'slave labour' from 1902, before his visit to Lisbon with Matthew Stober, head of the Angola Evangelical Mission and associate of ASAPS.[19] Cadbury was persuaded into procrastination by the FO. The report he commissioned from Joseph Burtt was delayed, but eventually revealed even more damning evidence than Nevinson's.

Restrained British criticism over Portuguese West Africa was fashioned by the need for the sixty thousand Mozambicans who worked in South African gold mines by 1902. Portugal also behaved like an ally through the Boer War.[20] But the Cadbury trial in 1909 brought the issue to a head. Cadbury was a prominent humanitarian, a model employer at Bournville, supporter of the Congo Reform Association, and member of the ASAPS from 1893.[21] Yet, *The Standard*, accused him of ignoring 'slavery' for profit. Plentiful evidence of abuse stretched back decades. As early as April 1884, the Baptist missionary in the Congo, William Holman Hunt, accused the Portuguese of reviving slavery everywhere they trod. They simply changed its name and called it 'ten-year contracts.'[22] Writing from Cape Town at the end of 1889, the Australian historian and explorer D. C. F. Moodie encountered the Portuguese on the southern border of Natal. He observed that they wrecked the lives of the Mabudto people of Amatongaland by selling them cheap rum: 'The wretched people do not care about dying as long as they die drunk'. They even armed tribes to fight against one another.[23] British Consuls sent negative reports from Luanda with regularity. From Lourenço Marques, Roger Casement observed Portuguese brutality in putting down Mozambican resistance, before enacting forced labour.[24] In Gomba in the Congo, in 1902, he considered the forced labour system amounted to slavery. Yet, the Consuls provoked no action from the FO.[25] But over São Tomé, specifically, Sir Martin Gosselin testified at the trial that he had informed Cadbury about slave conditions during the latter's visit to Lisbon in March 1903.[26] In fact, Cadbury's correspondence with Harry Johnston and E. D. Morel shows he was alerted the previous year.[27]

Such evidence, long in the public domain, has made historians as sceptical of Cadbury as *The Standard's* editor, the Tory C. Arthur Pearson. Even Nevinson sided with him, against Cadbury. But Tories had a longer-running agenda. George Cadbury's *Daily News* had embarrassed the Government over 'Chinese slavery' – the supply of cheap labour into the Transvaal – at the 1905 election. Here was a chance for revenge. William Cadbury said he had been leaned on by the FO to go easy on 'Portuguese slavery' to guarantee the labour flow from Mozambique. He believed that labourers in São Tomé and Principé were better off than in the Congo or South Africa.[28] But the court's verdict awarding miniscule damages of one farthing was really one of hypocrisy unproven on Cadbury's 'problematic ethics.'[29]

The background to the Cadbury trial intensified ASAPS activity. Belligerent members like Secretary, Henry Fox Bourne favoured the FO threatening the Portuguese with gunboats. J. G. Alexander disagreed: 'Philanthropy cannot, any more than Christianity, be forced upon a people by gunboats.'[30] John Harris deplored Palmerstonian rhetoric in favour of the right to search. An open letter, 'A Surviving Slavery', was published in *The Spectator* and *The Times*, and was signed by the Committee, plus prominent Leftists such as Ramsay MacDonald, H. G. Wells and John Galsworthy. Citing Burtt's report, it pulled no punches:

> The natives are obtained by purchase, capture, or trickery in the interior, are brought down to the coast in gangs, usually tied together at night with wooden shackles, are sold to recognised agents in the coast towns, and those that are destined for the islands are labelled and despatched in the ordinary steamers, running about once a fortnight. By this means an increasing supply of labourers for the islands is maintained, and the number of natives exported annually, which averaged four thousand three years ago, has now reached nearly five thousand. The consent of the natives is hardly even nominal; and they are sold at a recognised price. The climate in the cocoa plantations is very unhealthy, and in the first year many die of home-sickness and misery.[31]

A mass meeting in December 1908 sent a motion to Grey for a boycott 'unless Portugal took meaningful steps to halt slavery.'[32] Grey, unsurprisingly, rejected their suggestion.[33]

Duffy saw 1909 as the turning point in the campaign, although it is difficult to see why it was more significant than Burtt's report, or Nevinson's before that. If 1909 was a turning-point, perhaps it was because of the broader political context. The Cadbury trial ran concurrently with the Parliamentary passage of the 'People's Budget' and the subsequent constitutional crisis. At the FO, Grey was not anxious to get drawn into a squabble between a chocolate manufacturer and a newspaper at a time when the Government was fighting for its life.[34] But Harris and friends would not let him rest. As soon as the trial ended they accelerated political propaganda. Grey received constant demands to pressure the Portuguese. Networking amongst sympathetic MPs engendered debates that raised awareness, as did public meetings. Boycotts ratcheted-up the economic pressure.[35] And, the Press provided a running commentary.

Typical of this was the co-operation between Harris, on behalf of the ASAPS, and *The Spectator*. Harris doubted the authenticity of the boycott announced by the cocoa manufacturers. He questioned whether they really knew the origins of much of the cocoa they purchased, or much challenged it. Consequently, he advised the ASAPS to insist on much tighter checks on supply, and for manufacturers to provide evidence they were satisfying requirements. When many of them failed to guarantee this, he urged *The Spectator* to support his demands. At this stage, Strachey[36] was only prepared to urge the manufacturers to form their own committee of enquiry. This did not satisfy Harris, but it was, nonetheless, the beginning of a longer campaign of co-operation.[37]

Between 1909 and 1913 the Portuguese flattered to deceive in sustaining the labour recruitment ban to the cocoa islands from Angola. Duffy argues that pressure from the FO was more responsible than that from the ASAPS. This rather ignores the causes of the FO's shift towards greater activity in the first place. Grey was certainly dead-batting the ASAPS delegation that saw him, as late as July 1910.[38] Harris went away disappointed, accompanied by Lord Mayo, George Cadbury, Henry Nevinson and six other MPs.[39] A few months before, in April, Grey had still been defending the reform efforts of the Portuguese administration which his own Consul in Luanda, Drummond-Hay, had described as 'elastic.'[40]

In October 1910, Strachey gave a cautious welcome to the Revolution as an opportunity to end slavery. But his discourse was couched in a conditionality born of distrust. He predicted a Royalist counter-revolt, in the event of which the Republicans would need allies.[41] John Harris agreed over giving the Portuguese a chance but was even more cynical. Moral indignation was all well and good, he wrote, but there was a strategic interest at play. Harris was informed by a report, earlier in 1910, by the botanist at South Africa College, Professor Henry Pearson,[42] that revealed utter chaos on the borderland between German Damaraland (SW Africa) and Angola. The Portuguese authorities were spending large amounts of their time looking for native labourers who had fled a system of 'compulsory service' unchanged since Livingstone passed through in the 1850s. The Germans were well aware of this vulnerability, and the possible opportunity it offered. Border security was little better in relation to the Congo (Belgian) or Barotseland (British Rhodesia). Harris was looking for a deal that gave the Portuguese a guarantee about their colonies in return for attending to slavery.[43]

In November 1910, Harris and several other leading members of the ASAPS, were invited to Lisbon by the Portuguese Government. They did not meet seriously with government members but were fobbed off with Cadbury's friend, Alfredo da Silva, professor at the Porto Industrial and Commercial Institute and a founder member of the Portuguese Anti-Slavery Society.[44] Foreign Minister, Bernardino Machado had greeted them, then disappeared.[45] Harris broke with Cadbury's pussy-footing after this disappointment.[46] Such treatment needs to be borne in mind when criticising Harris for a blind humanitarianism that denigrated Portuguese efforts, harassing the FO, and disregarding governmental evidence.[47]

The Harrises spent parts of 1911–12 back in the Congo, then more briefly in São Tomé and Principé, from which John drew evidence for his subsequent publications. He also provided primary evidence for Strachey to argue for an end to the Alliance if the Portuguese did not improve.[48] Duffy echoes Eyre Crowe's smear, that *The Spectator*'s campaign was trying to have the colonies transferred to Germany,[49] as if the Anglo-German negotiations to that effect had never happened.[50] As the FO conspired with Cadbury to play their double game over 'slavery' in the cocoa islands, it was as well that somebody was trying to hold them to account.

Recently returned from West Africa, and armed with primary evidence, Harris presented it to an ASAPS public meeting at the Westminster Palace Hotel on 25 June 1912. Nevinson could not attend, but sent a letter urging all to listen carefully to him. The debate hinged on Strachey's motion that the Alliance should be ended unless Portugal 'terminates the conditions at present existing.' He justified this with the neo-colonialist assertion that Britain had every right to do this because it stood in a different relationship to Portugal than to any other power. Portugal was practising 'virtual slavery.'

Portuguese attendees circulated a defensive pamphlet arguing that repatriation was really an act of cruelty because Africans could not fend for themselves. Strachey thought that was like saying that all prostitutes should be eternally confined to their brothels because they could not cope without their tender loving care.[51] One of them dug himself in deeper by arguing that the natives did not have family feelings 'like ourselves'. Harris retorted that his wife Alice would put him right over this, later. It transpired that the Portuguese had never been to São Tomé, so Harris described the scenes of starvation he had seen. But he was convinced that 'the God of ethics is also the God of economics' because planters were becoming convinced that free labour was more profitable.

Alice spoke of her admiration for the familial emotions of African women. They were custodians of ancient stabilising traditions for their societies, not irresponsible and untrained savages. She identified how the repatriation system contained nefarious gender discriminations. Repatriation was only for the male labourer. If he accepted, he had to leave his family behind. What happened then? Often the deserted women had no choice but to 'marry' from the new labour intake. After forced recruitment was suspended in 1909, these were increasingly free labourers from Mozambique, not men from Angola. Alice poignantly described how the women were treated like bartered goods.[52] The Portuguese continued to insist on the near-perfection of life in the cocoa islands,[53] but then suspended labour recruitment.

The ASAPS urged Grey to call an international commission,[54] but a Commons debate in July only discussed transferring the Portuguese colonies.[55] The white paper in August was seen as a fudge by the ASAPS. Harris went with Travers Buxton on 22 October to the FO but the meeting ended in animosity. Eyre Crowe thought Harris inclined to shoot his mouth off. Harris had compared some conditions in the British Empire unfavourably with the Portuguese.[56] A second White Book, in February 1913, was dismissed by the ASAPS as complicity with the slavery system.[57] With black humour, Strachey accused the FO of trying to bury slavery in a shallow grave.[58] Direct negotiation ceased.

The ASAPS networked to produce a great Lords' debate in July 1913 and boasted of exposing the White Book as a cover-up. The Earl of Mayo[59] and the Archbishop of Canterbury both criticized the FO's dilatoriness. The Earl of Cromer implied the Alliance had become an embarrassment that might require Britain to take up arms to defend 'a slave State.'[60] Several contextual factors impacted on the debate. Firstly, in April and July 1913, Royalist incursions into Northern Portugal were abetted by the Spanish monarchy which allowed refugee status to rebels. It seemed possible that Spain might invade Portugal. Secondly, the Anglo-German negotiations over the Portuguese colonies were ongoing. While Portuguese propaganda painted ASAPS supporters as in league with the Germans, the real picture was more differentiated. Strachey, Morel and Cadbury were Germanophile, but Cromer, and Harris, himself, more sceptical.[61] Thirdly, Roger Casement's report into the Putamayo atrocities (1912) revealed British investment in the Peruvian Amazonian Company. Its rubber workers, some recruited from the Caribbean, suffered conditions as bad as in the Congo.[62]

Cromer tried to reduce the 'line of cleavage' between 'the enthusiasts and the officials.' But he blamed Eyre Crowe most at the FO, for spinning that the slaves were legally free. Still, Cromer gave the benefit of the doubt to Portuguese intentions.[63] To allay Portuguese suspicions that the British were plotting expropriation of the cocoa plantations, he urged the British public to pay more for cocoa products. At the same time, he refuted the arguments of the apologists that repatriation was no farce. Cromer reminded of John Harris' opinion that even Mozambique had a freer labour system.[64]

In December 1912 the FO had shot itself in the foot by publishing the Wyllie Report.[65] In arguing that free labour was more profitable than 'slavery' it confirmed much of what the reformers had been saying. Macieira, Portuguese Foreign Minister, announced that the ASAPS was not only anti-slavery, but anti-Portuguese. His conspiracy theory had it leading a campaign to ruin the planters, buy out the land cheaply and take over future cocoa production.[66] The irony was that Wyllie was far from an ASAPS supporter. He had plantation interests[67] and had translated a Portuguese defence of the plantation system, *The Boa Entrada Plantations*, by Monteiro de Mendonça, in 1907. Later, he had hounded Nevinson, accusing him of anti-Portuguese prejudice, then substituting his own racist defence of the cocoa plantations. In their 'native state' their labourers were like monkeys in a zoo:

> The islands, deadly as they may be for Europeans, are a veritable paradise for the blacks, or would be so could the Angolan realise his ideal – absolute idleness, plenty of rum and no care for the morrow.[68]

Nevinson's fault had been to recount the sad tale of the alcoholic Angolan he had found near Bihé. The man had sold all his children, then his wife, into slavery, to the very local Portuguese trader who supplied him with rum.[69] Nevinson blamed the Portuguese, not the Angolan.

Harris welcomed a third White Paper of April 1914, as a step towards calling-out slavery. But as the lights went out all over Europe in August, the torch of British public opinion was turned away from Portuguese West Africa. Harris accepted a war role of monitoring German colonial abuses. War needs dragged the old Alliance back into the spotlight; Angola, São Tome and Principé were cast into the shadows.[70] The ASAPS did more to expose the contradictions of British diplomacy in relation to the slavery question than in reforming actual conditions. But Grey could dance on a pinhead. In 1912 he had said that to abandon the Alliance in order to divide Portugal's colonies would be 'shameful.' On the other hand, it 'would be morally indefensible' to protect 'the scandalous state of things.'[71] When negotiations with the Germans over Portugal's colonies lapsed in 1914, after more than two years, Grey's dilemma was resolved. He still had a derelict empire for an ally. Whether the miserable labourers of São Tomé, Principé and Angola were really slaves had proved a tortured discourse. The pain lay not only in establishing their economic conditions objectively, but also in disclosing their status as subalterns in the great diplomatic game.

4 Alice and John

Alice Seeley married John Harris on 6 May 1898. They had met through the evangelical crusader, Rev. F.B. Meyer, and arrived in the

Congo in August. Alice had given up the Civil Service, John plumbing. She was the elder and the graduate in an unconventional partnership, but they were to enjoy equality as 'the most influential leaders of British anti-slavery in the first half of the twentieth century.'[72] As Baptists they were, by 1900, in dispute with Catholic Belgian authorities whom, Roger Casement reported in 1903, were committing atrocities against Congolese.[73] Savagery compelled Alice and John to go on the offensive. Alice fought back with photography that visually politicized E. D. Morel's Congo Reform Association. At home, William Cadbury helped organise a lantern-slide lecture tour in 1905 that turned a humanitarian crusade into a mass protest over 'the moral authority of empire in Edwardian Britain.'[74] Morel made the Harrises salaried joint secretaries of the CRA, although on tour Alice spoke more rarely than John.[75] But her work impacted upon Edwardian society's male gendering of photography. Her detractors projected images of muscular Christianity in a skirt and, worse, on the make. The Harrises boosted the CRA's finances tremendously, through establishing a Nonconformist network of support. But they split with Morel over whether economic development in Africa was more important than Christianity. The moral conscience the Harrises hoped to evoke resided largely within middle-class radicalism. Within pre-1914 humanitarian politics, evangelical philanthropy gradually won out over economic liberalism.[76]

Historians have debated the extent to which missionaries acted as 'cultural imperialists' who helped 'other' empire within the metropole.[77] Andrew Porter offers a pluralist model of missionary dynamics, useful in understanding the role of the Harrises. They were not state agents bearing 'cultural imperialism' to Africans. Quite the opposite in some respects. They criticized state lethargy in dealing with its problems. They acted as bridgeheads, reaching both ways: proselytisers in Africa, pressure-group activists in the metropole. Their Bible was no particular ally of the flag; their mission transnational in its critique of empire.[78] Their pluralism could be sectarian, though, for example in their religious opposition to Catholic missions in the Congo, and their rejection of Morel's political economy – the 'New Radicalism.'[79] None of this should obscure their underlying neo-colonial conviction that empires, reformed, were worth saving.

After splitting with Morel, the Harrises became joint secretaries of the British and Foreign Anti-Slavery and Aborigines' Protection Society.[80] John Harris had been in temporary charge since the death of Henry Fox Bourne in February 1909.[81] They shed a beacon of new light upon a dark room of fossils. Alice's photographic talent illuminated a turn towards the modern. If John was more traditionally inclined towards writing and rhetoric, his Nonconformist networking was a vital transferable skill from the CRA. Alice discreetly sheltered her greater charisma beneath the umbra of John's organisational aptitude.

5 John Harris: Witnessing 'Portuguese Slavery'

As Secretary of the ASAPS from 1910, John Harris' work as 'the primary spokesman of the humanitarians'[82] extended beyond the Congo to other errant empires like the Portuguese. By 1912 he was in Portuguese West Africa. His work there has a less extensive historiography than that in the Congo and has been comparatively neglected. As yet, there is no full biography of Harris.[83] In 1912, he published an article on 'Portuguese Slavery.'[84] In 1913, came a full-length book by the same title.[85] In 1914, a further book, *Dawn in Darkest Africa*, contained a third chapter on 'Portuguese Slavery.'[86] In addition, Harris jointly authored a pamphlet with other members of the ASAPS, addressed to Sir Edward Grey.[87] In the Foreign Secretary's in-tray it co-habited with a mass of material about political prisoners, about whom Grey needed no reminding.

Harris's *Contemporary Review* piece was evidenced largely from his brief visit to Portuguese West Africa. It ruffled feathers in the FO which cast doubt on his valuation of 'slavery.'[88] Within the year he published a full-length study that offered a much wider range of evidence. *Portuguese Slavery: Britain's Dilemma* was aimed at a broader public. Harris had not then interfaced with the political prisoners' campaign. Lord Cromer was a key link, providing an introduction for *Dawn in Darkest Africa* (1914).

Harris's methodology in *Portuguese Slavery* is to put British responsibility 'on trial.' A catalogue of witnesses accumulates the evidence of 'Portuguese slavery', adding to *The Spectator*'s case for withdrawing from the Alliance, later echoed by the BPC. Harris shared with Cromer and Strachey a fierce realism. Harris doubted the Portuguese had any particular 'aptitude for colonisation' beyond charming their way out of a 'crime against civilisation and African humanity.'[89] Cromer flirted with eugenics in citing Freire d'Andrade, Portuguese Foreign Minister's comment to Arthur Hardinge, that many slave traders were transported convicts 'and their half-caste progeny.'[90]

Harris's first witness was deceased. Henry Morton Stanley, famous for meeting David Livingstone in 1871, died in 1904. Harris used some of his correspondence to create a long-term context of 'Portuguese slavery.' Stanley had worked as an emissary for Leopold and was no angel either, admitting to the violent 'chastisement' of the local peoples.[91] He found the Portuguese record mixed. On the one hand, the influence of Portuguese commerce and trade had made the natives around Lake Stanley friendly. On the other, he deplored the pitiless condition of black men around Boma brought on by the sordid Portuguese rum sellers. By the time of the 1884 Berlin Conference Stanley, like Bismarck, opposed the Congo falling under Portuguese rule because it would become a British puppet.[92] This seemed more important than any moral objection to 'Portuguese slavery.' Harris was aware of the layers of ambiguity embedded in Stanley's discourse on slavery. To clarify matters, he extricated only text that suited his purpose.

The Brethren missionary, Charles Swan, published *The Slavery of To-Day* in 1909.[93] Willliam Cadbury had secretly financed him to return to Portuguese Africa to investigate slave conditions, and Swan felt called by the Lord to do the work. Born in in Sunderland in 1861, Swan had become interested in Africa through reading David Livingstone. He was in Angola and the Congo between 1883 and 1903, and then in Lisbon until his death in 1934. Brethren were notoriously reluctant to be called by politics, but Swan saw nothing anti-Portuguese in simply encouraging them to apply their own laws. Harris selected some of his more sensational discoveries. Near Benguela in Angola, in October 1908, Swan found cast-off shackles and slave skeletons. At Sangongola in December slaves told him that they expected to be there for life.[94] His evidence supports much that identified the planters as the main law evaders. They wrote off British criticism as a contrivance for bargaining away Portugal's colonies. However, in actively campaigning against them, Swan went further than most Brethren missionaries.[95] He proved a role model for Harris whose own Christian activism conveyed the missionary's findings in the periphery into the cultural discourse of the centre.

Harris suspected the British Government had, for many years, covered up Swan's evidence of Portuguese slavery. The FO did have a long track record of instructing Consuls in Angola to turn a deaf ear.[96] We know for sure that Swan presented a report to the Foreign Office on 2 June 1909 and on 22 June he wrote to *The Times* enclosing a statement signed by all the male Protestant missionaries he had been able to reach in Angola. That letter, 'Slave Grown Cocoa', emphasized that natives did not go voluntarily to São Tomé, which they dreaded. Amidst the buying and selling, labourers did not understand their rights. Repatriation was a myth. Swan knew no man or woman who had ever returned from the islands. In conclusion, he stressed the findings were not just his own, but the collective opinions of a group of missionaries for presentation to the FO. In the same edition, the Secretary of the Manufacturing Confectioners' Alliance pledged that it would continue with its boycott of São Tomé cocoa. He emphasized that, contrary to some suggestions emanating from Lisbon, this was for ethical reasons and at considerable expense to themselves.[97]

Harris thought Henry Nevinson 'that prince of journalists . . . [whose] . . . passion for humanity is coupled . . . [with] . . . purity of motive.'[98] They had become reconciled after falling out in 1908 over Cadbury.[99] Nevinson had accused chocolate manufacturers of deliberately putting profits before labour conditions. The *Manchester Guardian* had to issue an apology for the article, although Nevinson was prepared to go to court. Harris thought Nevinson behaved foolishly. Nevinson lambasted Harris as 'a slimy serpent' for pandering to Cadbury.[100] Nevinson was a loose cannon who could be dismissive of all Portuguese.[101] He visited Angola and the islands between 1904 and 1905, several years before Harris. He shirked little, sharing a slave boat for eight days to cross from Benguela to São Tomé. *Modern Slavery* (1906) was the composite of several articles commissioned by *Harper's Magazine*. Before Swan, he found the human remains of the slave trade and interviewed the bought and sold. He shared Harris's cynicism about the British Government doing anything for Portuguese Africans. But even the opinionated Nevinson had to watch his step to earn a living. He also worked for the *Daily News*, owned by George Cadbury.[102] But he resigned from it over its refusal to condemn the forced feeding of suffragettes.

Harris emphasized the breadth of Nevinson's experience in extending from Angola to the islands. He mapped the 'bleached highway' of captivity, signposted by shackled and dying Angolans often finished off in the most brutal of ways.[103] He estimated that half the population in Angola was enslaved in some way.[104] There lay the root of the evil, not in the islands where there had been too much focus on the obduracy of the Portuguese planters defeating a solution.[105]

Colonel Colin Harding's account of his 8,000-mile journey from Rhodesia to Angola proved a seminal text for the English reader of the slave traffic across this region.[106] Harris regretted that it had been largely ignored. Harding began his career as an uncritical servant of the Crown. He played a leading role in quelling the risings of the Mshona and Matabele in the late 1890s, participated in the Jameson Raid, and fought in the Boer War. In 1902, he accompanied the Paramount Chief of Barotseland, King Lewanika, to England.

He was a dispassionate observer of Portuguese achievements and atrocities alike.[107] As an Army officer, and Commandant of the Barotse Native Police in NW Rhodesia, he provided unique regional evidence of Portuguese slaving. Harris cites his meeting with a 'Portuguese half-caste' on his way to buy slaves in exchange for 120 yards of calico each. This trader forcibly loaded enough young slaves to people a caravan. Harding also confirms the generous dissemination of brandy by the Portuguese in lubricating relationships with local slavers.[108] He recites the familiar tale of routes strewn with disused shackles, bleached bones, and makeshift graves. These revelations marked the beginning of Harding's slow demise. Eventually he was forced out by the Rhodesia Chartered Company as too sympathetic to the natives. The face of the former bricklayer, miner, and solicitor's clerk did not fit as colonial administrator.

Daniel Crawford published *Thinking black* only in 1912, having pursued his missionary work for the Brethren for over twenty years. Harris cites Crawford's caricatured attitudes of Portuguese lethargy: 'the average attitude is notoriously one of repose . . . Portuguese with a long romantic moustache, lolling about on chairs . . . is the commonest sight of the day . . . with sleepy, sun-baked senses, he loses himself in long time-effacing reveries . . . so you see what slavery has done for the Portuguese.'[109] Crawford was forty-two when he published *Thinking black*. He was born in the Firth of Clyde coastal village of Gourock, famous for its superstitions. Young Daniel found more comfort in evangelical Christianity, and left for Africa when he was just nineteen and remained until his death in 1926, except for a four-year return to Britain just before the First World War. Harris' slightly inaccurate imperialist condescension observed, 'During this long period he never once returned to civilisation.'[110] In keeping with the Brethren, Crawford distrusted the worldliness of politics. He is marked out from other contemporary Christian missionaries by his willingness to cede agency to the African. For him, the African was equal in the sight God. Crawford's Christianity held Europeans to be as sinful as Africans. He disassociated himself from the 'contamination theories' about racial mixing causing national decline. African culture was not to blame for the degenerate moral values of the European.[111]

Joseph Burtt was employed by Cadbury and the British cocoa firms to investigate conditions of production in Portuguese Africa. Burtt had no anti-slavery record and in 1906, had even welcomed the appointment of the dictator João Franco by King Carlos.[112] Nevinson ran into him in São Tomé in June 1905, and suggested he was wet behind the ears.[113] Burtt spent nearly two years between June 1905 and April 1907, in the islands, then Angola, after learning Portuguese. But he found that few slaves spoke it. His report met a brick wall at the Lisbon Colonial Conference in November 1907.[114] Only then, after Nevinson and the *Daily Graphic* accused him of using slave labour, did Cadbury announce a boycott and switch to the Gold Coast for supplies.[115] The *Graphic* backed down when Cadbury threatened to sue.[116]

Burtt's report generated strong Portuguese criticism, but he replied by asking why it was that free labourers tried to escape so often. Nevinson had observed, a sad lack of island geography usually defeated them. The route home to Angola always terminated on the seashore.[117] A best-known slave song began, 'In São Tomé there is a door to go in, but none to come out.'[118] Sleeping sickness also encouraged escape. It had been brought in by imported cattle from Gabon in the 1820s, only becoming a serious problem in the 1890s.[119] Harris also credits Burtt with exposing the British Government's duplicity in covering-up the smuggling of slaves he had witnessed with own eyes.[120] But Harris is too generous to Cadbury and the other manufacturers for backing an end to the slave cargoes. In pursuit of his own agenda, he was inclined to excuse Cadbury's procrastinations and the press's role in exposing them.

George Bailey Beak was appointed a vice-consul in Katanga in May 1907, one of a group investigating conditions in the Belgian Congo.[121] Beak confirmed for Harris the existence of a porous and turbulent frontier between the Portuguese and Belgian empires that assisted slavers. In 1895, a dissident group of Congolese soldiers – *Révoltés* – created an autonomous zone in the south west. They were deserters from the *Force Publique*. The latter were mainly black conscripts, at first drawn from other empires like the British, but by 1895 mostly from the Congo itself. Abysmally treated by their white Belgian officers, they revolted against their brutality and murdered the base commander. In it up to their necks, the *Révoltés* established themselves in enclaves, and with help from local chiefs fought off attacks from the *Force Publique*. Yamba Yamba, the leader cited by Harris, continued the revolt until his death in 1908. Hochschild identifies him as one of two corporals who had succeeded to the leadership after the initial revolt of 1895. He also estimates that the force was only four to five hundred strong, far below the Belgian estimate of seven thousand, cited by Harris.[122] Having discontinued military operations, this group of *Valleci* (as the Portuguese called them) began trading slaves for guns and ammunition across Portuguese West Africa. They were not unusual, for as Beak pointed out, the illegal trading of rubber and ivory by similar renegade extra-state groups was commonplace. Beak's experience of the *Valleci* was confirmed by Burtt who reported that Portuguese trading stations positioned along the Congo border relied upon such groups for supplies of slaves. Burtt further revealed why they were so feared:

They are cannibals, living mostly on human flesh, and when a native whom they had sold was asked why they had not eaten them, he replied that he had a companion with him, and that both their arms had been scratched by the *Valleci*, and after tasting the blood, they sold him, and ate his companion.[123]

A less gruesome story of the *Révoltés* came from Nevinson. He met a young man in Benguela who had been purchased by a Portuguese trader, then sold to an Englishman, who freed him. He amused his peers by telling them he was no longer a cannibal but had become a cook.[124]

Beck's evidence valuably elucidates some complexities of the Portuguese slave trade. Even if Portuguese Governments could be persuaded to honour international agreements, the situation on the ground conspired against this. The Portuguese empire in West Africa possessed only a notional identity. Frontiers were porous. 'Labour' moved from one undemarcated imperial space to another. Intra-imperial conflict, such as the Belgian-*Révoltés* wars, destabilized populations, causing flows across invisible borders. This might be sparked by the extreme militarisation of armies, but equally by economic incentives. What began as a conflict over rubber and ivory in the Congo led to movement of militarized labour into Angola and the consequential recourse to slave trading for an alternative subsistence economy. Beak's *Valleci* wars were paralleled in other parts of Portuguese West Africa. For example, between 1902 and 1909 the *Bailundu w*ar in Angola was a sporadic tribal revolt against Portuguese incursions into complex local autonomies, including over slave trading and the wild rubber economy.[125] Angolan rubber prices collapsed between 1901 and 1913.[126] For domestic opinion, the Portuguese propagandized these as 'passifications' employing Social Darwinist language about race similar to that used in the cocoa islands.

John and Alice Harris's own testimony was methodologically rigorous despite only spending a month in Portuguese West Africa. John was aware of the problems presented by taking oral testimony at face value, alluding to the sensitivity of his hosts and the constraints upon what slaves could reveal. John favoured the surprise visit to outlying districts, where slaves were more distantly supervized by their masters. The FO official A. C. Cummings criticized Harris for relying on interpreters, to whom 'The Angola native or any other nigger never tells the truth. He simply says what he thinks will please the listener.'[127] John Harris's methodology was unimpaired by such racism. But he does romanticize the condition of the free labouring Angolan compared with slaves in the islands. The former were happier, 'full of jolly quips and sallies; lightheartedly he wields his axe, paddle or machete, to the rhythm of his song.'[128]

The silent witness was William Cadbury, who Harris may have excluded because of their earlier spat. In 1910, Cadbury published the findings from a visit he and Burtt had made to the islands and Angola at the end of 1908.[129] He spares the *serviçais* (forced labourers) his condescension, which he reserves for the 'natives' – the mixed race, planter class. Cadbury dismisses the 'native' class as a racial mix, from Brazil, Gabon, Guinea, and Portuguese convicts' descendants. They are a 'decadent race . . . a brown-skinned individual, insolent, lazy, and lawless. His women, some of whom, I am told are possessed of a certain dusky comeliness, are notoriously loose in character . . . I have never seen a more degraded race.'[130] Without irony, Cadbury passes from his misogynistic, racist, symbiosis of the planter class to deplore their nerve in looking down on the *serviçais*. Then damning all, he recalls the words of an old priest he had met in Lisbon six years before, 'in his despair he sometimes wished that the islands might be swallowed in the depths of the sea and all their troubles ended.'[131]

His assessment of the origin of the islands' labour problem in Angola was more perceptive. There he found that war had torn society apart, creating a breeding ground for slavery. Prisoners of war were sold to the highest bidder, their family members distributed as spoils. The Governor, Paiva Couceiro (who rose against the First Republic), he found apathetic, only tampering with the contract system. The Illiterate *serviçal* used his contract to light his pipe, or dropped it overboard, thereby abandoning his necessary evidence for repatriation.[132] Cadbury's solution was drawn from the ideological resources of Liberal Imperialism. To preserve Anglo-Portuguese relations the senior party must teach the junior that the great victory for human liberty cannot be reversed.[133] In Cadbury's paternalist world view, the 'decadent and degraded race' were simply bad students.

In comparison, Harris prioritized the psychological self-emancipation of slaves. Mistrust of whites was a first step and this depended on releasing the slave psyche from the mystification that there was no way out of servitude. This was the missionary's task, he argued, seeming to forget that s/he was also white. Harris mistook demoralization for belief. Slaves did express resistance in interviews; some even tried to escape. But Harris' spiritualism demanded psychological emancipation, voiced by the missionary in the metropole. *Portuguese Slavery: Britain's Dilemma* invited the charge that it was a Christian polemic, reliant on translated oral testimony and the research of others. That did not, necessarily, render it ineffective as a propagandist text.

6 'The price of a cup of cocoa'

When H. N. Brailsford said there was no one better at explaining the price of a cup of cocoa, he was referring to Henry Nevinson, not John Harris. Harris's estimate in 1912 that a healthy slave cost eighteen pounds was below Nevinson's 1904 figure of twenty-five to forty, and Burtt's of thirty, in 1905. Cocoa demand drove slave prices high, as the UK alone took one third of São Tomé's exports by 1910.[134] Harris also under-estimated the volume of labour flow. He thought 25,000 slaves had been brought to the islands in the two and a half decades to 1905. Actually, some 70,000 arrived into 'perpetual indenture' and another 50,000 on short-term contracts, between 1880 and 1908. Angolans and Mozambicans were joined by fourteen thousand Cape Verdeans, fleeing the famine of 1903. Masters largely ignored the 1903 instruction from Lisbon to raise rates, placing them below levels in British West Africa. This, and the high death rate of slaves arriving in poor health, kept productivity low.[135]

'Tell Mr Cadbury from me that cocoa is blood,'[136] the American missionary William E. Fay told Joseph Burtt in 1906, referring to the brutally competitive internal market. Blood was drawn by the *palmatória* – a piece of hard, flat wood – and the *chicote* – a whip. One dental torturer had all his slave's teeth pulled out.[137] The Cadbury inquiry heard that there was as much beating under the Republic as the Monarchy.[138] The Republic did improve primary education, and abolished Sunday working, but nutritional levels stagnated. Leisure was tightly regulated for fear of drunkenness breeding rebellion. Masters had no faith in missionaries' reforming qualities.[139]

Harris's gender analysis elucidates the double bind of the female slave. Portuguese officials were complicit with plantation owners in abuse. A prospector told Nevinson he had bought a young girl from an elderly official for twenty-five pounds. Harris implies he felt no shame because it was standard practice.[140] Harris describes a sexual market in which beautiful black women always brought good prices. One he met had been transported two thousand miles from Lake Tanganyika to the mouth of the Congo. When her planter owner no longer wanted her, she would be sold on.[141] Another woman provided a similarly shocking example of forced trans-imperial migration. She was enslaved by a white trader on false charges of theft, sold on to a tribe, then to another trader, who then expected to sell her to a planter.[142] Dehumanisation extended beyond gender. One plantation owner talked of breeding slaves like cattle. He did not bother much with names, especially for indentured children who inherited the names of the deceased. This was why campaigners like

Harris found it impossible to establish reliable birth and death rates.[143]

7 'The paralysis of power': Official narratives and compliant diplomacy

Harris came to realize that he was confronting a double cover-up, British as well as Portuguese. From Lisbon, Hardinge sent evidence to Grey of Portuguese carrying off slaves from the Belgian Congo. Grey knew most of this already and tried to offload responsibility onto Portugal's government. Mounting public pressure forced him into greater appeasement at home. Francis Villiers warned him in 1911 that the anti-Portuguese slavery campaign could become as big as the Congo one.[144] For Harris, the Cadbury trial had already exposed the FO's cover-up, as well as endorsing the value of a free press. Harris implies that Grey's natural posture was to sit on evidence embarrassing to the Portuguese. During the trial, Grey declined to comment on whether the FO had pressurized Cadbury's not to stop cocoa imports – a main plank of its defence.[145] As Nevinson, observed, with customary irascibility, Grey was 'quite useless for either side.'[146]

The transnational character of the population on the cocoa islands could have proved a legal minefield. Forced labourers included British, Belgian and German subjects, all with different languages and tribal customs. Both Crawford and Hardinge reported on this, before Harris, and Hardinge raised it with the Portuguese.[147] Harris ridiculed the idea that natives from other empires would freely enter into five-year contracts to travel three thousand miles to unknown Portuguese islands. Such preposterous distortions served only to cover-up the origins of the slaves.

As anti-slavery campaigner, Harris made a best attempt at objectivity. He conceded that material conditions of existence on the islands, particularly housing, were reasonably good. But the free labour contract was a fiction, and repatriation a part of it. The few who were returned to the mainland were simply dumped, disorientated and without means. Harris saw through the haze cast by the official narrative:

> In the Colonies there is always a bewildering unreality about Portuguese regulations, a sense of oppressive helplessness grips the mind of the investigator as he endeavours to reconcile mentally the legal documents of Downing Street with actual conditions; it all

seems so unreal, so grotesque, that relief is often found in an outburst of laughter which is only arrested by realising the tragedy of it all.[148]

Nothing illustrated the hypocrisy of the official narrative better, for Harris, than the repatriation scheme. By 1908 it was actually thirty eight pounds in deficit. He complained bitterly that the fund had become a euphemism for dumping the old and sick in Angola. It has been argued that, 'From the British perspective, the issue was mobility. Workers not free to leave their jobs were slaves.'[149] But, for Harris, the issue was far broader. He was concerned about material working conditions, forced migration from the mainland, the effects of slave recruitment on relations between empires, and ultimately about relations between the two nation states and their effects upon the stability of European empires generally. All of these grievances combined to make him a very unhappy man.

For Harris, the British government acted like ghost writers of the Portuguese narrative. The Portuguese were the masters of bureaucratic mystification, but Belgians and Germans were equally complicit. 'The almost unceasing stream of regulations which go out from the Tagus by almost every steamer'[150] was intended to induce paralysis. The sleeping sickness regulations of 1910, alone, were enough to send the reader of the thirty, long sections to sleep. Harris found no-one observing them in 1912.

The benefit of regulatory paralysis was an open door to illegal imports of *serviçais* from Angola.[151] 'My wife and I saw many slaves landed in a destitute condition,'[152] Harris wrote. The roadsides of Benguela were littered with the starving and abandoned.[153] Strachey reported that the Portuguese deliberately left the sick to die, to discourage slaves from falling down.[154] The cartographer T. S. Schindler came across an appalling slave waiting camp in Angola, at the end of 1911:

> Close to these men were three women, all middle aged, who were in a most pitiable condition. One said that she had been ill for some time, and looked very anaemic; another had both her feet, her knees, and her elbows literally full of jiggers.[155] Each foot was one huge sore filled with these insects, and the knees and the elbows were the same, and she was quite helpless. The third one was lying in a stupor and was difficult to rouse. Then a fourth woman came along limping, who suffered from elephantiasis in her left foot . . . I inquired of a young man whether any had died, and he told me that several had died, two of them just outside the camp, and that they were left where

they had died . . . the hyaenas [sic] had carried off every bit of the corpse.'[156]

Harris was better at rooting out British complicity than penetrating the intricate web of centre–periphery relations that sustained Portuguese slavery. He did observe the frequent recall of colonial officials with reforming intentions, a practice unchanged under the Republic. Behind this lay the institutionalisation of planter interests in the metropole. Slave capital circulated along many arteries, and pro-Royalist feeling was widespread. Harris met one 'rags to riches' planter who contributed some of his profits to finance Royalists in Portugal, itself.[157] Cadbury met the Count of Vale Flór in Lisbon in 1903. He had left Portugal at sixteen, in 1871. In São Tomé he worked as a store clerk; at twenty-seven, he was a large plantation owner. But in Lisbon he lived in a grand residence in the Baixa area reconstructed by Pombal after the 1755 earthquake. He also had an apartment in Paris, of which his wife was particularly fond. Such examples of upward social mobility were not uncommon. The first baron of Água-Izé was born to a mixed-race mother and a white Brazilian father on Principé in 1816. He rose from slave trader to governor of Benguela district in Angola by buying up plantations in São Tomé from religious houses.[158]

The planter interest was well organised in Lisbon from 1899 through the key propaganda organ of *Centro Colonial*. By 1913 it was only one of five lobby groups active there. A key activist was Francisco Manteiro who used his Mozambican plantations to supply labour to São Tomé and Principé. António de Sousa Lara became rich on sugar cane and rubber in Angola after fleeing Brazil, then diversified into São Tomé cocoa and even gunpowder manufacture in Lisbon.[159] A measure of *Centro Colonial*'s influence is the small propaganda war it conducted in the early months of 1913. In February, Hugh Gaisford, *Chargé d'Affaires* in Lisbon, complained about the falsification of British government dispatches implying that he accepted the Portuguese had put an end to slavery. Harris fully supported Gaisford, accusing *Centro Colonial* of 'a deliberate garbling . . . with the object of confusing the public mind.'[160] He then rushed up to Newcastle to move a resolution on Portuguese slavery to the Free Church Congress, followed by a lecture tour of Switzerland.[161] There he was criticized by an unlikely defender of *Centro Colonial*, Mr L. McHale from Timperley in Cheshire. McHale condemned Harris for hypocrisy on the grounds that his own evidence in *Dawn in Darkest Africa* was equally twisted. Did Harris not realise that the 'slaves' enjoyed the journey from Angola to the islands for its novelty value?[162]

Harris's analysis of 'Portuguese paralysis' countered official narratives. It revealed 'paralysis' as the goal of Government policy, not the unintended outcome. Hardinge was told by Vasconcelos, the Portuguese Foreign Minister, on 16 March 1912, that his Government 'had been to a great extent paralysed by the power of the vested interests, European and native.'[163] But this was the false impression of helplessness the Government wished to convey: ' the question deliberately organised to confuse the issues and bluff civilisation,'[164] as Harris put it. It was after all the same Republican Government that 'blazes upon the housetops its devotion to the cause of human freedom'[165] that also recalled Governor Coelho from Angola for 'indiscretions' when he imprisoned a slave trader.[166]

Harris was inclined to take a high moral tone over the FO's indolence. But he understood the strategy behind its buying into Lisbon's official narrative. He hoped to gain some leverage over the secrecy of the deep state. But as fast as he exposed the camouflage around free contracts and repatriation, Whitehall retreated further into the darkness. Harris' Gladstonian idealism made little impression upon the Liberal Imperialism dominating Cabinet. He came to realize that exposing slavery was not enough. Political campaigning against diplomatic cover-ups was necessary. So he appealed, over the heads of a disreputable government, directly to the public for policy change. With *The Spectator* and the BPC, he demanded withdrawal from the Alliance, and the honouring of 'the traditions of Clarkson, Wilberforce, Buxton, Sturge and Livingstone.'[167] As dishonourable minds in government focused increasingly upon the Balkans, in May 1914, the ASAPS published the pamphlet *Portuguese Slavery: Britain's Responsibility*. Harris jointly authored it with four other committee members.[168] It took the form of an open letter to Edward Grey. Lord Cromer's introduction set the tone: end the Alliance if slavery persisted.

But as the Portuguese political prisoners left prison, there was still no prospect of freedom for the *serviçais* in West Africa. If Harris and the ASAPS achieved rather less than the BPC, then their task had been immensely more difficult. Its triumph was to take the anti-slavery issue to the moral heart of middle-class radicalism. It had not flinched at confronting FO realism with its moral idealism. Harris has been labelled a 'Christian imperialist' who made a qualitative distinction between British and other colonialisms. He thought the British empire encouraged 'sacrifice and service', while others provoked rebellion. Harris did prefer a liberal imperialism, but he was not a Liberal Imperialist. He was not starry-eyed about the British Empire. For him, the moral test of empire was slavery. The Portuguese failed it, and the

British Government condoned it. He went on to support the Mandate system after the First World War. But he continued his anti-slavery work undeterred and worked through the League of Nations to set up the Anti-Slavery Convention in 1926.[169] After the First World War, his somewhat old-fashioned liberal imperialism evolved into arguing for a 'new commonwealth' of self-government for the colonies, that fell short of independence. He was, briefly but very actively, Liberal MP for North Hackney between 1923 and 1924. Knighted in 1933, he died aged 65 in 1940, more of an establishment figure than might have been predicted in 1914. From missionary to pressure group campaigner, to MP and back again, he never lost his deep moral resentment of racial discrimination.[170]

But, to 1914, Harris failed to shift either the Portuguese or British state over the 'slavery question.' By the time he died, the *Estado Novo* of Salazar, had dug forced labour deep into colonial law. State and empire were represented in what Afonso Costa, not Salazar, had called a 'single, indivisible whole.'[171] In the year Harris died, a children's fun park was opened at Santa Clara e Castelo Viegas, near Coimbra, in the region of Beira Litoral. It was the brainchild of Professor Bissaya Barreto, a *Salzarista*, who, with the architect Cassiano Branco, sought to educate the 'men of tomorrow' as 'national human capital' in the values of nation and race.[172] In the Overseas Section of *Portugal dos Pequenitos*[173] an inscription celebrated colonialism in São Tomé and Principé: 'The Portuguese colonized them in such a way that they now produce excellent coffee and the finest cocoa in the world.'[174] Absent was any reference to enduring slavery. Harris had fought for a different outcome, but a world war, a military coup, and a dictatorship later, the continuity of the Portuguese colonial state proved stronger.

Yet, there had seemed more cause for optimism before 1914. The anti-Portuguese slavery campaign taught Harris that the illiberal state hid in silences and darkness. He had witnessed at first hand, the obstructions of Belgian and Portuguese colonialism. If he did entertain a higher opinion of the British Empire, he remained deeply critical of its imperial diplomacy. Like Roger Casement, he was pushed to grasp the inter-connections and mutual dependencies of the growing global system. Slavery was immoral, but it was also functional. Harris remained too religious for Casement – the diplomat's response to the missionary. But, as compulsive activists, they had much in common. Casement travelled across Portuguese Africa and the Congo before Harris and, like him, had been disillusioned by the South African War. But Casement was the superior political scientist. Empirically, he developed a systemic analysis of imperialism that linked its excesses to the globalising demands of capitalism. Like Harris, he did not spare Grey and the FO the wrath of his wisdom. As Andrew Porter has said, he 'remained perpetually torn between belief in the reforming capacity of the liberal state and experience of its vacillation, incompetence, and corruptibility.'[175]

This could also be said of Harris. As a foreign policy critic of his own party, he became an ambivalent Liberal. The lesson learned about Liberal Imperialism was that, in its acceptance of factoring 'slavery' into the national interest, it elided with Conservatism. This ran directly up against a liberal idealism that rejected the morality of strategic realism. Slowly, he came to recognize that such policy responses were structurally embedded in state institutions like the FO. The labyrinth of the deep state reached below politicians, into the bowels of diplomacy itself. There, resided an unyielding resistance to severing the continuity of the Portuguese alliance. Meaningful challenge required counter-organisation and a counter-narrative of the state. This was Harris' greatest challenge once he realized that retreat into isolated missionary solace was a cul-de-sac. The evidence and moral argument he relied on in Africa were paper weapons in the face of institutional conservatism. All around him from 1910–14, the organisation of trades unions, women, Irish nationalists and Unionists flagged up the lesson, although he never drew comparisons, or called for mass action. Quite probably, he appreciated that urging people onto the streets out of compassion for Africans was a fool's errand. Getting them along to lantern-slide lectures was hard enough. So, the ASAPS was targeted as a narrowly-focused pressure group to chip away at the margins of power. It published, networked, lobbied, held public meetings, with less success than the CRA had over the Congo, but with just as much clamour. The 'slaves' remained unfree, but a counter-narrative of the Portuguese and British states damaged the reputation of liberalism in both.

E. M. Tenison had led a secluded life until 1913. From then, she needed to learn how to make a public noise, and John Harris proved a finely trained voice coach. No matter that his religion took him into the arms of the black people that she distanced herself from. He knew how to run a campaign and had pressed the flesh along the corridors of power. There is no evidence that he gave Tenison and the BPC tutorials on pressure group organisation, but it must be counted unlikely they did not discuss tactics at all. The evidence we do have shows Tenison imitating his networking skills. The replication of tactics – press propaganda, public meetings, lobbying MPs, down to the use of the same venue on one occasion (the Westminster Palace Hotel) – all fall into a pattern. These are the specifics that assisted the

BPC. But, more generally, Harris and the entire anti-slavery movement provided an exemplary culture of public agitation. It sustained a discourse of suspicion that kept Portugal under constant scrutiny.

Conclusion

The argument of this book has been for a dual reading of 'The Locusts' across historical time and space. The methodology has been to establish a dialogue between the years 1910–14 and the conceptualisation of the past historians call the Old Alliance, reconfigured as neo-colonialism. As a pressure group reacting to the immediate consequences of the 1910 Revolution they were of limited importance. A set of parallel personal agents knitted together in temporary coalition to achieve a specific objective. They agreed on certain core values: representative government, the rule of law, Christian morality, imperialism; but differed over much else. At every level disaggregation was visible: Conservatives from Liberals; Catholics and Anglicans from agnostics; racists from anti-slavery activists; men from women; lower middle class from aristocracy; young from old. As a political campaign, it exhibited a rich ambiguity, combining political dilettantism with an increasing organisational modernity. Although it claimed a dubious success in freeing political prisoners, in pursuing that goal its use of civic instruments, like the press and public meeting, its parliamentary lobbying and general networking was impressively modern. It was far more sophisticated than the bunch of 'British innocents' that one historian has dismissed it as.[1]

Absences are also significant. Socialists distanced themselves from the barely disguised Royalism of the Campaign. So too did women who prioritized gendered politics. Indeed the Campaign generated resistance from Socialists like Bax and Swinny, both defenders of the Republic, and from Suffragettes.

A few years before '5 October' 1910 brought attitudes towards Portuguese political prisoners into focus, the Boer War had done the same for South African. The working class had been indifferent to that campaign, too; Radical Liberalism failing to build any coalition to its Left.[2] The BPC learned to be better at coalition politics, although it reached from the Right to the Centre, from irate Monarchists to libertarians. The Boer War had activated jingoism amongst the lower middle classes.[3] Their colonial condescension towards the Dutch in South Africa was analgous to that exhibited towards the Portuguese. A difference, however, was that jingoism was a populist expression of colonialism; the BPC was deiberately esoteric. Narrowly focused socially, it contained public mobilization, relying heavily on individual agency and charismatic leadership to appeal to power.

However, a dual reading of the historical significance of 'The Locusts' suggests they may have been of greater importance within the *longue durée* of Anglo-Portuguese history. The successful campaign to free political prisoners can be read as an outcome of British neo-colonialist relations with Portugal. Although these had taken on particular forms by the early twentieth century, they emerged from older *mores* embedded in the construct of the Old Alliance. The sense of entitlement that instructed the Republic on how to behave was derived from the ideological righteousness of a defensive Christianity. It was underpinned by historical power imbalances and perceptions of subalterneity. Of course, Braudel's original conceptualisation of the *longue durée* was materialist.[4] But, it can also allude to persistent continuities in historical consciousness. The collective memory in Britain of Portugal's past drew upon deep and enduring structures of thought little altered over time. There was never one Portugal, nor one First Republic in the collective memory, but several competing ideas. But the argument of this book has been that there was a dominant one.

Public action in Britain, 1910–14, was legitimated by a shared narrative of a degenerate nineteenth-century Portugal. Although this could not be a universally shared imaginary, British neo-colonialism did pass on a dominant ideology. This still left space for contested narratives over events, as a reading of the press accounts of the 1910 Revolution shows. But these narratives were read within entrenched parameters of interpretation. Revolutions and atheism were subordinate to the rule of law and religious morality. The Portuguese chaos was derived from historic weaknesses. This was the explanation of some Portuguese, themselves, who detected a *sonderweg*[5] of exceptionality – a descending linearity from empire to semi-colonized status.

Modern Portuguese historiography has offered a counter-narrative of 1910, now interpreted as a popularly supported revolution. This was based on agreement that restoring even the minimum of stable government required the removal of a flawed Monarchy, deadlocked and unreformable as it was. The Republic was designed to repair governmental instability, financial crisis, economic backwardness and civic anomie. If this was a utopian vision of '5 October,' it was at least a progressive one committed to a better democracy. Improved education, separation of church and state, and protection of Empire, would all make for a stronger national culture.[6] This progressive vision challenged the older collective memory of degeneration. It reimagined that bad government was the problem, not national, or even racial, inferiority. National decline became a challenge, not a fate: the pre-condition for regeneration. Republicanism rediscovered optimism in the national character. But in pre-war Britain, Byron's glistening Tagus was long forgotten, submerged beneath an unrelieved gloom.

In October 2010, as Portugal celebrated the centenary of its Revolution, there was not so much gloom as silence – the traditional British response towards Portuguese history. Since the 'Locust years' the British have declined into a collective historical dementia about '5 October'. What remains is an etiolated historical memory. Historians work to fill gaps in the past, as best they can. Since Aubrey Bell hosted in 'The Locusts' they have disappeared with hardly a trace. This book has attempted to restore a lapsed memory of how the First Portuguese Republic was received in Britain. 'The Locusts' campaigned hard for the freedom of political prisoners, and one for 'slaves.' Both are still with us, but not in a Portugal that has restored its democracy since 1974 and decolonized its empire. Just like the '5 Ocotber' 1910, the Portuguese achieved this for themselves – an outcome that might have surprised 'The Locusts.'

Notes

Introduction

1. Aubrey F..G. Bell, *Portugal of the Portuguese* (New York: Charles Scribner's and Sons, 1916), p. v.
2. Rose Macaulay, *They Went to Portugal* (London: Jonathan Cape, 1946), and *They Went to Portugal Too* (Manchester: Carcanet, 1990).
3. Douglas L Wheeler, *Republican Portugal: A political history, 1910–1926* (Madison: University of Wisconsin Press, 1978).
4. V. de Bragança-Cunha, *Revolutionary Portugal, 1910–26* (London: James Clarke, 1937).
5. Kathleen C. Schwartzman, *The Social Origins of Democratic Collapse: The First Portuguese Republic in the Global Economy* (Lawrence: University Press of Kansas, 1989).
6. See, Patrick Chabal, *Amílcar Cabral: Revolutionary Leadership and People's War* (Cambridge: Cambridge University Press, 1983).

1 'Descending like locusts': Britain and the First Portuguese Republic

1. Finot had been born into a Jewish family in Warsaw in 1858, but spent most of his adult life in France as a journalist and social scientist. He was one of the foremost critics of Social Darwinism. In *Le préjuge de races* (*Bias of Races*), 1905, he had opposed Aryan and other notions of racial purity with a strong defence of the historical benefits of interbreeding. See, Jennifer Michael Hecht, "The Solvency of Metaphysics: The Debate over Racial Science and Moral Philosophy in France, 1890–1919", *Isis*, 90, 1 (1999), pp. 18–22.
2. Jean Finot, "The First of February in Lisbon", *The Contemporary Review*, January, 1 (1908), p. 287.
3. Paulo Jorge Fernandes, Filipe Ribeiro de Meneses, Manuel Baiôa, "The Political History of Twentieth-Century Portugal", *e-Journal of Portuguese History*, 1, 2 (2003), p. 10.
4. E. P. Thompson, *The Making of the English Working Class* (Harmondsworth: Pelican, 1968), p. 13.
5. Luís Trindade, "Introduction: Unmaking Modern Portugal" in Luís Trindade, ed., *The Making of Modern Portugal* (Newcastle: Cambridge Scholars Publishing, 2013), p. 6.
6. There are only three published histories of the First Republic in English: V. de Bragança-Cunha, *Revolutionary Portugal 1910–26* (London:

James Clark, 1937), Douglas L. Wheeler, *Republican Portugal: A Political History 1910–26* (Madison: University of Wisconsin Press, 1978) and Kathleen C. Schwartzman, *The Social Origins of Democratic Collapse: The First Portuguese Republic in the Global Economy* (Lawrence, KS: University Press of Kansas, 1989). Richard Herr and António Costa Pinto, eds, *The Portuguese Republic at One Hundred* (Berkeley: University of California Press, 2012) situates the First Republic within its longer-term context. See also, J.D. Vincent-Smith, *Britain and Portugal 1910–16*, PhD, University of London, 1971; and, "The Portuguese Republic and Britain, 1910–1914", *Journal of Contemporary History*, 10, 4 (1975), pp. 707–727.

7   John Vincent-Smith, "Britain, Portugal and the First World War", *European Studies Review*, 4, 3 (1974), pp. 207–238; and, "The Anglo-German Negotiations over the Portuguese Colonies in Africa", *The Historical Journal*, 17, 3 (1974), pp. 620–629; R.T.B. Langhorne, "Anglo-German Negotiations Concerning the Future of the Portuguese Colonies, 1911–14", *The Historical Journal*, 1, 2 (1973), pp. 361–387.
8   Wheeler, *Republican Portugal*, p. 99.
9   *Hansard Parliamentary Debates*, HC, 28, 13 July 1911.
10 V. de Bragança-Cunha, "Mr Ramsay MacDonald and Portugal", *The New Age*, 3 August 1911.
11 Wheeler, *Republican Portugal*, pp. 98–99.
12 Fernandes, Meneses and Baiôa, *Political History of Twentieth-Century Portugal*, p. 5.
13 For example, see A. H. de Oliveira Marques, *History of Portugal*, vol. 2 (New York: Columbia University Press, 2nd edn., 1976), pp.149–150.
14 *Ibid.*, p. 2.
15 Daniel Alves, "Crise, e republicanismo no discurso dos lojistas de Lisboa (1890–1910)", *Análise Social*, 47, 205 (2012), pp. 766–791.
16 Fernando Catroga, "In the Name of the Nation", in Fernando Catroga and Pedro Tavares Almeida, eds, *Res Publica 1820–1926: Citizenship and political representation in Portugal* (Lisbon: Assembleia da República/ Biblioteca Nacional de Portugal, 2011), p. 48.
17 Pedro Tavares de Almeida, "Elections and Parliamentary Recruitment in Portugal", in Pedro Tavares de Almeida and Javier Moreno Luzón, eds, *The Politics of Representation: Elections and Parliamentarism in Portugal and Spain, 1875–1926* (Brighton: Sussex Academic Press, 2017), p. 7.
18 *Ibid.*, pp. 11–12, 21 and 32.
19 Darlene J. Sadlier, "Modernity and Modernism in Portugal: the Questão Coimbra and the Generation of 1870", *Nineteenth Century Prose*, 32, 1 (2005). Online.
20 Walter J. Schnerr, "Ramalho Ortigão and the Generation of 1870," *Hispania*, 44, 1 (1961), pp. 42–46.
21 Queen Ameilie was French, as was her Maurras-admiring biographer, Lucien Corpechot.

22 Most notably in *The City and the Mountains*.
23 Quoted in Bragança-Cunha, *Revolutionary Portugal*, p. 81.
24 Antero de Quental, "Causes of the Decline of the Peninsular Peoples in the Last Three Centuries", speech 27 May 1871, *Portuguese Studies*, 24, 2 (2008), pp. 67–94.
25 Richard Herr, "What was meant by a Republic in 1910?", in Herr and Costa Pinto, eds, *Portuguese Republic*, pp. 32–34.
26 Sebastianism originated in the myth that King Sebastian had survived the Battle of Ksar El Kebir, Morocco in 1578 and disappeared, destined to reappear as a Portuguese Messiah.
27 Fernando Catroga, "Decadence and Regeneration in the Portuguese Republican Imagination at the End of the Nineteenth Century", *Portuguese Literary and Cultural Studies*, 12 (2004), pp. 297–319. (The discourse of 'The Locusts' shared Republicanism's degeneration thesis, but offered little hope of redemption).
28 Patrick Wilken, *Empire Adrift: The Portuguese Court in Rio De Janeiro, 1808–1821* (London: Bloomsbury, 2004).
29 Donald Southgate, *The Most English Minister: The politics and policies of Palmerston* (London: Macmillan, 1966), p. 75.
30 *Ibid.*, p. 196.
31 'For the English to see.' Inspectors were directed to slave-free ships, or those with hidden slave cargoes.
32 David Brown, *Palmerston: A Biography* (New Haven and London: Yale, 2010), p. 240.
33 Oliveira Marques, *History of Portugal*, vol. 2, pp. 86–88.
34 John St Loe Strachey. The phrase referenced back to the political 'enslavement' of the thirteen colonies by the theory of 'virtual representation.'
35 Nuno G. Monteiro and António Costa Pinto, "Cultural Myths and Portuguese National Identity", in António Costa Pinto, ed., *Contemporary Portugal: Politics, society and culture* (Boulder USA: Social Science Monographs, 2005), p. 48.
36 Oliveira Marques, *History of Portugal*, vol. 2, p. 110.
37 Teresa Pinto Coelho, "*Lord Salisbury s 1890 Ultimatum to Portugal and Anglo-Portuguese Relations*" (2006), p. 6. Online.
38 Luís Trindade, "The System of Nationalism: Salazarism as Political Culture", in Trindade, ed., *Making of Modern Portugal*, pp. 250–252, which employs Benedict Anderson's concept of 'imagined communities.' See also, Monteiro and Costa Pinto's argument that 1890 produced an 'imperialist nationalism', in Costa Pinto, *Contemporary Portugal*, p. 52.
39 Angela Guimarães, "At Home and Abroad: Anglo-Portuguese Colonial Rivalries and Their Domestic Impact in the Work of Raphael Bordallo Pinheiro", *The Oxford Art Journal*, 8, 1 (1985), pp. 29–39.
40 *Ibid.*, p. 31.
41 See, Homi K. Bhabha, *The Location of Culture* (London: Routledge, 1994).

42 Langhorne, *Anglo-German Negotiations*, p. 379.
43 *The Saturday Review*, 10 February 1912.
44 Nuno Severiano Teixeira, "Between Africa and Europe: Portuguese Foreign Policy 1890–2000", in Costa Pinto, ed., *Contemporary Portugal*, pp. 85–97.
45 Charles Boxer, "Second Thoughts on the Anglo-Portuguese Alliance 1661–1808", *History Today* (June 1986), p. 22. Born in 1904, Boxer was at school during much of the First Republic. See, Dauril Alden, assisted by James S. Cummins and Michael Cooper, *Charles R. Boxer: An Uncommon Life* (Lisbon: Fundação Oriente, 2001).
46 V.G. Kiernan, "The Old Alliance: England and Portugal", *The Socialist Register 1973* (London: Merlin Press, 1973), p. 261.
47 Tom Gallagher, "Anglo-Portuguese Relations since 1900", *History Today* (June, 1986), pp. 39–45.
48 Edgar Prestage, "The Anglo-Portuguese Alliance", *Transactions of the Royal Historical Society*, 4, 17 (1934), pp. 69–100.
49 Boxer, *Second Thoughts*, p. 22.
50 António de Figueiredo, "Charles Boxer", obituary, *The Guardian*, 16 May 2000.
51 Defined as one that failed to integrate the competing sectors of capital. Ironically, through 1989, any murmur of interest in the Portuguese case study was overtaken by debate over the 'disarticulation' of the Eastern European satellite economies in relation to the USSR.
52 Analogous to the corporatist school, for which see, António Costa Pinto, *Salazar's Dictatorship and European Fascism: Problems of Interpretation* (New York and London: Columbia University Press, 1995), pp. 61–67.
53 Douglas Wheeler, review of Schwartzman, *American Historical Review*, 96, 3 (1991), pp. 892–893.
54 António Costa Pinto, "Republican Portugal: The Long Road to Democracy", in Herr and Costa Pinto, eds, *Portuguese Republic*, pp. 1–6.
55 Stanley G. Payne, "Portugal's First Republic in the Comparative Perspective of Its Era", in Herr and Costa Pinto, eds, *Portuguese Republic*, p. 21.
56 Initiated by David Blackbourn and Geoff Eley, *The Peculiarities of German History: Bourgeois Society and Politics in Nineteenth-Century Germany* (Oxford: Oxford University Press, 1984).
57 Jeffrey S. Bennett, *When the Sun Danced: Myth, Miracles, and Modernity in Early Twentieth-Century Portugal* (Charlottesville: University of Virginia Press, 2012), p. 34.
58 Although that never got much beyond the planning stage.
59 Schwartzman, *Social Origins*, p. 33.
60 Tom Gallagher, "The Catholic church and the *Estado Novo* of Portugal", in Jim Obelkovich, Lyndal Roper, Raphael Samuel, eds, *Disciplines of Faith: Studies in Religion, Politics and Patriarchy* (London: Routledge and Kegan Paul, 1987), p. 518.

61 Cited in R. A. H. Robinson, "The religious question and the Catholic revival in Portugal, 1900–1930", *Journal of Contemporary History*, 12 (1977), pp. 360–361.
62 Three children, cousins, claimed that the Virgin Mary had appeared to them six times between May and October, 1917.
63 Robinson, *The religious question*, p. 350.
64 Bennett, *When the Sun Danced*, p. 94.
65 Education is another example. See, Stephen R. Stoer and Roger Dale, "Education, State, and Society in Portugal, 1926–1981", *Comparative Education Review*, 31, 3 (1987), pp. 400–418.
66 Chabal, *Amílcar Cabral*, p. 186.
67 Jock McCulloch, *In the Twilight of the Revolution: The Political Theory of Amílcar Cabral* (London: Routledge and Kegan Paul, 1983), p. 93.
68 'Revolution in Guinea' (1969), quoted in Ronald H. Chilcote, *Amílcar Cabral's Revolutionary Theory and Practice: A Critical Guide* (Boulder and London: Lynne Reiner, 1991), p. 31.
69 McCulloch, *In the Twilight*, p. 117.
70 Amílcar Cabral, "Le Portugal est-il imperialist?", *Afrique-Asie*, 3 (1972), pp. 34–35.
71 Cabral was assassinated in 1973, well before Said's *Orientalism*, for example, was first published in 1978.
72 Desmond Gregory, *The Beneficent Usurpers: A History of the British in Madeira* (London: Associated University Presses, 1988), pp. 42–46.
73 Valentim Alexandre, "The Colonial Empire", in Costa Pinto, ed., *Contemporary Portugal*, p. 83.
74 Lucien Corperchot, *Memories of Queen Amélie of Portugal* (London: Eveleigh Nash, 1915; reprinted Ticehurst, East Sussex: Royalty Digest, 1996), p. 185.
75 Finot, *First of February in Lisbon*, p. 290.
76 Paulo Jorge Fernandes, "The political role and functioning of the Portuguese Parliament", in Almeida and Luzón, eds, *The Politics of Representation*, p. 108.
77 Clements R. Markham, "Oceanographic Researches of His Late Majesty King Carlos of Portugal", *The Geographical Journal*, 31, 5 (1908), pp. 514–518.
78 Known as the Municipal Library Elevator Coup after the place where most of the arrests took place.
79 Malcolm Howe, *Dom Manuel II. The Last King of Portugal: His Life and Reign* (London: Book Press, 2009), p. 31.
80 Quoted in Bragança-Cunha, *Revolutionary Portugal*, pp. 80–81.
81 Victim of infanticide, in Eça de Queirós' great critique of the Church under the last years of the Monarchy, *The Crime of Father Amaro*.
82 Howe, *Dom Manuel*, p. 13.
83 Filipe Ribeiro de Meneses, *Afonso Costa* (London: Haus, 2010), p. 4.
84 Tom Gallagher, *Portugal: A Twentieth-Century Interpretation* (Manchester: Manchester University Press, 1983), p. 18.

85 Meneses, *Afonso Costa*, p. 11.
86 Bennett, *When the Sun Danced*, p. 35.
87 Finot, *First of February in Lisbon*, pp. 298–299.
88 José Miguel Sardica, "O poder visível: D. Carlos, a imprensa e a opinião pública no final da monarquia constitucional", *Análise Social*, 47, 203 (2012), pp. 344–368.
89 Joana Estorninho de Almeida, "Liberal State and Images of Civil Servants", in Trindade, ed., *Making of Modern Portugal*, p. 139.
90 Sardica, *O poder visível*, pp. 357–361, which informs most of this section.
91 An historian, Martins' Iberianism was criticized as unpatriotic and in denial of national identity. See, José Miguel Sardica, "The cultural discourse of Contemporary Portuguese Iberianism", *International Journal of Iberian Studies*, 27, 1 (2014), pp. 55–70.
92 Sardica, *O poder visível*, p. 365.
93 Fernando Catroga, "The Parliamentary Model of the First Portuguese Republic: Legacies and Discontinuities", in Almeida and Luzón, eds, *The Politics of Representation*, p. 136.
94 Howe, *Dom Manuel*, p. 19.
95 *Ibid.*, p. 37.
96 E. J. Dillon, "Republican Portugal", *Contemporary Review*, 98 (1910), p. 517.
97 *Ibid.*, p. 521.
98 Lord Burnham's description, cited in Joseph O. Baylen, "Dillon, Emile Joseph (1854–1933)", *Oxford Dictionary of National Biography* (Oxford University Press, 2004).
99 *The Times*, 3 February 1908.
100 Meneses, *Afonso Costa*, pp. 23–24.
101 Wheeler, *Republican Portugal*, pp. 45–47. The original call came from the Republican poet, Guerra Junqueira.
102 Francis Fukuyama, "The End of History?", *The National Interest*, 16 (1989), pp. 3–18.
103 Romania being the main exception.
104 Catroga and Almeida, eds, *Res Publica 1820–1926*, for example.
105 António Costa Pinto, "Twentieth-Century Portugal: An Introduction", in Costa Pinto, ed., *Contemporary Portugal*, p. 5.
106 Costa Pinto and Almeida, *On Liberalism*, p. 13.
107 Costa Pinto, *Twentieth-Century Portugal*, pp. 2–3.
108 Monteiro and Costa Pinto, *Cultural Myths*, p. 54.
109 Rui Ramos, "A Tale of One City? Local Civic Traditions under Liberal and Republican Rule in Portugal (Late 18th Century–Early 20th Century)", *Citizenship Studies*, 11, 2 (2007), p. 182.
110 António Costa Pinto, "Portugal: Crisis and Early Authoritarian Takeover", in Dirk Berg-Schlosser and Jeremy Mitchell, eds, *Authoritarianism and Democracy in Europe 1919–39: Comparative Analyses* (London: Palgrave Macmillan, 2002), p. 360.

111 Maria Manuela Aguiar, "1910: Portuguese Republican Women out of the Shadows", in Herr and Costa Pinto, eds, *Portuguese Republic*, pp. 185–190.
112 Costa Pinto, *Portugal: Crisis and Early Authoritarian Takeover*, p. 356.
113 *Ventura Terra, Architect. The useful and the beautiful*, Exhibition, West Tower, Praça do Comércio, Lisbon, July 13th to October 21st, 2017.
114 Used by historians of Portugal to describe the new industrial journalism; after Burke's 'Fourth Estate' (the Press).
115 Sardica, *O poder visível*, pp. 345–354.

2 Reporting the Revolution

1 Stephen Koss, *The Rise and Fall of the Political Press in Britain, vol. 2: The Twentieth Century* (London: Hamish Hamilton, 1984), p. 235.
2 Quoted in Keith Robbins, *Sir Edward Grey: A Biography of Lord Grey of Fallodon* (London: Cassell, 1971), p. 372.
3 J.A.S. Grenville, "Foreign Policy and the Coming of War", in Donald Read, ed., *Edwardian England* (London: The Historical Association, 1982), p. 164.
4 Peter Rowland, *The Last Liberal Governments: The Promised Land 1905–1910* (London: Barrie and Rockcliff, the Cresset Press, 1968), p. xvii.
5 Glyn Stone, "The Foreign Office and Forced Labour in Portuguese West Africa 1894–1914", in Keith Hamilton and Patrick Salmon, eds, *Slavery, Diplomacy and Empire: Britain and the Suppression of the Slave Trade 1807–1975* (Brighton: Sussex Academic Press, 2009), pp. 165–195.
6 Payne, *Portugal's First Republic*, p. 20.
7 Donald Read, "Crisis Age or Golden Age?", in Read, ed., *Edwardian England*, pp. 15–27.
8 Robbins, *Sir Edward Grey*, p. 135.
9 *Ibid.*, p. 224.
10 *Ibid.*, p. 244.
11 *Ibid.*, p. 223.
12 Viscount Grey of Falloden, *Twenty Five Years, 1892–1916, vol. 1* (New York: Fred. A. Stokes Co., 1925), p. 293.
13 Vincent-Smith, *Britain and Portugal 1910–16*, p. 48.
14 To Goschen, Ambassador in Berlin.
15 Langhorne, *Anglo-German Negotiations*, p. 369.
16 Cited in *ibid.*, p. 377.
17 *Daily Chronicle*, 6 October 1910.
18 Dan Stone, "Race in British Eugenics", *European History Quarterly*, 31, 3 (2001), pp. 397–425.
19 Angela V. John, *War, Journalism and the Shaping of the Twentieth Century: The Life and Times of Henry W. Nevinson* (London: I.B. Tauris, 2006), p. 29.
20 *Evening Post*, 20 October 1910.

266 | Notes to Chapter 2

21 *Daily Chronicle*, 7 October 1910.
22 Miguel Bombarda, "Portugal", *The British Medical Journal*, 1, 2318 (1905), pp. 1214–1215.
23 Russell E. Benton, *The Downfall of a King: Dom Manuel II of Portugal* (Washington: University Press of America, 1977), p. 89.
24 Bragança-Cunha, *Revolutionary Portugal*, p. 90.
25 Other sources suggest more Republican coercion (See, Benton, *Downfall of a King*, p. 102).
26 Diego Palacios Cerezales,"Weak State and Civic Culture in Liberal Portugal (1851–1926)", in Trindade, ed., *Making of Modern Portugal*, pp. 44–64.
27 *Daily Chronicle*, 7 October 1910.
28 Ibid.
29 Ibid., 8 October 1910.
30 Ibid.
31 Ibid., 7 October 1910.
32 Until the Revolution, Lisbon had been a well-lit city. The year before, it was powered by an impressive combination of 692 kerosene, 293 electric, and 10,000 gas lights. See, Bruno Cordeiro, "Technological Modernization and Disuse in the Making of Portugal's Capital: Street Lighting from the 1840s to the 1960s", in Trindade, ed., *Making of Modern Portugal*, p. 114.
33 *Daily Chronicle*, 7 October 1910.
34 Ibid.
35 Ibid.
36 Ibid.
37 Martin S. Briggs, "S. John's Chapel in the Church of S. Roque, Lisbon", *The Burlington Magazine for Connoisseurs*, 28, 152 (1915), pp. 50–51.
38 *Daily Chronicle*, 8 October 1910.
39 Portuguese press sources estimated up to a hundred deaths, plus over 700 wounded. Civilians outnumbered the military (See, Benton, *Downfall of a King*, p. 110).
40 Ibid., p. 107.
41 *Daily Chronicle*, 10 October 1910.
42 Ibid.
43 Ibid.
44 John, *Journalism and the Shaping of the Twentieth Century*, p. 29.
45 Koss, *Rise and Fall*, p. 33.
46 In 7 October 1910 edition.
47 *Daily Mail*, 6 October 1910.
48 Ibid.
49 Later, the Republic's second elected President, when he succeeded Arriaga in 1915.
50 Fernando Vernâncio, "'Quick, Fleeting Sketches': Literary History in Portugal in the 19th Century", *Yearbook of European Studies* 12 (1999), p. 192.

51 Alan Freeland, "The People and the Poet: Portuguese National Identity and the Camões Tercentenary (1880)", in Clare Molinero-Mar and Angel Smith, eds, *Nationalism and the Nation in the Iberian Peninsula: Conflicting Identities* (Oxford: Berg, 1996), pp. 59–63.
52 Edgar Prestage, "Reminiscences of Portugal", in H. V. Livermore, ed., *Portugal and Brazil: An Introduction* (Oxford: Clarendon Press, 1953), p. 4.
53 Aubrey Fitz Gerald Bell, "Portuguese Literature", in Livermore, ed., *Portugal and Brazil*, p. 109.
54 Bragança-Cunha, *Revolutionary Portugal*, p. 97.
55 Monteiro and Costa Pinto, *Cultural Myths*, p. 53.
56 Catroga, *In the Name of the Nation*, p. 44.
57 *Daily Mail*, 6 October 1910.
58 Wheeler, *Republican Portugal*, p. 74.
59 *Daily Mail*, 7 October 1910.
60 Ibid.
61 G. Valentine Williams, *The World of Action* (London: Hamish Hamilton, 1938). Another, was much Portuguese. He bastardizes the language with both Spanish and French in his careless attempts to reconstruct conversations he had there.
62 Ibid., p. 197.
63 Ibid., p. 194.
64 Ibid., p. 195.
65 In the inter-war period it became the favourite haunt of intellectuals like the poet Fernando Pessoa. It is possible that Williams was in another cafe in Rossio Square.
66 The *Daily Mail* also reported this.
67 Williams, *World of Action*, p. 199.
68 Ibid., p. 200.
69 One of Machado's fourteen children might have got to the door before him. Twelve appear in a photograph in the *Daily Mail*, 7 October 1910.
70 Williams, *World of Action*, p. 200.
71 *Daily Mail*, 5 October 1910.
72 Ibid., 6 October 1910.
73 Ibid.
74 Ibid., 7 October 1910.
75 *Manchester Guardian*, 8 October 1910.
76 *Daily Mail*, 6 October 1910.
77 Ibid.
78 Ibid.
79 William Magear Tweed (1823–78), who dominated the Tammany Hall politics in the mid-nineteenth century with the patronage of his Democratic Party machine.
80 Edward Said, *Orientalism* (New York: Vintage Books, 1979).
81 *The Times*, 8 April 1910.

82 *Ibid.*, 6 October 1910.
83 *Ibid.*, 7 October 1910.
84 *Ibid.*
85 *Ibid.*
86 *Ibid.*
87 *Ibid.*
88 John Villiers, "Sir Francis Villiers and the End of the Portuguese Monarchy", p. 10.
89 *Ibid.*, p. 16.
90 *Ibid.*, p. 17.
91 Oliveira Marques, *History of Portugal*, vol. 2, pp. 72–73.
92 *Ibid.*, p. 74.
93 *The Observer*, 9 October 1910.
94 Dillon, *Republican Portugal*, p. 523.
95 *Dominion*, 9, 2600, 23 October 1915, p. 13.
96 Baylen, *Dillon, Emile Joseph*.
97 Dillon, *Republican Portugal*, p. 525.
98 *Ibid.*, p. 531.
99 Chief of Royal Police.
100 Paiva Couceiro led the artillery defence of the north of the city. He later led Royalist incursions into Northern Portugal from Spain.
101 Luís Trindade, "The System of Nationalism", in Trindade, ed., *Making of Modern Portugal*, p. 256.
102 Bragança-Cunha, *Revolutionary Portugal*, p. 101.
103 Apart from Dillon, there was only the Positivist, S. H. Swinny and the Marxist, Belfort Bax, of any note.
104 Peter Whitebrook, *William Archer: A Biography* (London: Methuen, 1993), p. 15.
105 J. P. Wearing, "Archer, William (1856–1924)", *Oxford Dictionary of National Biography* (Oxford: Oxford University Press, 2004).
106 William Archer, "The Portuguese Republic", *Fortnightly Review*, 539, (1911), p. 244.
107 Even at the great Jerónimos monastery, Belém, where he saw a priest saying mass to three old women.
108 Payne, *Portugal's First Republic*, pp. 18–20.
109 Fernandes, *Political role and functioning of Portuguese Parliament*, pp. 107–118.
110 Fernandes, Meneses, and Baiôa, *Political History of Twentieth-Century Portugal*, pp. 1–18.
111 Jeffrey S. Bennett, "Symbolic Inversion in the 1910 Republican Revolution in Portugal", *History and Anthropology*, 23, 3 (2012), p. 298.

3 Changing Places: King Manuel into Exile

1. *The Times*, 10 October 1910.
2. *Daily Chronicle*, 8 October 1910.
3. *Manchester Guardian*, 10 October 1910.
4. *Daily Chronicle*, 10 October 1910.
5. *Ibid.*
6. Finot, *First of February in Lisbon*, p. 294.
7. *The Times*, 7 October 1910.
8. *Daily Chronicle*, 10 October 1910.
9. *Ibid.*
10. *Daily Chronicle*, 8 October 1910.
11. *The Times*, 4 July 1932.
12. Howe, *Dom Manuel*, p. 81.
13. *Ibid.*, p. 51.
14. Benton, *Downfall of a King*, p. 127.
15. The family's popularity with France's Republican Government was not improved by the marriage of Amélie, the Duke's sister, to Prince Carlos of Portugal. See, *The Times*, 3 June 1886.
16. *The Times*, 29 March 1926, Obituary.
17. Howe, *Dom Manuel*, p. 73, who miscalculates the age gap as five.
18. Benton, *Downfall of a King*, p. 174.
19. *Daily Chronicle*, 11 October 1910.
20. *Manchester Guardian*, 8 October 1910.
21. *Ibid.*, 13 October 1910.
22. *Ibid.*, 12 October 1910.
23. Cited in Benton, *Downfall of a King*, p. 123.
24. Most likely, *vinho verde*, a prized wine of the Minho, in NW Portugal. If so, Desa was unkind in describing it as '*vin ordinaire*'.
25. *Daily Chronicle*, 13 October 1910.
26. *Ibid.*, 19 October 1910.
27. *Ibid.*, 20 October 1910.
28. Williams, *World of Action*, p. 196.
29. Foreign Minister, 1895–7; Envoy to UK, 1897–1910.
30. *Manchester Guardian*, 10 0ctober 1910.
31. Williams, *World of Action*, p. 196.
32. *The Times*, 29 June 1906.
33. Later, Archbishop of Canterbury, 1928–42.
34. *Manchester Guardian*, 10 October 1910.
35. *Ibid.*
36. Benton, *Downfall of a King*, p. 203.
37. *The Observer*, 9 October 1910.
38. *Daily Mail*, 5 October 1910.
39. Rev. Roger T. Stearn, "Maclean, Sir Harry Aubrey de Vere (1848–1920)", *Oxford Dictionary of National Biography* (Oxford: Oxford University Press, 2004).

270 | Notes to Chapter 4

40 L. De Sousa Rebelo, "A Plan for the Restoration of the Monarchy in Portugal", *Portuguese Studies*, 1 (1985), p. 208.
41 *Ibid.*, pp. 205–206.
42 Benton, *Downfall of a King*, p. 141.
43 De Sousa Rebelo, *A Plan for the Restoration*, p. 207.
44 *Ibid.*, p. 209.
45 *Ibid.*, pp. 209–211.
46 Howe, *Dom Manuel*, pp. 60–61.
47 *Ibid.*, p. 63.
48 *Ibid.*, p. 65.
49 Between 23–26 April thirty-nine deaths were reported, over a hundred injured and a further one hundred and twenty missing. Manuel turned up in a motor car, to visit the injured in their tents and shelters, accompanied by two surgeons with medical supplies. Lisbon's bakers sent 20,000 loaves. See, *The Times*, 26 April 1909; Benton, *Downfall of a King*, pp. 75–76.
50 Howe, *Dom Manuel*, p. 65.
51 De Sousa Rebelo, *A Plan for the Restoration*, p. 208.
52 Benton, *Downfall of a King*, p. 154.
53 *Morning Post*, 5 September 1913.
54 *Ibid.*, 26 September 1913.
55 Howe, *Dom Manuel*, p. 67.
56 *Morning Post*, 11 September 1913.

4 The Catholic

1 John Horgan, "The Irishness of Francis McCullagh", in Kevin Rafter, ed., *Irish Journalism Before Independence: More a Disease than a Profession* (Manchester: Manchester University Press), p. 106.
2 John Horgan, "'The great war correspondent': Francis McCullagh, 1874–1956", *Irish Historical Studies*, 36, 144 (2009), p. 549.
3 Horgan, *Irishness of Francis McCullagh*, p. 108.
4 John Horgan, "Journalism, Catholicism and Anti-Communism in an Era of Revolution: Francis McCullagh, War Correspondent, 1874–1956", *Studies: An Irish Quarterly Review*, 98, 390 (2009), pp. 169–173.
5 Robinson, *The religious question*, p. 348.
6 It took its name from the distinguished Portuguese naturalist, Félix Avelar Brotero (1744–1828).
7 Francisco Malta Romeiras, "The journal Brotéria (1902–2002): Jesuit science in the 20th century", *Journal of the History of Science and Technology*, 6 (2012), pp. 100–109.
8 *Journal des Dibats*, letter from M. Maurice Muret, its correspondent in Lisbon; reprinted in *The Tablet*, 5 November 1910.
9 Thomas F. Glick, *The Comparative Reception of Darwinism* (Chicago: University of Chicago Press, 1988), p 431.
10 *The Tablet*, 5 November 1910.

11 Francis McCullagh, "Driving Jesuits from Portugal", *The Sacred Heart Review*, 44, 21 (1910), p. 367.
12 *Ibid.*, p. 368.
13 *Ibid.*
14 *The Scotsman*, 21 October 1910.
15 *Ibid.*, 9 November 1910.
16 *Ibid.*
17 Ken and Jeanette Newton, eds, *The Brethren Movement: Key Information* (Lockerbie: Opal Trust, 2015), pp. 50–51.
18 *The Tablet*, 19 November 1910.
19 Meneses, *Afonso Costa*, p. 18.
20 Francis McCullagh, "Some Causes of the Portuguese Revolution", *Nineteenth Century and After*, 29–30, 405 (1910), p. 944.
21 A Portuguese edition *Portugal Ignorado* was published in 1912, to include his thoughts on the 1910 Revolution.
22 Cited in, Francis McCullagh, "The Portuguese Revolution", *The Dublin Review*, 168 (1911), p. 91.
23 McCullagh, *Portuguese Revolution*, pp. 92–93.
24 De Sousa Rebelo, *A Plan for the Restoration*, p. 211.
25 José Madueiro Pinto, "Sociology in Portugal: Formation and Recent Trends", in Ana Nunes de Almeida, ed., *Challenges, Controversies and Languages for Sociology and the Social Sciences in the 21st Century* (Madrid: International Sociological Association, 1998), p. 58.
26 Marcello J. Borges, *Chains of Gold: Portuguese Migration to Argentina in Transatlantic Perspective* (Leiden: Koninklijke Brill, 2009), p. 26.
27 *The Tablet*, 22 October 1910.
28 Francis McCullagh, "The Portuguese Separation Law", *Dublin Review*, 169 (1911), pp. 126–142.
29 Wheeler, *Republican Portugal*, p. 68.
30 Susana Goulart Costa, "Politics and the Azorean Church under the First Portuguese Republic", in Herr and Costa Pinto, *Portuguese Republic*, pp. 58–59.
31 Diogo Duarte, "State, Church and Society: The 1911 Law of Separation and the Struggle for Hegemony over a Common Subject", in Trindade, ed., *Making of Modern Portugal*, pp. 227–240.
32 E. P. Thompson, *Customs in Common* (London: Penguin Press, 1993), pp. 1–15. For the 'moral economy of the crowd', see chapters IV and V of the same volume.
33 McCullagh, *The Portuguese Separation Law*, p. 141.
34 Oliveira Marques, *History of Portugal*, vol. 1, pp. 21–25.
35 Francis McCullagh, "The Separation of Church and State in Portugal", *Irish Ecclesiastical Record*, 29 (1911), pp. 595–596.
36 R.A.H. Robinson, "'Salus, Ecclesiae Suprema Lex': Monarchists, Catholics and the Portuguese First Republic, 1910–1926", in T.J. Dadson, R.J.P. Oakley & P.A. Odber de Baubeta, eds, *New frontiers in*

Hispanic and Luso-Brazilian Scholarship (Lampeter: Edwin Mellen, 1994), p. 41.
37 Oliveira Marques, *History of Portugal*, vol. 2, pp. 129–130.
38 Gallagher, *Portugal*, p. 126.
39 Francis McCullagh, "Separation of Church and State in Portugal", *Catholic World*, 63 (1911), p. 371.
40 McCullagh, *The Separation of Church and State*, p. 599.
41 *Ibid.*, p. 601.
42 *Ibid.*
43 McCullagh, *The Portuguese Separation Law*, pp. 141–142.
44 McCullagh, *Separation of Church and State in Portugal*, p. 376.
45 *Ibid.*
46 Bennett, *When the Sun Danced*, p. 172.
47 Wheeler, *Republican Portugal*, pp. 52; 81–82; 87–89.
48 Goulart Costa, *Politics and the Azorean Church*, p. 62.
49 Duarte, *State, Church and Society*, pp. 241–246.
50 Robinson, *The religious question*, pp. 360–361.
51 Camille Torrend, "Anti-clerical policy in Portugal", *Dublin Review*, 150 (1912), pp. 128–151.
52 *Ibid.*, p. 139.
53 *Ibid.*, pp. 150–151.
54 Sylva Doria, "Church and State in Portugal", *The Oxford and Cambridge Review*, 14 (1911), p. 19.
55 *Ibid.*, p. 9.
56 *Ibid.*, p. 28.
57 Almeida, *Liberal State and Images of Civil Servants*, p. 140.
58 *New York Times*, 21 May 1911.
59 Catroga, *Parliamentary Model of First Portuguese Republic*, p. 143.
60 *New York Times*, 21 May 1911.
61 "Sebastião de Magalhães Lima, Political and Republican Journalist", *Correio de Vouga*, 13 May 2014.
62 João Moreira dos Santos, "Roots of Public Relations in Portugal: Changing an Old Paradigm", *Public Relations Review*, 42 (2016), p. 794.
63 *New York Times*, 21 May 1911.
64 *The Times*, 27 April 1911.
65 Horgan, *The Great War Correspondent*, p. 555. The War Office report, however, noted that his Bulgarian was not up to much.
66 Wheeler, *Republican Portugal*, p. 89.
67 Francis McCullagh, "How the *Carbonária* Saved the Portuguese Republic", *Contemporary Review*, 561 (1912), pp. 350–361.
68 Francis McCullagh, "Freedom in Portugal", *The Living Age*, 268 (1911), p. 629.
69 *Ibid.*
70 Francis McCullagh, "The Portuguese Republic and the Press", *The Dublin Review*, 154 (1914), pp. 314–329.

71 Ibid., pp. 323–324.
72 Ibid., p. 318.
73 Ibid., p. 319.
74 Ibid., p. 320.
75 Ibid., pp. 327–329.
76 Ibid., p. 326.
77 Francis McCullagh, "Portugal: the Nightmare Republic", *Nineteenth Century and After*, 75 (1914), pp. 148–170.
78 McCullagh, *Nightmare Republic*, p. 168.
79 Horgan, *The Great War War Correspondent*, p. 547.
80 McCullagh, *Nightmare Republic*, pp. 168–169.
81 Ibid., p. 170.
82 Horgan, *The Great War Correspondent*, p. 562.

5 The Disgruntled Royalist

1 V. de Bragança-Cunha, *Eight Centuries of Portuguese Monarchy: A Political Study* (New York: James Pott and Co., 1911).
2 Bragança-Cunha, *Revolutionary Portugal*, p. 97.
3 *The Spectator*, 22 March 1913.
4 They were then the *Braganzas*, but the letter z was removed from the Portuguese alphabet by the orthographic reforms of 1911.
5 "House of Chandor", *Frontline (India's National Magazine)*, 24, 6 (2007).
6 Rekha Mishra, *History of the Press in Goa*, PhD, Goa University (2004), p. 147.
7 Sushila Sawant Mendes, *Luís De Menezes Bragança and the Emergence of Political Consciousness in Goa*, PhD, Goa University (2012), pp. 80–91.
8 Teotónio R. de Souza, "Castes, Social Mobility and Politics in Goa", *Herald (Goa)*, 25 September 2012.
9 Mendes, *Luís De Menezes Bragança*, pp. 170–171.
10 Ibid., p. 22.
11 Ibid., pp. 50–69.
12 Maria Aurora Couto, *Goa: A Daughter's Story* (New Delhi: Penguin Viking, 2004), p. 374.
13 Teotónio R. de Souza, "Portuguese Impact upon Goa: Lusotopic, Lusophonic, Lusophilic?", in Philip J. Havik and Malyn Newitt, eds, *Creole Societies in the Portuguese Colonial Empire* (Newcastle upon Tyne: Cambridge Scholars Publishing, 2015), p. 246.
14 C. B. Brettell, "Portugal's First Post-Colonials: Citizenship, Identity, and the Repatriation of Goans", *Portuguese Studies Review*, 15, 2 (2007/8), p. 7.
15 Ibid., p. 6.
16 Couto, *Goa*, p. 396.

17 Ibid., p. 307.
18 Mendes, *Luís De Menezes Bragança*, pp. 288–289.
19 Ibid., p. 308.
20 De Souza, *Portuguese Impact upon Goa.*, p. 250.
21 Parag D. Parobo, "Tristão Bragança Cunha and Nationalism in Colonial Goa: Mediating Difference and Essentialising Nationhood", *Economic and Political Weekly*, 50, 31 (2015), p. 63.
22 Pramod Kale, "Goan Intellectuals and Goan Identity: An Unresolved Conflict", *Economic and Political Weekly*, 29, 16/17 (1994), p. 910.
23 C. R. Boxer, *Race Relations in the Portuguese colonial empire 1415–1825* (Oxford: Clarendon Press,1963).
24 Cited in Parobo, *Tristão Bragança Cunha*, p. 65.
25 Ibid.
26 Ibid., p. 62.
27 Portuguese cultural imperialism.
28 Nishtha Desai, "The Denationalisation of Goans: An Insight into the Construction of Cultural Identity", *Lusotopie* (2000), p. 472.
29 Nicholas Owen, "The Soft Heart of the British Empire: Indian Radicals in Edwardian London", *Past & Present*, 220, 1 (2013), p. 147.
30 An Indian student shot the India Office official, Sir Curzon Wyllie, in July 1909.
31 Parobo, *Tristão Bragança Cunha*, p. 64.
32 Notably for Goa, Brettell, *Portugal's First Post-Colonials*. See also, Malyn Newitt, *Emigration and the Sea: An Alternative History of Portugal and the Portuguese* (London: C. Hurst and Co., 2015).
33 W. H. Koebbel, "Eight Centuries of Portuguese Monarchy, V. de Bragança Cunha," *The Academy and Literature*, 24 June 1911, p. 784.
34 Bragança-Cunha, *Revolutionary Portugal*, p. 23.
35 Michael Burleigh and Wolfgang Wipperman, *The Racial State: Germany 1933–1945* (Cambridge: Cambridge University Press, 1991), p. 30.
36 Bragança-Cunha, *Revolutionary Portugal*, p. 34.
37 Piet de Rooy, "Moens, Marie Herman (1875–1938)", Netherlands Biographical Dictionary, 4 (The Hague, 1994). Online.
38 Bragança-Cunha, *Revolutionary Portugal*, p. 100.
39 Catroga, *Parliamentary Model of First Portuguese Republic*, p. 125.
40 Patrícia Ferraz de Matos, *The Colours of the Empire: Racialized Representations during Portuguese Colonialism* (New York and Oxford: Berghahn Books, 2006), p. 140.
41 Bragança-Cunha, *Revolutionary Portugal*, p. 102.
42 Cited in *Ibid.*, pp. 114–115.
43 Norihito Yamada, "George Canning and the Spanish Question, September 1822 to March 1823", *The Historical Journal*, 52, 2 (2009), pp. 343–362.
44 Douglas Hurd, *Choose Your Weapons. The British Foreign Secretary: 200 Years of Argument, Success and Failure* (London: Phoenix, 2011), p. 64.

45 Norohito Yamada, "Canning, the principle of non-interference and the struggle for influence in Portugal, 1822–5", *Historical Research*, 86 (2013), pp. 661–683.
46 Bragança-Cunha. *Eight Centuries*, p. 135.
47 *Ibid.*, p. 141.
48 *Ibid.*, p. 191.
49 David Kaunda, father of Kenneth. See, Andrew C. Ross, "Laws, Robert (1851–1934)", *Oxford Dictionary of National Biography* (Oxford: Oxford University Press, 2004).
50 Bragança-Cunha, *Eight Centuries*, pp. 204–218.
51 Bragança-Cunha, *Revolutionary Portugal*, p. 71.
52 *Ibid.*, p. 74.
53 *Ibid.*, p. 83.
54 Bragança-Cunha, *Eight Centuries*, p. 252.
55 Michael Derrick, "A Disgruntled Royalist", *The Tablet*, 24 September 1938.
56 Bragança-Cunha, *Revolutionary Portugal*, pp. 106–107.
57 *Ibid.*, p. 17.
58 *Ibid.*, p. 128.
59 *Ibid.*, p. 169.
60 V. de Bragança-Cunha, "Portugal", *The New Age*, 5 January 1911, pp. 219–220.
61 It was probably a pun on the Spanish *es verdad* ('it is true').
62 S. Verdad, *The New Age*, October 12, 1911.
63 Wallace Martin, *The New Age under Orage: Chapters in English Cultural History* (Manchester: Manchester University Press, 1967), p. 15.
64 Tom Villis, "Early modernism and exclusion: the cultural politics of two Edwardian periodicals, 'The New Age' and 'The New Witness'", *University of Sussex Journal of Contemporary History*, 5 (2002), p. 1.
65 Kenneth O. Morgan, "Edwardian Socialism", in Read, ed., *Edwardian England*, p. 100.
66 Villis, *Early modernism and exclusion*, p. 8.
67 Tom Villis, *Reaction and the Avant-Garde: The Revolt Against Liberal Democracy in Early Twentieth Century Britain* (London: I.B. Tauris, 2004), p. 10 (who discounts the rumour).
68 Christos Hadjiyiannis, "Conservative Politics, Modernist Poetics: J. M. Kennedy's 'Tory Democracy'", *English Literature in Translation 1880–1920*, 58, 3 (2015), pp. 385–394.
69 V. de Bragança-Cunha, "Republicanism in Portugal", *The New Age*, 2 February 1911, pp. 318–319.
70 Gallagher, *Portugal*, p. 23.
71 Bragança-Cunha, *Revolutionary Portugal*, p. 171.
72 V. de Bragança-Cunha, "Republican Portugal", *The New Age*, 18 May 1911, p. 52.

276 | Notes to Chapter 5

73 *Hansard Parliamentary Debates*, HC 28, 13 July 1911.
74 V. de Bragança-Cunha, "Mr Ramsay MacDonald and Portugal", *The New Age*, 3 August 1911, p. 318.
75 Bragança-Cunha, *Revolutionary Portugal*, p. 160.
76 He died in November, 1937 having stepped down as Prime Minister of the National Government in June, 1935.
77 V. de Bragança-Cunha, "Signs of the Times in Portugal", *The British Review*, 5, 1 (1914), pp. 39–40.
78 *The Times*, 11 January 1911.
79 *Ibid.*
80 *The Scotsman*, 30 November 1910; letter from Stuart E. McNair.
81 Mark Bevir, "Ernest Belfort Bax: Marxist, Idealist, and Positivist", *Journal of the History of Ideas*, 54, 1 (1993), p. 120. E. P. Thompson thought 'there *was* something funny about Belfort Bax. The truth is that he was an owl. There was a good deal in him of the music-hall professor – the sudden fits of abstraction, the completely unpractical caste of mind, the essential lack of proportion which revealed itself in a blank absence of a sense of humour' in *Willliam Morris: Romantic to Revolutionary* (London: The Merlin Press, 1955), p. 373.
82 E. Belfort Bax, "Reaction v. Republicanism", *The New Age*, 28 December 1911, pp. 198–199. He was replying to V. de Bragança-Cunha, "Triumphant Republicanism", *The New Age*, 16 November 1911, pp. 56–57.
83 Belfort Bax, letter, "Reaction v. Republicanism", *The New Age*, 28 December 1911, p. 199.
84 V. de Bragança-Cunha, letter, "Reaction v. Republicanism", *The New Age*, 4 January 1912, pp. 236–237.
85 Belfort Bax, letter, "Reaction v. Republicanism", *The New Age*, 11 January 1912, pp. 258–259.
86 *Ibid.*, 1 February 1912, pp. 317–318.
87 *Ibid.*, 8 February 1912, p. 341.
88 V. de Bragança-Cunha, "The Portuguese Republic and the Working Classes", *The New Age*, 15 February 1912, pp. 367–368.
89 V. de Bragança-Cunha, "Portugal Next I", *The New Age*, 12 December 1912, p. 127. See also, "Signs of the Times in Portugal", *The British Review*, 5, 1 January 1914, pp. 31–46.
90 V. de Bragança-Cunha, "An Englishman in Portugal", *The New Age*, 11 April 1912, 571–572.
91 V. de Bragança-Cunha, letter, "British journalists in Portugal", *The New Age*, 27 March 1913, p. 510.
92 Bragança-Cunha, *Portugal Next I*, p. 128.
93 Bragança-Cunha, "Portugal Next II", *The New Age*, 19 December 1912, pp. 149–151.
94 Emigration was very high, averaging 80,000 per annum 1911–13. See, Victor Pereira, "The Papers of State Power: Passports and the Control of Mobility", in Trindade, ed., *Making of Modern Portugal*, p. 31.

95 V. de Bragança-Cunha, "Insane Portugal II (concluded)", *The New Age*, 29 May 1913, p. 111.
96 Wheeler, *Republican Portugal*, p. 60.
97 V. de Bragança-Cunha, "Insane Portugal I", *The New Age*, 22 May 1913, p. 81.
98 Wheeler, *Republican Portugal*, p. 17.
99 V. de Bragança-Cunha, "Portugal: Her Fate", *The New Age*, 27 November 1913, p. 105.
100 V. de Bragança-Cunha, "The Portuguese Amnesty", *The New Age*, 12 March 1914, p. 585.
101 *Ibid*.
102 Bragança-Cunha, *Signs of the Times in Portugal*, p. 38.
103 He describes the 22 April 1913 meeting as 'memorable' without indicating whether he was in personal attendance (*Revolutionary Portugal*, p. 145).
104 Bragança-Cunha, *Revolutionary Portugal*, p. 146.
105 *The Spectator*, 22 March 1913.
106 Bragança-Cunha, *Revolutionary Portugal*, p. 147.
107 *Ibid*., pp. 143 and 149.
108 *Daily Chronicle*, 16 May 1913.
109 *The Nation*, 5 July 1913.
110 *Ibid*., 26 July 1913.
111 *Ibid*., 2 August 1913.
112 *Ibid*., 9 August 1913.
113 Davitt was imprisoned for over seven years in the 1870s for Fenian conspiracy and twice more in the early 1880s for agitating against the Liberal Government for land reform.
114 *The Nation*, 23 August 1913.
115 Bragança-Cunha, *Revolutionary Portugal*, pp. 150–151.
116 José Miguel Sardica, "O jornalismo e a intelligentsia portuguesa nos finais da Monarquia Constitucional", *Comunicacão e Cultura*, 7 (2009), pp. 28–33.
117 *Ibid*., p. 22.
118 Military leader of the Royalist risings in Northern Portugal.

6 The Lusophile

1 Macaulay, *They Went to Portugal*.
2 José Saramago, *Journey to Portugal: In Pursuit of Portugal's History and Culture* (London: Harcourt, 2000).
3 Aubrey F. G. Bell, *In Portugal* (London: John Lane, The Bodley Head, 1912), p. 5.
4 Bell, *In Portugal*, pp. 8–10.
5 *Ibid*., p. 84.
6 Oliveira Marques, *History of Portugal*, vol. 2, p. 68.
7 Wheeler, *Republican Portugal*, p. 64.

8   *Ibid.*, p. 46.
9   *Ibid.*, p. 39.
10 *Ibid.*, p. 84.
11 Bell, *In Portugal*, pp. 221–222.
12 *The Spectator*, 12 April 1913.
13 Aubrey F. G. Bell, "The Portuguese Republic", *Contemporary Review*, 101 (1912); Aubrey F. G. Bell, "Portugal under the Republic", *The National Review*, 60 (1913).
14 Bell, *Portuguese Republic*, p. 371.
15 Wheeler, *Republican Portugal*, pp. 78–87.
16 Bell, *Portuguese Republic*, pp. 370–371.
17 See, Robert Gellately, *Backing Hitler: Consent and Coercion in Nazi Germany* (Oxford: Oxford University Press, 2001); Orlando Figes, *The Whisperers: Private Life in Stalin's Russia* (London: Penguin, 2008); Richard Overy, *The Dictators: Hitler's Germany and Stalin's Russia* (London: Penguin, 2005).
18 Bell, *Portugal under the Republic*, pp. 70–71.
19 Bell, *Portuguese Republic*, p. 374.
20 Gallagher, *Portugal*, p. 23.
21 Bell, *Portuguese Republic*, p. 375.
22 Bell, *Portugal under the Republic*, pp. 66–67.
23 Bell, *Portuguese Republic*, p. 372.
24 *Ibid.*, p. 378.
25 Aubrey Bell, "Portugal and the Republic", *The National Review*, 63 (1914), p. 311.
26 *Morning Post*, 27 October 1913.
27 *Ibid.*
28 *Ibid.*
29 Vincent-Smith, *Britain and Portugal*, p. 105.
30 *Tenison Papers*, Portugal Box, Addenda, Portugal and Brazil.
31 *The Spectator*, 1 November 1913.
32 H.V. Livermore, ed., *Portugal and Brazil: An introduction, made by friends of Edgar Prestage and Aubrey Fitz Gerald Bell in piam memoriam* (Oxford: Clarendon Press, 1953).
33 *Ibid.*, p. 19.
34 *Ibid.*, p. 18.
35 Wheeler, *Republican Portugal*, p. 98.
36 *Morning Post*, 27 December 1913.
37 Charles Emmerson, *1913: The World before the Great War* (London: Vintage, 2013), p. 3.
38 *Morning Post*, 29 April 1913.
39 *Ibid.*, 2 May 1913.
40 Peter Clarke, *Hope and Glory: Britain 1900–1990* (London: Penguin, 1996), p. 70.
41 Frederico Ágoas, "Science, State and Society: The Emergence of Social

Notes to Chapter 6 | 279

      Research in Portugal", in Trindade, ed., *Making of Modern Portugal*, p. 166.
42 *Morning Post*, 14 March 1913.
43 *Ibid.*, 23 April 1913.
44 *Ibid.*, 3 April 1913.
45 *Ibid.*
46 *Ibid.*, 4 March 1913.
47 *Ibid.*, 15 March 1913.
48 *Ibid.*, 3 April 1913.
49 *Ibid.*, 24 March; 5 April 1913.
50 *Ibid.*, 4 April 1913.
51 *Ibid.*, 21 April 1913.
52 *Ibid.*, 23 April 1913.
53 *Ibid.*
54 Wheeler, *Republican Portugal*, p. 96.
55 Bragança-Cunha, *Revolutionary Portugal*, p. 173.
56 *Morning Post*, 2 May 1913.
57 *Ibid.*, 7 and 8 May 1913.
58 *The Spectator*, 8 February 1913.
59 *Ibid.*, 8 March 1913.
60 *Ibid.*, 12 April 1913.
61 *Ibid.* 26 April 1913.
62 *Ibid.*, 31 May 1913.
63 *Morning Post*, 30 April 1913.
64 *Ibid.*, 16 August 1913.
65 *Ibid.*, 26 May 1913.
66 *Ibid.*, 5 June 1913.
67 *Ibid.*, 11 June 1913.
68 *Ibid.*, 13 June 1913.
69 *Ibid.*, 18 June 1913.
70 *Ibid.*, 26 June 1913.
71 *Ibid.*, 15 July 1913.
72 Hugh Kay, *Salazar and Modern Portugal* (London: Eyre and Spottiswoode, 1970), p. 21.
73 Cited in *Morning Post*, 19 July 1913.
74 *Ibid.*, 19 July 1913.
75 *Ibid.*, 26 July 1913.
76 *Ibid.*, 21 July 1913.
77 *Ibid.*, 28 July 1913.
78 *Ibid.*, 29 July 1913.
79 *Ibid.*
80 *The Times*, 7 March 1911.
81 Élisée Reclus, *The Earth and its Inhabitants*, Vol. 1, *Europe* (New York: D. Appleton and Company, 1883). pp. 469–501. Online.
82 João Freire, *Freedom Fighters: Anarchist intellectuals, workers, and*

soldiers in Portugal's history (Montreal and London: Black Rose Books, 2001), pp. 64–65.
83 *The Times*, 4 March 1911.
84 *Morning Post*, 16 August 1913.
85 Freire, *Freedom Fighters*, pp. 42–46.
86 Joana Dias Pereira, "Labour Movements, Trade Unions and Strikes (Portugal)", in Ute Daniel, Peter Gatrell, Oliver Janz, Heather Jones, Jennifer Keene, Alan Kramer, and Bill Nasson, eds, *1914–1918: Online. International Encyclopedia of the First World War* (Berlin: Freie Universität Berlin, 2014).
87 Freire, *Freedom Fighters*. p. 22.
88 *The Times*, 21 March 1911.
89 *Morning Post*, 12 August 1913.
90 *Ibid.*, 26 August 1913.
91 Ruth Scurr, *Fatal Purity: Robespierre and the French Revolution* (London: Vintage, 2012).
92 *Morning Post*, 3 September 1913.
93 *Ibid.*, 19 September 1913.
94 *Ibid.*, 26 September 1913.
95 *Ibid.*, 1,13, and 21 October 1913.
96 *Ibid.*, 14 October 1913.
97 *Ibid.*
98 *Ibid.*, 24 October 1913.
99 *Ibid.*, 29 October 1913.
100 *Ibid.*, 23 October 1913.
101 *Ibid.*, 22 October 1913.
102 *Ibid.*, 23 October 1913.
103 *Ibid.*, 25 October 1913.
104 *Ibid.*, 29 October 1913.
105 *Ibid.*, 27 October 1913.
106 *Ibid.*
107 *Ibid.*
108 *Ibid.*, 1 November 1913 ('The Portuguese People, Virtues and Defects').
109 *Ibid.*, 15 November 1913.
110 *Ibid.*, 18 November 1913.
111 *Ibid.*, 22 November 1913.
112 *Ibid.*, 24 November 1913.
113 *Ibid.*, 26 November 1913.
114 *Ibid.*, 5 December 1913.
115 Wheeler, *Republican Portugal*, p. 101.
116 *Morning Post*, 12 December 1913.
117 *Ibid.*, 17 December 1913.
118 *Ibid.*, 17 January 1914.
119 *Ibid.*, 22 January 1914.
120 Wheeler, *Republican Portugal*, p. 102.

121 *The Times*, 13 January 1914.
122 *The Spectator*, 17 January 1914.
123 *Morning Post*, 22 January 1914.
124 *Ibid.*, 28 January 1914.
125 *Ibid.*
126 *Ibid.*, 20 February 1914.
127 Wheeler's estimate is lower and less certain at 1–2,000 (*Republican Portugal*, p. 104).
128 *Morning Post*, 7 March 1914.
129 *Ibid.*, 9 March 1914.
130 *Ibid.*, 24 February 1914.
131 *Ibid.*, 26 February 1914.
132 *Ibid.*, 27 February 1914.
133 *Ibid.*, 28 February 1914.
134 *Ibid.*, 27 March 1914.
135 Wheeler, *Republican Portugal*, p. 165.
136 *Ibid.*, p. 106.
137 Bell, *Portugal and the Republic*, p. 308.
138 *The Spectator*, 4 July 1914.
139 Bell, *Portugal of the Portuguese*, p. v.
140 António Costa Pinto, *The Blue Shirts: Portuguese Fascists and the New State* (New York: Columbia University Press, 1999), pp. 32–44.
141 Bell, *Portugal of the Portuguese*, p. 257.
142 Kenneth Maxwell, *Pombal* (Cambridge: Cambridge University Press, 1995), pp. 87–110.
143 This is to leave unmentioned his substantial body of work on Spanish culture.

7 The Secretary

1 Mabel and Amy. Two Mabels in the house must have been confusing, even though the younger was always called Mab. Why she declined to use Eva remains a mystery. Julian Tenison had found the house and persuaded Aunt Mabel to buy and restore it.
2 Robert Innes-Smith, "Tenison, Eva Mabel (1880–1961)", *Oxford Dictionary of National Biography* (Oxford: Oxford University Press, 2004).
3 E. M. Tenison Papers, Templeman Library, University of Kent; *Rosemary for Remembrance*; "Unexpected Activities, 1912–14." In Hamlet, Act 4, Scene 5, Ophelia says, 'There's rosemary, that's for remembrance; pray, love, remember: and there is pansies, that's for thoughts.' I am grateful to Sue Crabtree for this reference.
4 I have negotiated this problem by never citing Tenison's quotations of other people's, or her own, reported speech from 1912–14. I merely summarize them. I quote only her own opinions in 1954.
5 Dorothea Gerard (1855–1915) was a romantic novelist. But, in 1913 she

282 | Notes to Chapter 7

published *The Austrian Officer at Work and Play*, which argued that the officer class, composed of the constituent nationalities of the Austrian Empire, became a cohesive military force and distinct social class.

6 Almeida was one of many Miguelists who had sort refuge in Austria alongside the Pretender.
7 In 1912, probably *Chivalry and the Wounded. The Hospitaliers of St. John of Jerusalem, 1014–1914*, published two years later.
8 *Unexpected Activities*, p. 4. (I have inserted pagination, although the original typed manuscript contains changes, as well as handwritten corrections within the text).
9 *Tenison Papers*, Rosemary for Remembrance, Autobiography, Postscript.
10 *Daily Mail*, 17 September 1912.
11 Ibid.
12 Ibid. Almeida was still in the Penitenciária in December 1913, when he was visited by Philip Gibbs.
13 Daughter of the 8th Baron Clifford of Chumleigh, she became Count de Torre-Diaz's second wife in 1892. He had been Gentleman of the Bedchamber to the King of Spain, and member of the Spanish Senate until the Revolution of 1868. From then, he went into merchant banking in London.
14 He was killed in action in August 1916. See, E. M. Tenison, "Tenison, Julian, A Character – sketch of Lieutenant Commander Julian Tenison, Born June 22, 1885. Died for his King and Country, August 15, 1916", (1920).
15 *Unexpected Activities*, p. 12.
16 Ibid., pp. 14–15.
17 Ibid., pp. 17 and 18.
18 Ibid., p. 19.
19 Known to friends as Madame Eça.
20 Tenison made one final and unsuccessful attempt to get him to join the BPC in mid 1913, but he did not turn up (*Unexpected Activities*, p. 128c).
21 *The Tablet*, 9 March 1912.
22 Ibid., 3 February 1912.
23 A working-class Catholic born in the Lower Falls, Belfast in 1871, Devlin was first elected for Kilkenny in 1902, he took Belfast West from the Unionists in 1906, and became a champion of labour issues in the textile trades.
24 *Hansard Parliamentary Debates*, HC, 34, 1 March 1912.
25 Liberal Member for North Somerset.
26 Conservative Member for Sheffield Central.
27 *Hansard Parliamentary Debates*, HC, 35, 5 March 1912.
28 Unionist Member for Kingston upon Hull.
29 *The Spectator*, 8 February 1913.
30 The Duchess later confessed that she had assumed Tenison was a man

Notes to Chapter 7 | 283

because in *The Spectator* article of 8 February her style seemed so concentrated, brief and forceful (*(Unexpected Activities*, p. 139b). On meeting her for the first time Thomas Glas Sandeman, cousin of Dona Julia de Brito, also expressed astonishment that she was not 'Mr E. M. Tenison' (*Unexpected Activities*, p. 150).
31 *Unexpected Activities*, p. 26.
32 *Ibid.*, p. 30.
33 *The Spectator*, 8 March 1913.
34 *Ibid.*, 15 March 1913.
35 *Ibid.*, 22 March 1913.
36 *Tenison Papers*, Portugal Box, Correspondence, letters to Duke of Bragança, 10 March 1954, 22 May 1957, 29 December 1958, 26 March 1959.
37 *Ibid.*, letter from Duke of Bragança to Tenison, 10 January 1959, for example.
38 *Unexpected Activities*, p. 31.
39 *Ibid.*, p. 34.
40 *Ibid.*, p. 38.
41 *Ibid.*, p. 42.
42 Tenison took her identity to the grave.
43 *Unexpected Activities*, p. 48.
44 *Ibid.*, p. 50.
45 *The Spectator*, 1 November 1913.
46 *Unexpected Activities*, p. 64.
47 *Ibid.*, p. 66.
48 *Ibid.*, p. 72.
49 *Ibid.*, p. 75.
50 *Ibid.*, p. 76.
51 Possibly, Archduchess Maria Theresa.
52 *Unexpected Activities*, p. 92.
53 *Ibid.*, p. 104.
54 Editor, 1904–18. Donald had relinquished the chance to be the Liberal and Progressive candidate for West Ham (North) to take the job. He went on to be elected President of the Institute of Journalists in 1913. See, A. J. A. Morris, "Donald, Sir Robert (1860–1933)", *Oxford Dictionary of National Biography* (Oxford: Oxford University Press, 2004).
55 *Unexpected Activities*, p. 106.
56 *Ibid.*, p. 109.
57 *Ibid.*, p. 108.
58 Tragically, for the historian, the Campaign's accounts perished in the fire at Yokes Court in 1952, along with much of Tenison's personal correspondence over Portugal.
59 He never reported doing this.
60 Philip Gibbs, *The Pageant of the Years* (London: Heinemann, 1946), p. 109.

284 | Notes to Chapter 7

61 *Unexpected Activities*, p. 115.
62 He succeeded his father, Alexander, as Conservative MP for Kingswinford (NW Staffordshire), 1905–18. He later joined the BPC.
63 *Unexpected Activities*, p. 119.
64 *Hansard Parliamentary Debates*, HC, 51, 10 April 1913.
65 *Ibid.*, HC, 53, 27 May 1913.
66 Stephen Koss, *The Rise and Fall of the Political Press in Britain, vol. 1: The Nineteenth Century* (Chapel Hill, NC: University of North Carolina Press, 1981), p. 364.
67 *Westminster Gazettte*, 25 April 1913.
68 *Ibid.*, 19 December 1913.
69 *Unexpected Activities*, p. 125.
70 *Ibid.*, p. 127.
71 *Ibid.*, p. 128. *La Libre Parole* was founded by the anti-Semite, Eduard Drumont, in 1892, and lapsed into an ultra-conservative nationalism from 1910. Vergnet published *France in Danger*, warning of Pan-Germanism, the same year.
72 Inflammation of the nervous system.
73 *Unexpected Activities*, p. 128d.
74 On 9 February 1914.
75 *Will England Save Portugal?* (London: L. Upcott Gill and Son, 1914), pp. 12–15.
76 *Unexpected Activities*, p. 136.
77 Writing in 1954, Tenison probably exaggerated her premonition of war.
78 *Unexpected Acitivities*, p. 137a. The pagination has been altered in Tenison's hand in the original MS.
79 Morrell had an open marriage and several children by different women.
80 Sir Arthur Conan Doyle, a BPC supporter, had publicly denounced Suffragette incendiarism at the Nevill Ground cricket clubhouse, Tunbridge Wells. Shortly afterwards, Sir Arthur's gardener discovered the letterbox of his house in Windlesham was filled with thick black glue. The two events may have been related. Sir Arthur's letters survived the glue reasonably well (*The Times*, 26 May 1913).
81 *Unexpected Activities*, p. 139.
82 *The Spectator* reported the Howard Association organized the meeting jointly with the BPC (23 January 1914), although this is omitted in *Unexpected Activities*.
83 Scott (1846–1932) owned the *Manchester Guardian* from 1905, when he ceased to be Liberal MP for Leigh.
84 Tenison also received phone calls at 51 Berkeley Square from contacts such as him, evidence of use of the new medium for political communication.
85 *Unexpected Activities*, p. 147.
86 *Ibid*.
87 Edgar Prestage, "Reminiscences of Portugal", in Livermore, ed., *Portugal and Brazil*, p. 8.

88 *Ibid.*, p. 9.
89 *Ibid.*, p. 7.
90 *Ibid.*, p. 10.
91 *The Spectator*, 21 February 1914.
92 *Ibid.*, 28 February 1914.
93 *Ibid.*
94 *Ibid.*, 1 November 1913.
95 *The Portuguese Amnesty* (London: L. Upcott Gill and Son Ltd, 1914), p. 7.
96 *Ibid.*, p. iv.
97 Macaulay, *The Went to Portugal*, p. 173.
98 *Unexpected Activities*, p. 163. Almeida married that other distinguished ex-political prisoner, Dona Constança Telles da Gama, shortly after the Amnesty. After the defeat of the Austro-Hungarian Empire in 1918, he followed the ex-Emperor Charles into exile in Madeira. He ended his days a contented citizen of Salazar's Portugal, and died in 1950 aged 83 (*Unexpected Activities*, p. 199).
99 *Ibid.*, p. 166.
100 *Ibid.*
101 *Ibid.*, p. 191.
102 *Tenison Papers*, Portugal Box, Addenda, Portugal and Brazil, p. 2.
103 *Tenison Papers*, Portugal Box, letter to the Duke of Bragança, 10 March 1954.
104 *Unexpected Activities*, p. 29.
105 Robert Innes-Smith, "The Witch of Yokes Court", *The Lady*, 20 July 2010.

8 The Duchess

1 Bill Forsythe, "Russell, Adeline Mary, duchess of Bedford (1852–1920)", *Oxford Dictionary of National Biography* (Oxford: Oxford University Press, 2004).
2 Lucia Zedner, *Women, Crime and Custody in Victorian England* (Oxford: Oxford University Press, 1991), p. 4.
3 F. K. Prochaska, *Women and Philanthropy in Nineteenth-Century England* (Oxford: Clarendon, 1980), p. 172.
4 *Ibid.*
5 Adeline M. Bedford, "Fifteen Years' Work in a Female Convict Prison", *The Nineteenth Century and After*, 68, (1910), p. 616.
6 Zedner, *Women, Crime and Custody*, p. 246.
7 *Ibid.*, pp. 253–254.
8 Jason Tomes, "Lytton, Victor Alexander George Robert Bulwer, second earl of Lytton (1876–1947)", *Oxford Dictionary of National Biography* (Oxford: Oxford University Press, 2004).
9 Constance Lytton and Jane Warton, Spinster, *Prisons and Prisoners: Some Personal Experiences* (London: Wm. Heinemann, 1914), pp. 62–

63. Jane Warton was the pseudonym Lady Lytton adopted to get rearrested after being released from Newcastle prison for what she believed were reasons of rank.
10　Jose Harris, "Lytton, Lady Constance Georgina Bulwer (1869–1923)", *Oxford Dictionary of National Biography* (Oxford: Oxford University Press, 2004).
11　Bill Forsythe, "Women Prisoners and Women Penal Officials 1840–1921", *British Journal of Criminology*, 33, 4 (1993), p. 532.
12　W. J. Forsythe, *Penal Discipline, Reformatory Projects, and the English Prison Commission, 1895–1939* (Exeter: University of Exeter press, 1990), p. 45.
13　Bedford, *Fifteen Years' Work*, p. 625.
14　Forsythe, *Penal Discipline*, p. 51.
15　*Ibid.*, p. 79. Imprisoned Suffragettes were to learn, tactically, from this.
16　Zedner, *Women, Crime and Custody*, p. 237.
17　*Ibid.*, pp. 249–250.
18　Forsythe, *Women Prisoners*, p. 532.
19　Lytton, *Prisons and Prisoners*, pp. 86–87.
20　Sean McConville, *English Local Prisons 1860–1900: Next Only to Death* (London: Routledge, 1995), p. 323.
21　Bedford, *Fifteen Years' Work*, pp. 628–629.
22　Quoted in Zedner, *Women, Crime and Custody*, p. 285.
23　Bedford, *Fifteen Years' Work*, p. 623.
24　Zedner, *Women, Crime and Custody*, idem.
25　Forsythe, *Women Prisoners*, p. 528.
26　Anne Logan, *Feminism and Criminal Justice: A Historical Perspective* (London: Palgrave, 2008).
27　Margaret L. Arnot and Cornelie Usborne, *Gender and Crime in Modern Europe* (Cambridge: Cambridge University Press, 1999), p. 5.
28　Forsythe, *Women Prisoners*, pp. 538–539.
29　*New York Times*, 13 April 1913.
30　Bedford, *Fifteen Years' Work*, pp. 630–631.
31　*The Times*, 5 April 1913.
32　Narrow iron grate.
33　*The Times*, 5 April 1913.
34　*Ibid.*, 7 April 1913.
35　*Daily Mail*, 7 April 1913.
36　*The Spectator*, 12 April 1913.
37　*Daily Mail*, 7 April 1913.
38　*The Spectator*, 12 April 1913.
39　*Manchester Guardian*, 7 April 1913.
40　*The Observer*, 19 April 1913.
41　*Ibid.*, 27 April 1913.
42　*Ibid.*, 4 May 1913.
43　*Ibid.*, 30 May 1913.

44 See, *The Nation*, 12 May 1913.
45 *Manchester Guardian*, 12 May 1913. Sir Arthur Conan Doyle dismissed Swinny in favour of Aubrey Bell's reporting for the *Morning Post*. 'Mr Swinny has been shown what the authorities desired him to see, and he is quite unwittingly helping to bolster up a most cruel system.' (*Daily Chronicle*, 16 May 1913).
46 *The Times*, 15 April 1913.
47 *Ibid.*, 17 April 1913
48 *Ibid.*
49 E. D. Ross, Rev. John Gurney, "Browne, Edward Granville (1862–1926)", *Oxford Dictionary of National Biography* (Oxford: Oxford University Press, 2004).
50 *The Times*, 13 May 1913.
51 *The Observer*, 23 April 1913.
52 *The Times*, 28 April 1913.
53 *Ibid.*, 30 December 1913.
54 *Ibid.*
55 *Ibid.*, 3 January 1914.
56 The Wolfram Mining and Smelting Company's principal use of the manufactured tin was in the production of sardine cans. Online. www.bhs**portugal**.org/time-line?sort_by=title&sort_order, 25 June 2018.
57 *The Times*, 8 January 1914.
58 *Ibid.*, 9 March 1914.
59 *Manchester Guardian*, 7 February 1914.
60 *Ibid.*, 20 February 1914.
61 *The Times*, 14 April 1920.
62 *The Spectator*, 1 May 1920.

9 Captives, Campaigners and Citizens

1 Wheeler, *Republican Portugal*, p. 104.
2 Linda Colley, *Captives: Britain, Empire and the World 1600–1850* (London: Jonathan Cape, 2002), p. 12.
3 Colley, *Captives*, p. 13.
4 *Portuguese Political Prisoners: A British National Protest* (London: L. Upcott Gill and Son, 1913).
5 *Ibid.*, p. 3.
6 *Ibid.*, p. 6.
7 Who broke from Costa's Democrats in 1911 and set up a League of Opposition by 1913 (Wheeler, *Republican Portugal*, pp. 84 and 101).
8 *Portuguese Political Prisoners*, pp. 10–14.
9 *Ibid.*, pp. 25–26.
10 *Ibid.*, p.15.
11 *Ibid.*, p.18.
12 *Ibid.*, p.19.

288 | *Notes to Chapter 9*

13 *Ibid.*, p. 23
14 António Vaz Monteiro Gomes, *Portuguese Political Prisoners: Reply to Duchess of Bedford's statements*, Lisbon 1913 (BLPES, Special Pamphlets Collection), pp. 5–6.
15 *Ibid.*, p. 7.
16 *Ibid.*, p. 8. (Tenison accused Monteiro Gomes of misrepresenting Figueiredo's opinion of *Penitenciária* conditions).
17 *Ibid.*, p. 9.
18 *Ibid.*, p. 10.
19 *Ibid.*, p. 11.
20 *Unexpected Activities*, p. 60.
21 *Ibid.*, p. 61.
22 *Ibid.*, p. 57.
23 Passed 25 April 1913, three days after the Aeolian Hall meeting.
24 Almeida, *Liberal State and Images of Civil Servants*, p. 129.
25 Pedro Tavares Almeida, "Electors, voting and representatives", in Catroga and Almeida, eds, *Res Publica*, p. 63.
26 *Ibid.*, pp. 65–87.
27 J. J. Gomes Canotilho, "Between the representative form of government and representation of nothing in Portuguese constitutional law", in Catroga and Almeida, eds, *Res Publica*, p. 143.
28 Cited in Luis Salgado de Matos, "The Military brought liberal political representation to Portugal", in Catroga and Almeida, eds, *Res Publica*, p. 179.
29 Maria Rita Lino Garnel, "Doctors and public health in the Republican Parliament", in Catroga and Almeida, eds, *Res Publica*, pp. 230–257.
30 Fátima Moura Ferreira, "The legal profession and political representation", in Catroga and Almeida, eds, *Res Publica*, pp. 216–229.
31 Fernando Farelo Lopes, "Parties and political representation during the liberal period in Portugal", in Catroga and Almeida, eds, *Res Publica*, p. 271.
32 *Ibid.*, p. 269.
33 Tenison thought him 'One of our best speakers' because he had been won over from an enlightened republicanism by the BPC's evidence (*Unexpected Activities*, p. 60).
34 The Liberal MP for Kilmarnock Borough, Tenison describes him as an early supporter motivated by a sense of the rightness of the cause (*Unexpected Activities*, p. 60).
35 Tomes, *Lytton*.
36 *Portuguese Political Prisoners*, p. 74.
37 *Ibid.*, p. 76.
38 Vincent-Smith, *Britain, Portugal and the First World War*, pp. 210–219.
39 Wheeler, *Republican Portugal*, p. 97.
40 A.J.P. Taylor, "Prologue; the year 1906", in Read, ed., *Edwardian England*, p. 5.

41 Cited in Keith Robbins, "The Spiritual Pilgrimage of the Rev. R. J. Campbell", *The Journal of Ecclesiastical History*, 30, 2 (1979), p. 268.
42 Richard Price, *An Imperial War and the British Working Class: Working Class Attitudes and Reactions to the Boer War, 1899–1902* (London: Routledge and Kegan Paul, 1972), pp. 40–43.
43 *The Glasgow Herald*, 2 March 1956, obituary.
44 Robbins, *Spiritual Pilgrimage*, p. 271.
45 Keith Robbins, *History, Religion and Identity in Modern Britain* (London: The Hambledon Press, 1993), p. 83.
46 Keith Robbins, "The Churches in Edwardian Society", in Read, ed., *Edwardian England*, p. 121.
47 *New York Times*, 1 August 1907.
48 The Government denied using corporal punishment.
49 *Portuguese Political Prisoners*, p. 80.
50 *Ibid.*, p. 88.
51 Sixth Baronet of Sledmere from 1913.
52 Lawrence James, "Sykes, Sir Mark, sixth baronet (1879–1919)", *Oxford Dictionary of National Biography* (Oxford: Oxford University Press, 2004).
53 *Portuguese Political Prisoners*, p. 90.
54 Roland Oliver, "Johnston, Sir Henry Hamilton (1858–1927)", *Oxford Dictionary of National Biography* (Oxford: Oxford University Press, 2004).
55 Charles G. Fenwick, "Common Sense in Foreign Policy by Harry Johnston", review, *The American Political Science Review*, 8, 1 (1914), p. 128.
56 Ernesto J. de C. Vasconcellos, "Portugal Colonial", review, *The Geographical Journal*, 54, 5 (1919).
57 Sir Harry H. Johnston, "Livingstone as Explorer", *Science*, 37, 964 (1913), p. 923.
58 Undine Lodge 3,394. Online. http://www.undinelodge.org.uk/index.php/mnu-homepage/mnu-about-us, 9 December 2018.
59 Which also helped provide the Campaign with its allegory of Neapolitan barbarism.
60 David Cannadine, *G.M. Trevelyan: A Life in History* (London: HarperCollins, 1992), p. 184.
61 *Portuguese Political Prisoners*, p. 98.
62 Letter to Lord Aberdeen, cited in Philip Magnus, *Gladstone: A Biography* (London: John Murray, 1954), p. 99.
63 Cannadine, *G.M. Trevelyan*, pp. 57–92.
64 Francisco Ferrer, 1849–1909, was unjustly accused of fomenting anti-clerical violence in Barcelona in July 1909. His execution caused European-wide protests, including one in Trafalgar Square.
65 *Portuguese Political Prisoners*, p. 100.
66 *The Times*, 17 April 1913.
67 *Morning Post*, 23 April 1913.

10 The Portuguese Pimpernel

1. Gibbs, *Pageant of the Years*, p. 109.
2. Philip Gibbs, *Adventures in Journalism* (London: Heinemann, 1923), p. 129.
3. Gibbs, *Pageant*, p. 109.
4. *Ibid.*
5. Philip Gibbs, *The Tragedy of Portugal* (London: Upcott Gill, 1914), pp. vii–viii.
6. Gibbs, *Pageant*, p. 7.
7. *Ibid.*, p. 68.
8. Martin, Kerby, *Sir Philip Gibbs and English Journalism in War and Peace* (Basingstoke: Palgrave, 2016), p. 44, gets the date wrong at 1911. This may be because he followed the author's own account in *Adventures in Journalism* (1923), p. 137. Gibbs had an unreliable memory for dates.
9. Gibbs, *Adventures*, pp. 132–133.
10. In *Adventures* Gibbs calls him 'Mr Jones', showing Gibbs did not take time to correlate the two books. Gibbs says the stranger also claimed they had met before, at the Savage Club (*Adventures*, p. 138).
11. Gibbs, *Pageant*, pp. 110–111.
12. Gibbs, *Adventures*, p. 140. In *Pageant*, the account is slightly different. There were two telegrams, one entirely in code, and 'arriving London Saturday' is omitted. Gibbs is being unreliable again.
13. *Ibid.*
14. Cited in, Reginald Pound, Rev. A. J. A. Morris, "Gibbs, Sir Philip Armand Hamilton (1877–1962)", *Oxford Dictionary of National Biography* (Oxford: Oxford University Press, 2004).
15. Gibbs, *Tragedy*, p. 6.
16. *Ibid.*, p. 10.
17. *Ibid.*, p. 14.
18. *Ibid.*, p. 15.
19. *Ibid.*, p. 20.
20. *Ibid.*, p. 21.
21. Wheeler, *Republican Portugal*, p. 101.
22. *The Daily Chronicle*, 13 January 1913.
23. Gibbs, *Tragedy*, p. 23.
24. Wheeler, *Republican Portugal*, p. 96.
25. *Ibid.*
26. Gibbs, *Tragedy*, p. 25.
27. *Ibid.*, p. 55.
28. The *Limoeiro* is located in one of the oldest parts of Lisbon, between the Alfama and St George's Castle. Later, it became infamous as the PIDE (secret police) headquarters under the Salazar dictatorship.
29. Gibbs, *Tragedy*, p. 33.
30. *Ibid.*, p. 36.

31 Subject of the *Daily Mail* letter, of September 1912, that had originally motivated E. M. Tenison.
32 For example, Oliveira Marques does not mention events on the Elvas-Badajoz border region (*History of Portugal*, vol. 1, pp. 427–429).
33 Designated a UNESCO world heritage site in 2012. The cells in which political prisoners were kept are open to public visit.
34 Gibbs, *Tragedy*, p. 41.
35 *Ibid.*, p. 49.
36 Wheeler, *Republican Portugal*, p. 99.
37 *Ibid.*
38 *Westminster Gazette*, 19 December 1913.
39 Philip Gibbs, "The Tyranny in Portugal", *Contemporary Review*, 557 (1914), pp. 30–38. Reprinted in, Gibbs, *The Tragedy of Portugal* (1914).
40 Gibbs, *Tragedy*, p. 76.
41 Gibbs, *Pageant*, p. 221.
42 Philip Gibbs, *Life's Adventure* (London: Angus and Robertson, 1957), Chapter 2.
43 *Ibid.*, p. 23.
44 Tenison, *Unexpected Activities*, p. 183.

11 The Missionary

1 João Pedro Marques, *The Sounds of Silence: Nineteenth-Century Portugal and the Abolition of the Slave Trade* (New York and Oxford: Berghahn Books, 2006), pp. 53–68.
2 *Ibid.*, p. 130.
3 R. J. Hammond's phrase, discussed in Marques, pp. 230–232.
4 James Duffy, *A Question of Slavery: Labour Politics in Portuguese Africa and the British Protest, 1850–1920* (Cambridge, Mass.: Harvard University Press, 1967), pp. 60–63.
5 Cristina Nogueira da Silva, "Political Representation and citizenship under the Empire", in Catroga and Almeida, eds, *Res Publica*, p. 97.
6 Ferraz de Matos, *Colours of Empire*, p. 112.
7 Jerónimo, *Civilising Mission*, p. 90.
8 Miguel Bandeiro Jerónimo, "The States of Empire", in Trindade, ed., *Making of Modern Portugal*, p. 68.
9 Jerónimo, *States of Empire*, p. 79.
10 Cited in Duffy, *Question of Slavery*, p. 99.
11 Cited in Lowell J. Satre, *Chocolate on Trial: Slavery, Politics and the Ethics of Business* (Athens, US: Ohio University Press, 2005), p. 45.
12 *Anti-Slavery Reporter*, October, 1911, p. 105.
13 Satre, *Chocolate on Trial*, p. 135.
14 Jerónimo, *Civilising Mission*, p. 59.
15 *Ibid.*, pp. 195–198.
16 Ferraz de Matos, *Colours of Empire*, p. 216.
17 *Ibid.*, p. 85.

292 | Notes to Chapter 11

18   Alexandre, *The Colonial Empire*, p. 63.
19   Jerónimo, *Civilising Mission*, p. 42.
20   Duffy, *Question of Slavery*, pp. 190–196.
21   Satre, *Chocolate on Trial*, pp. 23–25.
22   *The Times*, 14 April 1884.
23   *Ibid.*, 7 January 1890.
24   Andrew Porter, "Sir Roger Casement and the international humanitarian movement", *The Journal of Imperial and Commonwealth History*, 29 (2001), p. 63.
25   Stone, *Foreign Office and Forced Labour*, pp. 165–174.
26   Satre, *Chocolate on Trial*, p. 24.
27   Jerónimo, *Civilising Mission*, p. 47.
28   John Galsworthy agreed with him. See *The Times*, 14 January 1909.
29   Kevin Grant, *A Civilised Savagery: Britain and the New Slaveries in Africa, 1884–1926* (Abingdon: Routledge, 2005), p. 112.
30   *Anti-Slavery Reporter*, Oct.–Nov. 1908, pp. 125–143.
31   *Spectator*, 21 November 1908.
32   Satre, *Chocolate on Trial*, pp. 121–122.
33   Stone, *Foreign Office and Forced Labour*, p. 176.
34   Satre, *Chocolate on Trial*, pp. 161 and 170.
35   *Ibid.*, p. 187.
36   John St Loe Strachey, Chair of Angola sub-committee of the ASAPS; Liberal Unionist; Editor of *The Spectator*, 1887–1925.
37   *Spectator*, 13 August 1910.
38   Duffy, *Question of Slavery*, p. 213.
39   Jerónimo, *Civilising Mission*, p. 67.
40   Stone, *Foreign Office and Forced Labour*, pp. 179–181.
41   *The Spectator*, 15 October 1910.
42   Pearson was born in Suffolk in 1870, won a scholarship to Cambridge, and in 1903 was appointed Professor of Botany at the South Africa College. The report Harris read, "Travels of a Botanist in S W Africa", was submitted to the Royal Geographical Society in 1910. See, A. C. Seward, "H. H. W. Pearson", *Annals of Botany*, 31, 122 (1917), pp. i–xviii.
43   *Spectator*, 15 October 1910. Duffy overlooks the tactical subtlety in Harris's approach.
44   Jerónimo, *Civilising Mission*, p. 70.
45   *Anti-Slavery Reporter*, January 1911, pp. 187–189.
46   Satre, *Chocolate on Trial*, pp. 191–192.
47   Duffy, *Question of Slavery*, p. 219.
48   Stone, *Foreign Office and Forced Labour*, p. 181.
49   Duffy, *Question of Slavery*, p. 219. Eyre Crowe was, then, Secretary of the African Department with responsibility for the Portuguese colonies in Africa.
50   Stone, *Foreign Office and Forced Labour*, p. 190; and Langhorne, *Anglo-German Negotiations*, pp. 361–387.
51   *Spectator*, 29 June 1912.

52 *Anti-Slavery Reporter*, October 1912, pp. 216–235.
53 *The Times*, 2 July 1912.
54 Stone, *Foreign Office and Forced Labour*, pp. 182–183.
55 Satre, *Chocolate on Trial*, pp. 197–198.
56 *Ibid.*, pp. 198–199.
57 *Ibid.*, p. 185.
58 *Spectator*, 8 March 1913.
59 Mayo knew Portuguese West Africa well and as early as 1882 had denounced the labour system in the cocoa islands as 'slavery.' See, Higgs, *Chocolate Islands*, p. 14.
60 *Spectator*, 23 July 1913.
61 Satre, *Chocolate on Trial*, pp. 203–204.
62 *Ibid.*, p. 204.
63 *Spectator*, 16 August 1913.
64 *Ibid.*, 30 August 1913.
65 John Wyllie, retired army officer, favoured forming a society 'to protect the world' against the suffering inflicted by 'rabid humanitarians'. See, Higgs, *Chocolate Islands*, p. 150.
66 Satre, *Chocolate on Trial*, pp 183–188.
67 John, *War, Journalism and the Shaping of the Twentieth Century*, pp. 52–53.
68 *The Times*, 28 September 1909.
69 Henry Nevinson, *A Modern Slavery* (Castle Hedingham: Background Books, 1963), pp. 58–59.
70 Satre, *Chocolate on Trial*, p. 207.
71 *Ibid.*, p. 183.
72 Grant, *A Civilised Savagery*, p. 31.
73 Kevin Grant, "Christian Critics of Empire: Missionaries, Lantern Lectures and the Congo Reform Campaign in Britain", *Journal of Imperial and Commonwealth History*, 29, 2 (2001), pp. 32–33.
74 *Ibid.*, p. 30.
75 *Ibid.*, pp. 46–48.
76 *Ibid.*, p. 53.
77 Andrew Porter, "'Cultural imperialism' and protestant missionary enterprise, 1780–1914", *The Journal of Imperial and Commonwealth History*, 25, 3 (1997), pp. 367–391.
78 Jerónimo, *Civilising Mission*, pp. 109–110.
79 Bernard Porter, *Critics of Empire: British Radical Attitudes to Colonialism in Africa 1895–1914* (London: Macmillan, 1968), pp. 158–160.
80 Grant, *A Civilised Savagery*, pp. 59–78.
81 Higgs, *Chocolate Islands*, p. 148. Fox Bourne died suddenly after catching bronchitis while on holiday in Torquay.
82 Satre, *Chocolate on Trial*, pp. 183–184.
83 In her ODNB entry, Sybil Oldfield omits any reference to his work on Portuguese West Africa.

84 John Harris, "Portuguese Slavery", *Contemporary Review*, 557 (1912), pp. 635–645.
85 John Harris, *Portuguese Slavery: Britain's Dilemma* (London: Methuen and co., 1913).
86 John Harris, *Dawn in Darkest Africa* (London: Smith, Elder and Co., 1914).
87 *Portuguese Slavery. Britain's Responsibility* (London: Edward Hughes and co., 1914).
88 Stone, *Foreign Office and Forced Labour*, p. 182.
89 Harris, *Portuguese Slavery: Britain's Dilemma*, p. 13.
90 *Spectator*, 16 August 1913.
91 Felix Driver, "Stanley, Sir Henry Morton (1841–1904)", *Oxford Dictionary of National Biography* (Oxford: Oxford University Press, 2004).
92 Tim Jeal, *Stanley: The Impossible Life of Africa's Greatest Explorer* (London: Faber and Faber, 2007), pp. 11, 202, 240, 271, 290.
93 Charles A. Swan, *The Slavery of To-Day or, The Present Position of The Open Sore of Africa* (Glasgow: Pickering and Inglis, 1909).
94 *Ibid.*, pp. 19–22.
95 Tim Grass, "Brethren and the São Tomé cocoa slavery controversy: the role of Charles A. Swan (1861–1934)", *Brethren Archivists' and Historians' Network Review*, 5, 1 (2007), pp. 98–113.
96 Duffy, *Question of Slavery*, p. 182.
97 *The Times*, 22 June 1909.
98 Harris, *Portuguese Slavery: Britain's Dilemma*, p. 23.
99 Satre, *Chocolate on Trial*, p. 106.
100 *Ibid.*, p. 121.
101 Duffy, *Question of Slavery*, p. 190.
102 Angela John, "A New Slavery", *History Today* (June, 2002), pp. 34–35.
103 Harris, *Portuguese Slavery: Britain's Dilemma*, pp. 23–26.
104 Harris, *Dawn in Darkest Africa*, p. 175.
105 Harris, *Portuguese Slavery: Britain's Dilemma*, pp. 27–30.
106 Colin Harding, *In Remotest Barotseland* (London: Hurst and Blackett, 1904).
107 Duffy, *Question of Slavery*, pp. 137, 173–174.
108 Harding, *In Remotest Barotseland*, p. 81.
109 Daniel Crawford, *Thinking black* (London: Morgan and Scott, 2nd edition, 1913), p. 5.
110 Harris, *Portuguese Slavery: Britain's Dilemma*, p. 35.
111 Mark Sweetnam, "Dan Crawford, Thinking Black, and the Challenge of a Missionary Cannon", *Journal of Ecclesiastical History*, 58, 4 (2007), pp. 709–715.
112 Satre, *Chocolate on Trial*, p. 94.
113 *Ibid.*, p. 32.
114 *Ibid.*, p. 50.

115 Grant, *A Civilised Savagery*, pp. 123–129.
116 Jerónimo, *Civilising Mission*, p. 52.
117 Nevinson, *Modern Slavery*, p. 117.
118 W. G. Clarence-Smith, "Struggles over Labour Conditions in the Plantations of São Tomé and Príncipé, 1875–1914", in Michael Twaddle, ed., *From Chattel Slavery to Wage Labour in Africa, the Caribbean and England* (London: Frank Cass, 1993), p. 149.
119 Higgs, *Chocolate Islands*, p. 58.
120 Harris, *Portuguese Slavery: Britain's Dilemma*, p. 40.
121 Dean Pavlakis, *British Humanitarianism and the Congo Reform Movement, 1896–1913* (Abingdon: Routledge, 2016), p. 220.
122 Adam Hochschild, *King Leopold's Ghost: A Story of Greed, Terror and Heroism in Colonial Africa* (London: Pan Books, 2002), pp. 127–128.
123 Harris, *Portuguese Slavery: Britain's Dilemma*, p. 44.
124 Nevinson, *Modern Slavery*, p. 30.
125 Satre, *Chocolate on Trial*, pp. 50–51. See also, Linda Heywood, *Contested Power in Angola, 1840s to the present* (Woodbridge: Boydell & Brewer, 2000), pp. 1–30.
126 Alexandre, *The Colonial Empire*, pp. 65–66.
127 Satre, *Chocolate on Trial*, p. 194.
128 Harris, *Portuguese Slavery: Britain's Dilemma*, p. 46.
129 William A. Cadbury, *Labour in Portuguese West Africa* (London: Geo. Routledge and Sons, 1910).
130 *Ibid.*, pp. 22–23.
131 *Ibid.*, p. 71.
132 *Ibid.*, pp. 84–94.
133 *Ibid.*, p. 99.
134 Jerónimo, *Civilising Mission*, p. 63.
135 William Gervase Clarence-Smith, "The Hidden Costs of Labour on the Cocoa Plantations of São Tomé and Príncipé, 1875–1914", *Portuguese Studies*, 6, 1 (1990), pp. 165–167.
136 Higgs, *Chocolate Islands*, p. 95.
137 Clarence-Smith, *Struggles over Labour Conditions*, p. 158.
138 Harris, *Portuguese Slavery*, p. 640.
139 Clarence-Smith, *Struggles over Labour Conditions*, pp. 151–160.
140 Harris, *Portuguese Slavery: Britain's Dilemma*, p. 58.
141 Harris, *Dawn in Darkest Africa*, p. 183.
142 *Ibid.*, p. 178.
143 *Ibid.*, pp. 176 and 190.
144 Satre, *Chocolate on Trial*, pp. 110–111.
145 *Ibid.*, p. 152.
146 *Ibid.*, p. 174.
147 *Ibid.*, p. 87.
148 Harris, *Portuguese Slavery: Britain's Dilemma*, p. 95.
149 Catherine Higgs, "Happiness and Work: Portuguese Peasants, British

296 | *Notes to Conclusion*

  Laborers, African Contract Workers, and the Case of São Tomé and Príncipe, 1901–1909", *International Labor and Working Class History*, 86 (2014), p. 56.
150 Harris, *Portuguese Slavery: Britain's Dilemma*, p. 108.
151 *Ibid.*, pp. 97–99.
152 *Ibid.*, p. 99.
153 *Ibid.*, p. 106.
154 *Spectator*, 17 August 1912.
155 Sand fleas that burrow into the skin and lay eggs causing swelling, itching and infection that can kill.
156 Harris, *Portuguese Slavery: Britain's Dilemma*, p. 105.
157 Harris, *Dawn in Darkest Africa*, p. 179.
158 Higgs, *Chocolate Islands*, pp. 16–17 and 28–29.
159 William Gervase Clarence-Smith, *The Third Portuguese Empire, 1825–1975: A Study in Economic Imperialism* (Manchester: Manchester University Press, 1985), pp. 104–105.
160 *Spectator*, 1 February 1913.
161 *Ibid.*, 1 March 1913.
162 *Ibid.*, 15 February 1913.
163 Harris, *Portuguese Slavery: Britain's Dilemma*, p. 108.
164 *Ibid.*, p. 126.
165 Harris, *Dawn in Darkest Africa*, p. 195.
166 Harris, *Portuguese Slavery: Britain's Dilemma*, p. 109.
167 *Ibid.*, p. 127.
168 Thomas Fowell Buxton (President), J. St Loe Strachey, E.W. Brooks (Treasurer), Travers Buxton (Secretary).
169 Grant, *A Civilised Savagery*, pp. 137–148.
170 Lawrence Iles, "Campaigner Against Slavery", *Journal of Liberal History* 38 (2003), pp. 29–31.
171 Ferraz de Matos, *Colours of the Empire*, p. 45.
172 *Ibid.*, p. 217.
173 Portugal of the Little Ones.
174 Ferraz de Matos, *Colours of the Empire*, p. 255.
175 Porter, *Roger Casement*, pp. 68–72.

Conclusion

1 Vincent-Smith, *Portuguese Republic and Britain*, p. 720.
2 Price, *An Imperial War*, pp. 233–235.
3 *Ibid.*, pp. 176–177.
4 Braudel's question was: 'Is it possible somehow to convey simultaneously both that conspicuous history which holds our attention by its continual and dramatic changes – and that other, submerged history, almost silent and always discreet, virtually unsuspected either by its observers or its participants, which is little touched by the obstinate erosion of time?' See, Richard E. Lee, "Fernand Braudel, The Longue

Durée and World Systems Theory" in Richard E. Lee, ed., *The Longue Durée and World-Systems Analysis* (Albany, US: State University of New York Press, 2012), pp. 1–8.
5   Special path. The analogy is with modern German history. See, Blackbourn and Ely, *Peculiarities of German History*.
6   José Miguel Sardica, "The Memory of the Portuguese First Republic throughout the Twentieth Century", *e-Journal of Portuguese History*, 9, 1 (2011), pp. 1–8.

Bibliography

Primary Sources

Unpublished

E. M. Tenison Papers, Templeman Library, University of Kent, Canterbury.

Published

Official Publications: Parliamentary Papers

HC Deb. 28, 13 July 1911, Portuguese Republic.
HC Deb. 34, 28 February 1912, Portugal (Political Prisoners).
HC Deb. 34, 1 March 1912, Political Prisoners (Portugal).
HC Deb. 35, 5 March 1912, Portugal (Political Prisoners).
HC Deb. 35, 11 March 1912, Portuguese Political Prisoners.
HC Deb. 51, 10 April 1913, Portugal (Political Offenders).
HC Deb. 52, 1 May 1913, Portuguese Prisons.
HC Deb. 53, 27 May 1913, Political Prisoners.
HL Deb. 14, 23 July 1913, Native Labour in Portuguese West Africa.
HL Deb. 17, 27 July 1914, Portuguese West Africa.

HC Africa. No. 2, 1912, Correspondence respecting contract labour in Portuguese West Africa, Cd. 6322.
HC Africa. No. 2, 1913, Further correspondence respecting contract labour in Portuguese West Africa, Cd. 6607.

Newspapers

Anti-Slavery Reporter
The Daily Chronicle
The Daily Mail
The Evening Post
The Glasgow Herald
The Manchester Guardian
The Morning Post
The New York Times
The Observer
The Saturday Post
The Scotsman
The Times

Periodicals

Catholic World
Science
The Academy and Literature
The American Political Science Review
The British Review
The Contemporary Review
The Dublin Review
The Fortnightly Review
The Geographical Journal
The Irish Ecclesiastical Record
The Nation
The National Review
The New Age
The Nineteenth Century and After
The Oxford and Cambridge Review
The Positivist
The Sacred Heart Review
The Spectator
The Tablet
The Westminster Gazette

Contemporary Sources: Books

Bell, Aubrey F. G., *In Portugal*, London: John Lane, The Bodley Head, 1912.

Bell, Aubrey F. G., *Portugal of the Portuguese*, New York: Charles Scribner and Sons, 1916.

Bragança-Cunha, V. de, *Eight Centuries of Portuguese Monarchy: A Political Study*, New York: James Pott and Co., 1911.

Bragança-Cunha, V. de, *Revolutionary Portugal, 1910–26*, London: James Clarke, 1937.

Cadbury, William A., *Labour in Portuguese West Africa*, London: George Routledge and Sons, 1910.

Corperchot, Lucien, *Memories of Queen Amélie of Portugal*, London: Eveleigh Nash, 1915.

Crawford, Daniel, *Thinking Black*, London: Morgan and Scott, 2nd edition, 1913.

Gibbs, Philip, *Adventures in Journalism*, London: Heinemann, 1923.

Gibbs, Philip, *The Pageant of the Years*, London: Heinemann, 1946.

Gibbs, Philip, *Life's Adventure*, London: Angus and Robertson, 1957.

Harding, Colin, *In Remotest Barotseland*, London: Hurst and Blackett, 1904.

Harris, John, *Portuguese Slavery: Britain's Dilemma*, London: Methuen and Co., 1913.

Harris, John, *Dawn in Darkest Africa*, London: Smith, Elder and Co., 1914.

Lytton, Constance and Warton, Jane, *Prisons and Prisoners: Some Personal Experiences*, London: Wm. Heinemann, 1914.

300 | *Bibliography*

Mantero, Francisco, *Portuguese planters and British humanitarians: The case for S. Thomé*, Translated by Lieutenant Colonel J. A. Wyllie, FRGS, Lisbon: Redacção da Reforma, 1911. Online. https://archive.org/stream/portugueseplante00mant/ portugueseplante00mant_djvu.txt
Nevinson, Henry, *A Modern Slavery*, Castle Hedingham, Essex: Background Books, 1963.
Swan, Charles A., *The Slavery of To-Day or, The Present Position of The Open Sore of Africa*, Glasgow: Pickering and Inglis, 1909.
Williams, G. Valentine, *The World of Action*, London: Hamish Hamilton, 1938.

Contemporary Sources: Articles

Archer, William, "The Portuguese Republic", *Fortnightly Review*, 539, February 1911, pp. 231–250.
Bedford, Adeline M., "Fifteen Years' Work in a Female Convict Prison", *The Nineteenth Century and After*, 68, October 1910, pp. 615–631.
Bell, Aubrey "The Portuguese Republic," *The Contemporary Review*, 101, March 1912, pp. 370–379.
Bell, Aubrey F. G., "Portugal under the Republic", *The National Review*, 60, February 1913, pp. 1003–1012.
Bell, Aubrey F. G., "Portugal and the Republic", *The National Review*, 63, March–April 1914, pp. 306–314.
Bland, J.O.B., "A Portuguese Jacobin", *Nineteenth Century and After*, 70, July 1911, pp. 145–151.
Bombarda, Miguel, "Portugal", *The British Medical Journal*, 1, 2318, 3 June 1905, pp. 1214–1215.
Bragança-Cunha, V. de, "Portugal", *The New Age*, 5 January 1911, pp. 219–220.
Bragança-Cunha, V. de, "Republicanism in Portugal", *The New Age*, 2 February 1911, pp. 318–319.
Bragança-Cunha, V. de, "Republican Portugal", *The New Age*, 18 May 1911, p. 52.
Bragança-Cunha, V. de, "Mr Ramsay MacDonald and Portugal", *The New Age*, 3 August 1911, p. 318.
Bragança-Cunha, V. de, "Triumphant Republicanism", *The New Age*, 16 November 1911, pp. 56–57.
Bragança-Cunha, V. de, "The Portuguese Republic and the Working Classes", *The New Age*, 15 February 1912, pp. 367–368.
Bragança-Cunha, V. de, "An Englishman in Portugal", *The New Age*, 11 April 1912, pp. 571–572.
Bragança-Cunha, V. de, "Portugal Next I", *The New Age*, December 1912, pp. 126–128.
Bragança-Cunha, V. de, "Portugal Next II", *The New Age*, 19 December 1912, pp. 149–151.

Bragança-Cunha, V. de,"Insane Portugal I", *The New Age*, 22 May 1913, pp. 80–81.
Bragança-Cunha, V. de, "Insane Portugal II", *The New Age*, 29 May 1913, pp. 111–113.
Bragança-Cunha, V. de, "Portugal: Her Fate", *The New Age*, 27 November 1913, pp. 104–105.
Bragança-Cunha, V. de, "Signs of the Times in Portugal", *The British Review*, 5, 1 January 1914, pp. 31–46.
Bragança-Cunha, V. de, "Camões: Man and Poet", *Westminster Review*, January 1914, pp. 552–562.
Bragança-Cunha, V. de, "The Portuguese Amnesty", *The New Age*, 12 March 1914, pp. 584–585.
Briggs, Martin S., "S. John's Chapel in the Church of S. Roque, Lisbon", *The Burlington Magazine for Connoisseurs*, 28, 152 (1915), pp. 50–51.
Derrick, Michael, "A Disgruntled Royalist", review, *The Tablet*, 24 September 1938.
Dillon, E. J., "Republican Portugal", *Contemporary Review*, 98, 1910, pp. 513–534.
Doria, Sylva, "Church and State in Portugal", *The Oxford and Cambridge Review*, 14, 1911, pp. 4–28.
Finot, Jean, "The First of February in Lisbon", *The Contemporary Review*, 93, 1908, pp. 287–300.
Gibbs, Philip, "The Tyranny in Portugal", *Contemporary Review*, 557, 1914, pp. 30–38.
Harris, John, "Portuguese Slavery", *Contemporary Review*, 557, May 1912, pp. 635–645.
Koebbel, W. H.,"Eight Centuries of Portuguese Monarchy, V. de Bragança Cunha", review, *The Academy and Literature*, 24 June 1911, p. 783.
McCullagh, Francis, "Driving Jesuits from Portugal", *The Sacred Heart Review*, 21, 1910, pp 367–368.
McCullagh, Francis, "Some Causes of the Portuguese Revolution", *The Nineteenth Century and After*, 68, 1910, pp. 931–944.
McCullagh, Francis, "'Freedom' in Portugal", *The Living Age*, 268, 1911, pp. 629–631.
McCullagh, Francis, "Portuguese Republicans 'Fiddling While Rome Burns'", *The New York Times*, 21 May 1911.
McCullagh, Francis, "Separation of Church and State in Portugal", *The Catholic World*, 63, 1911, pp. 371–379.
McCullagh, Francis, "The Portuguese Separation Law", *The Dublin Review*, 169, 1911, pp. 126–142.
McCullagh, Francis, "The Separation of Church and State in Portugal", *Irish Ecclesiastical Record*, 29, 1911, pp. 593–603.
McCullagh, Francis, "The Portuguese Revolution", *The Dublin Review*, 168, 1911, pp. 85–105.
McCullagh, Francis, "How the *Carbonária* Saved the Portuguese Republic", *Contemporary Review*, 561, 1912, pp. 350–61.

McCullagh, Francis, "Portugal: the Nightmare Republic", *Nineteenth Century and After*, 75, 1914, pp. 148–170.
McCullagh, Francis, "The Portuguese Republic and the Press", *The Dublin Review*, 154, 1914, pp. 314–329.
Johnston, Harry H., "Recent Portuguese Legislation on the Negro Question in Portuguese Africa", *Journal of the Royal African Society*, 3, 10, 1904, pp. 166–172.
Markham, Clements R., "Oceanographic Researches of His Late Majesty King Carlos of Portugal", *The Geographical Journal*, 31, 5, 1908, pp. 514–518.
Oldmeadow, Ernest, "'Clericalism' in Portugal", *The Tablet*, 23 May 1908.
Quental, Antero de, "Causes of the Decline of the Peninsular Peoples in the Last Three Centuries, speech 27 May 1871", *Portuguese Studies*, 24, 2, 2008, pp. 67–94.
Torrend, Camille, "Anti-clerical policy in Portugal", *Dublin Review*, 150, 1912, pp. 128–151.

Contemporary Sources: Pamphlets

Anti-Slavery and Aborigines' Protection Society, *Portuguese Slavery: Britain's Responsibility*, London: Edward Hughes and Co., 1914.
Gibbs, Philip, *The Tragedy of Portugal*, London: L. Upcott Gill and Son, 1914.
Gomes, António Vaz Monteiro, *Portuguese Political Prisoners: Reply to Duchess of Bedford's statements*, Lisbon: 1913, British Library of Political and Economic Science, Special Pamphlets Collection.
Portuguese Political Prisoners: A British National Protest, London: L. Upcott Gill and Son, 1913.
Tenison, E. M., *The Portuguese Amnesty*, L. Upcott Gill and Son Ltd., London, 1914.
Tenison, E.M., *Will England Save Portugal? Our Hereditary Obligations*, London: L. Upcott Gill and Son, 1914.
Tenison, E. M., *Tenison, Julian, A Character-sketch of Lieutenant Commander Julian Tenison, Born June 22, 1885. Died for his King and Country, August 15, 1916*, 1920.

Secondary Sources

Books

Alden, Dauril, *Charles R. Boxer: An Uncommon Life*, Lisbon: Fundação Oriente, 2001.
Almeida, Pedro Tavares de, and Luzón, Javier Moreno, eds, *The Politics of Representation: Elections and parliamentarism in Portugal and Spain, 1875–1926*, Brighton: Sussex Academic Press, 2017.
Arnot, Margaret L. and Usborne, Cornelie, *Gender and Crime in Modern Europe*, Cambridge: Cambridge University Press, 1999.

Batalha, Luís, *The Cape Verdean Diaspora in Portugal: Colonial Subjects in a Postcolonial World*, Lanham MD: Lexington Books, 2004.
Bennett, Jeffrey S., *When the Sun Danced: Myth, Miracles, and Modernity in Early Twentieth-century Portugal*, Charlottesville: University of Virginia Press, 2012.
Benton, Russell E., *The Downfall of a King: Dom Manuel II of Portugal*, Washington: University Press of America, 1977.
Bermeo, Nancy and Nord, Philip, eds, *Civil Society Before Democracy: Lessons from Nineteenth-Century Europe*, Lanham, Maryland: Rowman and Littlefield, 2000.
Berg-Schlosser, Dirk and Mitchell, Jeremy, eds, *Authoritarianism and Democracy in Europe 1919–39: Comparative Analyses*, London: Palgrave, 2002.
Borges, Marcello J., *Chains of Gold: Portuguese Migration to Argentina in Transatlantic Perspective*, Leiden: Brill, 2009.
Brown, David, *Palmerston: A Biography*, New Haven and London: Yale, 2010.
Catroga, Fernando and Almeida, Pedro Tavares, eds, *Res Publica 1820–1926: Citizenship and Political Representation in Portugal*, Lisbon: Assembleia da República, Biblioteca Nacional de Portugal, 2011.
Chabal, Patrick, *Amílcar Cabral: Revolutionary Leadership and People's War*, Cambridge: Cambridge University Press, 1983.
Chilcote, Ronald H., *Amílcar Cabral's Revolutionary Theory and Practice: A Critical Guide*, Boulder and London: Lynne Reiner, 1991.
Claeys, Gregory, *Imperial Sceptics: British Critics of Empire, 1850–1920*, Cambridge: Cambridge University Press, 2010.
Clarke, Peter, *Hope and Glory: Britain 1900–1990*, London: Penguin, 1996.
Coates, Timothy J., *Convict Labor in the Portuguese Empire, 1740–1932: Redefining the Empire*, Leiden: Brill, 2014.
Costa Pinto, António, *Salazar's dictatorship and European Fascism: Problems of Interpretation*, New York and London: Columbia University Press, 1995.
Costa Pinto, António, *The Blue Shirts: Portuguese Fascists and the New State*, New York: Columbia University Press, 1999.
Costa Pinto, António, ed., *Contemporary Portugal: Politics, Society and Culture*, Boulder: Social Science Monographs, 2005.
Clarence-Smith, William Gervase, *The Third Portuguese Empire, 1825–1975: A Study in Economic Imperialism*, Manchester: Manchester University Press, 1985.
Couto, Maria Aurora, *Goa: A Daughter's Story*, New Delhi: Penguin Viking, 2004.
Duffy, James, *A Question of Slavery: Labour Politics in Portuguese Africa and the British Protest, 1850–1920*, Cambridge, Mass: Harvard University Press, 1967.
Ferraz de Matos, Patrícia, *The Colours of the Empire: Racialized*

Representations during Portuguese Colonialism, New York and Oxford: Berghahn Books, 2006.
Freire, João, *Freedom Fighters: Anarchist Intellectuals, Workers, and Soldiers in Portugal's History*, Montreal and London: Black Rose Books, 2001.
Forsythe, W.J., *Penal Discipline, Reformatory Projects, and the English Prison Commission, 1895–1939*, Exeter: University of Exeter Press, 1990.
Grant, Kevin, *A Civilsed Savagery: Britain and the New Slaveries in Africa, 1884–1926*, Abingdon: Routledge, 2005.
Gregory, Desmond, *The Beneficent Usurpers: A History of the British in Madeira*, London: Associated University Presses, 1988.
Hall, Catherine, *Civilizing Subjects: Metropole and Colony in the English Imagination, 1830–1867*, London: Polity Press, 2002.
Hall, Catherine, ed., *Cultures of Empire: Colonizers in Britain and the Empire in the Nineteenth and Twentieth Centuries*, Manchester: Manchester University Press, 2000.
Havik, Philip J., and Newitt, Malyn, eds, *Creole Societies in the Portuguese Colonial Empire*, Newcastle: Cambridge Scholars Publishing, 2015.
Heywood, Linda, *Contested Power in Angola: 1840s to the present*, Rochester and Woodbridge: Boydell and Brewer, 2000.
Herr, Richard, and Costa Pinto, António, eds, *The Portuguese Republic at One Hundred*, Berkeley: University of California Press, 2012.
Higgs, Catherine, *Chocolate Islands: Cocoa, Slavery and Colonial Africa*, Athens, Ohio: Ohio University Press, 2012.
Hinsley, F. H., ed., *Cambridge History of Foreign Policy under Sir Edward Grey*, Cambridge: Cambridge University Press, 1977.
Hochschild, Adam, *King Leopold's Ghost: A Story of Greed, Terror and Heroism in Colonial Africa*, London: Pan Books, 2002.
Howe, Malcolm, *Dom Manuel II, the Last King of Portugal: His life and Reign*, London: Book Press, 2009.
Hurd, Douglas, *Choose Your Weapons: The British Foreign Secretary, 200 Years of Argument, Success and Failure*, London: Phoenix, 2011.
Jeal, Tim, *Stanley: The Impossible Life of Africa's Greatest Explorer*, London: Faber and Faber, 2007.
Jerónimo, Miguel Bandeira, *The 'Civilising Mission' of Portuguese Colonialism, 1870–1930*, Basingstoke: Palgrave Macmillan, 2015.
John, Angela V., *War, Journalism and the Shaping of the Twentieth Century: The Life and Times of Henry W. Nevinson*, London: I.B. Tauris, 2006.
Kerby, Martin, *Sir Philip Gibbs and English Journalism in War and Peace*, Basingstoke: Palgrave Macmillan, 2016.
Lee, Richard E., ed, *The Longue Durée and World-Systems Analysis*, Albany: State University of New York Press, 2012.
Livermore, H. V. ed., *Portugal and Brazil: An Introduction*, Oxford: Clarendon Press, 1953.
Logan, Anne, *Feminism and Criminal Justice: A Historical Perspective*, Basingstoke: Palgrave Macmillan, 2008.

McConville, Sean, *English Local Prisons 1860–1900: Next Only to Death*, London: Routledge, 1995.
McCulloch, Jock, *In the Twilght of Revolution: The Political Theory of Amílcar Cabral*, London: Routledge and Keegan Paul, 1983.
Macaulay, Rose, *They Went to Portugal*, London: Jonathan Cape, 1946.
Macaulay, Rose, *They Went to Portugal Too*, Manchester: Carcanet, 1990.
Magnus, Philip, *Gladstone: A Biography*, London: John Murray, 1954.
Martin, Wallace, *The New Age under Orage: Chapters in English Cultural History*, Manchester: Manchester University Press, 1967.
Marques, João Pedro, *The Sounds of Silence: Nineteenth-Century Portugal and the Abolition of the Slave Trade*, New York and Oxford: Berghahn Books, 2006.
Maxwell, Kenneth, *Pombal*, Cambridge: Cambridge University Press, 1995.
Maxwell, Kenneth, *The Making of Portuguese Democracy*, Cambridge: Cambridge University Press, 1995.
Meneses, Filipe Ribeiro de, *Portugal 1914–1926: From the First World War to Military Dictatorship*, Bristol: HiPLAM, 2004.
Meneses, Filipe Ribeiro de, *Afonso Costa*, London: Haus, 2010.
Molinero-Mar, Clare and Smith, Angel, eds, *Nationalism and the Nation in the Iberian Peninsula: Conflicting Identitites*, Oxford: Berg, 1996.
Motyl, Alexander J., *Imperial Ends: The Decay, Collapse and Revival of Empires*, New York: Columbia Press, 2001.
Newitt, Malyn, *Emigration and the Sea: An Alternative History of Portugal and the Portuguese*, London: C. Hurst and Co., 2015.
Oliveira Marques, A.H. de, *History of Portugal, Vols. 1 and 2*, New York: Columbia University Press, 2nd edition, 1976.
Pavlakis, Dean, *British Humanitarianism and the Congo Reform Movement, 1896–1913*, Abingdon: Routledge, 2016.
Porter, Bernard, *Critics of Empire: British Radical Attitudes to Colonialism in Africa 1895–1914*, London: Macmillan, 1968.
Porter, Bernard, *The Absent-Minded Imperialists: Empire, Society, and Culture in Britain*, Oxford: Oxford University Press, 2004.
Price, Richard, *An Imperial War and the British Working Class: Working Class Attitudes and Reactions to the Boer War, 1899–1902*, London: Routledge and Kegan Paul, 1972.
Prochaska, F.K., *Women and philanthropy in nineteenth-century England*, Oxford: Clarendon Press, 1980.
Read, Donald, ed., *Edwardian England*, London: The Historical Association, 1982.
Rich, Paul B., *Race and Empire in British Politics*, Cambridge: Cambridge University Press, 1986.
Robbins, Keith, *History, Religion and Identity in Modern Britain*, London: The Hambledon Press, 1993.
Said, Edward, *Orientalism*, New York: Vintage Books, 1979.
Said, Edward, *Cuture and Imperialism*, New York: Vintage Books, 1993.

Satre, Lowell J., *Chocolate on Trial: Slavery, Politics and the Ethics of Business*, Athens, Ohio: Ohio University Press, 2005.

Schwartzman, Kathleen C., *The Social Origins of Democratic Collapse: The First Portuguese Republic in the Global Economy*, Lawrence, Kansas: University Press of Kansas, 1989.

Southern, Paul, *Portugal: The Scramble for Africa*, Bromley: Galago Books, 2010.

Southgate, Donald, *The Most English Minister: The Politics and Policies of Palmerston*, London: Macmillan, 1966.

Stone, Dan, *Breeding Superman: Nietzsche, Race and Eugenics in Edwardian and Interwar Britain*, Liverpool: Liverpool University Press, 2002.

Thompson, E. P., *Willliam Morris: Romantic to Revolutionary*, London: The Merlin Press, 1977.

Thompson, E. P., *Customs in Common*, London: Penguin Press, 1991.

Trindade, Luís, ed., *The Making of Modern Portugal*, Newcastle: Cambridge Scholars Publishing, 2013.

Trindade, Luís, *Narratives in Motion: Journalism and Modernist Events in 1920s Portugal*, New York and Oxford: Berghahn Books, 2016.

Villis, Tom, *Reaction and the Avant-Garde: The Revolt Against Liberal Democracy in Early Twentieth Century Britain*, London: I.B. Tauris, 2004.

Wallerstein, Immanuel, ed., *The Modern World System in the Longue Durée*, Abingdon: Routledge, 2016.

Wheeler, Douglas L., *Republican Portugal: A Political History 1910–26*, Madison: University of Wisconsin Press, 1978.

Whitebrook, Peter, *William Archer: A Biography*, London: Methuen 1993.

Wilken, Patrick, *Empire Adrift: The Portuguese Court in Rio De Janeiro, 1808–1821*, London: Bloomsbury, 2004.

Zedner, Lucia, *Women, Crime and Custody in Victorian England*, Oxford: Clarendon, 1991.

Articles and Book Chapters

Alexandre, Valentim, "The Colonial Empire", in António Costa Pinto, ed., *Contemporary Portugal: Politics, Society and Culture*, Boulder: Social Science Monographs, 2005, pp. 63–84.

Almeida, Pedro Tavares de, "Elections and Parliamentary Recruitment in Portugal", in Pedro Tavares de Almeida, and Javier Moreno Luzón, eds, *The politics of representation: elections and parliamentarism in Portugal and Spain, 1875–1926*, Brighton: Sussex Academic Press, 2017, pp. 99–123.

Alves, Jorge Fernandes, "Primeira República, poder local e a saga parlamentar para um novo código administrativo", *Revista da Faculdade de Letras, Historia, Porto*, III, 11, 2010, pp. 33–61. Online. http://ler.letras.up.pt/uploads/ficheiros/9006.pdf; 30 November 2018.

Alves, Daniel, "Crise e republicanismo no discurso dos lojistas de Lisboa (1890–1910)", *Análise Social*, 48, 205, 2012, pp. 766–791.
Baiôa, Manuel, Fernandes, Paulo Jorge, and Meneses, Filipe Ribeiro de, "The Political History of Nineteenth-Century Portugal", *e-Journal of Portuguese History*, 1, 1, 2003, pp. 2–13.
Baylen, Joseph O., "Dillon, Emile Joseph (1854–1933)", *Oxford Dictionary of National Biography*, Oxford University Press, 2004.
Bennett, Jeffrey S., "Symbolic Inversion in the 1910 Republican Revolution in Portugal", *History and Anthropology*, 23, 3, 2012, pp. 283–300.
Bevir, Mark, "Ernest Belfort Bax: Marxist, Idealist, and Positivist", *Journal of the History of Ideas*, 54, 1, 1993. pp. 119–135.
Boxer, Charles, "Second Thoughts on the Anglo-Portuguese Alliance 1661–1808", *History Today*, June 1986, pp. 22–26.
Brettel, C. R., "Portugal's First Post Colonials: Citizenship, Identity, and the Repatriation of Goans, *Portuguese Studies Review*, 14, 2, 2006–7, pp. 143–170.
Cabral, Amílcar "Le Portugal est-il imperialist?", *Afrique-Asie*, 3, 2, 1972, pp. 34–35.
Cabral, M. V., "The Aesthetics of Nationalism: Modernism and Authoritarianism in Early Twentieth-Century Portugal", *Luso–Brazilian Review*, 26, 1, 1989, pp. 15–43.
Catroga, Fernando, "O laicismo e a questão religiosa em Portugal (1865–1911)", *Análise Social*, 29, 100, 1988, pp. 211–273.
Catroga, Fernando, "Decadence and Regeneration in the Portuguese Republican Imagination at the End of the Nineteenth Century", *Portuguese Literary and Cultural Studies*, 12, 2004, pp. 297–319.
Catroga, Fernando, "The Parliamentary Model of the First Portuguese Republic: Legacies and Discontinuities", in Pedro Tavares de Almeida, and Javier Moreno Luzón, eds, *The Politics of Representation: Elections and Parliamentarism in Portugal and Spain, 1875–1926*, Brighton: Sussex Academic Press, 2017, pp. 124–157.
Coelho, Maria Teresa Pinto, " 'Pérfida Albion' and 'Little Portugal': The Role of the Press in British and Portuguese National Perceptions of the 1890 Ultimatum", *Portuguese Studies*, 6, 1990, pp. 173–190.
Costa Pinto, António and Almeida, Pedro Tavares de, "On Liberalism and the Emergence of Civil Society in Portugal", in Nancy Bermeo and Philip Nord, eds, *Civil Society Before Democracy: Lessons from Nineteenth-Century Europe*, Princeton: Princeton University Press, 1998, pp. 3–21.
Costa Pinto, António, "Portugal: Crisis and Early Authoritarian Takeover", in Dirk Berg-Schlosser and Jeremy Mitchell, eds, *Authoritarianism and Democracy in Europe 1919–39: Comparative Analyses*, London: Palgrave, 2002, pp. 354–80.
Clarence-Smith, William Gervase, "The Hidden Costs of Labour on the Cocoa Plantations of São Tomé and Príncipe, 1875–1914", *Portuguese Studies*; 6, 1, 1990, pp. 152–172.

Clarence-Smith, William Gervase, "Struggles over Labour Conditions in the Plantations of São Tomé and Príncipe, 1875–1914", in Michael Twaddle, ed., *From Chattel Slavery to Wage Labour in Africa, the Caribbean and England*, London: Frank Cass, 1993, pp. 149–167.

Desai, Nishtha, "The Denationalisation of Goans: An Insight into the Construction of Cultural Identity", *Lusotopie*, 2000, pp. 469–476.

Dias Pereira, Joana, "Labour Movements, Trade Unions and Strikes (Portugal)", in Ute Daniel, Peter Gatrell, Oliver Janz, Heather Jones, Jennifer Keene, Alan Kramer, and Bill Nasson, eds, *1914–1918: Online. International Encyclopedia of the First World War*, Berlin: Freie Universität Berlin, 2014.

Fernandes, Paulo Jorge, Meneses, Filipe Ribeiro de, Baiôa, Manuel, "The Political History of Twentieth-Century Portugal", *e-Journal of Portuguese History*, 1, 2, 2003, pp. 1–18.

Fernandes, Paulo Jorge, "Elections and Parliamentary Recruitment in Portugal", in Pedro Tavares de Almeida and Javier Moreno Luzón, eds, *The Politics of Representation: Elections and Parliamentarism in Portugal and Spain, 1875–1926*, Brighton: Sussex Academic Press, 2017, pp. 7–38.

Fitzgerald, Robert, "Rowntree, Joseph (1836–1925)", *Oxford Dictionary of National Biography*, Oxford University Press, 2004.

Forsythe, Bill, "Women Prisoners and Women Penal Officials 1840–1921", *British Journal of Criminology*, 33, 4, 1993, pp. 525–540.

Freeland, Alan, "The People and the Poet: Portuguese National Identity and the Camões Tercentenary (1880)", in Clare Molinero-Mar and Angel Smith, eds, *Nationalism and the Nation in the Iberian Peninsula: Conflicting Identitites*, Oxford: Berg, 1996, pp. 53–67.

Gallagher, Tom, "Anglo-Portuguese Relations since 1900", *History Today*, June 1986, pp. 39–45.

Gallagher, Tom, "The Catholic church and the Estado Novo of Portugal", in Jim Obelkovich, Lyndal Roper, Raphael Samuel, eds, *Disciplines of Faith: Studies in Religion, Politics and Patriarchy*, London: Routledge and Keegan Paul, 1987, pp. 518–536.

Garcia, José Luis, Graça, João Carlos, Geronimo, Helena Mateus and Marques, Rafael, "Portuguese Sociology: A non-cesurial perspective", in *The European Handbook of Sociology*, Abingdon: Routledge, 2014, pp. 357–375.

Grant, Kevin, "Christian Critics of Empire: Missionaries, Lantern Lectures and the Congo Reform Campaign in Britain", *Journal of Imperial and Commonwealth History*, 29, 2, 2001, pp. 27–58.

Grass, Tim, "Brethren and the Sao Tomé cocoa slavery controversy: the role of Charles A. Swan (1861–1934)", *Brethren Archivists' and Historians' Network Review*, 5, 1, 2007, pp. 98–113.

Guimarães, Angela, "At Home and Abroad: Anglo-Portuguese Colonial Rivalries and Their Domestic Impact in the Work of Raphael Bordallo Pinheiro", *The Oxford Art Journal*, 8, 1, 1985, pp. 29–39.

Hadjiyiannis, Christos, "Conservative Politics, Modernist Poetics: J. M. Kennedy's 'Tory Democracy'", *English Literature in Translation 1880–1920*, 58, 3, 2015, pp. 385–394.

Hasian, Marouf Jr., "Alice Seeley Harris, the Atrocity Rhetoric of the Congo Reform Movements, and the Demise of King Leopold's Congo Free State", *Atlantic Journal of Communication*, 23, 3, 2015, pp. 178–192.

Higgs, Catherine, "Happiness and Work: Portuguese Peasants, British Laborers, African Contract Workers, and the Case of São Tomé and Príncipe, 1901–1909", *International Labor and Working Class History*, 86, 2014, pp. 55–71.

Horgan, John, "Journalism, Catholicism and Anti-Communism in an Era of Revolution: Francis McCullagh, War Correspondent, 1874–1956", *Studies: An Irish Quarterly Review*, 98, 390, 2009, pp. 169–184.

Horgan, John, " 'The great war correspondent': Francis McCullagh, 1874–1956", *Irish Historical Studies*, 36, 144, 2009, pp. 542–563.

Horgan John, "The Irishness of Francis McCullagh" in Kevin Rafter, ed., *Irish Journalism Before Independence: More a Disease than a Profession*, Manchester: Manchester University Press, 2011, pp. 106-119.

Howes, Robert, "The British Press and Opposition to Lord Salisbury's Ultimatum of January 1890", *Portuguese Studies*, 23, 2, 2007, pp. 153–166.

Innes-Smith, Robert, "The Witch of Yokes Court", *The Lady*, 20 July, 2010.

John, Angela, "A New Slavery", *History Today*, June 2002, pp. 34–35.

Kale, Pramod, "Goan Intellectuals and Goan Identity: An Unresolved Conflict", *Economic and Political Weekly*, 29, 16–17, 1994, pp. 909–911.

Kiernan, Victor, "The Old Alliance: England and Portugal", *The Socialist Register 1973*, London: Merlin Press, 1973, pp. 261–281.

Laidlar, John F., "Edgar Prestage: Manchester's Portuguese pioneer", *Bulletin of the John Rylands Library*, 74, 1, 1992, pp.75–94.

Langhorne, Richard, "Anglo-German negotiations concerning the future of the Portuguese colonies, 1911–1914", *Historical Journal*, 16, 2, 1973, pp. 361–387.

Livermore, H., "Consul Crawfurd and the Anglo-Portuguese Crisis of 1890", *Portuguese Studies*, 8, 1992, pp. 170–188.

Magone, José M., "Political recruitment and elite transformation in modern Portugal, 1870–1999: The late arrival of mass representation", in Heinrich Best and Maurizio Cotta, eds, *Parliamentary Representatives in Europe, 1848–2000*, Oxford: Oxford University Press, 2000, pp. 341–370.

Mata, Maria Eugénia, "Economic Ideas and Policies in Nineteenth-Century Portugal", *Luso-Brazilian Review*, 39, 1, 2002, pp. 29–42.

Marques, A.H. de Oliveira, "The Portuguese 1920s: A general survey", *Iberian Studies*, 2, 1973, pp. 32–40.

Meneses, Filipe Ribeiro de, "The Portuguese Empire", in Robert Gerwarth and Erez Manela, eds, *Empires at War*, Oxford: Oxford University Press, 2014, pp. 179–196.

Mourão, Paulo, "The Effect of the Establishment of the Portuguese Republic on the Revenue of Secular Brotherhoods – the Case of 'Bom Jesus de Braga'", *e-Journal of Portuguese History*, 14, 1, 2016, pp. 20–52.

Nunes, Ana Bela, Mata, Eugénia, Valério, Nuno, "Portuguese Economic Growth 1833–1985", *The Journal of European Economic History*, 18, 2, 1989, pp. 291–370.

Oldfield, Sybil, "Harris, Sir John Hobbis (1874–1940)", *Oxford Dictionary of National Biography*, Oxford University Press, 2004.

Owen, Nicholas, "The Soft Heart of the British Empire: Indian Radicals in Edwardian London", *Past & Present*, 220, 1, 2013, pp. 143–184.

Parobo, Parag D., "Tristão Bragança Cunha and Nationalism in Colonial Goa: Mediating Difference and Essentialising Nationhood", *Economic and Political Weekly*, 50, 31, 2015, pp. 61–68.

Pierson, Stanley, "Ernest Belfort Bax, 1854–1926: The Encounter of Marxism and Late Victorian Culture", *Journal of British Studies*, 12, 1, 1972, pp. 39–60.

Pinto, José Madueiro, "Sociology in Portugal, Formation and Recent Trends," in Ana Nunes de Almeida, ed., *Challenges, Controversies and Languages for Sociology and the Social Sciences in the 21st Century*, Madrid: International Sociological Association, 1998, pp. 57–65.

Porter, Andrew, " 'Cultural imperialism' and protestant missionary enterprise, 1780–1914", *Journal of Imperial and Commonwealth History*, 25, 3, 1997, pp. 367–391.

Porter, Andrew, "Sir Roger Casement and the international humanitarian movement", *The Journal of Imperial and Commonwealth History*, 29, 2, 2001, pp. 59–74.

Porter, Andrew, "Evangelical Visions and Colonial Realities", *Journal of Imperial and Commonwealth History*, 38, 1, 2010, pp. 145–155.

Prestage, Edgar, "The Anglo-Portuguese Alliance", *Transactions of the Royal Historical Society*, 4, 17, 1934, pp. 69–100.

Prestage, Edgar, "Reminiscences of Portugal", in H. V. Livermore, ed., *Portugal and Brazil: An Introduction*, Oxford: Clarendon Press, 1953, pp. 1–14.

Pound, Reginald, and Morris, Rev. A. J. A., "Gibbs, Sir Philip Armand Hamilton (1877–1962)", *Oxford Dictionary of National Biography*, Oxford University Press, 2004.

Ramos, Rui, "A Prisoner of Liberalism: The Strange Case of J. P. Oliveira Martins", *Portuguese Studies*, 16, 2000, pp. 52–82.

Ramos, Rui, "A Tale of One City? Local Civic Traditions under Liberal and Republican Rule in Portugal", *Citizenship Studies*, 11, 2, 2007, pp.173–186.

Rebelo, L. De Sousa, "A Plan for the Restoration of the Monarchy in Portugal", Portuguese Studies, 1, 1985, pp. 204–224.

Robbins, Keith, "The Spiritual Pilgrimage of the Rev. R. J. Campbell", *The Journal of Ecclesiastical History*, 30, 2, 1979, pp. 261–276.

Robinson, R. A. H., "The religious question and the Catholic revival in Portugal, 1900–1930", *Journal of Contemporary History*, 12, 2, 1977, pp. 345–362.

Robinson, R. A. H., "'Salus, Ecclesiae Suprema Lex': Monarchists, Catholics and the Portuguese First Republic, 1910–1926", in T.J. Dadson, R.J.P. Oakley and P.A. Odber de Baubeta, eds, *New frontiers in Hispanic and Luso-Brazilian Scholarship*, Lampeter: Edwin Mellen, 1994, pp. 411–442.

Romeiras, Francisco Malta, "The journal *Brotéria* (1902–2002): Jesuit science in the 20th century", *Journal of the History of Science and Technology*, 6, 2012, pp. 100–109.

Ross, Andrew C., "Laws, Robert (1851–1934)", *Oxford Dictionary of National Biography*, Oxford: Oxford University Press, 2004.

Ross, Christopher N. B. "Lord Curzon and E. G. Browne Confront the 'Persian Question'", *Historical Journal*, 52, 2, 2009, pp. 385–411.

Rooy, Piet de, "Moens, Herman Marie (1875–1938)", *Biographical Dictionary of the Netherlands*, 4, The Hague, 1994. Online. http://resources.huygens.knaw.nl/bwn1880-2000/lemmata/bwn4/moens 5 December 2018.

Sadlier, Darlene J., "Modernity and Modernism in Portugal: The Questão Coimbra and the Generation of 1870", *Nineteenth Century Prose*, 32, 1, Spring 2005. Online. http://www.thefreelibrary.com/Modernity+and+modernism+in+Portugal%3a+the+%22Questao+Coimbra%22+and+the...-a0208109739, 18 July 2014.

Santos, João Moreira dos, "Roots of Public Relations in Portugal: Changing an Old Paradigm", *Public Relations Review*, 42, 2016, pp. 792–800.

Sardica, José Miguel, "Imagens da República", *Comunicação & Cultura*, 8, 2009, pp. 9–24.

Sardica, José Miguel, "O jornalismo e a intelligentsia portuguesa nos finais da Monarquia Constitucional", *Comunicação e Cultura*, 7, 2009, pp. 17–38.

Sardica, José Miguel, "The Memory of the Portuguese First Republic throughout the Twentieth Century", *e-Journal of Portuguese History*, 9, 1, 2011, pp. 1–27.

Sardica, José Miguel, "O poder visível: D. Carlos, a imprensa e a opinião pública no final da monarquia constitucional", *Análise Social*, 203, 67, 2012, pp. 344–368.

Sardica, José Miguel, "The Portuguese Constitutional Charter of 1826", *Constitutional History*, 13, 2012, pp. 527–561.

Sardica, José Miguel, "The cultural discourse of Contemporary Portuguese Iberianism", *International Journal of Iberian Studies*, 27, 1, 2014, pp. 55–70.

Southern, Paul, "German border incursions into Portuguese Angola prior to the First World War", *Portuguese Journal of Social Science*, 6, 2007, pp. 3–14.

Souza, Teotónio R. de, "Castes, Social Mobility and Politics in Goa", *Herald (Goa)*, 25 September, 2012.
Stearn, Rev. Roger T., "Maclean, Sir Harry Aubrey de Vere (1848–1920)", *Oxford Dictionary of National Biography*, Oxford University Press, 2004.
Stone, Dan, "Race in British Eugenics", *European History Quarterly*, 31, 3, 2001, pp. 397–425.
Stone, Glyn, "The Foreign Office and Forced Labour in Portuguese West Africa, 1894–1914", in Keith Hamilton and Patrick Salmon, eds, *Slavery, Diplomacy and Empire: Britain and the Suppression of the Slave Trade, 1807–1975*, Brighton: Sussex Academic Press, 2009, pp. 165–195.
Sweetnam, Mark S., "Dan Crawford, Thinking Black, and the Challenge of a Missionary Cannon", *Journal of Ecclesiastical History*, 58, 4, 2007, pp. 705–722.
Vernâncio, Fernando, " 'Quick, Fleeting Sketches', Literary History in Portugal in the 19th Century", *Yearbook of European Studies*, 12, 1999, pp. 185–196.
Vincent-Smith, John, "Britain, Portugal and the First World War", *European Studies Review*, 4, 3, 1974, pp. 207–238.
Vincent-Smith, John, "The Anglo-German Negotiations over the Portuguese Colonies in Africa", *The Historical Journal*, 17, 3, 1974, pp. 620–629.
Vincent-Smith, John, "The Portuguese Republic and Britain, 1910–1914", *Journal of Contemporary History*, 10, 4, 1975, pp. 707–727.
Villis, Tom, "Early modernism and exclusion: The cultural politics of two Edwardian periodicals, 'The New Age' and 'The New Witness'", *University of Sussex Journal of Contemporary History*, 5, 2002, pp. 1–17.
Wearing, J. P., "Archer, William (1856–1924)", *Oxford Dictionary of National Biography*, Oxford University Press.
Wheeler, Douglas L., "The Portuguese revolution of 1910", *Journal of Modern History*, 64, 2, 1972, pp. 172–194.
Yamada, Norihito, "George Canning and the Spanish Question, September 1822 to March 1823", *The Historical Journal*, 52, 2, 2009, pp. 343–362.
Yamada, Norihito, "Canning, the principle of non-interference and the struggle for influence in Portugal, 1822–5", *Historical Research*, 86, 2013, pp. 661–683.

Unpublished papers

Coelho, Teresa Pinto, "Lord Salisbury s 1890 Ultimatum to Portugal and Anglo-Portuguese Relations," 2006. Online.
http://www.mod-langs.ox.ac.uk/files/windsor/6_pintocoelho.pdf,
30 December 2013.
Villiers, John, "Sir Francis Villiers and the End of the Portuguese Monarchy." Online.
www.mod-langs.ox.ac.uk/files/windsor/7_villiers.pdf,
20 August 2018.

Theses

Benmansour, Katarzyna, *In Portugal* (1912): *Aubrey Bell's depiction of Portuguese society under the First Republic*, MA, Universidade Nova de Lisboa, 2011. Online.

Mendes, Sushila Sawant, *Luís De Menezes Braganza (1878–1938) and the Emergence of Political Consciousness in Goa*, PhD, Goa University, 2012. Online.

Mishra, Rekha, *History of the Press in Goa*, PhD, Goa University, 2004. Online.

Tombat, Nishtha, *Tristao de Bragança Cunha (1891–1958) and the rise of Nationalist Consciousness in Goa*, PhD Goa University, 1995. Online.

Vincent-Smith, J.D., *Britain and Portugal 1910–16*, PhD, University of London, 1971.

Online Sources

Reclus, Élisée, *The Earth and its Inhabitants*, Vol. 1, Europe (New York: D. Appleton and Company, 1883).
 https://www.gutenberg.org/files/54760/54760-h/54760-h.htm

Oxford Dictionary of National Biography
 http://www.oxforddnb.com/page/free-odnb

Online. *International Encyclopedia of the First World War*, Berlin: Freie Universität Berlin, 2014.
 http://www.1914-1918-online.net/

Index

A Capita, 191
A Nação, 189
A República, 123, 127
Abercorn House, Richmond, 59
Acland, Sir Francis, 147
Aeolian Hall, public meeting (22 April 1913), 126, 128, 150–151, 180, 194–195, 198–209
Africa, 13, 84, 95, 199, 231
  Portuguese West, 5, 202, 231–239, 241, 245
  South, 204, 233–234
Agency, historical, 36, 96, 244
  women, 2, 160, 248
Água-Izé, Baron of, 251
Alfonso XIII (King of Spain), 56
Aljube prison (Lisbon), 134, 137, 174, 202, 214
Aljube prison (Porto), 219–220
Almeida, António José, 131, 134
Almeida, Dom João de, 142–144, 149–150, 161–162, 174, 222
Almeida, Moreira de, 81, 218
Alpoim, José Maria de, 23, 197
Amélie, (Queen of Portugal), 20, 50–51, 52, 55, 57, 59, 61, 229
America, 42
Amnesty (political prisoners 1914), 104, 126, 130, 132, 135–136, 159–160, 181, 183, 209
  limitations, 162
Anarchism, 129, 130–131
  Bakunin, 130
  Reclus, Elisée, 130
Anarcho-syndicalism, 131
Andrade, Alfredo Augusto Freire de, 232, 241
Anglo-German negotiations over Portuguese colonies, 14, 29, 103, 237–239
Anglo-Portuguese Alliance, 6, 14–15, 19, 23, 27, 29, 39, 47, 49, 52, 58, 61, 93, 95, 103, 104, 106–107, 121, 128, 162, 174–176, 180–181, 198–199, 203, 206, 228
  in 1913, 123–125
  Portuguese slavery, 233, 237–239, 241, 243, 245, 252, 254
Anglicanism, 68, 138, 141, 143, 144, 154, 156, 161, 167, 231, 256
Angola, 199, 232–233, 236–237, 239, 242, 244, 246–247, 249
Anti-clericalism, 8, 11, 16–17, 38, 40, 48, 64, 71–73, 77, 79, 97, 130, 138, 195
Anti-Slavery and Aborigines' Protection Society, 5, 156, 231, 233–236, 238–240, 252, 254
  public meeting (June 1912), 237
Apsley House, 194
Archer, William, 48–49
Army (Portugal), 30, 32, 39, 41, 45, 47, 68, 71, 80, 127, 131, 136, 196–197, 199, 215, 218, 225–226
Arriaga, President Manuel de, 132, 135–136
Arruella, José, 190
Assimilados, 89–90
Augustina Victoria of Hohenzollern, Princess, 61
Avila, Dr Lubo de, 220
Aylesbury prison, 166–171, 173, 185
Azores, 21, 38, 47, 55, 72, 76, 127, 174, 190, 217

Balfour, Arthur, 155
Baptists, 231, 234, 240
Barker, Lilian, 170
Barotseland (British Rhodesia), 236, 243–244
Barreto, Professor Bissaya, 253
Barroso, Dr Antonio, Bishop of Porto, 77
Bax, Ernest Belfort, 101, 256
  and Bragança-Cunha, 101–102

Beak, George Bailey, 245
Bedford, Adeline, Duchess of, 2, 5, 84,
    106, 121, 124, 126, 128, 140, 147,
    149–152, 154, 157–159, 163, 191,
    198, 202–203, 206, 210, 214
  Association of Lady Visitors
    (prisons), 166, 169, 171
  BPC, Vice-Chair, 173
  Christian philanthropy, 165–167,
    172
  Liberal social reform and First
    Portuguese Republic, 184–185
  penal reform in Britain, 167–172
  Portuguese prisons 172–185
  Press (British), 173–178
Bell, Aubrey, 1, 2, 5, 38, 106, 148, 151,
    156, 159, 161, 177, 201, 223
  arrest, 120–122, 133–134
  periodical press, 111–120
  Morning Post (1913–14), 123–138
Bentley, W. A., 177–178
Berkeley Square, 3, 141, 147, 158, 206
Berlin Conference (1884), 242
Birdwood, George, 180
Boer War, 14, 36, 48, 179, 195,
    200–201, 203, 233, 243, 256
Bombarda, Dr Miguel, 31, 83
Borstals, 168, 170
Bourne, Henry Fox, 234, 240
Boxer, Charles, 15, 90, 140
Braga, Teófilo, 10–11, 38–39, 45, 48,
    69–70, 79, 102, 104, 106, 125
Bragança, Duarte Nuno, Duke of
    (1907–1976), 149–150, 164
Bragança, Miguel, Duke of (1853–
    1927), 44, 61, 149
Bragança, Luís de Menezes, 88, 90
Bragança Cunha, Filomena de, 88
Bragança-Cunha, Tristão de, 88–91
Bragança-Cunha, Vicente de, 1, 2, 4,
    38, 139
  BPC, 105–107
  Costa, Afonso, 104
  family background (Goa), 87–91
  history, 91–98
  journalism, 98–105, 107–108
  Portuguese Empire, 103–104
Brahmins (Goa), 88
Brailsford, Henry Noel, 248
Branco, Cassiano, 253
Brazil, 12, 13, 24, 32, 35, 38, 67, 68,
    74, 84, 85, 130, 133, 136, 143,
    160, 221, 209, 233, 247, 251

Brethren, The, 67, 242, 244
Breyner, Thomaz de Mell, 53
British Protest Committee, 2, 5, 12, 19,
    162
  Bedford, Adeline, Duchess of,
    172–183
  Bell, A. F. G., 121
  Bragança-Cunha, V. de, 103, 105,
    106
  captives' narratives, 186–187
  cross-party co-operation, 146, 157,
    160, 163, 179, 184, 194, 208–209
  diversity, 8–9, 201
  Gibbs, P., 220, 226–227, 229
  Harris, J., 231, 241, 252, 254
  historical importance, 256–258
  McCullagh, F., 76, 81, 84
  public meetings, 126, 128, 150–151,
    157–160, 180, 183, 194–195,
    198–209
  Tenison, E. M., 142–164
Brito e Cunha, Dona Julia de, 129, 134,
    137, 148, 174
Brock, William, 232
Brotéria, 64, 74
Browne, Edward Granville, 178
Buchanan, M. A., 122
Buckle, George, 43
Buiça, Manuel do Reis da Silva, 21, 100
Bulgaria, 212
Burtt, Joseph, 233, 244–245, 247
  forced labour, 235, 248
Busaco, Battle of, 43
Buxton, Travers, 237, 252

Cabral, Amílcar, 2, 17–19, 43, 90
Cadbury, George, 234, 236, 243
Cadbury, William, 128, 233–238, 240,
    242–245, 247–249, 251
  racism, misogyny, 247
Camacho, Manuel de Brito, 69, 232
Camões, Luís, 35, 38, 66, 92, 96, 125,
    129, 161
Campbell, Reverend R. J., 177–179,
    198, 200, 209
  Christian Socialism, 200–201
Campolide College, 64–66, 68, 77, 83
Canada, 109, 122
Canning, George, 9, 106
Carbonária, 78–80, 112, 119, 125–127,
    137–139, 151, 156, 158, 161,
    173–176, 180, 182, 187, 194,
    202–203, 207, 215

Carbonária (continued)
  Gibbs. P., 213, 216–218
Carlos I, King of Portugal, 1, 14,
  20–23, 26, 30, 43, 45–46, 83, 96,
  100–101, 161, 180, 244
  assassination, 21–22
Carnegie, Sir Lancelot, 121, 125
Casement, Sir Roger, 234, 238, 240,
  253
Castle Hedingham (Essex), 164
Castro, General Jaime de, 221
Castro, José Luciano de, 23, 46
Catholic Review (Viseu), 189
Catholicism, 11, 17, 155–156, 203,
  210, 232, 203, 232
  anti-clericalism and religious revival,
  74
  Belgium, 240
  Bell, A. F. G., 139
  Bragança-Cunha, V. de, 87–88, 95
  Darwinism, 65
  Gibbs, P., 153, 211, 228
  journalism, 63–64
  McCullagh, F., 4, 72, 74, 76
Cecil, Evelyn, 195
Cecil, Lord Robert, 155
Centro Colonial, 251
Chardos, (Goa), 88
Charles, Princess of Bavaria, 60
Chocolate, *see* cocoa
'Chinese slavery', 234
Church of England, *see* Anglicanism
Churchill, Winston Spencer, 59, 198
Citizenship/Civil Society, 3–4, 24, 26,
  107–108
  Portugal, 11, 25, 107, 126, 195–198
  Goa, 89, 91
Clarkson, Thomas, 252
Class (social), 41–42, 148–151, 154,
  185
  'Portuguese slavery', 240
  Portuguese prisons, 173
Clientalism, 18, 25, 69, 134
Cocoa, 128, 233, 235–236, 238–239,
  242–244, 248–249, 251
Coelho, Lopes, 220
Coimbra, 10, 23, 36, 38, 67, 70, 89,
  97, 110–111, 119, 149, 129, 214,
  220, 224, 253
Colley, Linda, 186–187
Colonialism (Portugal), 2, 13, 15,
  17–19, 28, 88–89, 91, 232, 253
  compared with others, 252

'double colonialism' (Goa), 90
  Spanish in Portugal, 216
Colonies, Portuguese, 8, 13–14, 17–18,
  28–29, 38, 44, 58, 84–85, 89,
  103–104, 119, 124, 128, 130, 138,
  199, 204, 205, 232, 236–239, 242,
  249
  and Anglo-German relations, 14, 28,
  124
Combes, Émile, 131
Committee of British Residents in
  Portugal, 105, 146
Comte, Auguste, 11, 38, 197–198
Congo (Belgian), 14, 28, 179, 204, 209,
  234, 236–238, 240–242, 245–246,
  248, 249, 253–254
Congo Reform Association, 234, 240,
  254
Conservatism
  Britain, 141, 163, 165, 194–195,
  203, 254
  Portugal, 16, 38, 215
Constitution (Portugal),
  Constitutional Charters, 1826, 94;
  1834, 196
  1911 Constitution, 79, 89, 112, 139,
  194, 196, 225
Contemporary Review, 214
Corfe, Leonard, 158, 194
Correira Barreto, António Xavier, 47
Cortes (Portugal), 16, 31, 46, 89, 160,
  197, 232
Costa, Afonso 2, 19, 20, 27, 29, 32, 39,
  62, 65, 69, 72, 74–78, 82, 83, 93,
  97, 99, 104, 111, 119, 121,
  125–126, 128–136, 139, 149,
  151–152, 154–157, 159–160, 162,
  172, 174–178, 181–183, 185, 187,
  188–190, 195, 197, 199, 211,
  215–17, 219, 225–227, 253
  economy, 123
  Separation Laws, 74–75
  fall of Government (January 1914),
  135–136, 157
  Empire, 253
Costa, Alfredo Luís da, 20–21
Costa, Dr Constâncio Roque da, 220
Costa, Francisco de Melo, Count
  Ficalho, 191, 222
Couceiro, Henrique Mitchell de Paiva,
  2, 16, 47, 49, 60–61, 75, 78, 80,
  84, 108, 142–143, 189, 222, 247
Crawford, Daniel, 243, 249

Credito Predial, 46, 96
Cromer, Earl, Evelyn Baring, 238, 241, 252
Crowe, Sir Eyre, 162, 237–238
Cummings, A. C., 246
Cunha, Isidoro, 88
Cunha, Dr Ligorio da, 88
Cunha e Costa. José Soares da, 152, 225–226, 227

Daily Chronicle, 4, 5, 31, 36–37, 39, 41–43, 54–58, 106, 153, 155–156, 181
   Gibbs, P., 210–214, 216, 217, 224, 226, 228
   Revolution 1910, 30–37
Daily Express, 38, 211
Daily Graphic, 212, 245
Daily Mail, 29, 31, 59, 142–143, 146, 150, 175–176, 194, 211–213
   Revolution 1910, 37–43, 45
Daily News, 234, 243
Daily Telegraph, 23, 47, 99
Dawn in Darkest Africa (Harris), 241, 251
Dawson, Geoffrey, 174
Democracy (Portugal), 3, 8, 10, 16, 24, 42, 49, 97, 112, 121, 131, 153, 157, 186, 190, 257–258
Denunciations, 112, 119, 128, 175, 220–221
Deslys, Gabrielle, 52
Devlin, Joseph, 146
Dictatorships, 24, 112, 119
Dillon, Emile Joseph, 22–23, 46–48, 99
Disraeli, Benjamin, 209
Donald, Robert, 30, 153, 210
Donohoe, M. H., 31–40, 43, 47, 55, 57
Doria, Sylva, 77–78
Douglas, Rev. Arthur J., 125–126
Dover, Pact of, 61
Doyle, Sir Arthur Conan, 84, 106, 160, 179–180, 183, 214
Drummond-Hay, F. E., 236
Du Cane, Sir Edmund, 170
Duffy, James, 235–237

Eastern Telegraph Company, 31, 37
Economy (Portuguese), 119, 123
Edward VII, King, 14, 57–58
Edwardian Britain, 1–2, 5, 27, 200, 240
Eight Centuries of Portuguese Monarchy (Bragança-Cunha), 91–96

Elections (Portugal),
   1911, 112
   1913, 134, 218
Electoral Law (1911), 112
Elvas, 4, 110, 132, 177, 214, 222–224
   Forte da Graça, 223–224, 227, 230
Empire (Portuguese), 1–4, 7–8, 11–13, 15, 18–19, 27, 29–30, 35, 41, 43, 49, 69–70, 74–75, 79, 82, 84, 87, 89, 91–92, 94–95, 102–103, 124–125, 139, 199, 205, 231–239, 241–255
Ericeira, 50–51
Ervideira, Count, 128
Estado Novo, 253
Eugenics, 30, 41, 43, 168, 241
Evangelical Christianity, 240, 244
Evesham, 57

Fanon, Franz, 90
Fay, William E., 248
Feminism,
   Portuguese Republicanism, 25
   prison history, 168–169, 171
Ferdinand II, King ('Bomba') of Naples and Sicily (1830–59), 175, 178, 179
Ferraz de Matos, Patrícia, 233
Figueiredo, Father Avelino de, 189–190, 191, 224
Finot, Jean, 1, 7, 20–21, 45
First World War, 8, 39, 48, 86, 93, 157, 171, 198, 203, 206, 244, 252, 253
   origins and Portuguese colonies, 14
Forced labour, *see serviçais*
Force Publique, 245
Foreign Office, 6, 234, 235–238, 242, 246
   Portuguese slavery and diplomacy, 249–252, 254
Forster, Lys, 151
Forsythe, William J., 171
France, 10, 15, 18, 27, 41, 44–45, 54, 69, 74, 76, 92–93, 120, 130, 178, 189, 194, 195, 206
   Separation Laws (1904), 131
   French Revolution, 153, 171–172, 175, 216, 218
   Jacobinism, 125, 128, 157, 179, 194, 203, 208
Franchise (Portugal), 10, 16, 25, 38, 89, 131, 134, 157, 160, 195–196, 217

318 | Index

Franco, João, 17, 20, 22–23, 30, 31, 38, 43, 69, 78, 80, 96, 103, 244
Francophilia (Portugal), 10, 15, 59, 119–120, 161, 197
Freemasonry,
  Portugal, 11, 17, 21, 44, 68–71, 76, 80, 101, 161, 186, 195–196, 201
  Britain, 207
Freitas, João (Senator), 129
Freitas, Lomelino de, 190
Fulwell Park, Twickenham, 59

Gaisford, Hugh, 71, 251
Galsworthy, John, 235
Gama, Dona Constança Telles da, 105, 112, 125, 133, 148, 161, 174–175, 180, 202, 221
Garrett, Almeida, 110
Gender, 2, 25, 112, 131, 147, 148, 152, 156, 165, 168–169, 171–172, 221, 237, 240, 248, 256
  Harris, Alice, and photography, 240
  Harris, John, and forced labour, 248
  imprisonment in Portugal, 171
  prison reform, 171
'Generation of 1870', 10–12, 26, 38, 69, 79, 89, 97, 111, 119
George V, King, 55, 58, 59
Germany, 8, 14, 18, 22, 27, 28, 29, 41, 43, 44, 103, 119, 124, 144, 163, 184, 199, 209, 231, 233, 237, 238–239
  German Damaraland (SW Africa), 236
Goa, 3, 4, 84, 87–91, 92, 96, 98, 107
Godoy, Manuel de, 223
Gibbs, Philip, 2, 3, 5, 30, 105, 119, 141, 153–157, 159–160, 163, 177, 180, 181, 183
  autobiography, 211, 214
  Elvas, 222–224
  Coimbra, 224
  Catholicism, 227–229
  novels, 211
  Tenison, E. M., 210–211, 214
  Liberal humanitarianism, 228
  Lisbon, 212–218, 221–222, 224–225
  Porto, 218–221
Gibraltar, 52
Gillie, Reverend R. C., 160
Gladstone Committee and Act (1895), 166–167, 169

Gladstone, William Ewart, 207–209
Gladstone, Wiliam Gwynne Charles, 198, 206
Gomes, António Vaz Monteiro, 190–192, 199
Gomes, Manuel Teixeira, 80
Goodenough Lady, *née* Countess Anna Kinsky, 143, 149
Gordon, Dr Mary, 168
Gosselin, Sir Martin, 234
Grey, Sir Edward, 79, 99, 150, 155, 157–158, 160, 162, 173, 175, 181, 195, 209, 220
  diplomacy towards Portugal, 27–29, 125, 144, 147, 178–179, 239
  'Portuguese slavery', 235–236, 241, 249, 252, 254
Guerra Junqueiro, Abilío, 22, 110
Guild Socialism, 98
Gurney, Henry, 202

Haeckel, Ernst, 92–93
Harding, Colin, 243–244
Hardinge, Sir Arthur, 102, 104, 121, 146, 202, 241, 249, 252
Harford, Canon George, 142–144
Harmsworth, Alfred, 37, 43
Harper's Magazine, 233, 243
Harris, Alice, 239–241
  'Portuguese Slavery', 246
  repatriation and gender discrimination, 237
Harris, John Hobbis, 2, 3, 4, 125, 153, 156, 158, 210
  anti-racism, 247, 253
  British Empire compared with Portuguese, 238
  Christian imperialism, 247, 252
  Christianity and economics, 237
  networking, 231, 235, 238, 240
  'Portuguese Slavery', 241–247
  Secretary of ASAPS, 241
  Tenison, E. M., 231
  theory of the state, 254
Hedingham Hall (Essex), 141
Herbert, Aubrey, 198, 213
Hewitt, H. W., 181–182
Hindus (Goa), 89
Historiography, 171
  Anglo-Portuguese Alliance, 15–16
  First Republic, 1, 4, 7–8, 9, 80, 84, 257–258
  Portuguese West Africa, 233, 241

Hochschild, Adam, 245
Holden, Richard, 67–68
Homem Cristo, Francisco Manuel, 69, 106, 152, 188–189
Hope, James, 147
Horgan, John, 63, 82, 85
Howard Association, 132, 156, 162, 167
Hunt, William Holman, 234

Iberianism, 38
Imagined communities, 4, 89
Imperialism, 204, 256
  Cabral, A., 17–18
  cultural, 240
  diplomacy, 253
  London, 91
  McCullagh, F., 63–64, 85
  Positivism, 38
  Swinny, S. H., 106
In Portugal (Bell), 109–111, 138
  Elvas, 222–225
  Portuguese state, 110
India, 48, 54, 74, 81, 84, 88–92, 144, 155, 198
Indigenas, 90
Industry,
  Portuguese, 9, 16, 95, 107, 119, 120, 131
  British, 182
Inebriates' Act (1898), 169
Integralismo Lusitano, 164
Ionides, Mrs, 144
Ireland, 124, 196, 254
Ivory, 245–246

Jerónimo, Miguel Bandeira, 233
Jesuits, 49, 64–68, 74–76, 83, 106, 203
Jingoism (Britain), 200
Johnston, Sir Harry, 198, 204–206, 232, 234
Jones, Harry, 153
Journalism,
  France, 156
  Britain, 22–23, 36, 42, 57, 63, 82, 91, 98–105, 107–108, 122–138, 140, 151, 226
  Goa, 88
  empire, 233
  'new journalism', 4, 22, 25–26, 79
  Portugal, 21, 25–26, 107
Jowett, Benjamin, 165

Keir Hardie, James, 201
Kennedy, John McFarland, 98–99
  German Empire, 102
  Portuguese Empire, 103
Kiernan, Victor, 15
King, Joseph, 147
Kings College, London, 59
Konkani, 90

La Libre Parole, 156
Labour Party, 100
Laicisation, 72–73
Lang, Dr Cosmo, 58
Lansdowne, 5th Marquess, Henry Charles Keith Petty-Fitzmaurice, 156
Lara, António de Sousa, 251
Lavradio, Marquis of, 146
Laws, Dr Robert, 95
Le Play, Frédéric, 70
Leão, Eusebio, 37
Lencastre, Homero de, 214, 218–221, 222, 225
Leopold I, King of Belgium, 241–242
Liberalism,
  British, 2, 121, 124, 156, 175, 178–179, 185, 194, 198, 208, 211, 233, 252
  Portuguese, 94, 121, 203, 227
  Liberal Imperialism, 2, 41, 91, 200–201, 204–205, 252–254
  Cadbury, W., 247
  Liberal Internationalism, 208–209, 225
Libya, 63
Lima, Dr Oliveira, 220
Lima, Sebastião Magalhães, 44
Limoeiro prison (Lisbon), 110, 137, 147, 173, 175, 178, 188–189, 202, 214, 221–222, 224–225
Lisbon, 9–11, 16, 21–23, 25–26, 29–37, 39–45, 50–51, 53, 55, 59, 62, 65, 68–69, 77, 80–81, 83, 93–94, 100, 105, 110, 112, 119, 120–122, 126–127, 129–130, 132–137, 142, 144, 146–148, 151, 154, 159–162, 173, 175, 183, 187, 189, 191, 202–204, 211–218, 220–225, 228, 229, 233–234, 236, 242, 244, 248–249, 251–252
Livingstone, David, 241, 242, 252
Lockwood, Mark, 198, 207
Logan, Anne, 171

Longard de Longgarde, Madame, *née* Dorothea Gerard, 142–143, 146
Longue durée, 16–17, 45, 105, 109, 111, 120, 223, 257
Luis Felipe, Crown Prince, 1
Lusitanization, 89–90
Lusophony, 89, 107
Lytton, 2nd Earl, 128, 136–137, 144, 146, 153, 155, 158, 162, 166, 177, 180, 194, 198–199, 208–209, 210, 226
Lytton, Lady Constance, 166–167, 170, 199

McCullagh, Francis, 1, 2, 4, 40, 63, 150–151, 153–154, 159, 161
   Bragança-Cunha, 87, 103
   Constitution 1911, 78–79
   Freemasonry and anti-clericalism, 71–78
   Jesuits, 64–68
   Racism, 83, 85
   Republic as nightmare, 82–86
   Social theory, 68–71
McNair, Stuart E., 67–68
McHale, L., 251
Macau, 85
North China Daily News, 82
Macaulay, Rose, 1, 109, 162
MacDonald, James Ramsay, 99–100, 235
Machado, Bernardino, 23, 41, 47, 48, 58, 104, 136–137, 159–160, 162, 236
Maciera, António Caetano, 238
Mackie, Horatio G., 232
Maclean, Sir Harry, 59
Madeira, 19
Mafra, 50–52
Magalhães, Alfredo de, 125
Magalhães Lima, Sebastião de, 44, 79, 107
Majendie, Musette, 164
Manchester Guardian, 29, 36, 156, 158–159, 176–177, 183, 214, 243
Manteiro, Francisco, 151
Manuel II, King of Portugal, 4, 20, 22–23, 30–31, 40–42, 45, 46, 68–69, 96, 108, 161, 149, 151, 190, 194, 214, 229
   and BPC, 163, 182
   exiled, 50–62
   Gabby Deslys, 53
   marriage, 61–62
   pension, 59
   plan to restore monarchy, 60
   visit to England, 1909, 14
Maria Pia, Queen of Portugal, 40, 50–51, 53
Maria Theresa, Archduchess, 149–150
Martins, Oliveria, 22
Mascarenhas, Dom José, 188
Masculinity, and prison reform, 165–166, 169, 171
Mayo, 7th Earl of, Dermot Bourke, 156, 236, 238
Medeiros, Manuel Goulart de, 135
Mendonça, Monteiro de, 239
Meyer, Rev. Frederick Brotherton, 239
Miguelism, 12, 44, 60–61, 76, 94, 145, 149–150, 162–163, 182
Missionaries, 233, 240
   Angola, 242
   Harris, Alice and John, 231–255
   São Tomé and Príncipe, 248
   Swan, Charles, 242–243
Modern Slavery (Nevinson), 243
Moens, Herman Marie Bernelot, 92–93
Monarchism, 74, 201, 225
Monism, 92
Moodie, Duncan Campbell Francis, 234
Morel, Edmund Dene, 28, 179, 234, 238, 240
Morning Post, 5, 105, 109, 111, 120–138, 177, 202
Morrell, Philip, 158–159, 183
Motta, Dr Santos, 220
Mozambique, 13, 14, 18, 60, 77, 124–125, 199, 204, 233–234, 237–238, 251
Municipalism (Lisbon), 25
Muret, Maurice, 65

Naples, 175, 178–179, 181, 208–209
Nation, The, 105
National regeneration (Portugal), 12, 38, 84–85, 95
   Bragança-Cunha, V. de, 105
   Bell, A. F. G., 120
Nationalism,
   Goa, 88
   Portugal, 38, 84, 92–93, 96, 107, 216

India, 90
Navy (Portugal) 30, 32, 34, 36–37, 41, 56, 131, 196, 199
Neo-colonialism (Britain), 1, 2, 13, 15, 19, 42–43, 85, 94–95, 211, 231–232, 256–257
  Bell, A. F. G., 140
  Bedford, Adeline, Duchess of, 185
  Gibbs, P., 228
  Harris, J. and A., 240
  Johnston, H., 204
  Sykes, M., 204
  Strachey, J., 237
  Tenison, E. M., 211
Nevinson, Henry, 5, 36, 233, 235–237, 239, 243–246, 248–249
New Age, The, 87, 98
Nicholas I, Tsar of Russia, 55
Nietzsche, 98–99
Norfolk, Duke of, 143, 154

O Debate (Goa), 89
O Dia, 188, 218
O Heraldo (Goa), 89
O Intransigente, 190, 215, 218
O Mundo, 123, 128–129, 133, 187
O Nacionalista (Goa), 89
O Seculo, 128, 177
Observer, The, 46, 176–177, 179–180
Old Alliance, *see* Anglo-Portuguese Alliance
Oporto, Duke of, 50, 52
Oppositions' League' (Portugal), 215
Orage, A. R., 98–99
Oram, A. M., 37, 39, 112
Orleans, Duke of, 52–54, 56–57
Ornelas, Aires de, 60
Ortigão, Ramalho, 20, 21, 97, 102

Palmerston, Viscount, 12–13, 86, 106, 136, 157, 159, 162, 175, 179, 183, 209, 231–232, 234
Pankhurst, Chistabel, 158
Paris, 11, 41, 44, 53, 59, 80, 92, 96, 106, 119, 120, 151–152, 157, 182, 203, 216, 251
Parliament (British) and Portuguese colonies,
  White Papers, 238–239
  Wyllie Report, 238
  House of Lords' Debate, 238

Parties
  Centro Democrático (Goa), 89
  Nationalist Party of Portugal (Goa), 88
  Progressives, 46, 95
  Regenerators, 46, 94, 95, 197
  Democrats, 112, 123, 130–131, 134, 136, 138, 198, 200, 215
  Evolutionists, 112, 131, 135, 198
  Unionists, 112
Pearson, Sir Cyril Arthur, 234
Pearson, Professor Henry, 236
Penal Reform League, 166
Peninsular War, 67, 93, 148, 203, 223
Penitenciária prison (Lisbon), 134, 137, 142, 147, 149–150, 160, 174, 175, 178, 188, 190–193, 202, 214, 220, 222, 224
Persia, 178
Personalismo, 104
Phillips, Percival, 38
Pinheiro, Raphael Bordallo, 13
Pinto, Alexandre Serpa, 204
Plymouth, 56
Poinsard, Léon, 69–71
Political prisoners (Portugal), 1–5, 8, 19, 76, 81–84, 105–106, 111–112, 121, 125–128, 132, 136, 40, 145–147, 160, 256–258
  Bedford, Adeline, Duchess of, 165, 172–185
  captives' narratives, 186–190, 194
  counter-narratives, 190–193
  Gibbs, P., 216, 221–225
  Harris, J., 231, 241
  health, 189, 227
  public Meetings, 157–160, 198–209
  psychological trauma, 188
  Republic compared with Monarchy, 188, 190, 192–193, 224
  rule of law, 186
  Tenison, E. M., 153–160, 164
  tribunals, 225
Pombal, 64, 73, 139
Ponsonby, Arthur, 146
Porter, Andrew, 240, 254
Porto, 12, 13, 16, 25, 32, 36, 39, 45, 47, 69, 75, 77–78, 111, 129, 188, 213–214, 218–222, 224–225, 227–228, 236
Portugal of the Portuguese (Bell), 109, 138–140
Portuguese Anti-Slavery Society, 236

Portuguese Political Prisoners, 121, 128, 155, 176–177, 188–190, 194, 224
Portuguese Slavery: Britain's Dilemma (Harris), 232, 241–247
Portuguese Slavery: Britain's Responsibility (Harris et al.), 252
Positivism, 11, 17, 38, 69–70, 72, 101, 106, 196
Power, Father M. J., 67
Presbyterianism, 95
Press (British), 3–4, 8, 27, 55–56, 76, 107, 156, 160, 162, 173, 177, 180, 183, 199, 208, 235, 256–257
  Liberal Party, 28–29, 156
  'Portuguese Slavery', 235, 245
  Revolution 1910, 27–49
Press (Portuguese), 21–22, 53, 65, 81, 99, 107, 119, 123, 136, 139, 188
  repression, 81–82
Pressure groups, 1, 167, 231, 234, 240, 253, 256
  BPC compared with ASAPS, 254–255
Prestage, Edgar, 15, 38, 58, 81, 122, 150, 161
Prevention of Crime Act (1908), 168
Príncipe, 5, 232–234, 237, 239, 251, 253
Propaganda, 5, 8, 10, 60, 64, 80, 82–83, 96, 103, 176–177, 187, 191–193, 229, 235, 238, 247, 251, 254
Putamayo atrocities, 238

Queirós, José Maria Eça de, 10–11, 32, 111–112, 233
Queirós, Senhora de, *née* Emilia de Castro Pamplona Resende, 146
Queirós, Henrique Caldeira, 192–193
Quelhas Monastery, 40–41, 67
Quental, Antero de, 10–11, 38

Race, 15, 30, 37, 41–42, 48, 69, 84, 90, 92–93, 98–99, 205, 246, 251, 253
Racism, 77 (Torrend), 83, 84 (McCullagh), 90, 93, 98 (Orage), 232 (Brito Camacho), 239 (Wyllie), 246 (Cummings), 247 (Cadbury)
*Ralliement (*France), 74
Red Cross, 129, 160, 184
Relacão prison (Porto), 221

Religious revival in Portugal, 74–77
Republic, First Portuguese,
  early years (1910–14), 2, 16–17, 49, 99, 100–101, 201–202
  Campbell, R. J., 202–203
  Bedford, A., 204–206
  Johnston, H., 225
  Gibbs, P., 227
  First World War, 8
  historiography, 1–2, 7–8, 9–20, 80, 84, 197–198, 233, 241
  religious question, *see* anti-clericalism
Republicanism, 96, 196, 258
  Anarchism, 130–131
  Bell, A. F G., 110–111, 120
  Bragança-Cunha, V. de, 97–105
  BPC, 162, 164, 176–178, 195, 197, 202, 204
  Dillon, E. J., 47
  Europe, 204, 206
  Gibbs P., 215, 228
  Goa, 89–91
  in power, 25–29, 37–41, 42–49, 53, 64, 76, 82–84
  nationalism and race, 93
  middle class elite, 197
  origins and nature before 1914, 9–20, 23
Rességuier, Madame de, 145, 149
Révoltés (Valleci), 245–246
Revolution, 5 October 1910,
  beyond Lisbon, 36
  Bragança-Cunha, V. de, 97
  British Press, 27–49
  Gibbs, P., 215
  historiography, 24–26
Revolution 1974, 2
Revolutionary Portugal (Bragança-Cunha), 92, 96–98
Risings against Republic, 60–61, 76, 80, 84, 200, 220, 238, 190, 132–133, 182, (military coup 1926), 183
Rotativismo, 43, 46, 69, 70, 94, 96–97, 107, 111
Royal Commission on the Feeble-Minded (1908), 170–171
Royalism (Britain), 141, 175, 256
Royalism (Portugal), 4, 43, 49, 187, 236
  conspiracies, 219
Ruggles-Brise, Sir Evelyn, 167–170
Rubber, 238, 245–246, 251

Russia, 208
Russo-Japanese War (1904–5), 63, 80

Said, Edward, 42
Salazar, António de Oliveira, 129, 132, 139, 161, 164, 253
Salisbury, 3rd Marquess of, 95
Sandeman, Thomas Glas, 148
Santos, António Machado, 106, 127, 134, 215, 218
São Roque church (Lisbon), 35
São Tomé, 3, 4, 84, 129, 219, 232–234, 237, 239, 242–244, 248, 251, 253
Saramago, José, 109
Sardica, José Miguel, 107
Schindler, T. S., 249
Schroetter, Ernesto Driesel, 60
Schwartzman, Kathleen, 2, 15
Scott, Charles Prestwich, 158–159
Scovola, Caldeira, 219
Separation Law 1911 (Portugal), 10, 72–74, 76–78, 97, 131–132, 136, 139, 195, 198, 257
   McCullagh, F., 74–75
   Gibbs, P., 228
Serbia, 179–180, 212
Serviçais, 247, 249, 252
Silva, Alfredo da, 236
Sintra, 50, 110
Slavery (Portuguese), 4, 5, 8, 12–13, 27–28, 84, 95, 125, 127, 128, 153, 146, 199, 231, 234
   Abolitionists, 231
   global imperialism, 253–254
   planter interests, Lisbon, 251–252
   porous frontiers and wars, 245–247
   repatriation, 233, 242, 247, 250, 252
   Republic compared with Monarchy, 248, 252
   sleeping sickness, 245, 249
   sexual exploitation and dehumanisation, 248–249
   Tolerationists, 231
   Vagrancy laws, 232
Social Darwinism, 93, 170, 204, 246
Socialism,
   Britain, 8, 48, 98, 99–101, 178, 201, 209
   Goa, 88
   Portugal, 131, 215
Sociedade Propaganda de Portugal, 80, 103

Somers Cocks, Philip, 147, 151, 173
Sousa, Teixeira de, 23, 47, 50, 68
Soveral, Marquis of, 52, 55–57, 194
Spain, 41, 44, 78, 84, 125, 137, 216, 219, 222–223, 238
Spectator, The, 11, 127, 146, 148, 173, 176–177, 184, 187, 188, 199
   'Portuguese Slavery', 234–235, 241, 252
Spender, John Alfred, 155–156
Standard, The, 234
Stanley, Henry Morton, 204, 241
Staveley-Hill, Henry, 154, 157–158
Stober, Matthew, 233
Strachey, John St Loe, 145–146, 148, 235–238, 241, 249, 250
Strikes (Portugal),
   general strike, March 1911
   January 1914, 135
Sturge, Joseph, 252
Subalterneity, 2, 3, 13, 15, 18–20, 42, 89–90, 95, 120, 140, 162, 228, 239, 257
Suffragettes, 148, 166–167, 168, 180, 194, 199, 201, 243
   Cat and Mouse Act, 158, 196
Swinny, Shapland Hugh, 105, 177, 193
Switzerland, 194, 251
Sykes, Sir Mark, 147, 198, 203–204
Syndicalism
   Portugal, 127, 129, 132, 135, 137, 182, 186, 215, 224
   Britain, 124, 194

Teles, Basílio, 25–26
Tenison, Eva Mabel, 2, 3, 5, 81, 105–106, 121–122, 132, 173, 177, 179, 183, 210–211, 214, 226, 231, 254
   Amnesty, 162–163
   aristocracy, defence of, 148–151
   gender and identity, 147–148, 152, 156, 164, 171
   political networking, 144–148, 151–156
   Portugal after Amnesty, 164
   propaganda, 157–158, 187, 189–190
   Public meetings, 158–160, 194, 198, 202
Tenison, Julian, 81, 144, 148, 150, 152
The Portuguese Amnesty, 163
The Slavery of Today (Swan), 242
Thinking Black (Crawford), 244

Thompson, E. P., 7
Times, The, 80, 100, 103, 130, 150, 179, 184–185, 192, 194
   political prisoners, 173–176, 180–183
   'Portuguese slavery', 234, 242
   Revolution 1910, 29, 43–46
Tipping, Mary, 71
Torre Diaz, Countess de, *née* Hon. Bertha Mary Agnes Clifford, 143–144
Torrend, Camille, 64–68, 76–77
Trades unions,
   Britain 124, 254
   Portugal, 25, 215
Transvaal, 234
Trevelyan, George Macaulay, 152, 177–178, 194, 198, 207–20
Tribune, The, 212
Turkey, 203, 206
   Revolution 1908, 102, 178, 181

Ultimatum 1890, 13, 15, 21, 37, 43, 46, 79, 95, 204
Unexpected Activities (Tenison), 141–142, 164

Vale Flór, Count of, 251
Valleci, see Révoltés
Vasconcelos, Augusto de, 252
Vatican, 44, 73–74
Vauban, Sébastien Le Prestre de, 223
Veiga Beirão, Francisco da, 46
Velladas, Pedro, 220
Vergnet, Paul, 81, 156–157
Victoria, Queen, 54
Vienna, 44, 145, 149, 152, 154, 160, 162–163, 182, 211

Villiers, Sir Francis, 45, 47, 249
Viseu, Duke of, 150

Wellington, Duke of, 194
Wells, H. G., 235
Westminster Gazette, The, 155, 157
Westminster Palace Hotel,
   public meetings, ASAPS, 237; BPC, 157–160, 183
Wheeler, Douglas, 2, 104, 127, 219, 225–226
'White Ants', 119, 135, 137–139, 217
Wilberforce, William, 252
Will England Save Portugal?, 157, 159–160, 228
Williams, George Valentine, 39–41, 47, 57
Wingfield, Sir Charles, 122
Women, 202, 237, 247–248, 250
   (Africa)
   Britain, 2, 124, 158, 165–172 (prisons), 184–185, 194, 199, 254, 256
   Portugal, 10, 25, 83, 112, 131, 137, 173–174, 221–222 (prisons), 194, 202
Wood Norton, 52, 54–55, 57, 229
Working class (Portugal), 23, 76, 84, 97–98, 102, 217
World Systems Theory, 2, 15–17
Wyllie, John Alfred, 238–239

Yamba Yamba, 245
Yokes Court, 3, 141–142, 144, 149, 152–154, 156, 161, 164, 210

Zedner, Lucia, 165, 171